DIGITAL MARKETING MADE EASY

By Kevin Urrutia and Wilson Lin

Copyright © 2020 Kevin Urrutia and Wilson Lin

All rights reserved. No part of this publication may be reproduced, distributed, or transmitted in any form or by any means, including photocopying, recording, or other electronic or mechanical methods, without the prior written permission of the publisher, except in the case of brief quotations embodied in reviews and certain other non-commercial uses permitted by copyright law.

Dedication

Kevin

To my amazing family, Edwin, Jackie, Ashley, and my mother, Alicia -

You will learn many things along life's journey. One thing that you cannot teach is passion. That is a journey that you must find on your own. I am lucky to have found my passion, and I hope that you find your path that will make you happy.

Wilson

Thank you to my parents, David and Miranda for showing me what grit and determination look like. For raising me from day one with a growth and hustle mindset through tough love and leading through example.

And thank you to Kevin Urrutia, for that one night in Binghamton, where I hitchhiked onto your ride and joined you on this journey :) One simple request to help you with Photoshop led us down this crazy path. From product design to now building multiple successful businesses together.

About The Authors

Kevin Urrutia

Growing up and embracing New York City's hustle culture, Kevin has been described as a serial entrepreneur with an obsession and the willingness to grow new businesses in emerging markets. Before he set his sights onto e-commerce, Kevin worked for tech companies like Intuit and Zarly amidst the biggest tech rush in Silicon Valley.

Yet, that wasn't enough. Inevitably, Kevin sought out more opportunities and found his rightful lifelong passion in e-commerce. Since then he has built brands across multiple industries and earned himself the title of 4X e-com entrepreneur generating $50M revenue a year. He is also the Host of the hit marketing podcast, *Digital Marketing Fastlane*.

Twitter: @danest

Linkedin: https://www.linkedin.com/in/urrutia/

Wilson Lin

As a traveling entrepreneur and growth strategist for DTC brands, Wilson Lin prides himself on 4 fundamental values for scaling a successful business and self-growth: Have an appetite for learning, take action, incrementally improve and have realistic expectations.

Wilson is driven by numbers and allows creativity to flourish when it comes to positioning innovative products in the market. With a background in UI/UX and product management, his zen-like leadership style intersects at technology, strategy, and digital marketing - with the ROI to back it up.

Years into his entrepreneurial journey and two e-commerce businesses surpassing a revenue of $30 Million, Wilson is on a mission to propel Voy Media's performance marketing into unimaginable levels.

Linkedin: https://www.linkedin.com/in/wilson-voymedia/

For speaking and consulting engagements, contact Kevin or Wilson at kevin@voymedia.com or wilson@voymedia.com

Table of Contents

About The Authors iii
Introduction to Digital Marketing 1
Chapter 1: Content Marketing 13
Chapter 2: Landing Pages 71
Chapter 3: Creating Ads 133
Chapter 4: B2B Sales 191
Chapter 5: Facebook Advertising 249
Chapter 6: User Onboarding... 309
Chapter 7: A/B Testing.. 375
Conclusion 429

Introduction to Digital Marketing

Running an online business requires patience, tenacity, creativity, and skills to understand how to win your brand's target customer and to convert them into customers. But you don't need to just acquire customers. You need to attract the ones who will provide you with lifetime value for your business.

To keep your customers buying from you, you must keep improving your products and delivering the best services or products to solve their problems. You've got to learn about the changing trends in your industry as well as your customers' preferences and adapt your business to the changes.

This is because your clients' demands are evolving and increasing every day, and so are your competitors' products and services.

Learning growth marketing helps you to not only know your customers' buyer journey stages but to effectively learn about the entire customer life cycle. This digital marketing book will help you build your personal brand as you grow your online business and beat out your competitors for a larger market share.

Customer experience is increasingly becoming a top priority for customers. Research by Super Office shows that 86% of customers pay more because of the great customer experience they get from brands.

This book will guide you to increase your customer or user experience and stand out from the other brands you compete within the market.

In this book, I've covered the following topics with in-depth content to help you grow your online market, reach more leads, and increase your lead conversion and sales.

    Chapter 1: Content Marketing
    Chapter 2: Landing Pages
    Chapter 3: Creating Ads
    Chapter 4: B2B Sales
    Chapter 5: Facebook Ads
    Chapter 6: User Onboarding
    Chapter 7: A/B Testing

If your business is a start-up, you're going to learn great ways to grow it quickly online. You'll learn how to build trust with target customers and convert them into clients. This guide will work for you irrespective of your niche or speciality.

Learning the art of effective lead nurturing is essential for your business growth. If potential clients are not nurtured in the right way, they'll leave your email list. This will be a great loss to your business as you'll miss the chance to convert those leads into customers.

You must take every opportunity to convert your leads. This means nurturing leads not only before they become customers, but also after they become your customers. Most brands don't do this after leads become customers. This failure is a large contributor to customer churn or high customer turnover. A high customer churn rate can negatively affect the growth of your business.

A report by Statista shows that online retail brands have a 22% customer churn rate.

Customer churn rate in the United States in 2018, by industry

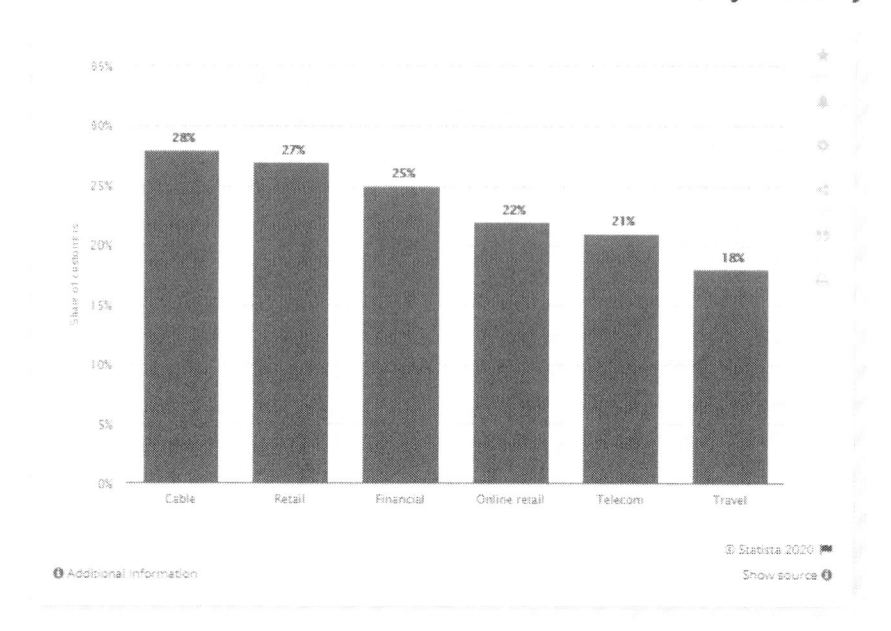

Industry	Churn Rate
Cable	28%
Retail	27%
Financial	25%
Online retail	22%
Telecom	21%
Travel	18%

You already know it costs more money, time, and resources to acquire new customers than it does to maintain existing ones. You'll learn from this book how to effectively onboard new customers and nurture existing customers to increase their value. This will help you reduce churn rate and boost your sales and revenue as you retain more customers for your business.

Growing online brands and increasing sales and revenue requires brands to target the right market and deliver exactly what the target clients want.

It's easy to grow your online business with the right [growth hacking techniques](). This book will help you make informed decisions that promote your brand's growth. Your decisions will be backed up with data and insights to help you reach the target market, win their trust, and sell them your products or services.

Digital Marketing Funnel

Your business will attract target customers who are at different buyer stages. You should be able to effectively nurture these customers at each stage.

Growth hacking is more profitable and measurable than traditional marketing. These are the stages that define the growth funnel.

Growth Hacking in Action

✓ **ACQUISITION**
Use a cost effective channel to deliver your product or service to your target audience.

✓ **ACTIVATION**
Get people to use your product.

✓ **RETENTION**
Engage with your users to create a long-lasting relationship.

✓ **REFERRAL**
Encourage existing customers to invite others to use your product.

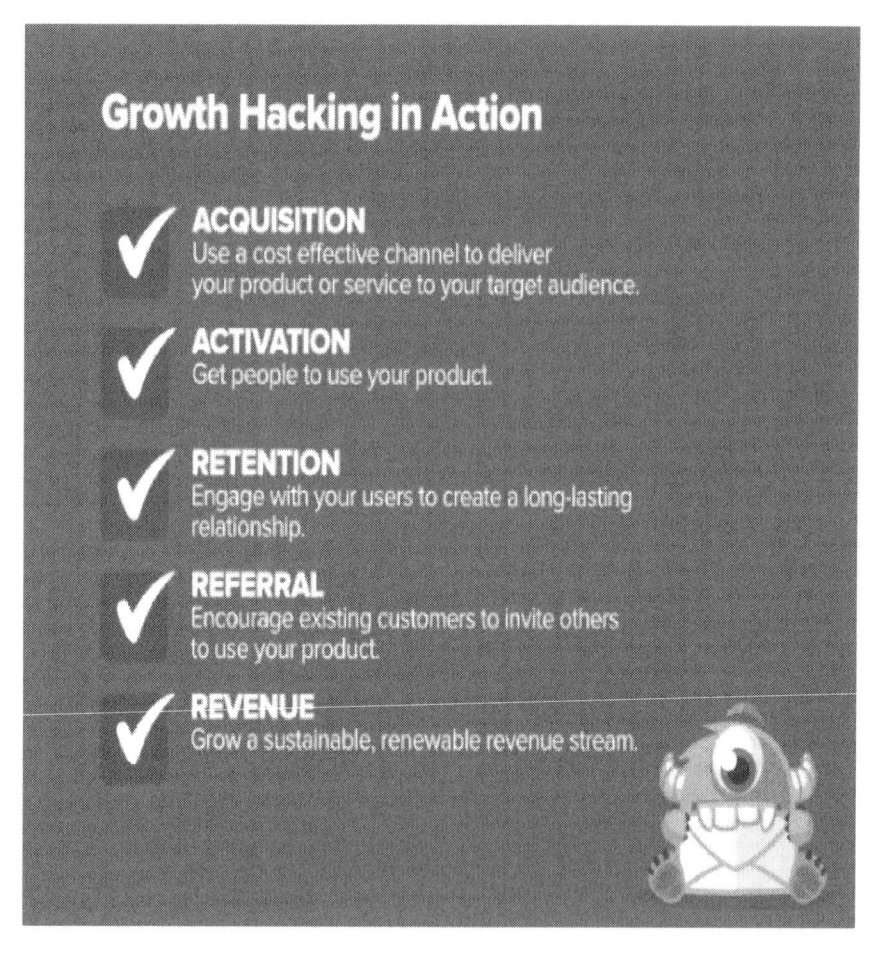

✓ **REVENUE**
Grow a sustainable, renewable revenue stream.

Image Source: https://optinmonster.com/growth-hacking/

A growth hacker uses all the key performance indicators (KPIs) and metrics necessary to ensure business success at every stage of growth.

Different potential clients will come to your business when they're at different buyer stages. To build trust and win potential clients at each stage, you'll learn how to create great content for your target market that meets them where they are to engage them with your business.

B2B brands encounter lots of challenges since the client acquisition and conversion chain is long and complicated. *Digital Marketing Made Easy* will, as it says, help make it easy to win potential clients' trust as you engage with them and nurture them. It will teach you how to walk your B2B clients through the sales funnel and increase conversions.

Facebook Ads

Running Ads for your business is one of the ways brands increase traffic to their websites as they engage target customers. Research by eMarketer shows that Google and Facebook have the highest share of spending on Ads.

Facebook* vs. Google Share of Total US Digital Ad Spending, 2016-2020
% of total digital ad spending

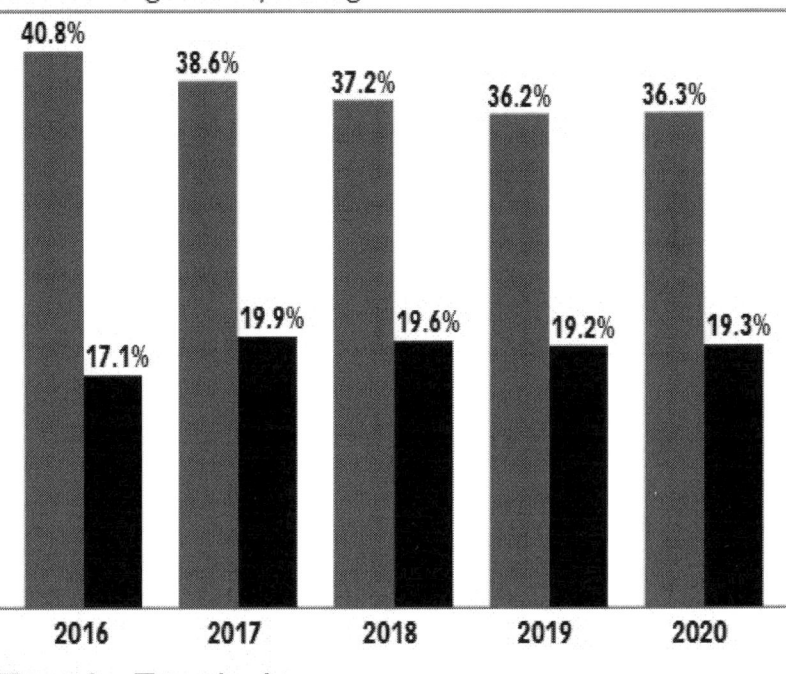

Year	Google	Facebook*
2016	40.8%	17.1%
2017	38.6%	19.9%
2018	37.2%	19.6%
2019	36.2%	19.2%
2020	36.3%	19.3%

Note: includes advertising that appears on desktop and laptop computers as well as mobile phones, tablets and other internet-connected devices, and includes all the various formats of advertising on those platforms; net ad revenues after companies pay traffic acquisition costs (TAC) to partner sites; *includes Instagram ad revenues
Source: eMarketer, March 2018

235954   www.eMarketer.com

Despite that spending, many brands fail to see a return on investment for ads.

This guidebook will teach you how to run Facebook Ads the right way to attract and convert leads into customers. By learning these essentials, you'll be able to choose the best advertising company when you want to run your business ads on Facebook.

Voy Media is an exceptional agency that can help you with your ads. Here are some examples of Voy Media testimonials from clients who used our services:

This guide will also help you choose the best agency to manage your ads so you can grow your brand, reach more leads, and convert them.

A/B Testing

Reaching more target customers and converting them to clients requires experimentation. Effectively gauging your business's performance by testing to see what works and then implementing it helps grow your business faster.

Among the various areas you need to test to improve the performance of your online business are landing pages, the content you write, and readers' engagement with your brand and calls-to-action (CTAs). Knowing how to run A/B tests for these different areas of your brand can help you increase web traffic and conversion rates.

This marketing guide will teach you how to run A/B tests for your business. You'll also learn how to implement changes based on your tests as you grow your brand online.

This will help you reduce the bounce rate and cart abandonment rate since target clients have different reasons for leaving your business's website.

Reasons For Online Shopping Cart Abandonment

- 56% — PRESENTED WITH UNEXPECTED COSTS
- 37% — I WAS JUST BROWSING
- 36% — FOUND A BETTER PRICE ELSEWHERE
- 32% — OVERALL PRICE TOO EXPENSIVE
- 26% — DECIDED AGAINST BUYING
- 25% — WEBSITE NAVIGATION TOO COMPLICATED
- 24% — WEBSITE CRASHED
- 21% — PROCESS WAS TAKING TOO LONG
- 18% — EXCESSIVE PAYMENT SECURITY CHECKS
- 17% — CONCERNS ABOUT PAYMENT SECURITY
- 16% — DELIVERY OPTIONS WERE UNSUITABLE
- 15% — WEBSITE TIME OUT
- 13% — PRICE PRESENTED IN A FOREIGN CURRENCY
- 11% — PAYMENT WAS DECLINED

% of Respondents
Respondents: 19k consumers, 153 Senior Retailers (Jan-Feb 2012)
SOURCE: WorldPay

Image Source: https://www.quicksprout.com/checkout-process-design/

Marketing Charts research showed that 51% of brands do A/B testing for their product offers to reduce the churn rate.

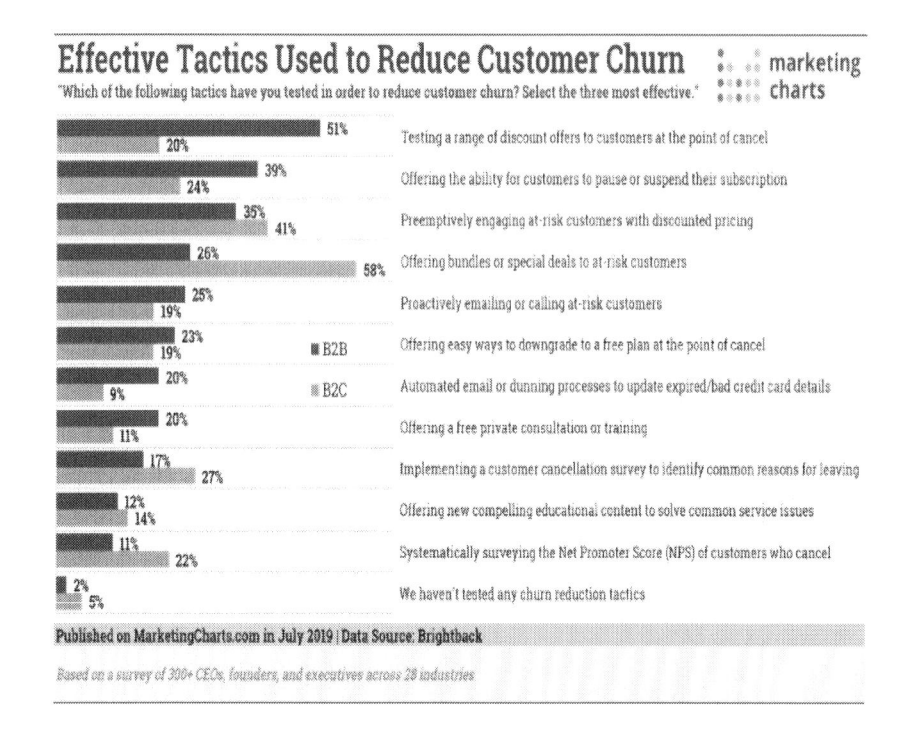

Effective Tactics Used to Reduce Customer Churn
"Which of the following tactics have you tested in order to reduce customer churn? Select the three most effective."

marketing charts

Tactic	B2B	B2C
Testing a range of discount offers to customers at the point of cancel	51%	20%
Offering the ability for customers to pause or suspend their subscription	39%	24%
Preemptively engaging at-risk customers with discounted pricing	35%	41%
Offering bundles or special deals to at-risk customers	26%	58%
Proactively emailing or calling at-risk customers	25%	19%
Offering easy ways to downgrade to a free plan at the point of cancel	23%	19%
Automated email or dunning processes to update expired/bad credit card details	20%	9%
Offering a free private consultation or training	20%	11%
Implementing a customer cancellation survey to identify common reasons for leaving	17%	27%
Offering new compelling educational content to solve common service issues	12%	14%
Systematically surveying the Net Promoter Score (NPS) of customers who cancel	11%	22%
We haven't tested any churn reduction tactics	2%	5%

Published on MarketingCharts.com in July 2019 | Data Source: Brightback

Based on a survey of 300+ CEOs, founders, and executives across 28 industries

This shows how important A/B tests are to your business growth. Another study by the same company showed that 33% of markets are testing their pages to increase their marketing campaigns' performance.

Introduction to Digital Marketing

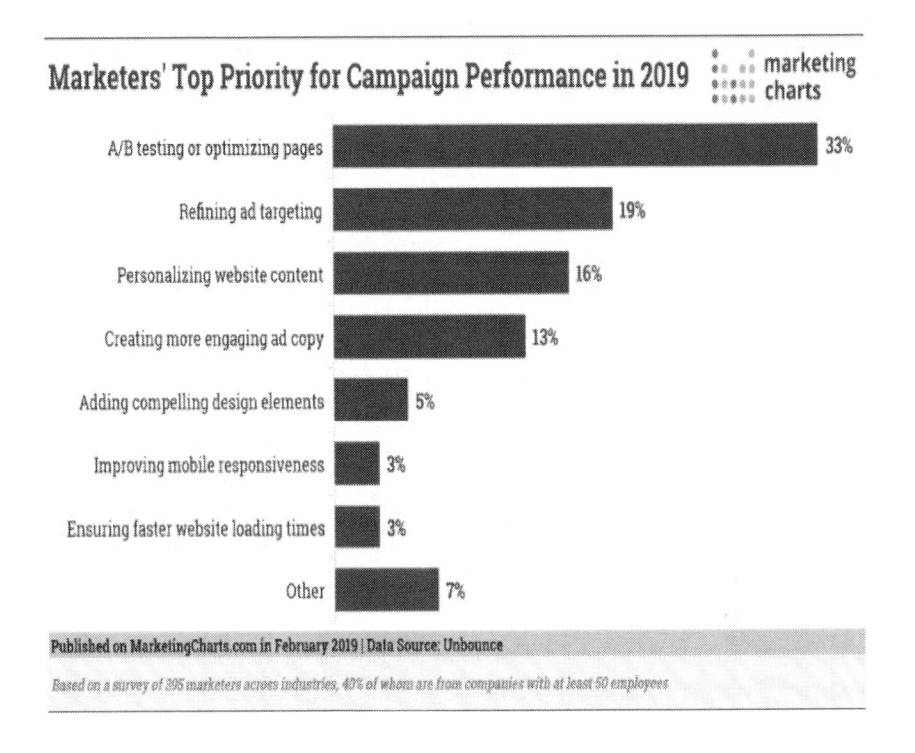

Marketers' Top Priority for Campaign Performance in 2019 — marketing charts

Priority	%
A/B testing or optimizing pages	33%
Refining ad targeting	19%
Personalizing website content	16%
Creating more engaging ad copy	13%
Adding compelling design elements	5%
Improving mobile responsiveness	3%
Ensuring faster website loading times	3%
Other	7%

Published on MarketingCharts.com in February 2019 | Data Source: Unbounce

Based on a survey of 395 marketers across industries, 40% of whom are from companies with at least 50 employees

Marketing Channels

Different marketing channels you can use to run your business ads accomplish different objectives. This guidebook covers these channels and how to run your marketing campaigns on them.

You'll learn great tips to create high-quality content that performs well in search engine results. Developing content that drives steady traffic to your business website is one of the major challenges brands encounter.

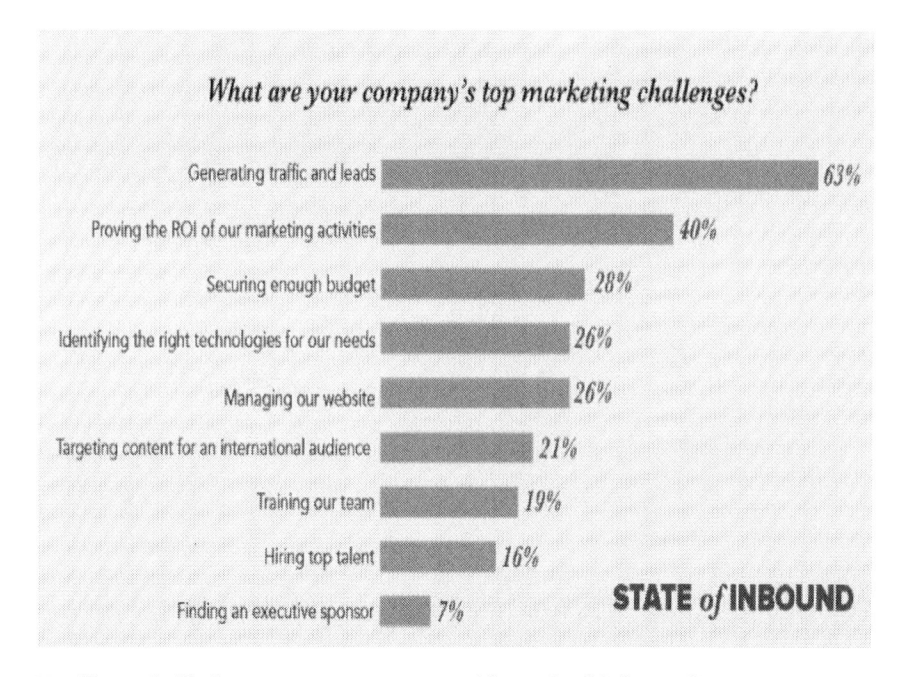

What are your company's top marketing challenges?

Challenge	Percentage
Generating traffic and leads	63%
Proving the ROI of our marketing activities	40%
Securing enough budget	28%
Identifying the right technologies for our needs	26%
Managing our website	26%
Targeting content for an international audience	21%
Training our team	19%
Hiring top talent	16%
Finding an executive sponsor	7%

STATE of INBOUND

You'll read all about ways to generate ideas for high-quality content that builds leadership authority in your niche and engages your target market. We'll cover the numerous tools that are out there to help you produce stellar content. We'll explain how to choose the right channel for each type of content.

It's essential to monitor marketing metrics for your content. You'll learn about the key metrics to monitor various marketing channels and the tools that can make monitoring easy.

Onboarding New Clients

Every marketer wants to see new customers who come to the business remain customers and sources of recurring revenue.

That being said, many customers shop just once and then go to your competitors.

This guide will help you learn how to onboard new customers in a way that ensures they like your products, know how to use them, and see how they can help them solve their pain points.

This stage is one of the most delicate parts of your business marketing. You've done your marketing, and your target customers have liked your

Introduction to Digital Marketing

products or services and purchased them. If they're not well onboard, you'll lose them quickly. After all that effort, you definitely don't want to lose those new customers, right?

No question. And that's why we'll help you learn how to onboard your customers effectively, turning them into lifetime customers. You'll learn the benefits of user onboarding and its effects on your online business growth.

To find out how important user onboarding is to your business, Totango did research that was compiled by Marketing Charts. It shows that 61% of customer success is attributed to user onboarding.

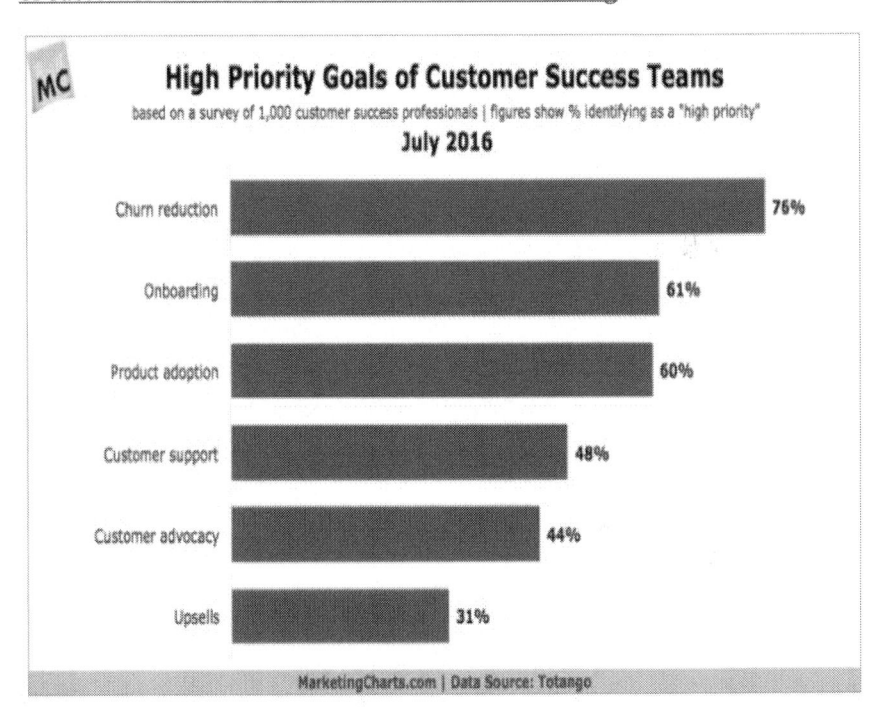

High Priority Goals of Customer Success Teams
based on a survey of 1,000 customer success professionals | figures show % identifying as a "high priority"
July 2016

Goal	%
Churn reduction	76%
Onboarding	61%
Product adoption	60%
Customer support	48%
Customer advocacy	44%
Upsells	31%

MarketingCharts.com | Data Source: Totango

Clearly, ensuring you onboard your customers the right way is key to success.

Research by Groove shows that two happy moments for your new customers are when they sign up for your services and when they see their brands achieve success by using your services.

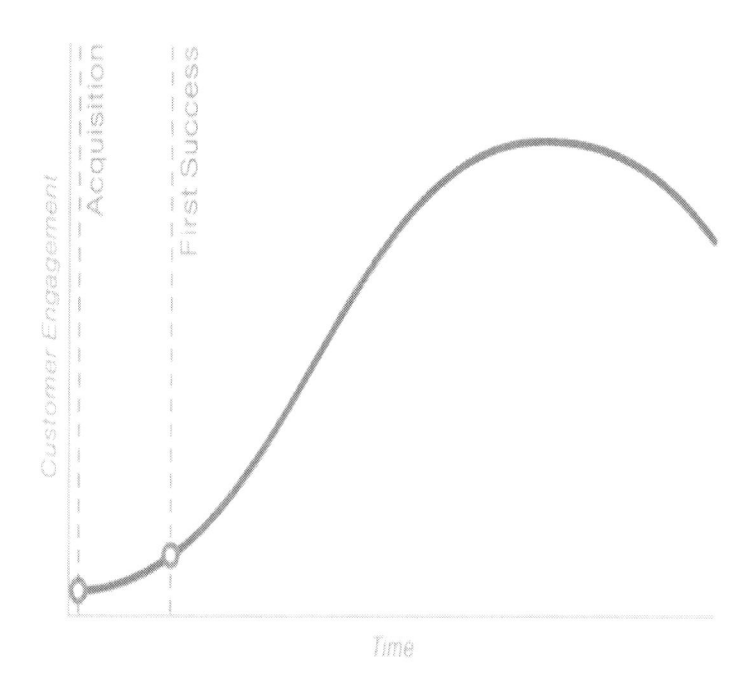

Therefore, your onboarding process should make sure your customer sees the success they're having as a result of using your service or product. If they don't see that value, they'll leave and join your competitors.

As you read, we'll teach you how to build more trust and credibility with new users as you onboard them and integrate them into your business services.

But first, chapter 1 will cover how you can successfully create and distribute powerful, attractive content. Read on to learn more!

Chapter 1: Content Marketing

Growing an online business takes time. You must first commit to building trust with your leads, then get them to interact and engage with your business, and, finally, convert them to clients.

What Is Content Marketing?

To start, let's define the term *content marketing*. It's a marketing approach that involves creating content to attract, engage, and convert specific target audiences into customers for your business.

Brands and individual business owners use content marketing for a variety of reasons. These are some of their objectives:

- Display thought leadership
- Drive sales
- Increase website traffic (SEO)
- Educate the market
- Engage customers/prospects
- Build trust with clients
- Attract new customers
- Grow loyalty among existing customers
- Generate email subscribers
- Increase brand awareness

How to Create High-Quality Content

Now that you know the definition and objectives of content marketing, let's look at how to create high-quality content that helps individuals and brands achieve those objectives. These are the steps you can take to make sure your content is some of the best out there.

Gather Insight

You have business competitors who are creating content to attract the same clients you want. You can start by reading their blog content. Then do in-depth research and create much better content for your audience.

Ensure your content is unique and offers actionable tips your clients can use to solve their pain points. How-to articles work better than other content types.

For instance, if you have a SaaS client who wants to generate leads for his business, you can create a blog post outlining "10 Tips to Generate Leads for Your SaaS Business." In the post, explain the ten tips step by step and show readers how to apply them.

For example, see this Voy Media blog post about the best video editing software. If a potential client needs to find an editor for his video, he'll get all the insight he needs from this blog because it covers the topic well and includes illustrations.

Be Concise

Long sentences are difficult to read. Use a mix of both long and short sentences, but don't make your sentences too long. Each paragraph should have less than four sentences.

You can also use a one-sentence paragraph.

Include lots of white space between your paragraphs. Where possible, use a combination of bullets and white space. A good example is Neil Patel's blog.

Address Clients' Pain Points

Your readers and potential clients search for content online because they're looking for solutions to problems. When developing your content marketing plans, focus on creating content that helps solve those problems.

First, understand your target clients so you can create content that's meaningful to them. A great way to go about this is to develop buyer personas that illustrate your clients' needs and pain points. Then, create content that educates them and introduces helpful solutions.

A Content Marketing Institute (CMI) report shows that 62% of marketers use buyer personas to help focus content for their readers.

Chapter 1: Content Marketing

Agency Content Marketers' Use of Personas in 2018

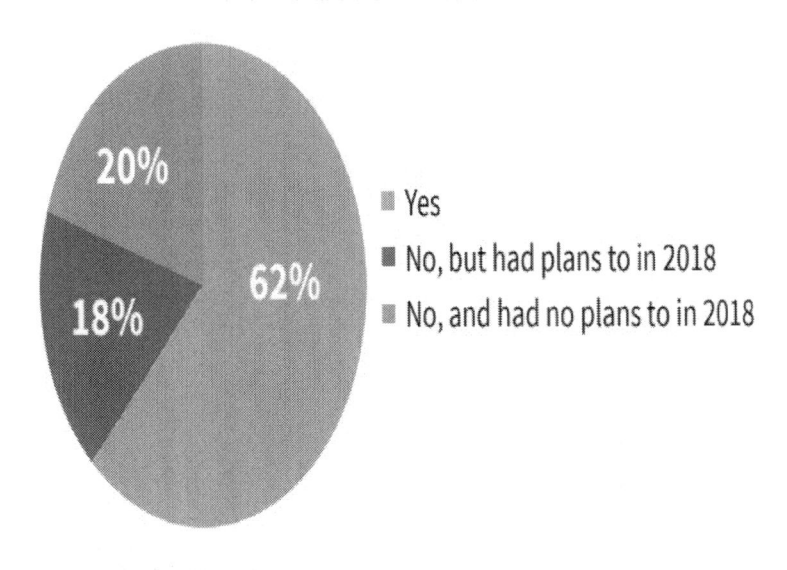

- 20%
- 62%
- 18%

■ Yes
■ No, but had plans to in 2018
■ No, and had no plans to in 2018

Base: Agency content marketers; aided list.

Agency Content Marketing 2019: Benchmarks, Budgets, and Trends—Content Marketing Institute/MarketingProfs

Include Screenshots and Images

Screenshots and other visual illustrations help readers understand and consume your content with ease. Include them to capture your readers' interest and engage them all the way through, to the end of the content.

Also, include statistics and data to support any claims you make and improve your content's credibility.

Use Keywords

Your target clients use keywords to search for useful content. Research by the CMI shows that 78% of marketers use keyword research techniques to create content.

Techniques Agency Content Marketers Use to Research Their Audience

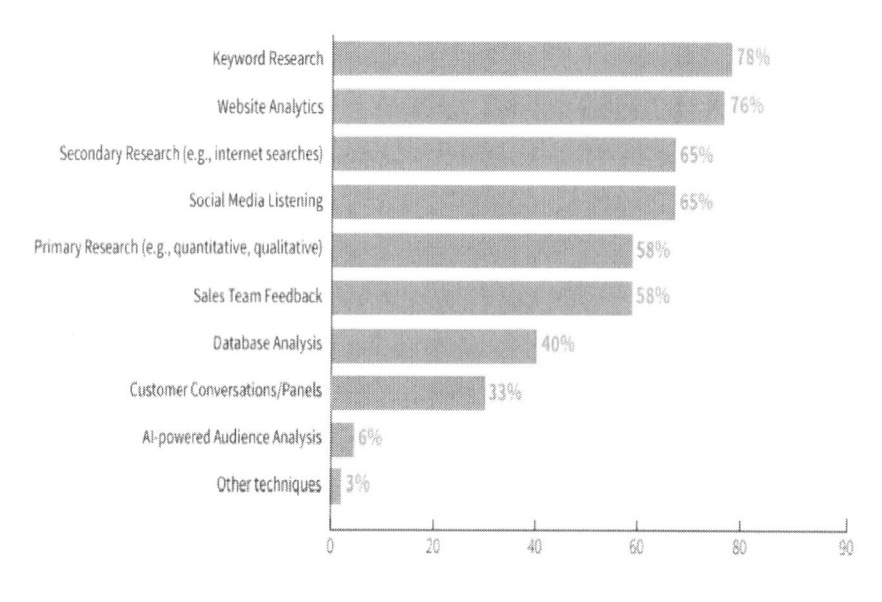

Technique	Percentage
Keyword Research	78%
Website Analytics	76%
Secondary Research (e.g., internet searches)	65%
Social Media Listening	65%
Primary Research (e.g., quantitative, qualitative)	58%
Sales Team Feedback	58%
Database Analysis	40%
Customer Conversations/Panels	33%
AI-powered Audience Analysis	6%
Other techniques	3%

Base: Agency content marketers who research target audiences. Aided list; multiple responses permitted.
Agency Content Marketing 2019 Benchmarks, Budgets, and Trends—Content Marketing Institute/MarketingProfs

Use keyword tools to find and analyze keywords you can use to create your content.

Optimize those keywords within your content so it will rank high in search engine results. Use them in the headlines, subheadings, meta tag descriptions, and article permalink.

Develop a Documented Content Strategy

Document your strategy for content creation. This will help you map out the type of content you'll create, and when you'll need it completed, to achieve your marketing goals.

This plan helps you increase your commitment to your content marketing. A report from the CMI shows that only 38% of organizations are extremely committed. Here are some benefits of documenting your content strategy.

Chapter 1: Content Marketing

How Agency Marketers Rate Their Organization's Commitment to Content Marketing

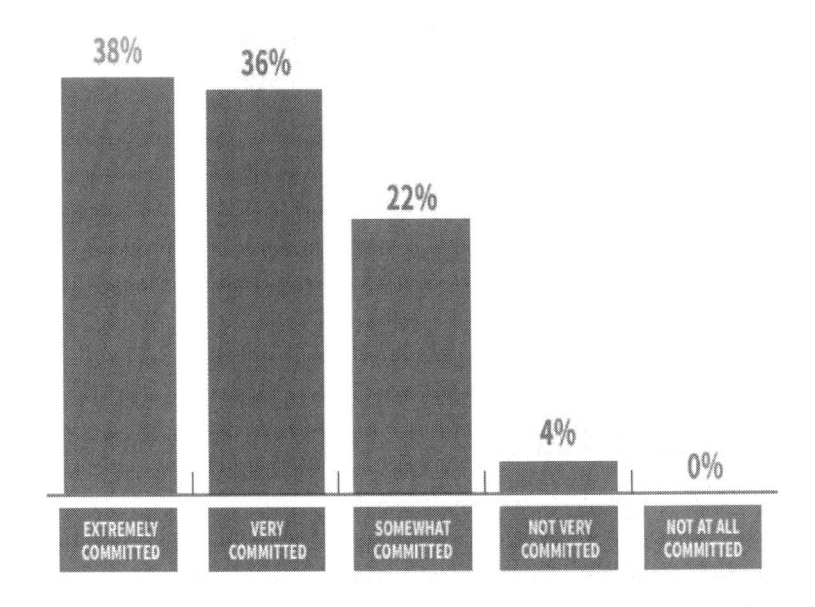

Extremely Committed	Very Committed	Somewhat Committed	Not Very Committed	Not At All Committed
38%	36%	22%	4%	0%

Base: Agency content marketers; aided list.

Agency Content Marketing 2019: Benchmarks, Budgets, and Trends—Content Marketing Institute/MarketingProfs

Generate Blog Content Ideas

To keep up with the content schedule outlined in your content strategy, you'll need a constant stream of blog ideas because you'll be writing frequently. It becomes difficult when you sit down to write a blog post for your readers only to find that you don't know what to write.

Here are some tools that can help you generate blog posts for your audience.

Hubspot Blog Ideas Generator

This is how it works: First, you enter a noun that you want to use as a keyword and add it. You can add more than one noun.

Here's my example. I've added *SaaS, business sales, leads,* and *build trust.*

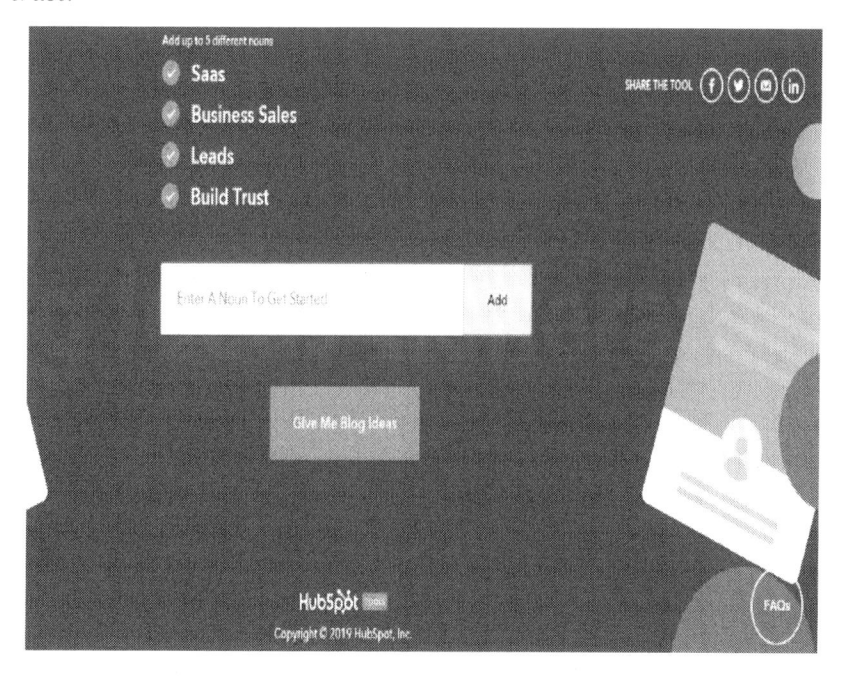

Then, click "Give Me Blog Ideas." Here are the results of my search:

Quora Search

You can use the Quora website to search for topics potential clients are discussing. A simple search should include keywords your target market uses to search for solutions.

I searched for "how to get clients for my eCommerce store," and here's what I found:

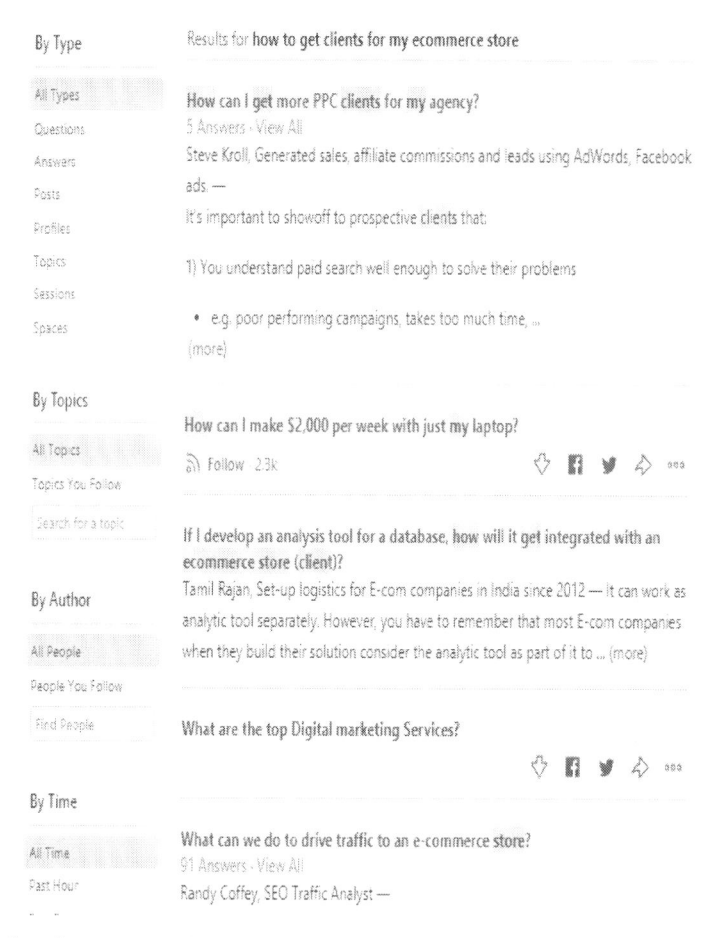

From the above questions, you can know that the first reader wants to learn how to get clients for his agency and the last one wants to draw website traffic.

You can then create content to address those pain points and provide an in-depth solution.

Portent's Content Idea Generator

Chapter 1: Content Marketing

In the search bar, enter the keywords you want to use in your blog post's headline. I used the keywords *increasing eCommerce sales*, and here's a headline that resulted:

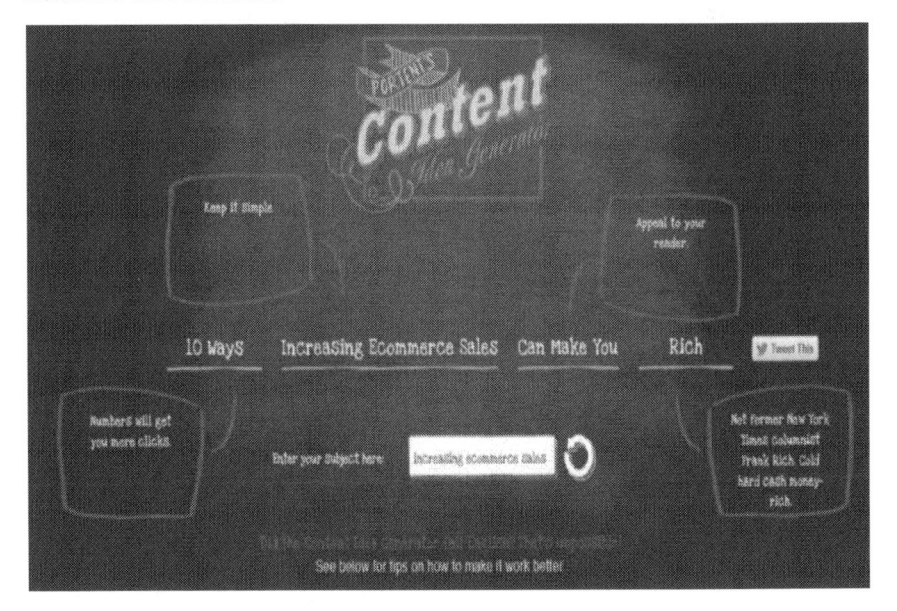

Google Trends

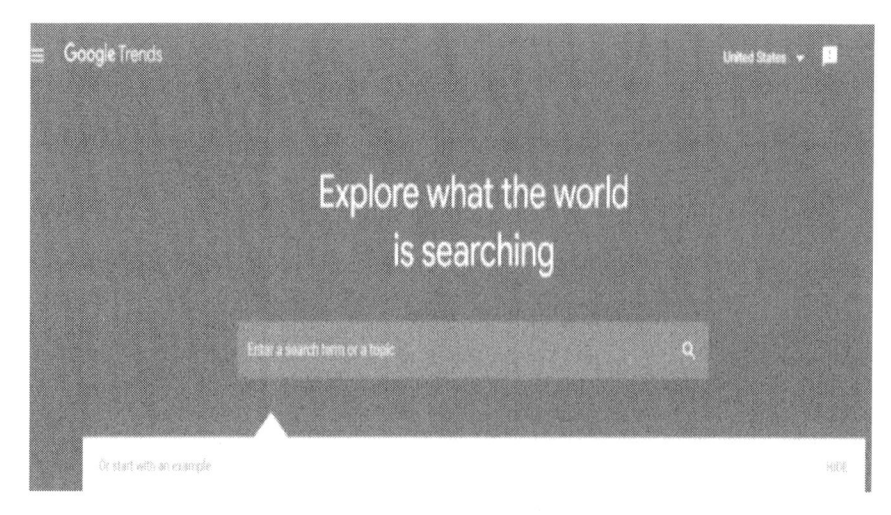

With Google Trends, you can search for the latest information in relation to your business. You can get the latest trends in your industry and use them to create content that's attractive to your target market.

UberSuggest

Neil Patel created this tool, and it can help you research top-performing keywords or content in your industry.

You can use it to generate blog ideas or search for content that contains your keywords. Enter either the domain of your competitor or a keyword.

Chapter 1: Content Marketing

The results will indicate the best-performing pages and blog posts of your competitors.

Use the information to create better content that ranks higher in search engine results.

Here are the results I got by typing in the Voy Media URL:

Domain Overview: voymedia.com

ORGANIC KEYWORDS	ORGANIC MONTHLY TRAFFIC	DOMAIN SCORE	BACKLINKS
11,692	3,340	68	3,749
			NoFollow: 1,260

TRAFFIC — 3,340 organic visitors per month

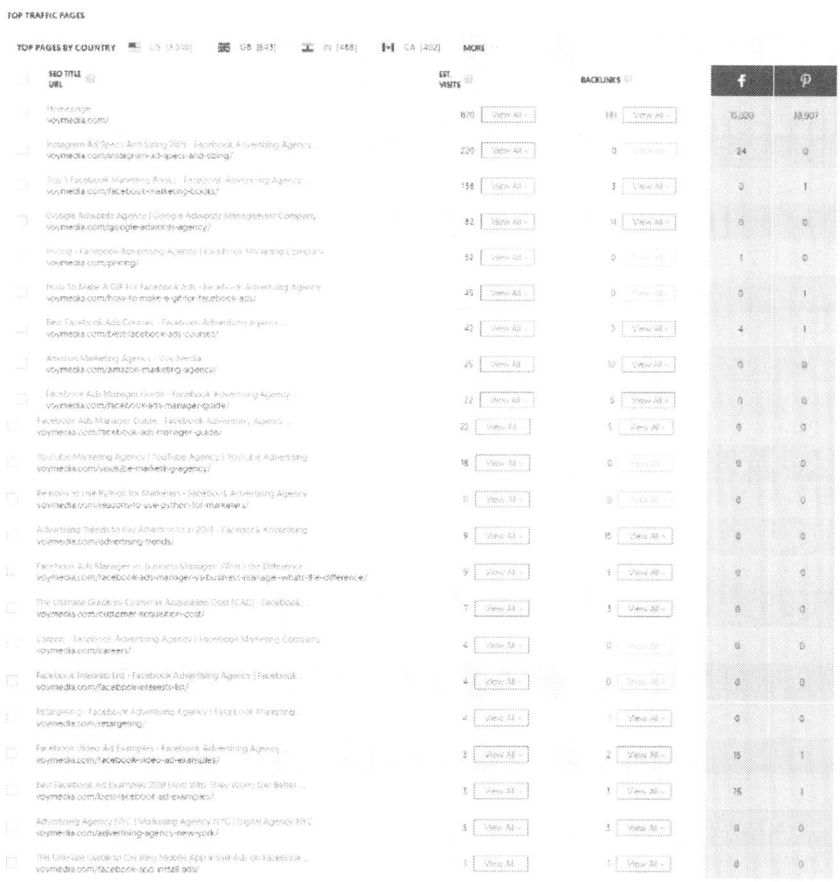

The above information shows you the blog post headlines that perform, and with that knowledge, you can create much better content for your readers.

Don't copy the information or the blog post content. Simply use it to gain insight, then rely on your own expertise to create much better and more detailed content for your readers.

Google Keyword Planner

You already know your target market and you've developed a buyer persona to represent it. Google Keyword Planner helps you find keywords your target market uses to search for content online that will solve their problems.

Using the keywords, you can generate content ideas and write to address their challenges and propose solutions.

Link Bait Generator

With Link Bait Generator, you simply type your keywords into the search bar and click "Get Headlines." Here are examples of blog post content ideas I generated with the keywords *increase free trials for business*.

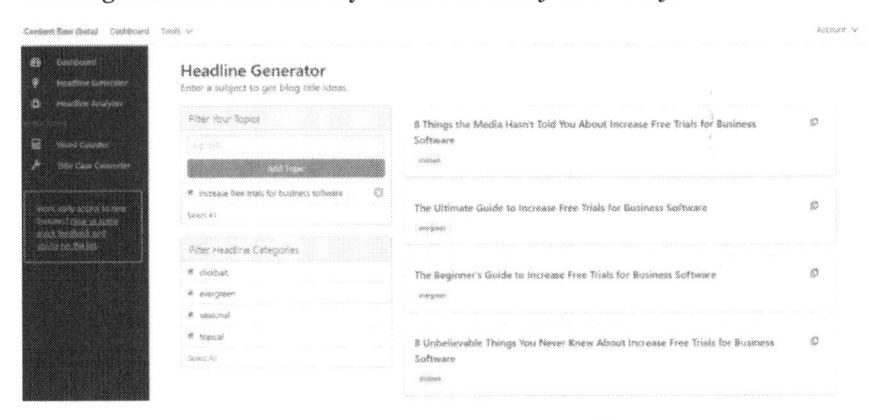

Other Methods

Apart from the above tools, here are some other ways to generate content ideas.

Read marketing content. The more you read, the more knowledge you gain about your market niche. Read both offline and online materials.

You learn more about your readers and generate ideas that you can share to attract, engage, and convert them to customers

Engage with readers in online forums. Take advantage of these forums and groups from different social media accounts. Through the groups and forums, you can ask and answer questions. As you engage with potential clients, you can learn more about them and use the information you gather to create content.

For instance, here are some LinkedIn groups you can join to participate in the discussion:

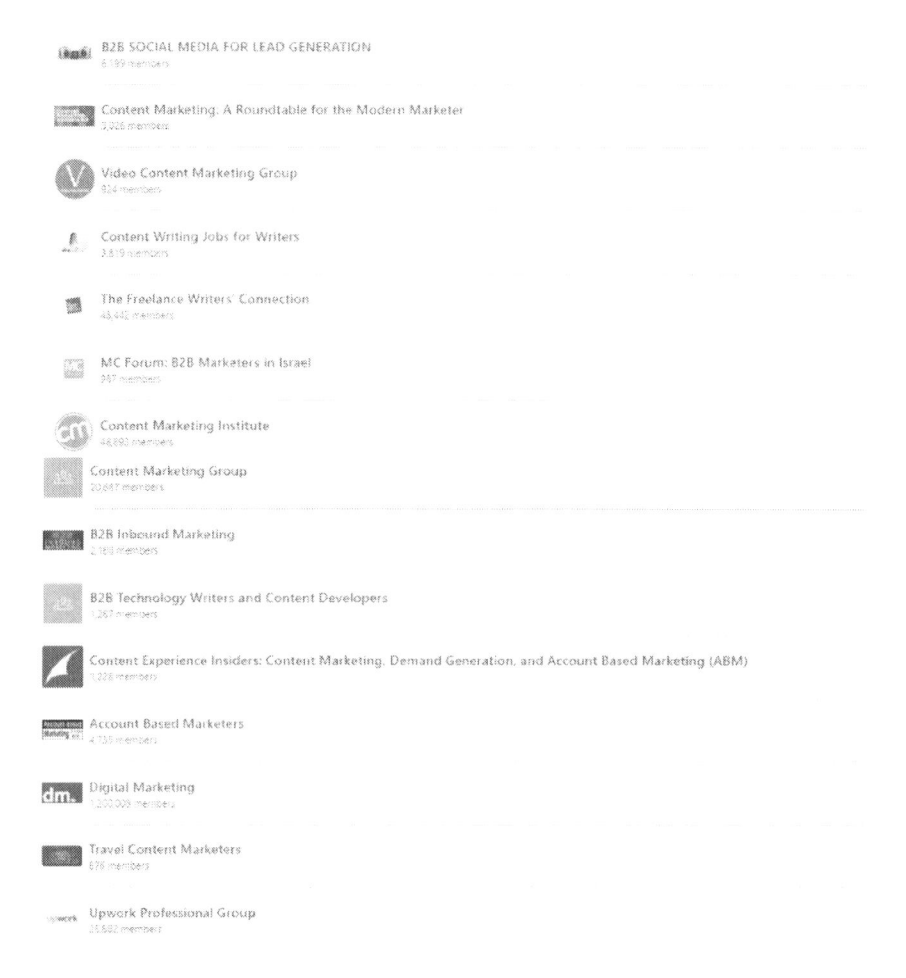

- B2B SOCIAL MEDIA FOR LEAD GENERATION
- Content Marketing: A Roundtable for the Modern Marketer
- Video Content Marketing Group
- Content Writing Jobs for Writers
- The Freelance Writers' Connection
- MC Forum: B2B Marketers in Israel
- Content Marketing Institute
- Content Marketing Group
- B2B Inbound Marketing
- B2B Technology Writers and Content Developers
- Content Experience Insiders: Content Marketing, Demand Generation, and Account Based Marketing (ABM)
- Account Based Marketers
- Digital Marketing
- Travel Content Marketers
- Upwork Professional Group

Tips: How to Write Engaging Content

Here are some pointers to help write stunning content.

Write a catchy headline

There's too much noise on the internet. To get clients to hear you and pay attention, you have to give them something worthy of their time. Spare no effort on your article headline. It's what will make potential clients click and read your content, thinking, "Hmm . . . I should check out this article. It sounds promising."

A great headline includes

>**A call-to-action.** It triggers readers to take immediate action. Call-to-action headlines catch readers' attention because they want to know what the article recommends for immediate action.
>
>**Numbers.** Readers love headlines with numbers, for example, "5 incredible ways to make money online from home."
>
>**A promise.** Your readers are likely to read an article that promises them something. But don't get carried away! Always ensure you deliver on your promise.

There are so many tools you can use to create awesome, captivating headlines for your content. One of these great tools is the CoSchedule Headline Analyzer.

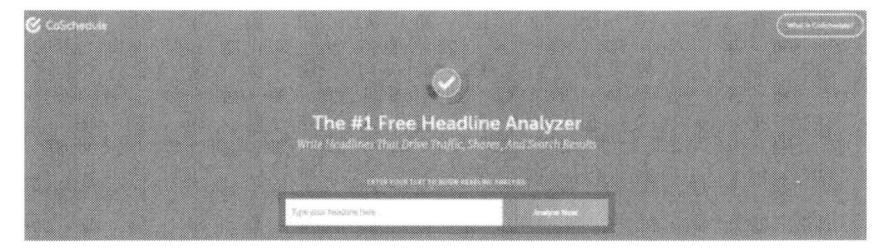

I ran a sample headline through the tool and this is what I got. The headline was "How to Actually Write Awesome Click-Irresistible Headlines":

How To Actually Write Awesome Click Irresistable Headlines

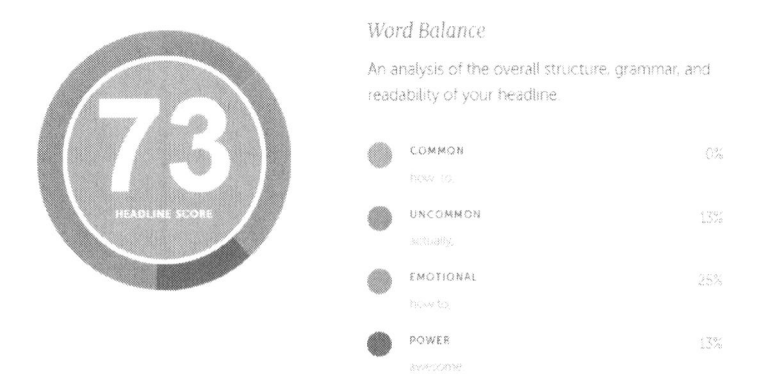

73 HEADLINE SCORE

Word Balance
An analysis of the overall structure, grammar, and readability of your headline.

- COMMON — 0%
  how to
- UNCOMMON — 13%
  actually
- EMOTIONAL — 25%
  how to
- POWER — 13%
  awesome

Write evergreen content

Write content that won't become obsolete in the near future. Update your posts if there are new technological and content advancements. That will keep your readers updated with the latest trends.

However, some content, like articles about holiday events, becomes outdated quickly. Find a way to tweak the content you deliver so it's always relevant. Clients are always searching for information to solve their problems. Good information is valuable and trustworthy.

Evergreen content ranks high in search engine results and has more likes, shares, and comments on social media.

Create content in line with your business brand. Include supporting content like screenshots, images, and linked videos to support the content's message. Your content should focus on the clients' needs and provide step-by-step guidance on how to solve their pain points.

Limit listicles

Do you write one type of article content, listicles? Well, readers get tired of reading content in the same format all the time. It's imperative that you write different types of headlines and unique content. Create a mix of interesting types of content for your readers.

Want to nurture your leads through the different buyer stages? Create effective content that builds trust, educates your leads about your business, and increases conversion rates and sales.

Readers need content that educates and informs them and is actionable. They need to know how they can implement the content's message to solve their pain points.

If you accomplish these goals, readers will like what you publish. They'll enjoy reading your work and your site will draw lots of traffic. With your actionable content, you can easily convert leads to clients.

Engage with Commenters

Once you've created outstanding content, encourage your readers to comment and share. Through the comments, you'll learn even more about your readers and their problems, and you'll have a chance to relate to them directly.

This will help you keep creating content that addresses those pain points, builds their trust, and converts them into loyal customers.

Improve Your Writing Skills

We've covered all the basics of creating high-quality content and you've put them into practice, but it's still not coming easy. What else can you do? Just as you go to the gym for your health and fitness, you need to stretch your writing muscle to keep creating awesome content for your readers. Here are some tips to improve your writing.

Practice, practice, practice

Writers are readers. Ensure you read widely to get content ideas and improve your vocabulary. Read articles on great sites like Forbes.com, Entrepreneur.com, Inc.com, and nytimes.com, among others.

This gives you experience and exposes you to high-performing content that's read by millions of people. You can imitate what you read on this site when creating your content, but incorporate your own expertise and information to make it unique.

Remove distractions when writing

Distractions interfere with your flow of creative juices. You can lose your train of thought if you're distracted during writing. Use tools to keep yourself focused as you work.

To ensure faster writing, write when your creativity is running high. Also, don't write and edit your content at the same time. Just get your rough draft down, and you can edit it later.

Set a writing target

You know your content strategy and the number of articles you need per week. Set a target for the number and length of articles you want to create. Enforcing a deadline for each article can help motivate you and eliminate procrastination.

Buyer Journey Stages

Your leads go through stages before they become clients. During each stage, you work to strengthen trust in your company from the leads' perspective as you show them how your services will help them. It's vital to commit and give your best effort to your leads at each stage to nurture them down the sales funnel.

Here are the stages leads go through to become clients.

Awareness

At this stage, the leads are not even aware of the challenges they're facing. You need to educate and inform them about their pain points. This process is crucial as it encourages them to recognize their problems and start considering solutions.

Your leads also need to know that your business can help them overcome their obstacles. This is a trust-building stage. The leads learn more about your business and how your products or services can help them.

Further, you should offer your leads informative and comprehensive content to highlight the challenges they experience in their business. Show them your business expertise as they learn more about your business and their own pain points. Some beneficial content types at this stage include

- videos
- documentaries

infographics

articles and blog posts

Consideration

Once leads have become aware of their difficulties, they move to the consideration stage. At this point, they're trying to consider the products that will help them solve their identified problems.

Expose your leads to different products and services you offer to help them see the best ones to use in their problem-solving. Provide them with valuable and educational content to support them in the decision-making process. Content types you can use at this stage are

> e-books
> videos
> in-depth blog posts
> guides
> templates
> spreadsheets

Decision-Making

Now your prospects have settled on the services or products they view as solutions.

They need more detailed information about the specific products they're considering. Research by Demand Generation shows that <u>40% of buyers consume three to five types of content</u> before buying.

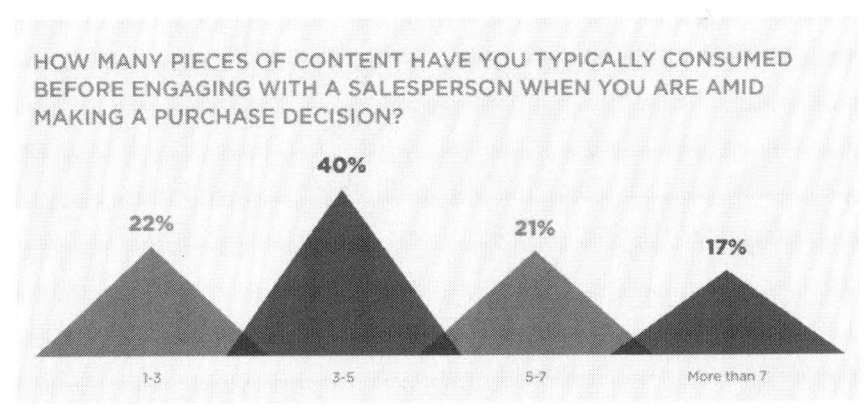

HOW MANY PIECES OF CONTENT HAVE YOU TYPICALLY CONSUMED BEFORE ENGAGING WITH A SALESPERSON WHEN YOU ARE AMID MAKING A PURCHASE DECISION?

- 1-3: 22%
- 3-5: 40%
- 5-7: 21%
- More than 7: 17%

Create a variety of content to help buyers make informed decisions. Suitable content for this stage includes

Case studies: Leads see examples of other customers who used the services and how they solved their problems.

Reports: Clients see data about other businesses that are using or have used your business products or services. This builds trust with the leads because prospects trust other businesses that have benefited from taking the route they're considering.

Reviews: Positive recommendations from customers strengthen the trust bond with your leads. Research by BrightLocal shows that 27% of buyers read online reviews before purchasing a product or service. Providing reviews and recommendations from previous customers makes it easy to convert leads into customers.

Blog posts and white papers: Inform leads at this stage in lead nurturing by offering in-depth knowledge about your business and positioning it as a thought leader in your industry.

Do you read online reviews for businesses?

Do you read online reviews for businesses?

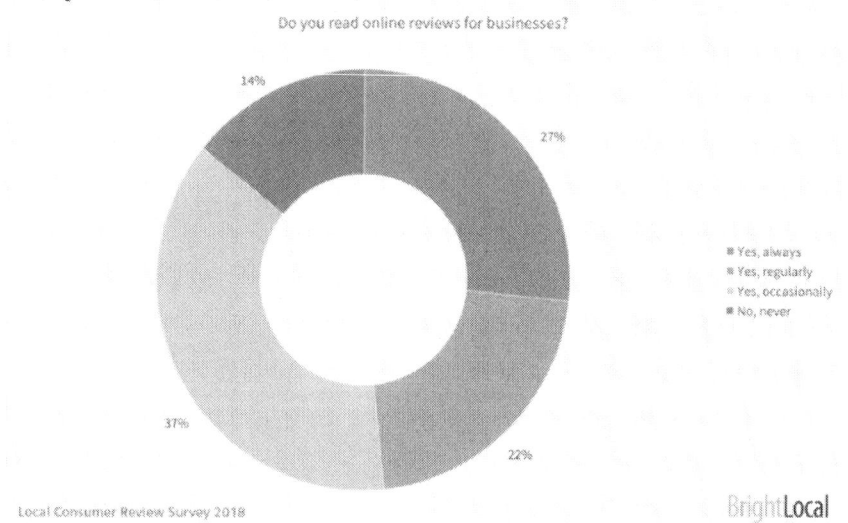

- Yes, always — 14%
- Yes, regularly — 27%
- Yes, occasionally — 37%
- No, never — 22%

Local Consumer Review Survey 2018 — BrightLocal

Content Marketing Metrics to Monitor

It's essential to evaluate and analyze the return on investment (ROI) of your content marketing efforts. ROI is the business revenue you generate as an outcome of your content marketing campaigns. Before we dive into the metrics, let's look at how to measure your content ROI.

Measuring Content Marketing ROI

These are the steps you can take to measure the returns from your content marketing.

Step 1: Calculate content production cost

How much does it cost to produce your content? You hire content creators and freelancers to write content for you. Or, if you don't hire writers, you pay your in-house employees to write the content.

Step 2: Calculate distribution cost

Once your content is ready, you don't just publish it. You distribute it to attract your target market's attention to your brand. You use a variety of means and tools to distribute the content, and most of those tools are not free.

Evaluate how much it costs you to distribute the content through different channels like social media or other websites, your cost per click (CPC), and any other associated expenses.

Step 3: Calculate content returns

The first two steps will give you the total cost of your content. Calculate the total sales you get from each piece of content.

This will give you a rough estimate of the returns from your content marketing. Here's a simple way to calculate the ROI:

How to Calculate Content Marketing ROI

$$\text{Content Marketing ROI (as percentage)} = \left(\frac{\text{Return} - \text{Investment}}{\text{Investment}} \right) \times 100$$

optinmonster

Image Source: https://optinmonster.com/how-to-measure-content-marketing-roi-metrics/

For example, let's say you spend $750 creating content and the resulting sales bring in $5,000 in revenue.

> Subtract the investment from the returns: $5000 - $750 = $4,250
>
> Divide the result by the amount of the investment: $4,250 / 750 = 5.6667
>
> Multiply by 100: 5.6777 × 100 = 568%
>
> Your ROI is 568%.

Other objectives, like content engagement and thought leadership or keeping up with your competitors, can't be fully measured. With that in mind, let's move on to the content marketing metrics you *can* monitor.

Content Marketing Metrics

You create content with various aims. Here are the metrics you can measure:

Shares

Quality content gets more shares among readers. Potential clients will share your content on social media if they see that the content is high quality and helps them solve their pain points.

High-value content enhances brand image, draws traffic to your website, and builds more trust with your potential clients.

Among the many tools that can help you with social shares tracking is SEMrush.

Chapter 1: Content Marketing

Here's an example of content shares for the Creative Revolt blog:

Bounce rate

This is the number of website visitors who "bounce" off or leave your site just after landing on it.

Bounce rate is calculated by dividing the number of visitors who leave immediately by the total number of visitors to the site. For example, if 500 visitors land on the homepage of a website, and 100 leave without clicking any other page on the site, then the bounce rate of that homepage is 100 / 500 = 20%.

A high bounce rate on your website is a clear sign that your content is not attractive and educational. This is even worse for an e-commerce site because a high bounce rate can result in no sales. Some ways to reduce bounce rate include

- Writing quality content

- Improving the user experience
- Attracting the right readers to your site
- Maintaining a responsive website
- Reducing page load time

The following diagram shows key factors in boosting your website's usability and reducing its bounce rate.

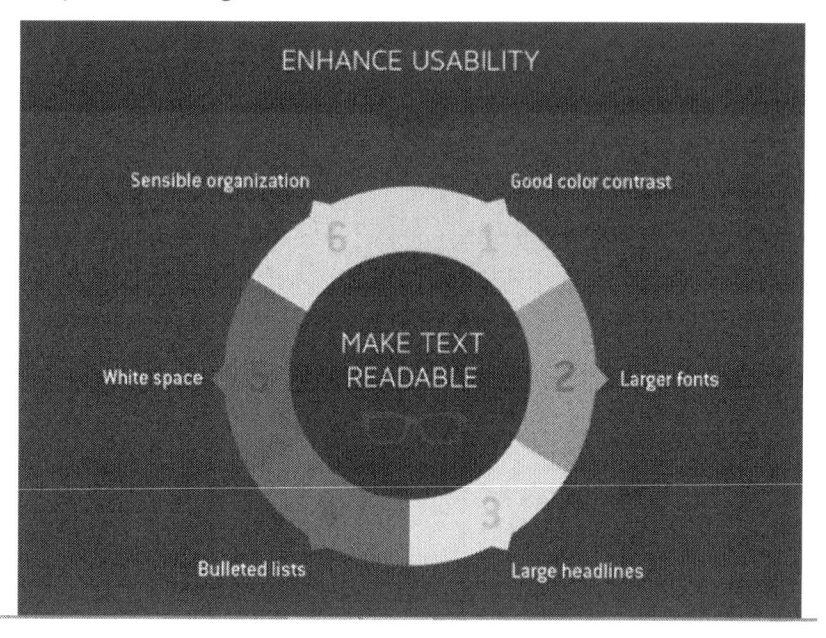

ENHANCE USABILITY

MAKE TEXT READABLE

1. Good color contrast
2. Larger fonts
3. Large headlines
4. Bulleted lists
5. White space
6. Sensible organization

Traffic

High website traffic shows that your content is performing better. One of the best tools for measuring traffic to your website is SimilarWeb.

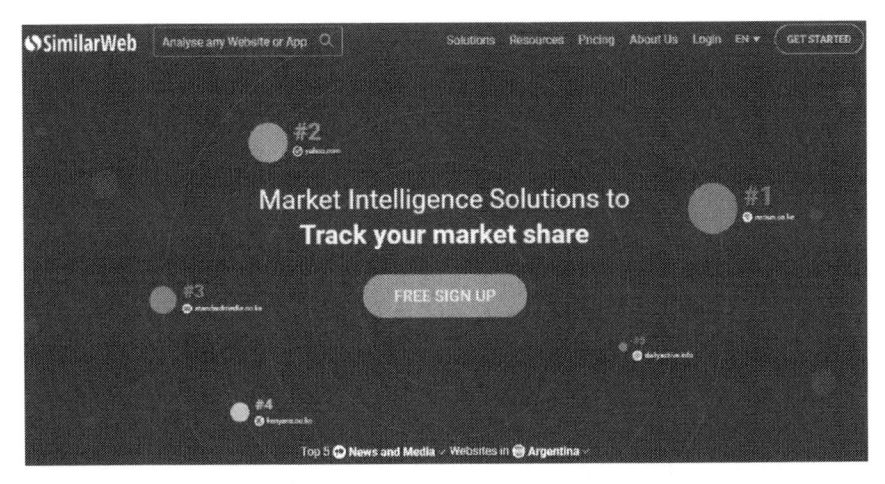

Traffic to your website indicates readers are loving your content and want to engage more with it.

The tools we've listed so far can tell you which marketing channels draw high traffic, and you should promote your content on those sites.

Reader comments

A high number of comments from readers shows that they like and want to engage with your content. When more and more readers continue to engage with your content through comments, you continue to develop trust and increase your brand awareness.

To keep engaging your readers, create in-depth content that guides readers to solve their problems. Here's an example of great reader engagement with a blog post by Brian Dean.

> # We Analyzed 5.2 Million Desktop and Mobile Pages. Here's What We Learned About Page Speed
>
> by Brian Dean
>
> We analyzed 5 million desktop and mobile pages to learn which factors impact page speed.
>
> First, we established worldwide benchmarks for TTFB, Visual Complete and Fully Loaded load time metrics.
>
> Then, we looked at how image compression, CDNs and hosting impact site loading speed.
>
> Our data revealed some very interesting (and surprising) insights.
>
> **Continue Reading**
>
> 448 Comments

Content mentions

When website visitors like your content, they'll share and mention it on social sites and attract other readers who can benefit from it.

In relation to mentions, listen to what your readers are saying about your content and brand. You can monitor the content mentions of your competitors and create far better content for your target audience.

Here are some of the best tools to use for social listening and content mentions:

> Hubspot (free or paid)
> Hootsuite
> Buffer
> TweetReach
> BuzzSumo
> SproutSocial
> Keyhole
> SumAll (free)
> Mention (free)
> Awario

Conversion rates

Conversion is an awesome way to measure the performance of your content campaigns. You can use your content to trigger conversions in different ways for your business.

Some numbers to keep track of are

> Email subscriber signups
> Email CTA click-throughs
> Landing page form completions
> Email open rates

Link-building

When other business owners and writers find your website content resourceful, they'll link to it. Great content encourages link building, which draws more traffic to your website.

You can use online tools to analyze your link building for your website content. For your outbound links, ensure you link to high-quality blogs in your market niche.

Page views

High page views from visitors indicate that your readers like the content on your site.

Monitor the number of views for each page and evaluate the content you've posted on it. If it's not attracting high traffic, then revisit your buyer personas and tweak the content.

Top Content Creation and Marketing Tools

The content creation process can be tedious. Luckily, there are tons of tools that can help you create and market your content.

The CMI studied some of the tools marketers use to create awesome content. Here's what they found:

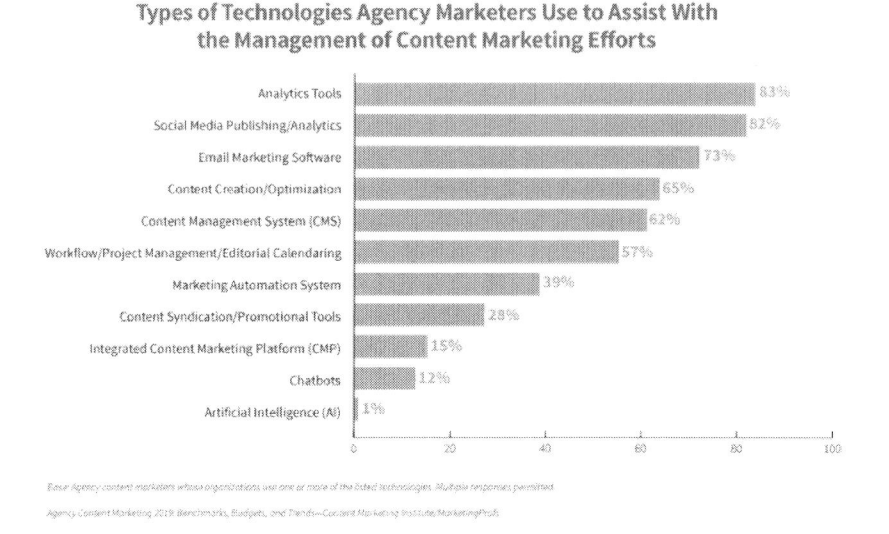

Types of Technologies Agency Marketers Use to Assist With the Management of Content Marketing Efforts

Technology	Percentage
Analytics Tools	83%
Social Media Publishing/Analytics	82%
Email Marketing Software	73%
Content Creation/Optimization	65%
Content Management System (CMS)	62%
Workflow/Project Management/Editorial Calendaring	57%
Marketing Automation System	39%
Content Syndication/Promotional Tools	28%
Integrated Content Marketing Platform (CMP)	15%
Chatbots	12%
Artificial Intelligence (AI)	1%

Base: Agency content marketers whose organizations use one or more of the listed technologies. Multiple responses permitted.
Agency Content Marketing 2019: Benchmarks, Budgets, and Trends—Content Marketing Institute/MarketingProfs

Let's analyze these tools, breaking them down into several categories.

Image Creation Tools

Images inspire your readers' first impressions. They attract readers and engage them in your content. Here are some tools to help create and source the best images to fit your content.

Chapter 1: Content Marketing

Stencil

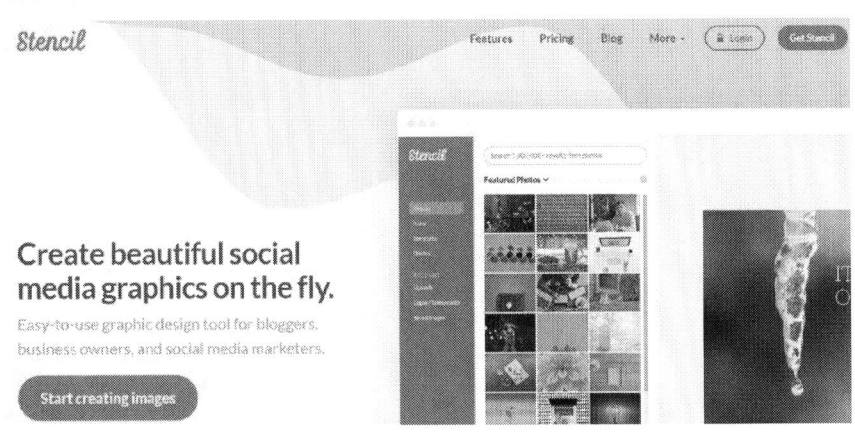

Stencil helps you design beautiful, high-quality images for your content. The tool offers royalty-free images that are simply stunning.

Here are a few of its awesome features:

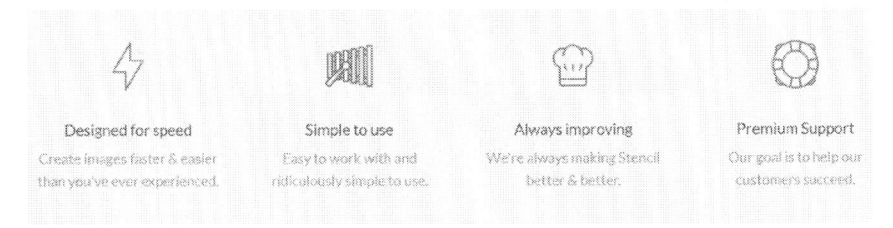

Designed for speed — Create images faster & easier than you've ever experienced.

Simple to use — Easy to work with and ridiculously simple to use.

Always improving — We're always making Stencil better & better.

Premium Support — Our goal is to help our customers succeed.

And here is its pricing model:

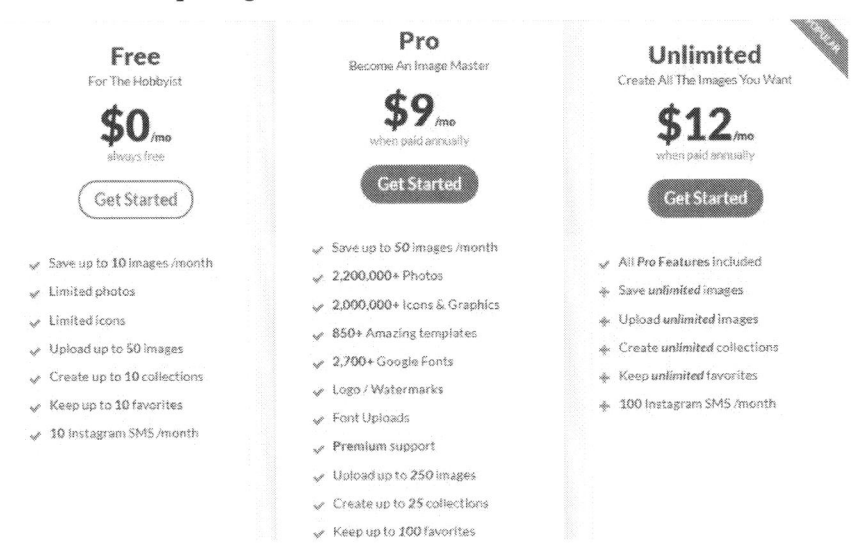

Free — For The Hobbyist
$0/mo always free
- Save up to 10 images /month
- Limited photos
- Limited icons
- Upload up to 50 images
- Create up to 10 collections
- Keep up to 10 favorites
- 10 Instagram SMS /month

Pro — Become An Image Master
$9/mo when paid annually
- Save up to 50 images /month
- 2,200,000+ Photos
- 2,000,000+ Icons & Graphics
- 850+ Amazing templates
- 2,700+ Google Fonts
- Logo / Watermarks
- Font Uploads
- Premium support
- Upload up to 250 images
- Create up to 25 collections
- Keep up to 100 favorites

Unlimited — Create All The Images You Want
$12/mo when paid annually
- All Pro Features included
- Save *unlimited* images
- Upload *unlimited* images
- Create *unlimited* collections
- Keep *unlimited* favorites
- 100 Instagram SMS /month

Pixlr

This tool can give you a serious advantage when it comes to editing your photos. Its user-friendly features let you create awesome images that attract and engage your readers.

Photo Collage

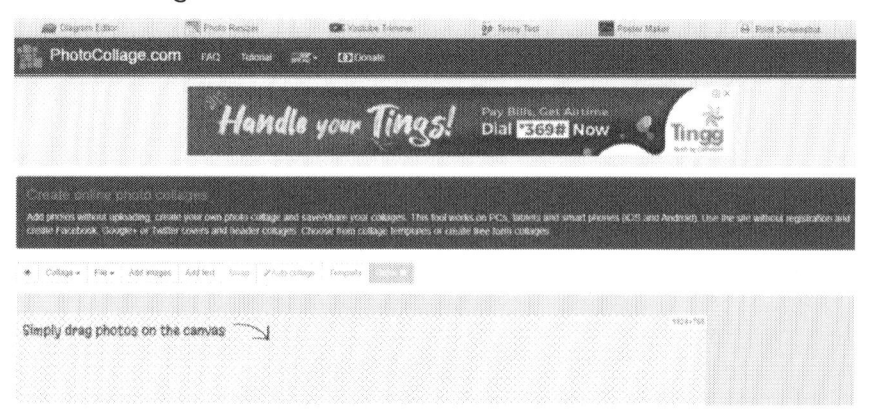

Create collages using this tool, which includes an awesome FAQ section that answers any questions you may have. You can watch the tutorial to learn more about how the tool works.

To drag your photos onto the canvas, ensure that they contain more than 50 pixels. Corrupt images can't be loaded into the canvas.

Chapter 1: Content Marketing

Fotor

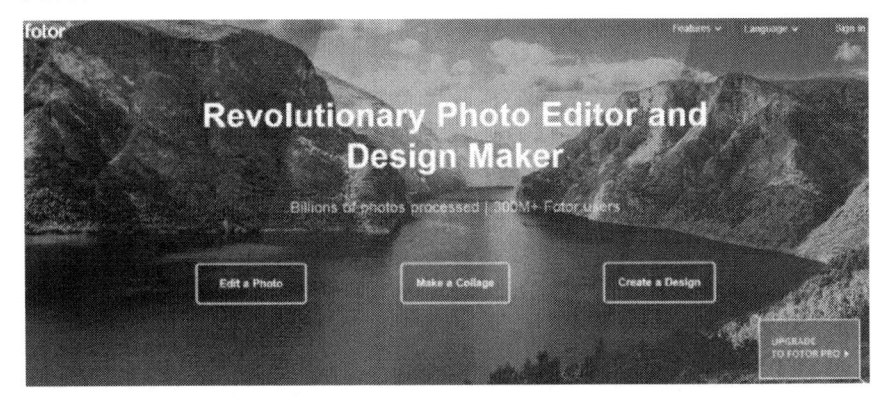

Fotor is a photo processing tool. Its site offers a few tutorial videos that show you how to use it. You can choose from basic and pro features.

Here is its pricing:

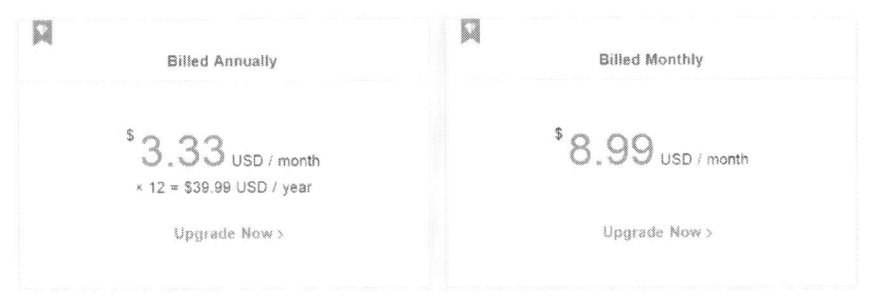

Adobe Spark

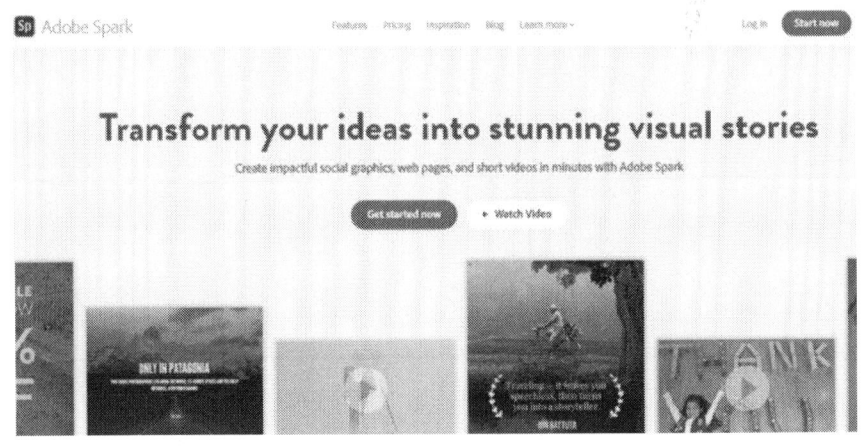

This tool can help you create beautiful images and visual content for your website.

Canva

With this tool, you can search for graphics, fonts, etc., and use the drag-and-drop feature to create an amazing design for your marketing content.

It also has digital cropping features that help you frame your images the way you want.

Snappa

Snappa helps you create a variety of graphics to go with your website content. You can put together the perfect images to go on your landing page, accompany your blog post, or draw attention to your social media account.

Chapter 1: Content Marketing

Its different photo types are editable and suitable for marketing needs. Snappa has awesome templates you can customize to match your content marketing goals.

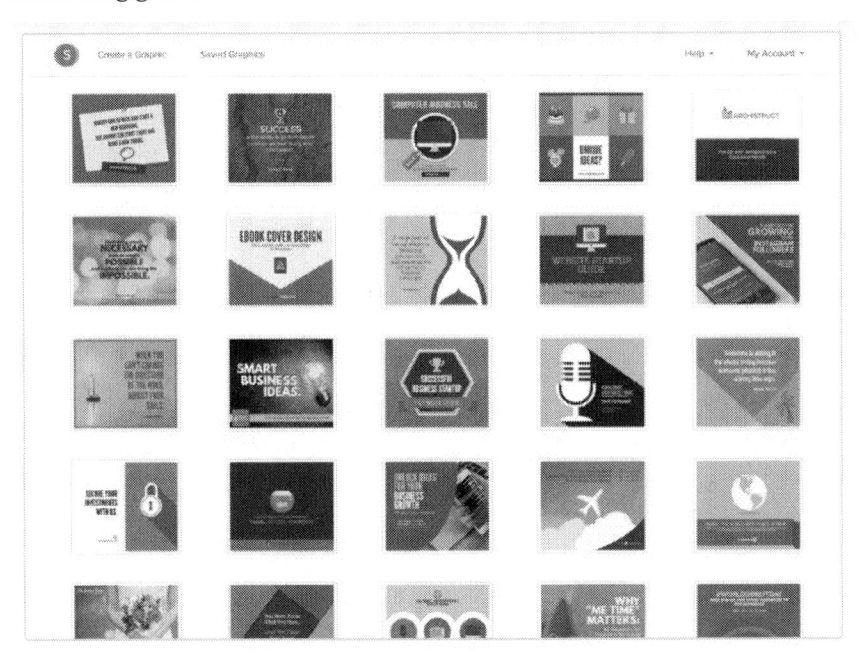

You can check out the Snappa pricing model below.

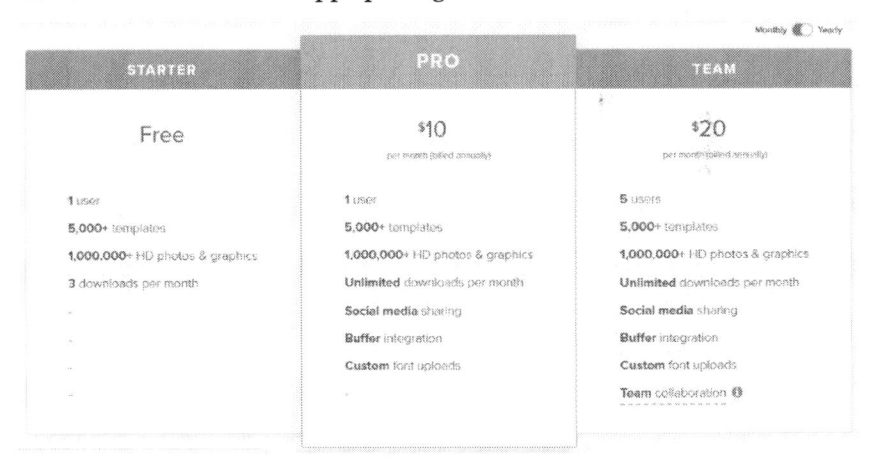

STARTER	PRO	TEAM
Free	$10 per month (billed annually)	$20 per month (billed annually)
1 user	1 user	5 users
5,000+ templates	5,000+ templates	5,000+ templates
1,000,000+ HD photos & graphics	1,000,000+ HD photos & graphics	1,000,000+ HD photos & graphics
3 downloads per month	Unlimited downloads per month	Unlimited downloads per month
	Social media sharing	Social media sharing
	Buffer integration	Buffer integration
	Custom font uploads	Custom font uploads
		Team collaboration

Content Editing Tools

Your content needs to be error-free and easy to consume. These tools help you edit your content so it'll not only be high-quality, but easy and enjoyable to read.

Grammarly

This tool helps you correct grammar, spelling, and punctuation and set the tone of your writing. Its many features include a plagiarism checker to let you know when content has been copied from other sites.

Readable

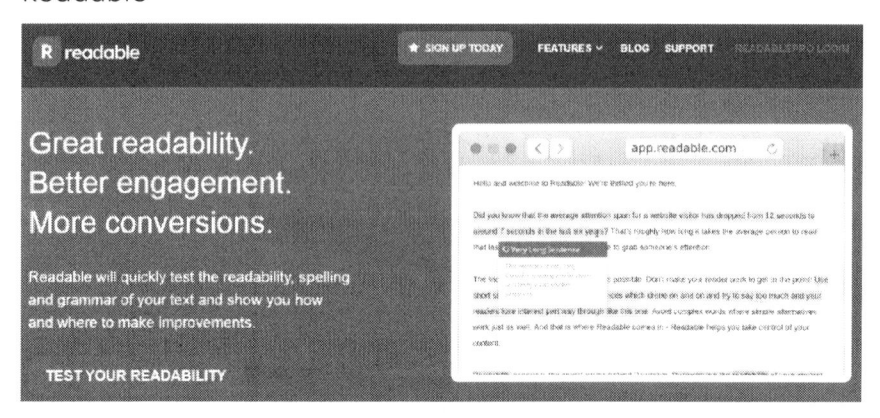

This tool offers suggestions to improve your content's readability. For example, it tells you when you should shorten paragraphs and sentences, incorporate transitional words, or add white space.

Below are some beneficial features of the tool.

Chapter 1: Content Marketing

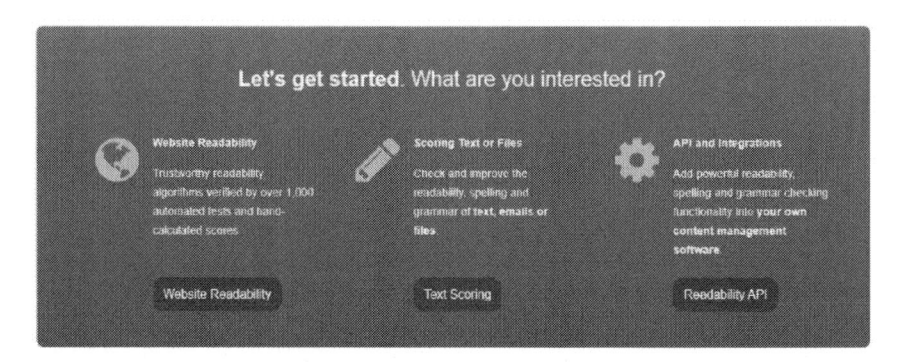

And here's what its readability score shows you.

Check out the Readable website to see its comprehensive pricing model.

After the Deadline

This excellent language checker's advanced grammar and spell-check uses artificial intelligence to identify and correct errors in writing.

You can use it as a plugin for your website's blog or as a search engine extension. It's also compatible with a myriad of languages, so you can choose the language you want for the writing and editing of your content.

ProwritingAid

Chapter 1: Content Marketing

This option has both free and paid features. You can check article errors or root out plagiarism. With the paid option, there's no limit to the content you can correct.

It can be incorporated into other tools like Google Docs, search engines, or Microsoft Word. Here's the tool pricing:

1-year	2-year	3-year	Lifetime
$70⁰⁰	$100⁰⁰	$140⁰⁰	$240⁰⁰
Purchase	Purchase	Purchase	Purchase
			Most popular

Content Marketing Tools

These tools are a great way to implement some of the principles and tips we've already covered while letting the computer do some of the work for you.

Yoast

Yoast helps you optimize your content for search engines. It guides you in the placement and use of keywords in different parts of your content.

Components, where you can place your keywords, include headlines, meta descriptions, subheadings, and body text.

It has a readability score tool to measure the ease of reading your content. It also offers SEO courses to teach marketers how to grow their website traffic through content optimization.

Ahrefs

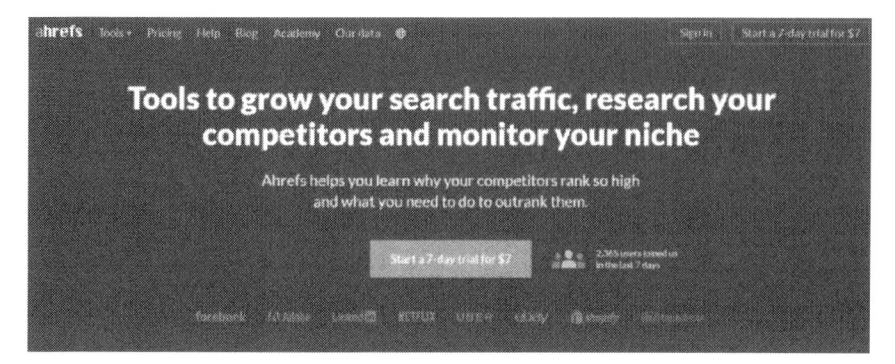

With Ahrefs, you learn more about why your competitors rank high and use the same tactics to grow your own traffic.

Its array of tools is essential for your content marketing.

You can visit the Ahrefs website to learn more about the tool and its pricing.

Chapter 1: Content Marketing

Google Docs

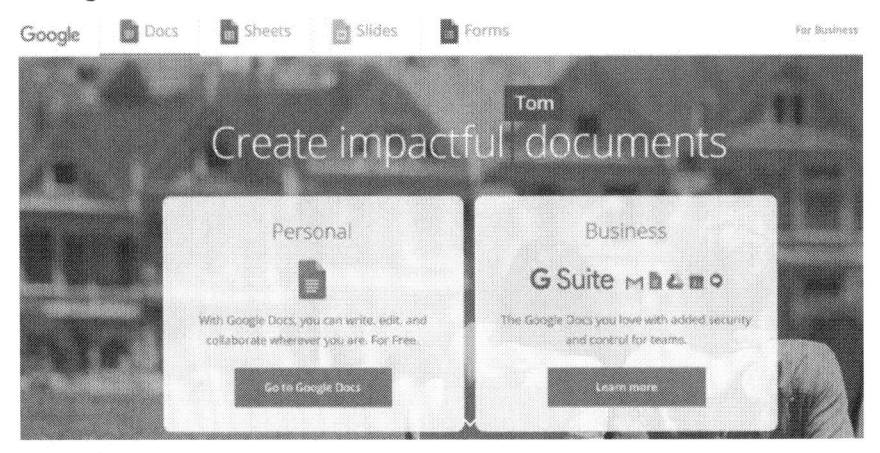

Google Docs is a word processing program that helps you edit, format, and share content with other users. You can use the tool for personal or business needs. However, you have to pay for more advanced business services.

Trello

This tool is a project management platform that helps you organize your content and business workflow efficiently.

Its pricing model varies depending on the nature and size of your business. Visit the company's website to choose the best option for you.

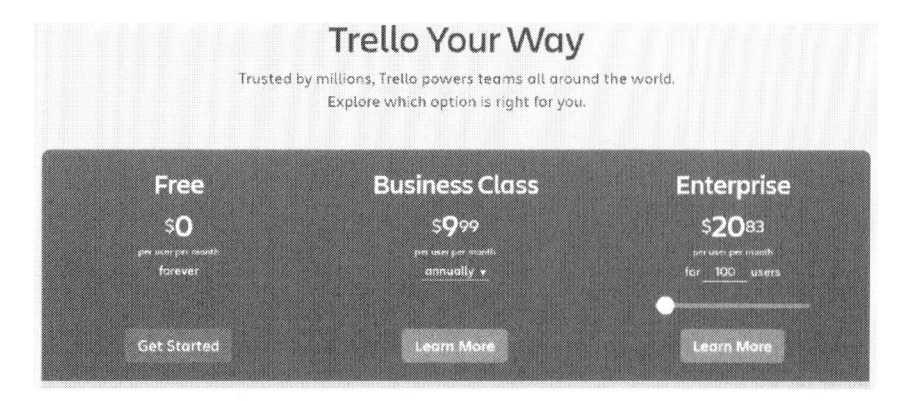

WordPress

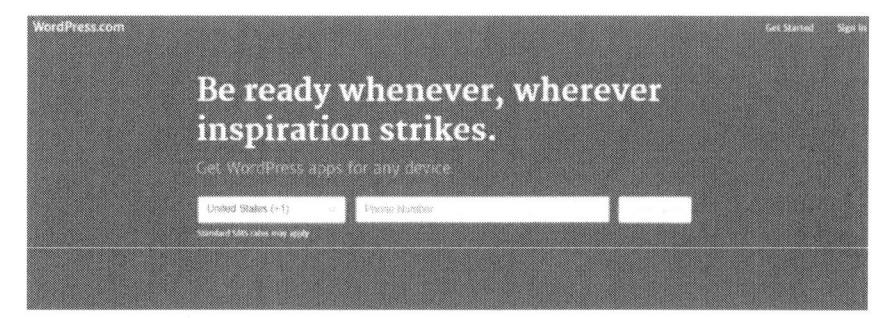

WordPress is a content management system that helps you run your blog page or website. With WordPress, you can customize your content for marketing purposes.

You can keep updating your blog post content or create new content for your website as needed.

Chapter 1: Content Marketing

Google Optimize

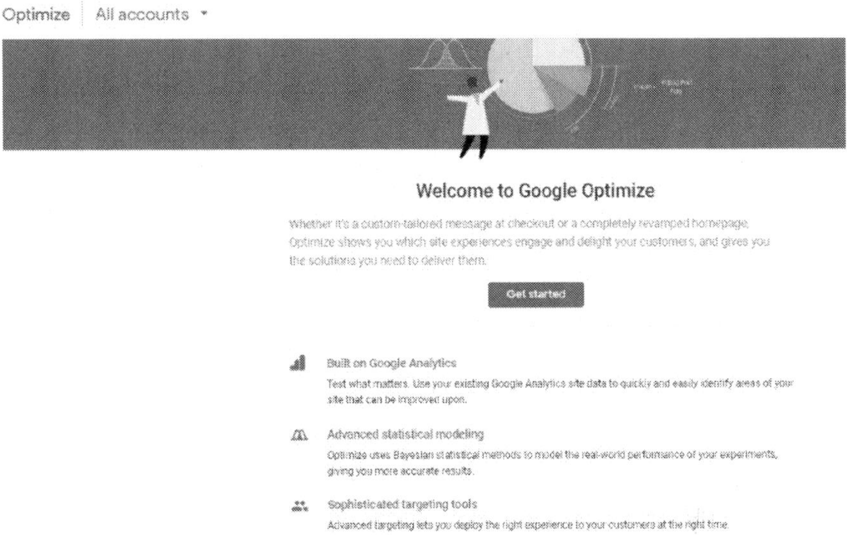

This tool helps you test and improve your user content experience. It helps you conduct an A/B test on your site to determine the best way to deliver your content to users.

For advanced features, use Google Optimize 360. Its advanced services help you understand how to market your brand and attract potential customers to your business.

Airtable

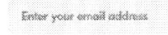

This platform has features of a database but works like a spreadsheet to help organize your work. You can use it to manage your customer relationship.

You can integrate the tool with your website to help share your content with your readers.

Here is its pricing model:

Visit the Airtable website for an in-depth view of the pricing model.

SEMrush

For your content to rank high on search engines, you need to include the keywords your potential customers use.

This tool helps you find those keywords. You can monitor your competitors' keywords, ads, and budgets to determine the right type of ads to invest in.

Chapter 1: Content Marketing

SEMrush helps you analyze link-building to find out what types of content your readers want. Then, you can create this type of content and distribute it through the right channels for your business marketing purposes.

SEMrush's pricing is shown here:

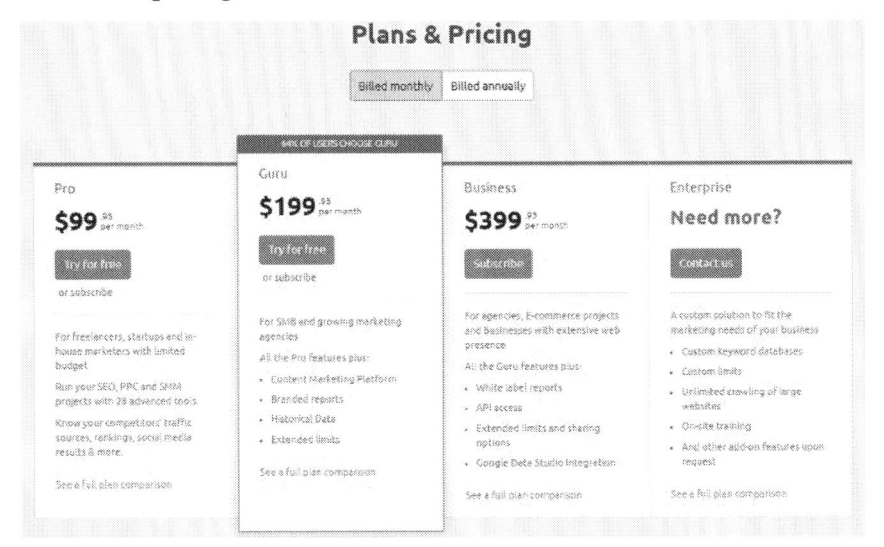

ClickFunnels

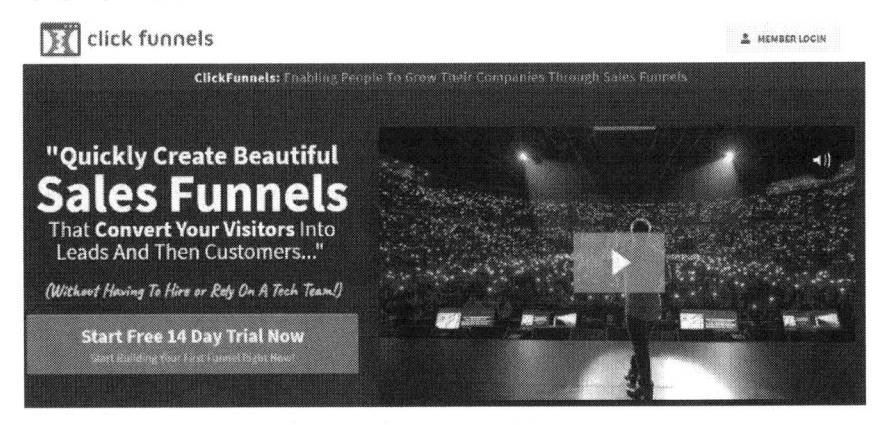

You create content for different sales cycles to help your readers take action at different buyer stages, right?

Well, you need to use the ClickFunnels tool. It helps you guide your visitors through the buyer journey. It aligns with your content so your readers don't feel confused about any stage of the sales funnel.

Content Promotion Tools

So you've created and edited the content, and you've added the images that will draw your readers in. It's perfect. Now it's time to get it out there for the world to see. These tools can help you put your content in front of the right people.

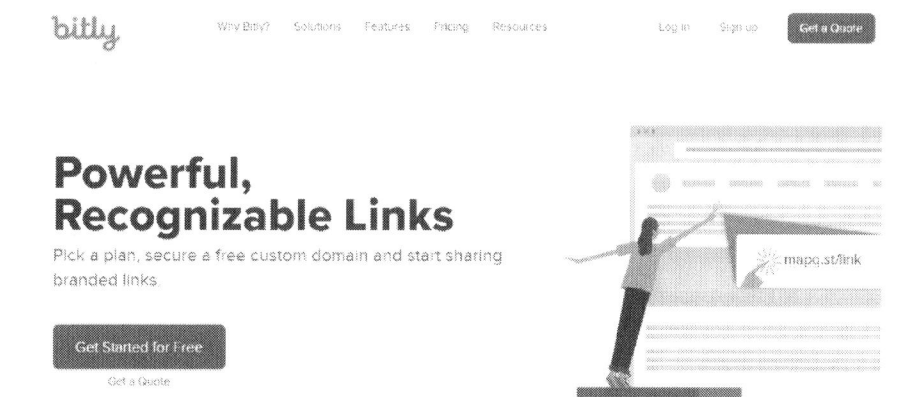

Bitly

This tool helps you shorten your content URLs so you can easily promote your content on different channels.

It's most suitable for promoting content on Twitter, which allows posts of up to only 280 characters.

Bitly has advanced features for your content promotion. Here's the pricing:

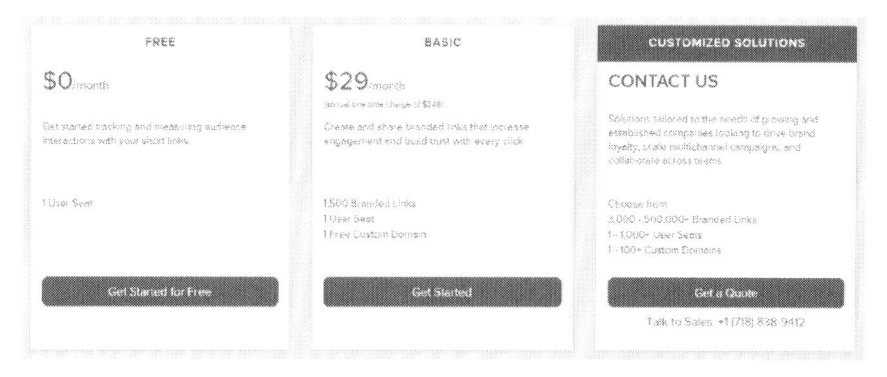

Chapter 1: Content Marketing

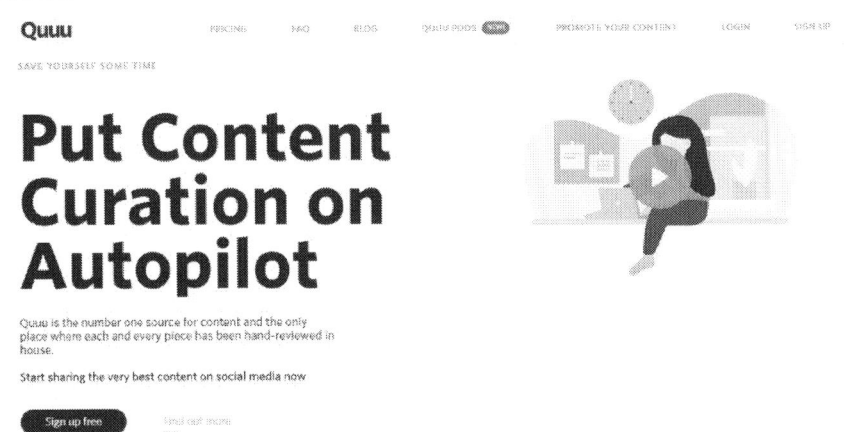

QUUU

Put Content Curation on Autopilot

This site helps promote curated content to social sites to increase engagement and traffic.

You can integrate the tool with other tools to help with content promotion. Following are the prices for the different Quu service packages:

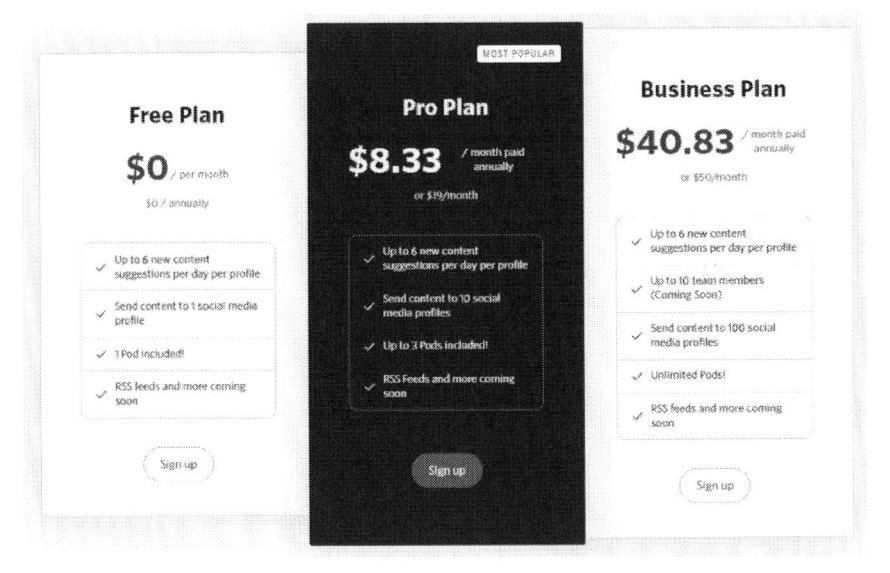

Meet Edgar

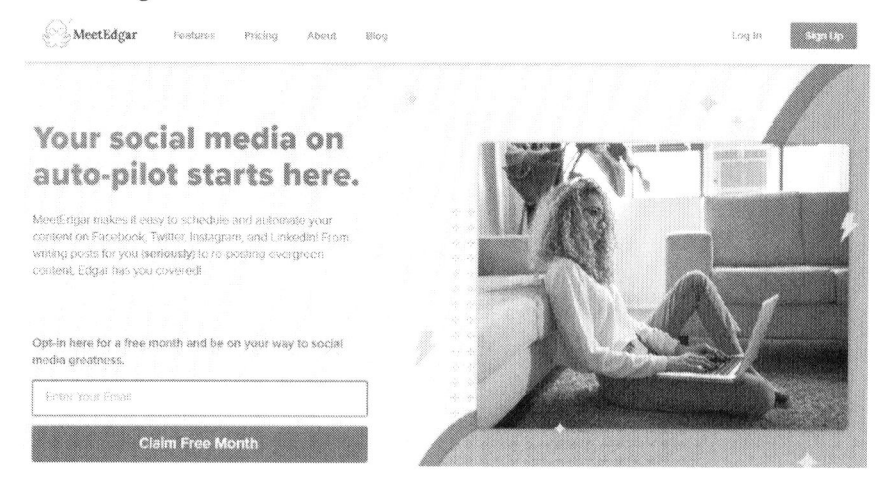

This tool functions as a sort of autopilot to schedule and post your content on social media. You can add your different content types and schedule when and where you want the tool to post them on social media.

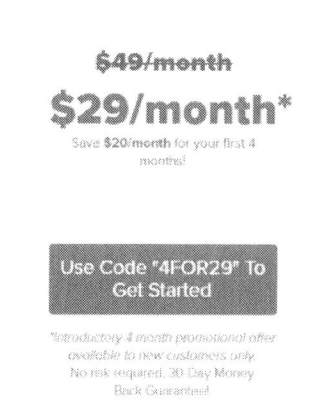

$49/month
$29/month*

Save $20/month for your first 4 months!

Use Code "4FOR29" To Get Started

Introductory 4 month promotional offer available to new customers only. No risk required. 30 Day Money Back Guarantee!

Works with:

For less than $2/day, you can set it and forget it! Load up your posts once, set your schedule, and Edgar takes it from there - he is the virtual social media assistant you didn't know you needed.

- ✓ 25 social media accounts
- ✓ Access to our smart composer that automatically writes status updates for you from articles or blog posts
- ✓ Unlimited library for your content (text, images, videos)
- ✓ Unlimited categories to organize your content
- ✓ Unlimited access to our support team
- ✓ Access to premium social media courses through our course hub, Edgar University.

Chapter 1: Content Marketing

Sprout Social

Build and grow stronger relationships on social

Sprout Social helps you promote content, engage your community, and monitor and analyze content performance.

You can visit the Sprout Social website for more details about its services and prices.

Zapier

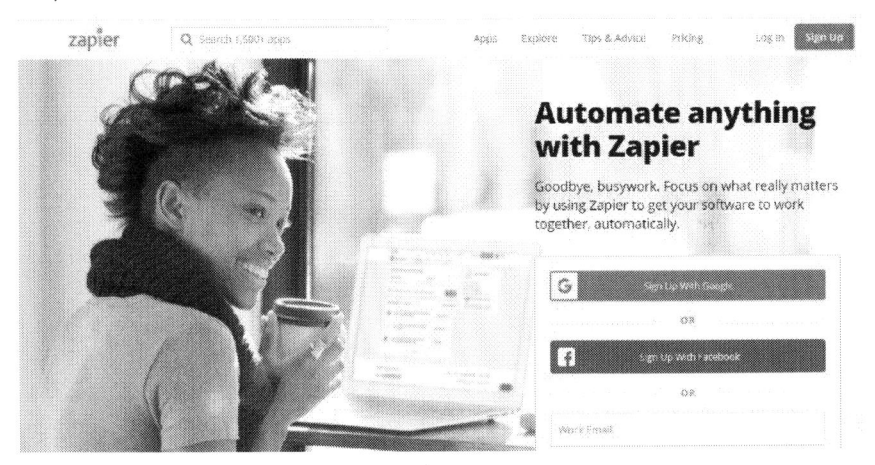

Automate anything with Zapier

You can integrate this app with email marketing tools to promote your content to readers.

Zapier automates the importation of new customers' contact information into your CRM the moment you get the data. You can visit the Zapier website for more details about how to use the app and its package pricing.

Email Marketing Tools

You'll also need to distribute your content directly to your readers to engage them and market your brand.

Here are some tools you can use to streamline your email campaigns.

Constant Contact

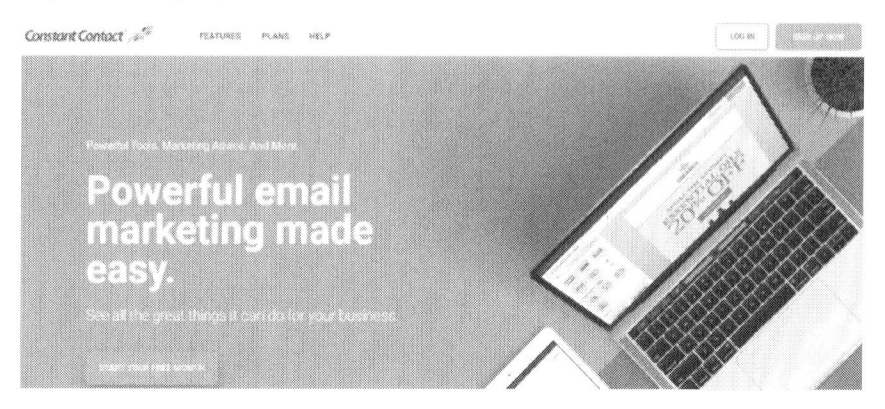

This tool provides templates to help you easily create and send emails to your target readers.

It helps you monitor your email open rates and automatically resend emails to readers who don't open them.

You can segment your readers and sent emails to different groups according to their buyer stage. Visit the website to review the company's comprehensive pricing structure.

AWeber

To engage readers, you need to send follow-up emails and content that help build more trust. AWeber helps you organize your email follow-ups and automatically sends them to your target readers.

Once you automate your content marketing, it's easy to learn more about your target readers' problems and deliver content that addresses those pain points.

Here is the AWeber service pricing structure:

	$19/mo 0-500 SUBSCRIBERS	$29/mo 501-2,500 SUBSCRIBERS	$49/mo 2,501-5,000 SUBSCRIBERS	$69/mo 5,001-10,000 SUBSCRIBERS	$149/mo 10,001-25,000 SUBSCRIBERS	25,000+ SUBSCRIBERS
	Get Started	Get Started	Get Started	Get Started	Get Started	Get a Quote
Unlimited Emails	✓	✓	✓	✓	✓	✓
Automation	✓	✓	✓	✓	✓	✓
Segmenting	✓	✓	✓	✓	✓	✓
Analytics	✓	✓	✓	✓	✓	✓
Customer Solutions	✓	✓	✓	✓	✓	✓
Sign Up Forms	✓	✓	✓	✓	✓	✓
Integrations	✓	✓	✓	✓	✓	✓
Image Hosting	✓	✓	✓	✓	✓	✓
6,060+ Stock Photos	✓	✓	✓	✓	✓	✓
700+ Email Templates	✓	✓	✓	✓	✓	✓
Edu. Resources	✓	✓	✓	✓	✓	✓

GetResponse

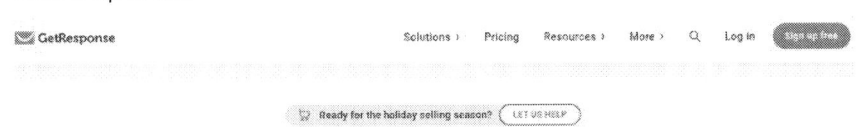

Free your marketing machine

Grow your audience, promote services, and sell products with marketing software that does the job for you.

SIGN UP FREE

This is a great tool to help with content marketing for your brand. It empowers you to create personalized landing pages with awesome content that attract potential customers to your website.

You can use its A/B testing features to analyze content performance and determine the right content to market to your leads.

Below is the pricing plan for the GetResponse tool:

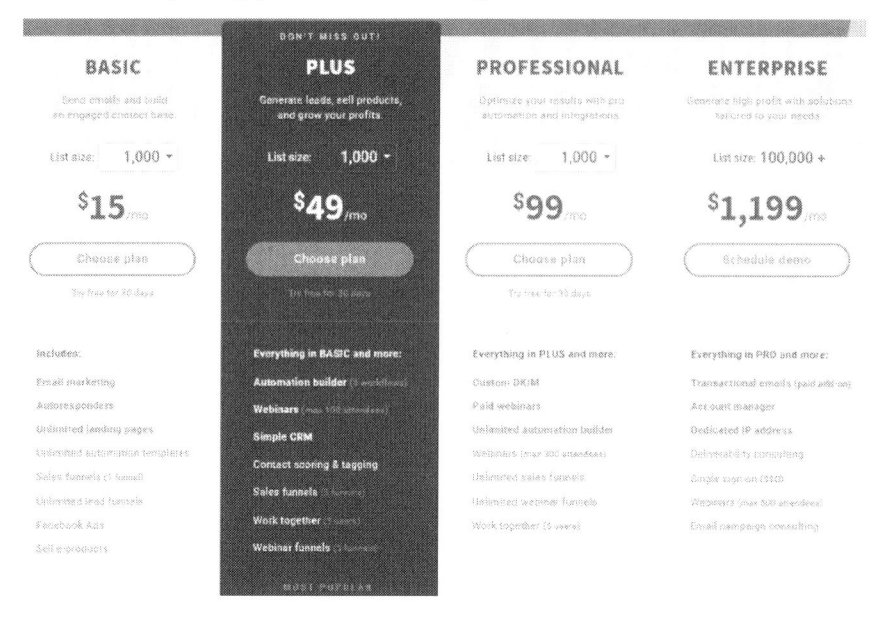

Drip

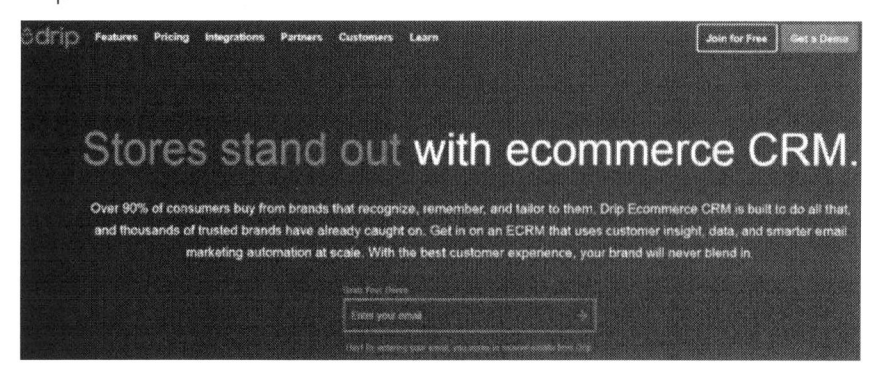

One goal of content marketing is to build trust as you educate and create thought leadership content.

Drip helps you build trust with e-commerce leads as you nurture them into customers. Its features show you the kinds of actions readers take with your content so you can create content that's attractive and engaging. Learn more about pricing from the Drip website.

Chapter 1: Content Marketing

ConvertKit

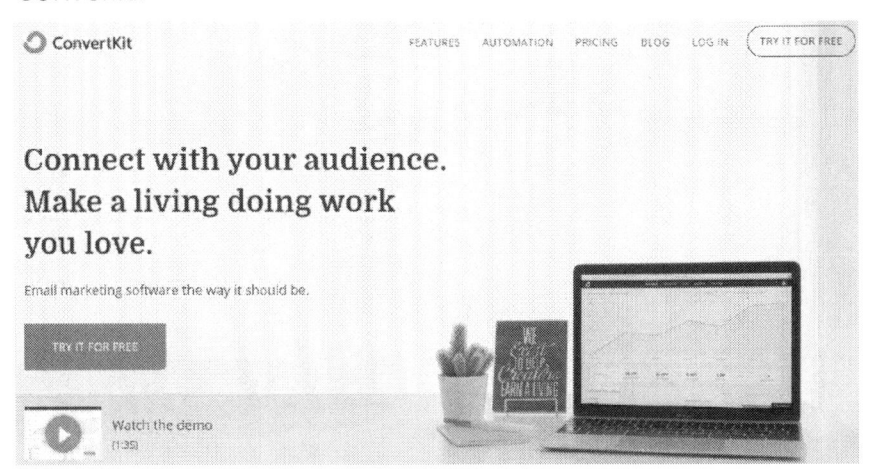

You need to grow your subscriber numbers to increase lead generation for your business.

This tool helps you recruit more subscribers and market your business content to them. Use it to create emails that increase conversions to your business. Below is the ConvertKit pricing plan:

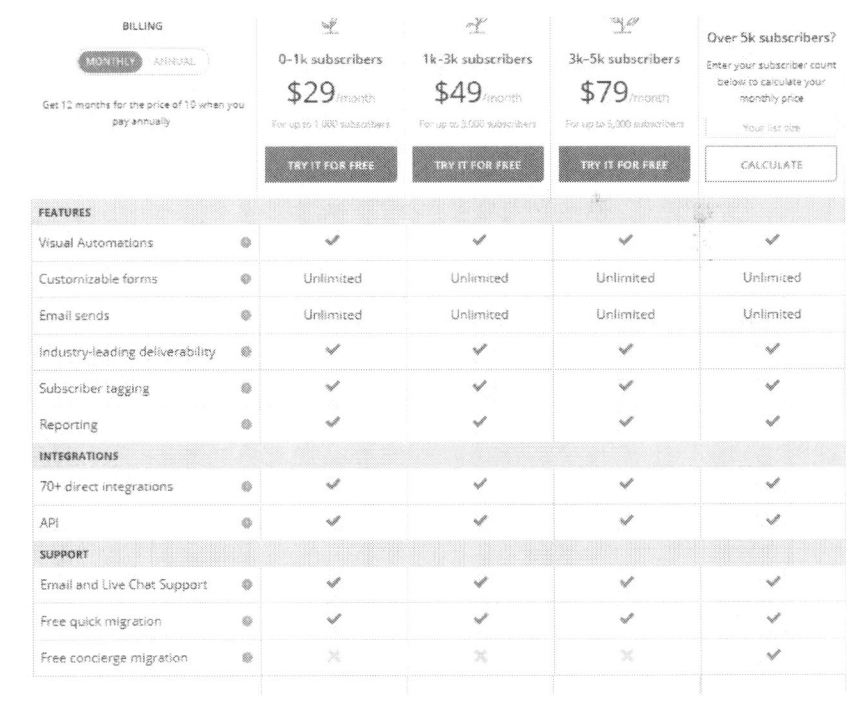

	0-1k subscribers	1k-3k subscribers	3k-5k subscribers	Over 5k subscribers
	$29/month	$49/month	$79/month	Calculate
FEATURES				
Visual Automations	✓	✓	✓	✓
Customizable forms	Unlimited	Unlimited	Unlimited	Unlimited
Email sends	Unlimited	Unlimited	Unlimited	Unlimited
Industry-leading deliverability	✓	✓	✓	✓
Subscriber tagging	✓	✓	✓	✓
Reporting	✓	✓	✓	✓
INTEGRATIONS				
70+ direct integrations	✓	✓	✓	✓
API	✓	✓	✓	✓
SUPPORT				
Email and Live Chat Support	✓	✓	✓	✓
Free quick migration	✓	✓	✓	✓
Free concierge migration	✗	✗	✗	✓

Where to Post Your Content

There are several places where you can post your content to achieve your content marketing goals.

Your Website

Since you have a running blog on your website, you should update it with fresh content.

Post most of your content on your website to engage readers and target clients with your brand. For example, here is Voy Media's list of recent blog posts.

> RECENT POSTS
>
> The importance of product launch marketing
>
> Guest Blogging: Why it is a powerful inbound strategy?
>
> Some Important Things to Note While Testing Salesforce
>
> Ready, Steady, Go: How to Achieve Your Goals in 50 Days
>
> How to sell on Amazon
>
> Best Video Editing Software
>
> Optimize Your Online Services with Facebook Lead Ads
>
> How to Embed Your Instagram Photos and videos on the website?
>
> What are the Best Features in Mobile Apps?
>
> How Can Effective PPC Management Transform the Conversion Rate of a Business?

Guest Posts

You can create your content and then post it on other reputable sites within your niche. This helps attract traffic to your website and build trust with your readers.

High-quality content in your guest posts attracts readers to your brand and engages them. Be sure to include backlinks in your content that will direct your readers to your website. Here's an example of a guest post on Forbes.com:

Why Cleaner Landing Pages Aren't Always Better

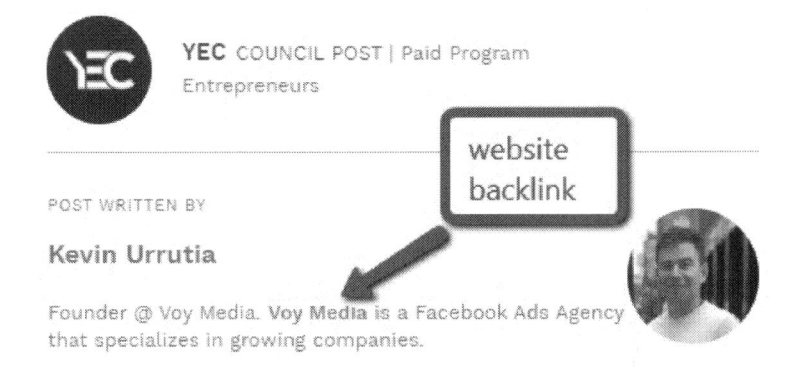

YEC COUNCIL POST | Paid Program
Entrepreneurs

POST WRITTEN BY

Kevin Urrutia

Founder @ Voy Media. **Voy Media** is a Facebook Ads Agency that specializes in growing companies.

website backlink

Medium

This is a platform where you can publish your marketing content to reach users who can benefit from it and attract them to your business's products or services.

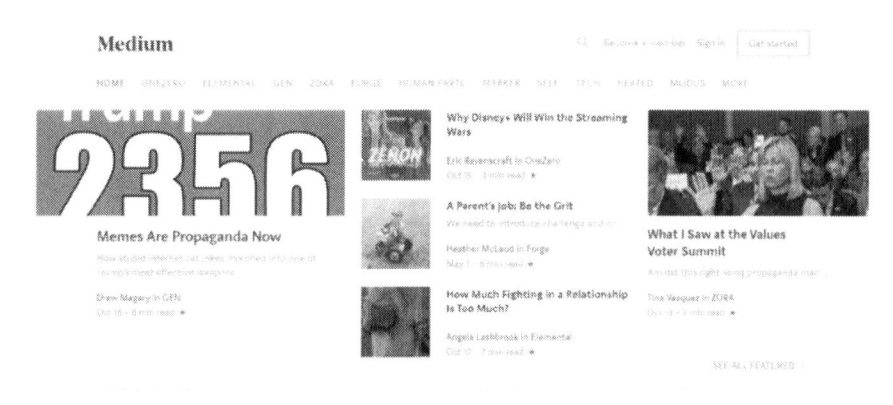

You can upgrade your Medium membership to access more of the platform's features, and this is its pricing structure:

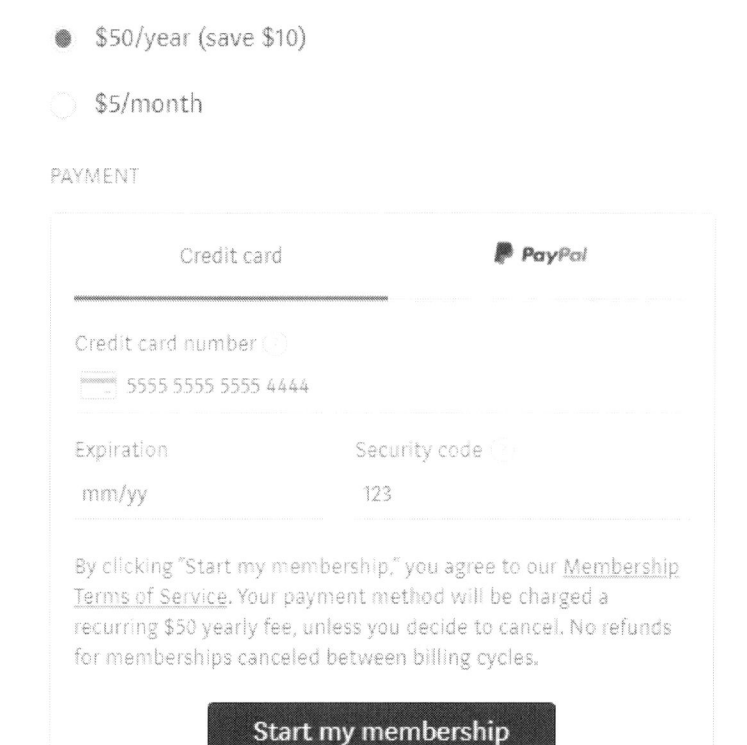

LinkedIn

LinkedIn is a professional social network that helps connect brands, employees, and customers.

You can create your business profile and link your website content to increase its exposure to potential customers.

Include content updates on your profile that will attract readers to your business. The content should be helpful to your target market and show your potential clients how to solve their problems. Video content has higher engagement rates than other content.

Create informative video content on your profile to attract and engage readers with your business.

SEO Tips: Optimize Your Content

You don't just need to create content, but content that ranks high in the search engine results for more visibility. Here are some tips.

Use Latent Semantic Keywords

In addition to using the main keywords for your content, include keywords that relate to your main keywords.

You can use a latent semantic tool to generate related keywords.

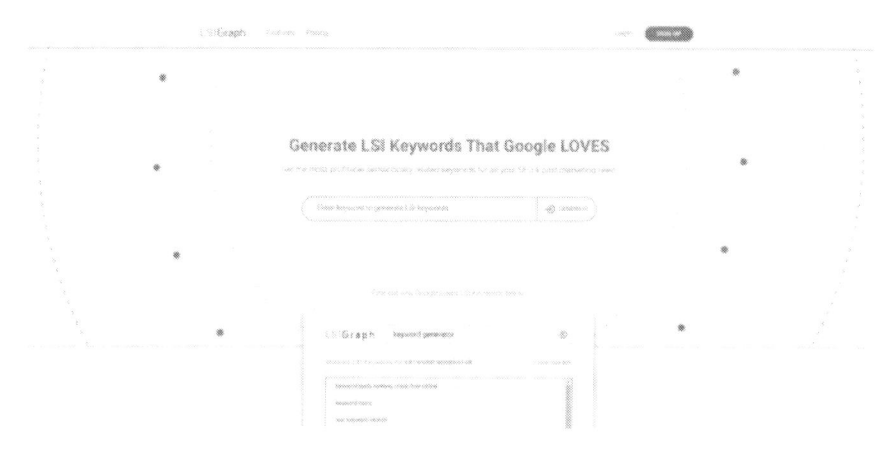

I ran a search for Facebook Ads on the tool and here are the latent semantic keywords I got:

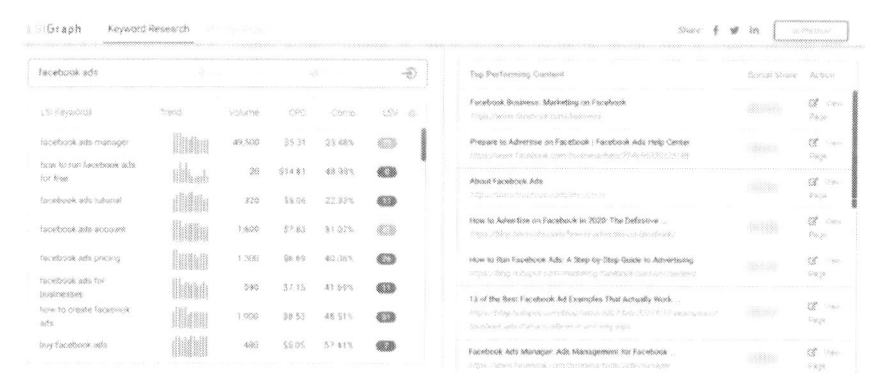

Include the related keywords throughout the content to enhance your main keywords' visibility and boost your content's rank.

Be Mindful of Content-Length

Google loves long, in-depth content. Don't just write long content, but content that's informative and educational and solves customers' problems. Include high-quality backlinks within your content.

HubSpot research shows that content with an average word count of 2,250 receives more organic traffic.

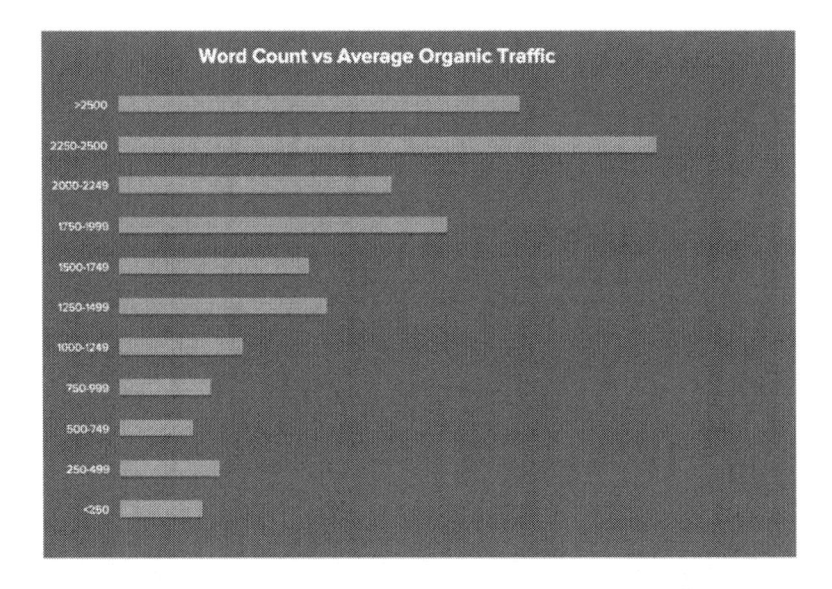

Backlinko's study shows that long-form content performs better on search engines. "Long-form" content is an average of 2,000 words.

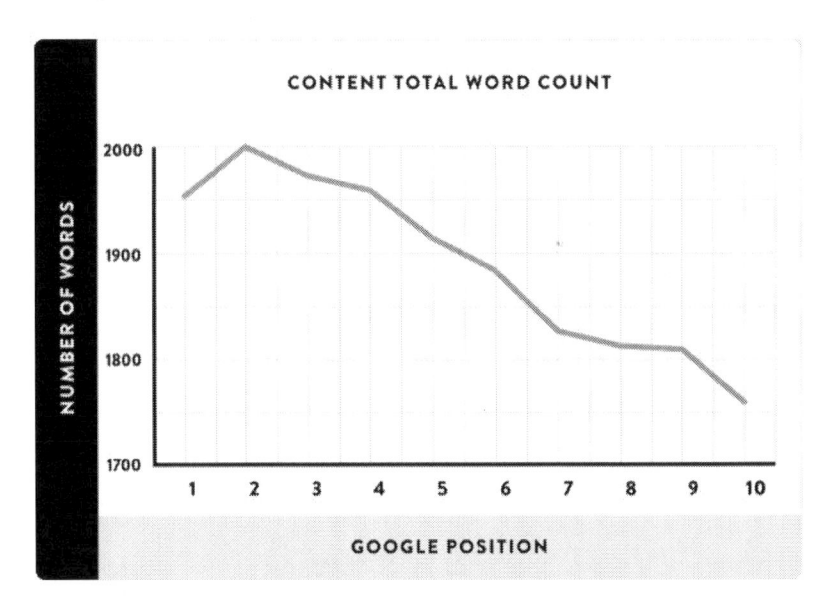

Image source: https://backlinko.com/search-engine-ranking

Prioritize the Visuals

Your content needs to be easy to read. It should be broken down into short paragraphs and feature screenshots, bullet points, and white space. A wall of text looks daunting and makes for tedious reading, and it'll scare your readers away.

Most readers use mobile devices to search for content. Make sure your content is mobile-friendly so it's easy to read on mobile devices.

Ensure that your images and videos load quickly. Incorporate more videos in your content. The captivating power of videos will draw more readers and increase traffic to your website.

A report by Cisco shows that videos will [contribute 80% of traffic](#) by 2021. Google favors high-quality, in-depth content.

Now that you know what makes good content and you've seen the many tools that can help you create it, read on. In chapter 2, we'll teach you everything you need to know about landing pages.

Chapter 2: Landing Pages

Your website needs landing pages to help market your business to your target clients: to attract traffic, build trust, and convert leads into new clients. To start with, you can ask yourself what a landing page is.

As the name suggests, a landing page is the first page a visitor lands on when they visit your business website. It could be your lead capture page, your product description page, or another page.

In this chapter, we'll discuss everything you need to know about how to create amazing landing pages that increase lead conversion and sales.

What Makes a Great Landing Page?

There are various factors you have to consider to create amazing landing pages with high conversions. Here are a few.

High-Quality Content

Your main goals in creating your landing page are to attract, build trust, and convert leads. To accomplish these, you don't just need content, but the right amount of content to communicate your message and convince your target clients.

As for the content's length, it doesn't matter as long as it can hold the customer's attention, convey the message you want to send, and convince your target audience. Different landing pages require different types of content with various lengths. For example, a blog page requires in-depth content on a topic.

A report by OrbitMedia showed that the average length of a blog post is 1,200 words.

Length of typical blog post

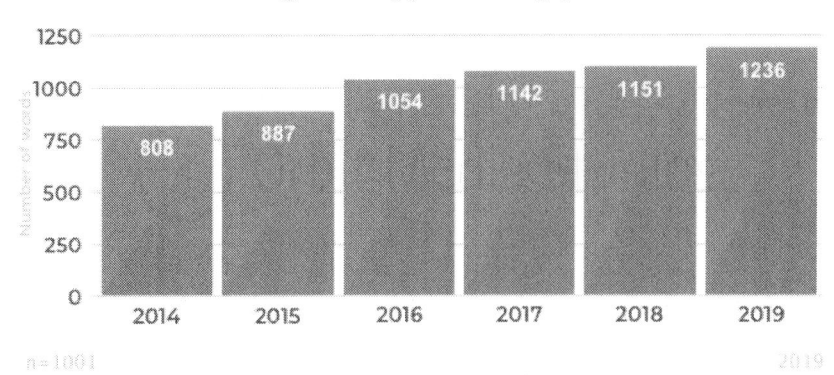

Year	Number of words
2014	808
2015	887
2016	1054
2017	1142
2018	1151
2019	1236

The same report shows that content containing more than 2,000 words has high conversion results.

Bloggers who report "strong results" based on length of typical article

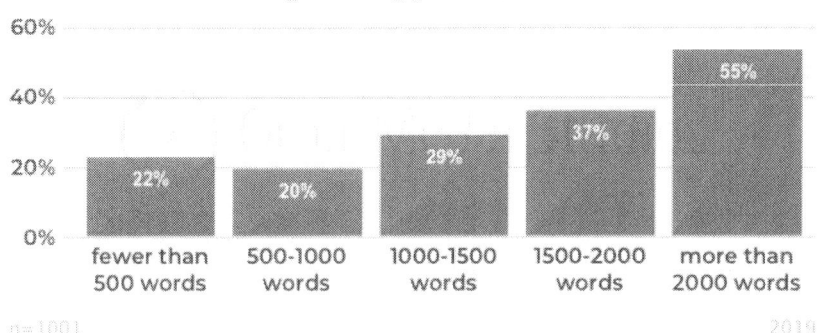

Length	Percentage
fewer than 500 words	22%
500-1000 words	20%
1000-1500 words	29%
1500-2000 words	37%
more than 2000 words	55%

To write an effective blog, ensure that your content convincingly relates your brand message to your target clients.

Statistics by MarketingSherpa show that 48% of marketers create new landing pages for their different marketing campaigns.

Chapter 2: Landing Pages

48% of marketers build a new landing page for each marketing campaign

MARKETINGSHERPA

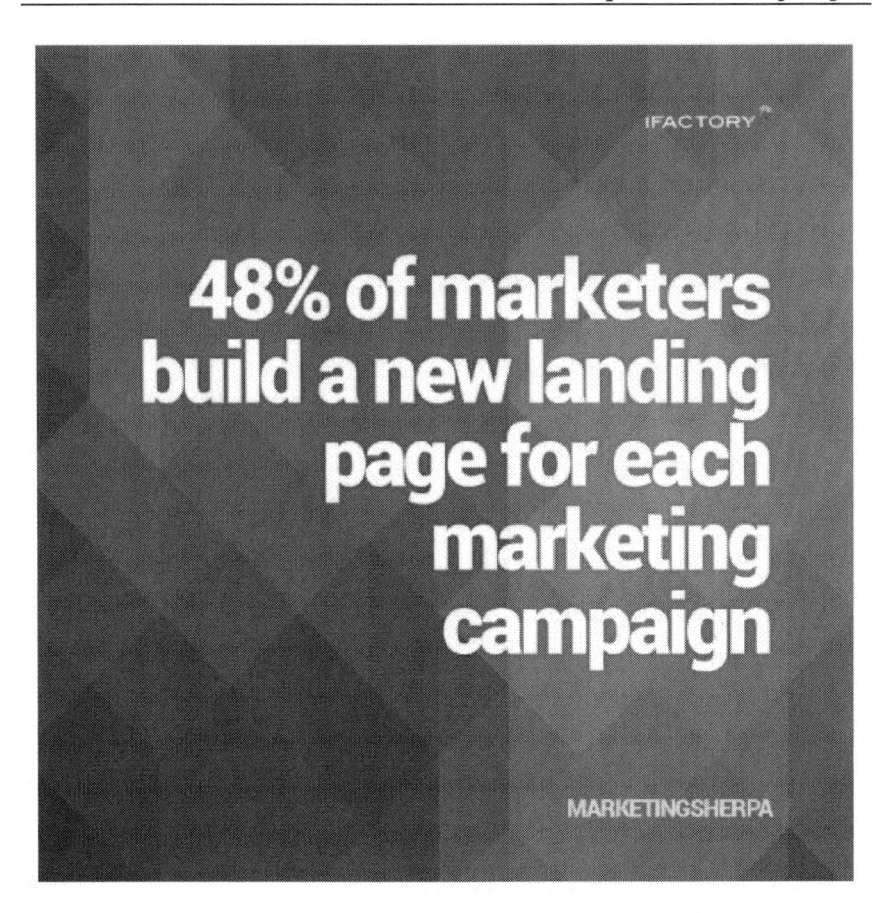

Image Source: *https://ifactory.com.au/insights/why-should-i-use-landing-pages/*

Trust Symbols

Your entire online business is founded on one thing: trust. If your target customers can't trust you, then they won't engage with your business and you'll lose them to your competitors.

One amazing way to earn this trust is by adding trust symbols to your landing pages. A great example is your business logo. Here are some other examples of trust badges that look good on a landing page:

When target clients see the trust seals on your pages, they have more confidence in your business's products and services.

The trust seals assure your visitors of safety as they engage with your brand. Visitors perceive your business as less likely to defraud them, overcharge them, or poorly handle their data.

You can also include SSL certificates as a trust seal on your website. Here's an example of trust seals on one of Voy Media's landing pages.

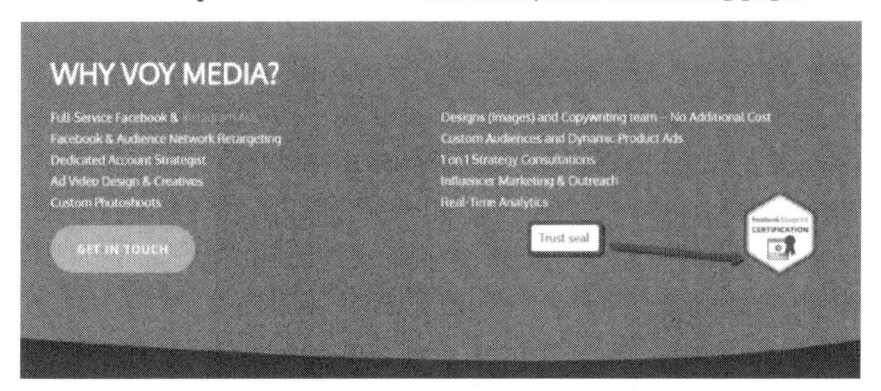

Chapter 2: Landing Pages

Images That Match Your Page Content

Your main goal is to ensure that, at the end of the day, you gain your readers' trust and engage them in your business.

To achieve this, use images that match the content on each web page. If you're explaining a product, include its image. Use the same images on your banner ads or your pay-per-click ads.

Research by CMI shows that the percentages of pay-per-click and banner ads are 57% and 35% respectively.

Types of Paid Content Distribution Methods Agency Marketers Use

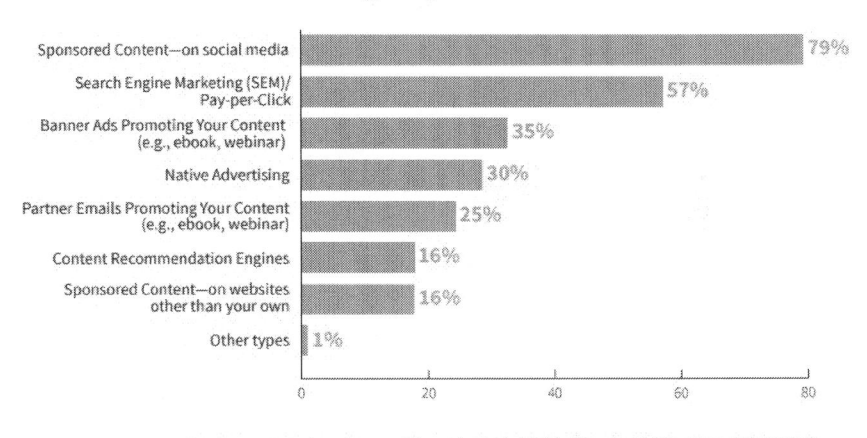

Method	%
Sponsored Content—on social media	79%
Search Engine Marketing (SEM)/Pay-per-Click	57%
Banner Ads Promoting Your Content (e.g., ebook, webinar)	35%
Native Advertising	30%
Partner Emails Promoting Your Content (e.g., ebook, webinar)	25%
Content Recommendation Engines	16%
Sponsored Content—on websites other than your own	16%
Other types	1%

Base: Agency content marketers whose organizations used paid methods in the last 12 months. Aided list, multiple responses permitted.
Agency Content Marketing 2019: Benchmarks, Budgets, and Trends—Content Marketing Institute/MarketingProfs

If potential clients notice that your images are inconsistent, their confidence in your product drops and they leave your business.

Great images forge an emotional connection with your target clients, increase user experience, and reduce bounce rates. The human brain is faster at processing images than words. Great images on your website help your target clients easily understand your business and engage with it.

Here's an example of compelling images on landing pages for Coca-Cola, one of the most well-known brands worldwide:

FRONT PAGE BRANDS
BRANDS
We Are Coca-Cola
and So Much More
READ THE STORY
fairlife
Simply Lemonade
CORE POWER
Minute Maid
Diet Coke
zero SUGAR
ciel

Chapter 2: Landing Pages

Social Proof and Testimonials

Potential clients like to hear feedback from people who have used your business's products or services. Include testimonials from your past clients on your landing pages to increase your trust-building process and lead conversions.

Here's an example of HubSpot's client testimonial:

> // I love how simple, yet very efficient HubSpot CRM is. The ability to customize properties has been a huge benefit to both my sales team and our reporting. //
>
> LEAH LAWRENCE
> Corporate Sales Manager | FoodJets

And another example of testimonials from Buffer clients:

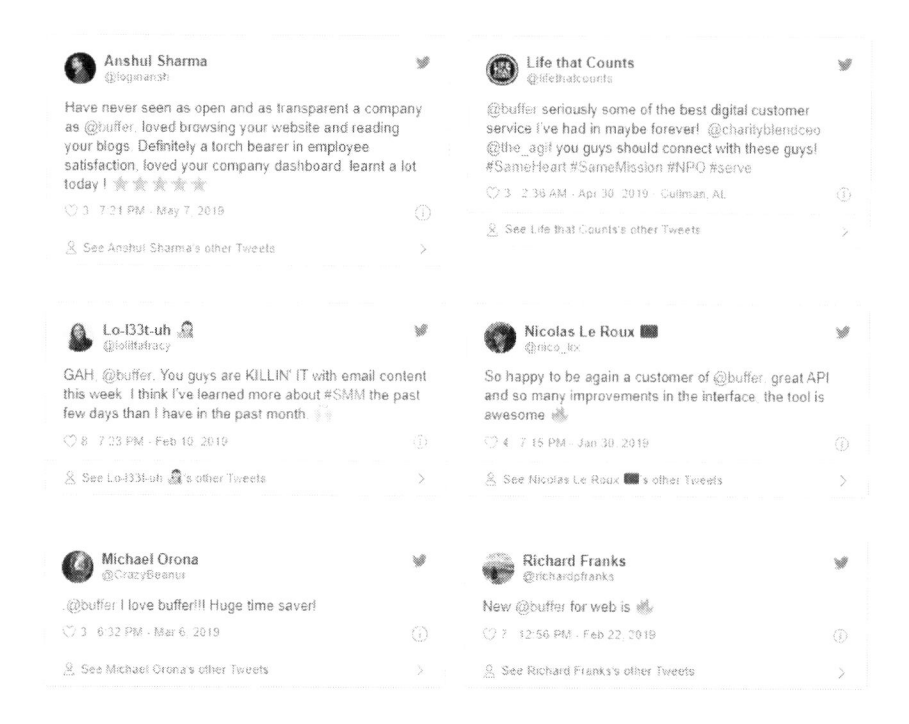

Mobile-Responsiveness

Many potential clients and readers use mobile devices to search for solutions to their pain points.

A report by Statista on internet usage shows that 51.65% of total internet traffic comes from mobile devices.

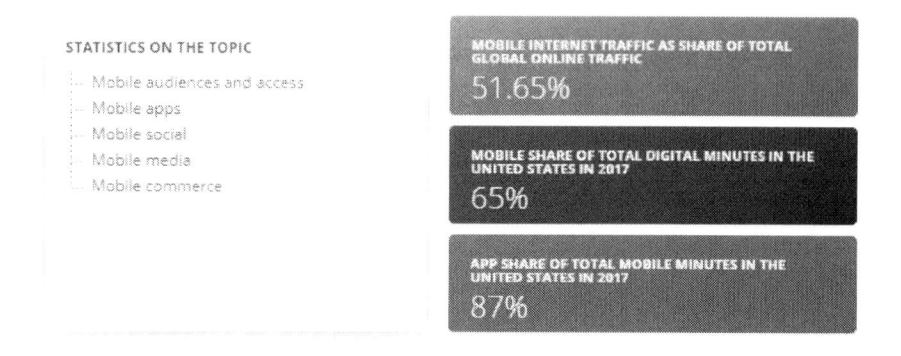

The number of people who use mobile devices to search for products or services online is staggering. As a marketer, you need to understand that optimizing landing pages for mobile searches is vital. If a potential client finds it hard to load your website or any of your landing pages on a mobile device, they'll leave you for your competitor.

Ensure your pages have faster loading speeds. Your website landing page should load within just three seconds.

As page load time goes from:

1s to 3s the probability of bounce **increases 32%**

1s to 5s the probability of bounce **increases 90%**

1s to 6s the probability of bounce **increases 106%**

1s to 10s the probability of bounce **increases 123%**

Create a click-to-call button to help potential clients reach you easily if they decide to use your products or services, or just want to learn more.

You can add a click-to-call button to your WordPress website using the WP call button plugin.

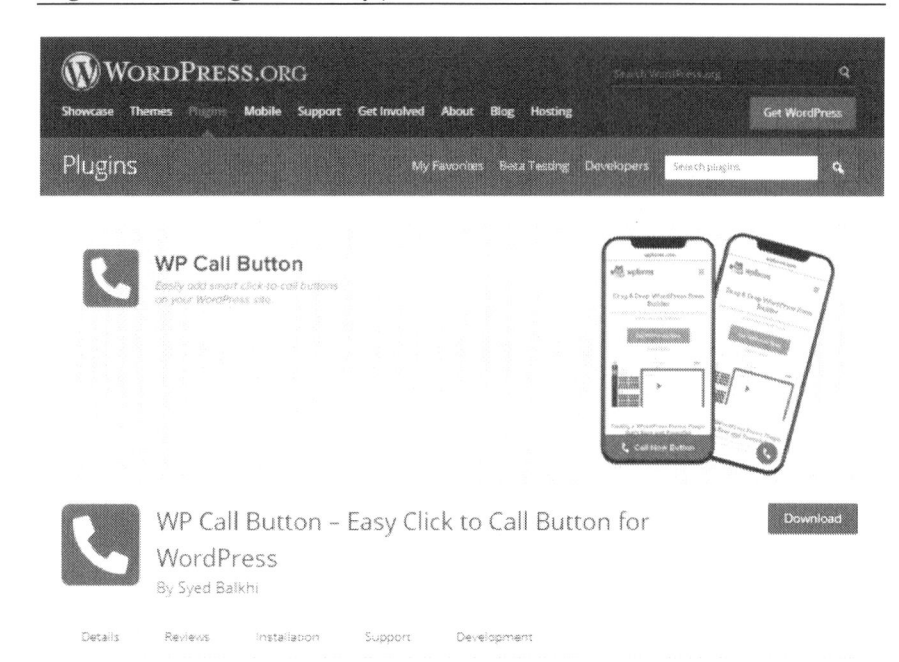

Since most potential clients skim content when using mobile devices, create short and to-the-point content that will attract and engage them. Use bullet points and keep your sentences and paragraphs concise.

Importance of Landing Pages

Marketers create different landing pages to help them achieve different goals for their business growth. Here are the benefits of creating landing pages.

Increase Lead Generation

To promote business growth, you need customers to buy your products or services. Landing pages are key to capturing these potential clients and engaging them with your business.

A good way to increase the chances of generating more leads for your business is to use a lead magnet. Here's a perfect example of a lead magnet that helps List Goal's website capture leads:

Chapter 2: Landing Pages

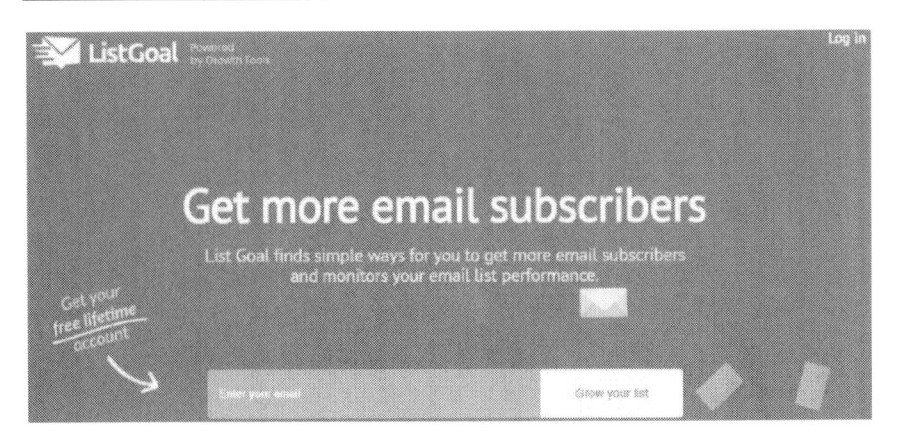

Once you've captured the leads, engage them in your business and nurture them through the buyer journey to convert them into clients.

Collect Customer Data

To effectively solve your clients' pain points, you need data and information about them. Brands also use landing pages to acquire information from prospective customers. Here's an example of a MarketingSherpa landing page:

This information helps you create a buyer persona for your clients, which in turn helps your brand create better services or products for your customers.

Other landing pages ask potential clients to provide more in-depth information about themselves. This long lead generation form collects more information from potential clients:

81

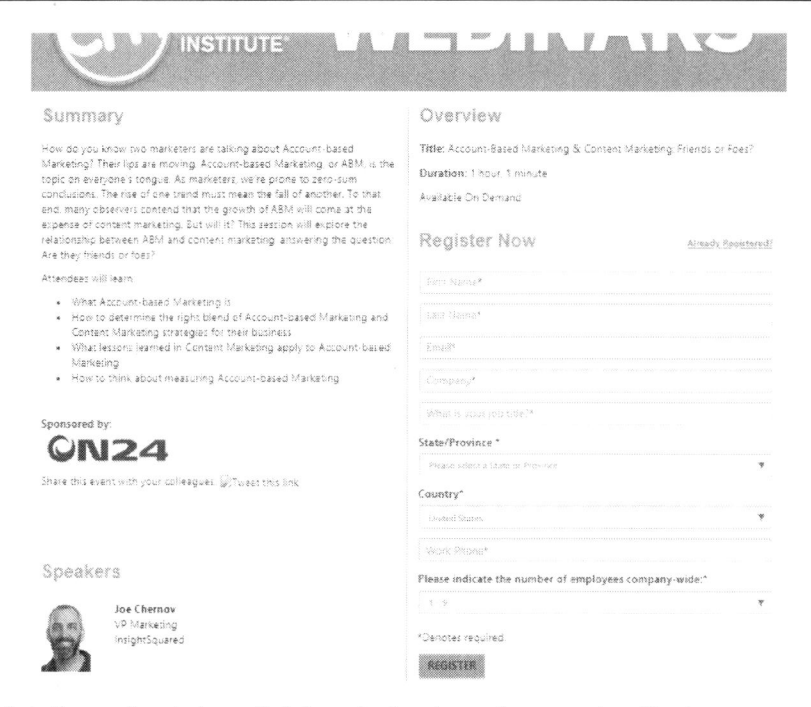

Such information is beneficial to the business because it tells them more about their target clients and how to serve them.

Increase Brand Awareness

Potential customers find it hard to do business with you if they don't know or trust your brand. Great landing pages help businesses increase brand awareness, engage more potential clients, and build trust.

Brand awareness draws traffic to your website and, according to the State of Inbound, this is a major challenge for brands.

Chapter 2: Landing Pages

What are your company's top marketing challenges?

Challenge	%
Generating traffic and leads	63%
Proving the ROI of our marketing activities	40%
Securing enough budget	28%
Identifying the right technologies for our needs	26%
Managing our website	26%
Targeting content for an international audience	21%
Training our team	19%
Hiring top talent	16%
Finding an executive sponsor	7%

STATE of INBOUND

Great landing pages enhance your brand across different marketing channels. Potential clients will recognize your business with ease, engage and increase the chances of converting into customers.

Encourage Prospects to Take Action

Brands create each landing page with a purpose. Landing pages can help drive leads to take a specific action, whether it's to sign up for a newsletter, download a book, make a purchase, or contact you for details.

That's why great landing pages are precise, direct, and to-the-point, giving readers all the necessary information to help them make a decision before taking action.

Here's an example of a ClickFunnels landing page that prompts potential clients to sign up for a free trial of the company's software.

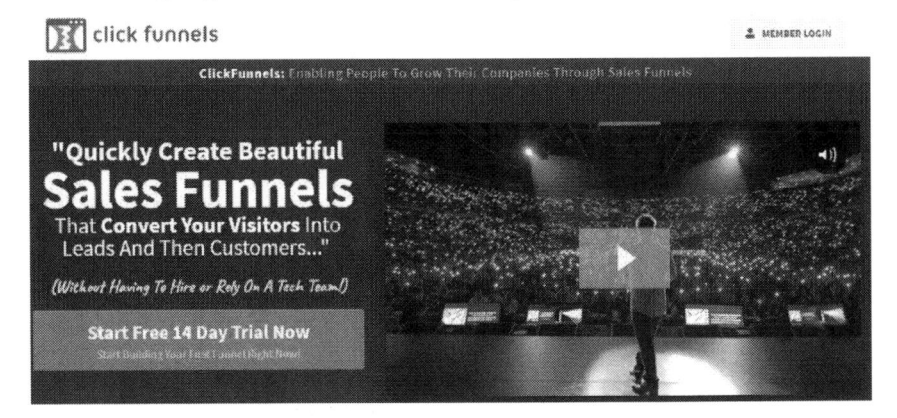

click funnels   MEMBER LOGIN

ClickFunnels: Enabling People To Grow Their Companies Through Sales Funnels

"Quickly Create Beautiful
Sales Funnels
That **Convert Your Visitors** Into Leads And Then Customers..."

(Without Having To Hire or Rely On A Tech Team!)

Start Free 14 Day Trial Now
Start Building Your First Funnel Right Now!

This second version of the landing page shows the potential customers the pricing model of the software package. Extra information like this helps the target customer make the decision about which package they'll purchase after the trial period.

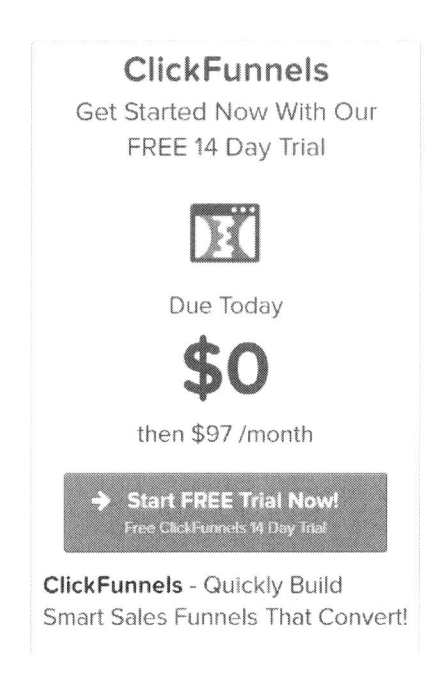

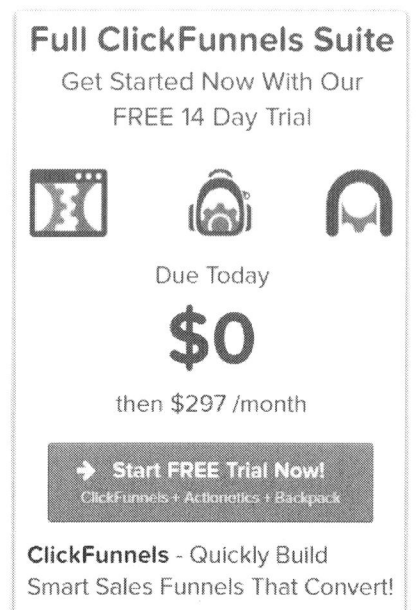

ClickFunnels	Full ClickFunnels Suite
Get Started Now With Our FREE 14 Day Trial	Get Started Now With Our FREE 14 Day Trial
Due Today	Due Today
$0	$0
then $97 /month	then $297 /month
→ Start FREE Trial Now! Free ClickFunnels 14 Day Trial	→ Start FREE Trial Now! ClickFunnels + Actionetics + Backpack
ClickFunnels - Quickly Build Smart Sales Funnels That Convert!	**ClickFunnels** - Quickly Build Smart Sales Funnels That Convert!

Track Customer Data

Since your potential customers provided you with some information when you provided the lead magnet, you can easily track them. This helps you know how they're engaged with your brand. For instance, you can send them emails with a CTA and track whether they opened the email or took any action.

You can use the customer data you collected to measure your business's marketing progress.

Grow Your Email List

Email marketing has a high ROI.

Chapter 2: Landing Pages

The average return for email marketing is **$38 for every dollar invested**, or an ROI of 3800%.

salesforce

To grow your email list, start with leads. Use an email campaign to nurture them and gradually convert them into clients.

Landing pages help you capture leads to build your email list. A report by the CMI shows that 73% of marketers use email marketing software.

Types of Technologies Agency Marketers Use to Assist With the Management of Content Marketing Efforts

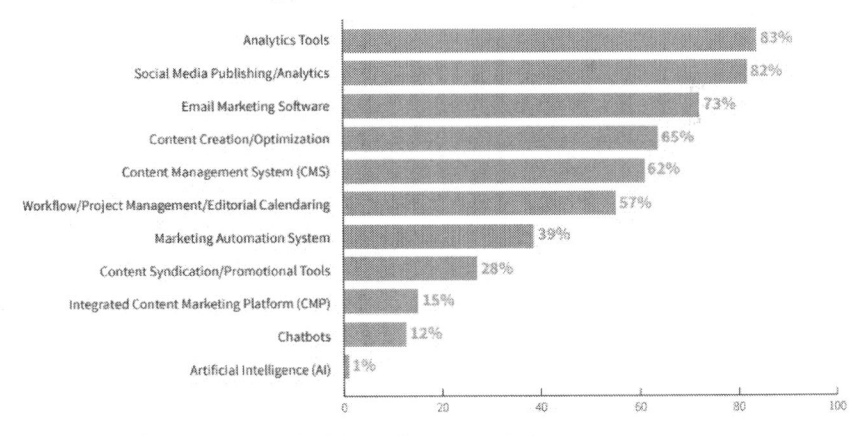

Technology	Percentage
Analytics Tools	83%
Social Media Publishing/Analytics	82%
Email Marketing Software	73%
Content Creation/Optimization	65%
Content Management System (CMS)	62%
Workflow/Project Management/Editorial Calendaring	57%
Marketing Automation System	39%
Content Syndication/Promotional Tools	28%
Integrated Content Marketing Platform (CMP)	15%
Chatbots	12%
Artificial Intelligence (AI)	1%

Base: Agency content marketers whose organizations use one or more of the listed technologies. Multiple responses permitted.
Agency Content Marketing 2019: Benchmarks, Budgets, and Trends—Content Marketing Institute/MarketingProfs

85

It's clear that email marketing is an essential marketing process. Effective landing pages help you create and grow your email list, nurture leads, and convert them into clients to increase sales.

Create First Impressions

Potential clients won't engage with your business if it doesn't impress them. One great way to capture the attention of potential readers is with attractive landing pages.

For example, if you're searching for an agency to help with your social media ads and you land on the Voy Media homepage, the page will capture your attention since it's designed well. The message is clear and simple and there are no distracting elements.

Another example is this landing page by Neil Patel Digital, a company that helps you increase your website traffic.

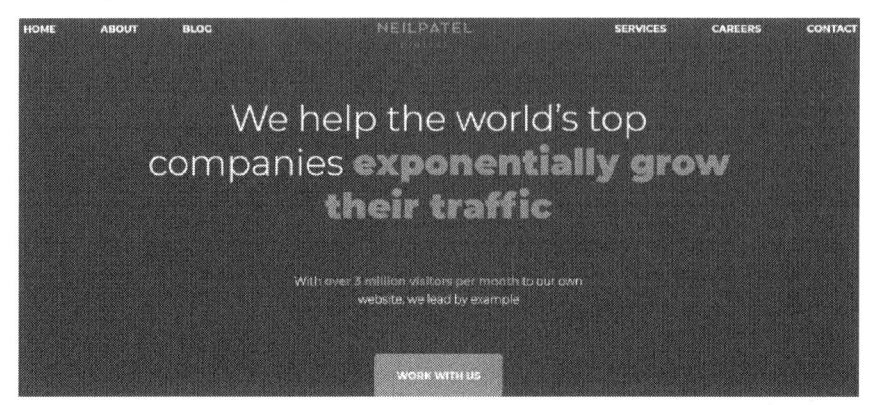

Chapter 2: Landing Pages

If you're searching for an agency to help bolster your web traffic, this bold text and simple design will catch your attention the moment you land on the site.

Promote Your Products or Services

Landing pages are awesome settings for product promotion. A well-designed landing page with compelling copy helps market your products to potential clients.

Here's an example of the [Buffer website](). The page helps the site promote its services to readers persuasively.

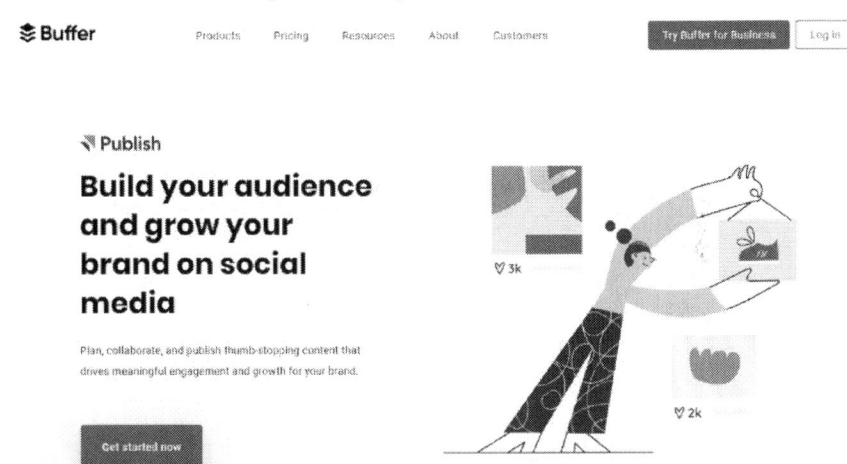

If you're searching for software to help you grow your business on social media, the landing page will draw you in. You'll learn more about the software, hear what other clients have to say, and probably become a client.

Improve SEO Ranking

Every business owner wants their website to appear on the top pages of the search engine results, which leads to more website visitors whom they can convert into clients.

Landing pages help brands rank high in these results. The content of good landing pages is keyword-optimized and uses the same keywords potential clients use to search for content.

More potential customers will see your landing pages, engage, and become clients. This increases business conversions, generates more sales, and increases the business's ROI.

Reinforce Your Brand to Customers

A strong personal brand plays a significant role in building trust and converting leads into customers.

However, to inspire potential customers to convert and the conversion rates to keep improving, you need to reinforce your brand. That's where landing pages come in. Your landing page tone and copy help cement the trust you've acquired through brand awareness and other marketing channels.

Even if leads don't convert immediately, it lays the groundwork for nurturing and convincing them to use your products or services later.

Types of Landing Pages

Online brands create different types of landing pages according to the goal they want to achieve. Here are a few examples of these types.

404 Landing Page

Sometimes things go wrong and your clients visit a page that has a 404 error. This is highly frustrating to the potential customer. When you give your readers a link that happens to be broken, they often leave your website and never come back.

You're in business to attract, engage, and convert leads into clients, not to break their trust and lose them, right? Well, to compensate for the loss and regain their trust, you can create a 404 landing page. Here's an example:

Chapter 2: Landing Pages

The page should offer your potential clients something to retain their trust and apologize for the mistake. A little humor goes a long way toward lightening the mood.

Here's another great 404 landing page from the OptinMonster website:

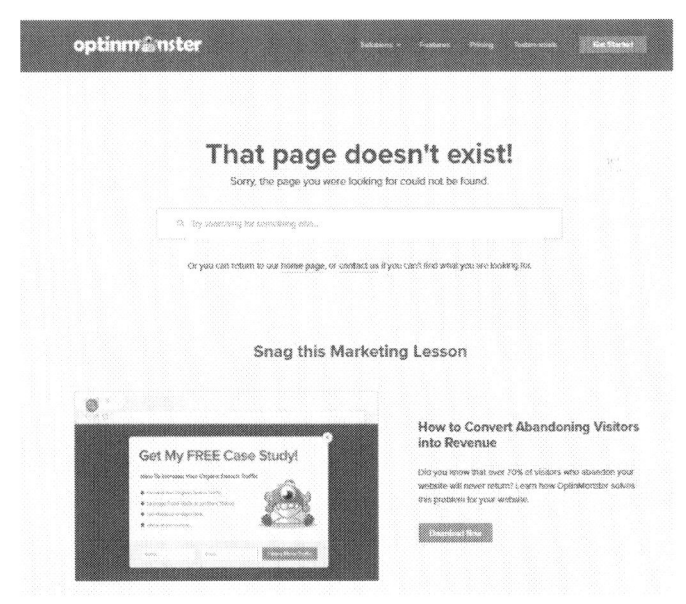

89

About Us Landing Page

Before clients do business with you, they need to know who you are, what you offer, and why they should trust and use your products or services.

Your About Us page helps clarify all these issues and answer your potential clients' questions. On this page, you can talk about why your company cares about the work it does and why you're qualified to do it. You may want to include testimonials from past clients and social media proof to build trust with potential customers. Here's the [Voy Media About Us page](#)

Long-Form Sales Page

As the name suggests, this landing page provides in-depth content that tells the potential clients more about the business's products or services.

The page is meant to attract, engage, and build trust with readers. Most of these types of landing pages feature a demo video that walks the potential clients through your business's processes and benefits.

Here's the [HubSpot long-form sales landing page](#):

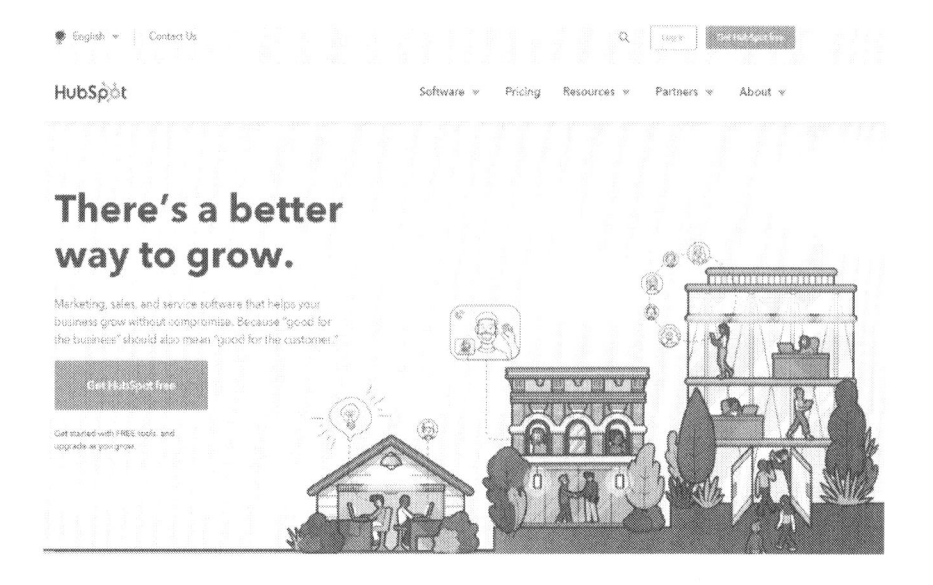

Chapter 2: Landing Pages

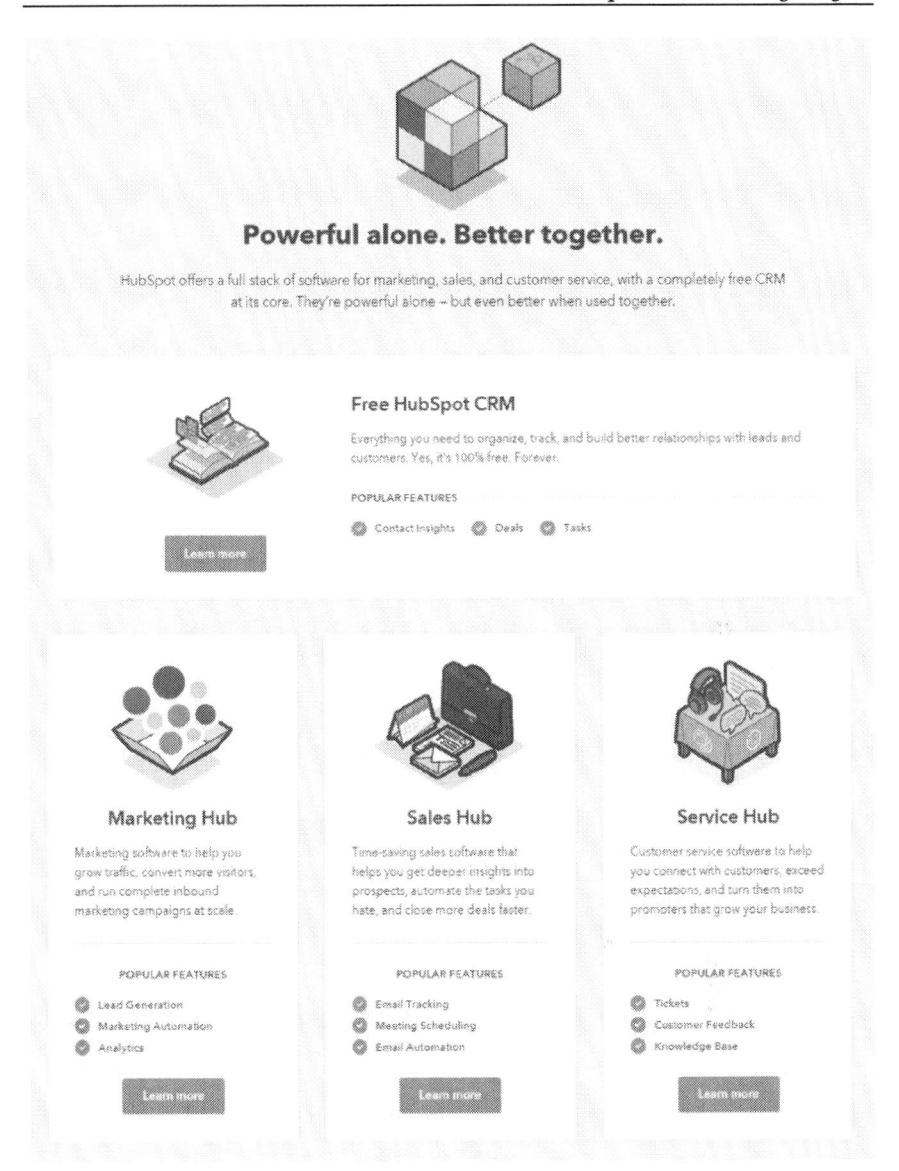

Get Started Landing Page

You've explained your business to your potential clients and detailed how you can help them solve their pain points.

They're now ready to use your products or services to better their lives. This page is essential to engage and get your clients started with your business.

The Lusha website has a spectacular example of this type of page:

And here's another example from the AWeber website:

The Pricing Landing Page

Your clients need to know how much your products or services cost. This landing page highlights your pricing model for the services or products you sell.

Here's an example of the GettyImages pricing model for its image, video, and editing services.

Chapter 2: Landing Pages

Large images 4K and HD videos		Medium images SD videos		Small images Low-res videos	
Single	$499 per download	Single	$350 per download	Single	$150 per download
○ 5 pack 2,250	$450 per download	○ 5 pack 1,500	$300 per download	○ 5 pack 675	$135 per download
○ 10 pack 4,250	$425 per download	○ 10 pack 2,700	$270 per download	○ 10 pack 1,250	$125 per download
BUY NOW		BUY NOW		BUY NOW	

Packs include any combination of royalty-free creative photos, videos, illustrations, vectors, and most editorial images, but exclude all rights-managed images. Packs don't expire as long as you sign in at least once a year.

The page provides detailed information about the different packages to show potential clients the perks of the packages they can purchase.

Squeeze Landing Page

One great way to grow your business is through lead generation. Email marketing is one of the most efficient ways to generate leads.

A report by CMI shows that 77% of marketers use email campaigns as a marketing method for their business.

Content Marketing Methods Agency Marketers Use to Nurture Their Audience

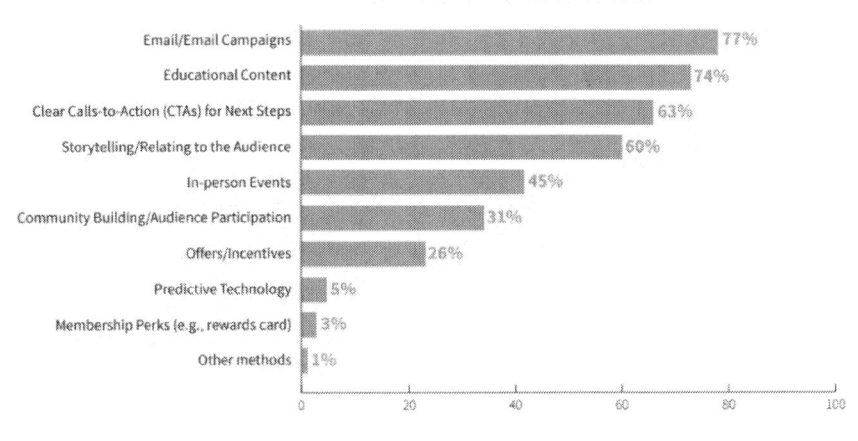

Method	%
Email/Email Campaigns	77%
Educational Content	74%
Clear Calls-to-Action (CTAs) for Next Steps	63%
Storytelling/Relating to the Audience	60%
In-person Events	45%
Community Building/Audience Participation	31%
Offers/Incentives	26%
Predictive Technology	5%
Membership Perks (e.g., rewards card)	3%
Other methods	1%

Base: Agency content marketers whose organizations nurture their audience. Aided list; multiple responses permitted.
Agency Content Marketing 2019: Benchmarks, Budgets, and Trends—Content Marketing Institute/MarketingProfs

This shows that they first have to acquire potential clients' email addresses. Their websites include a squeeze page to help capture that information.

Brian Dean of Backlinko has an awesome squeeze page on his website:

Lead Capture Landing Page

Like the squeeze page, this page aims at collecting customer details. However, the difference between the two is that this landing page collects more than just the customer's email address.

The information you want to gather depends on your business marketing goals. Here's an example of a lead capture landing page from HubSpot:

Chapter 2: Landing Pages

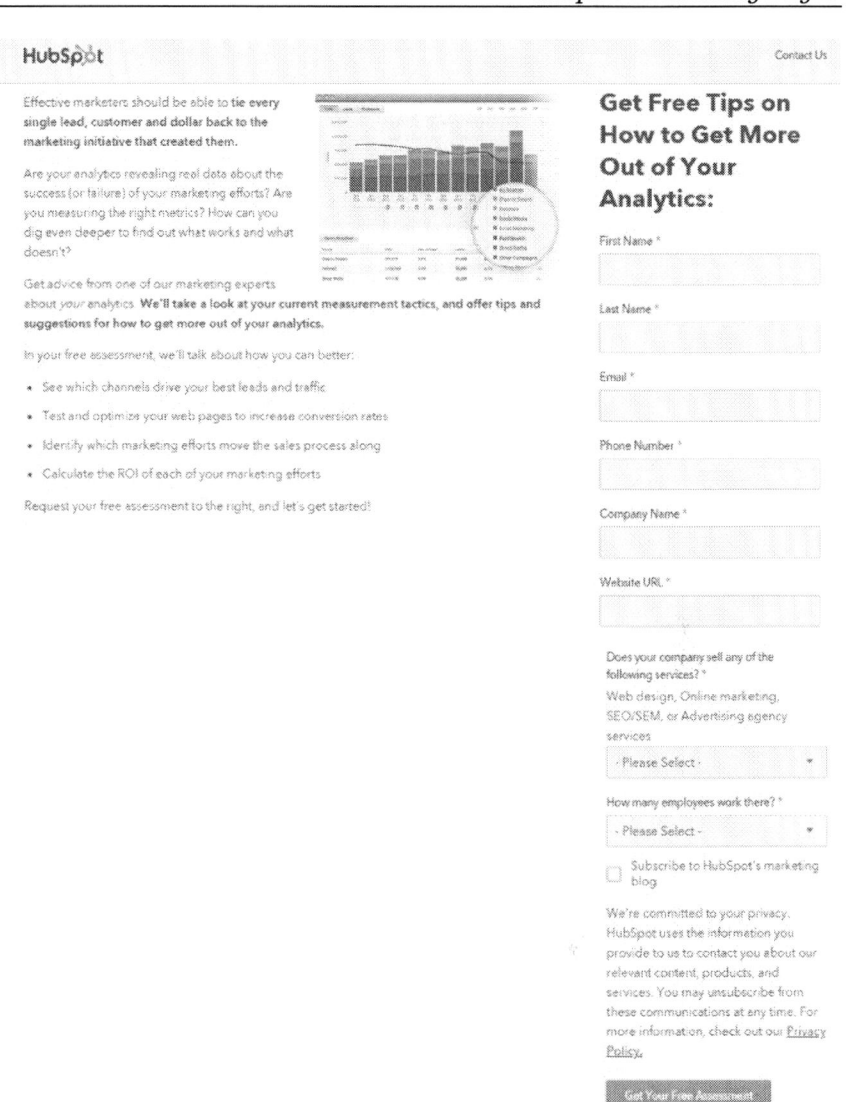

Unsubscribe Page

As your business grows and more customers come on board, some customers will eventually unsubscribe from your newsletter or email list. As a marketer, you need to know why they're leaving and collect information that can help improve your services and retain more customers.

With this page, you can offer your customers the ability to manage how they interact with your business. For instance, a subscriber may choose to unsubscribe from your business because you're sending too many emails and promotional offers.

An unsubscribe page can collect helpful data about why customers don't want to hear from you anymore. Here's an example from the Bonobos website:

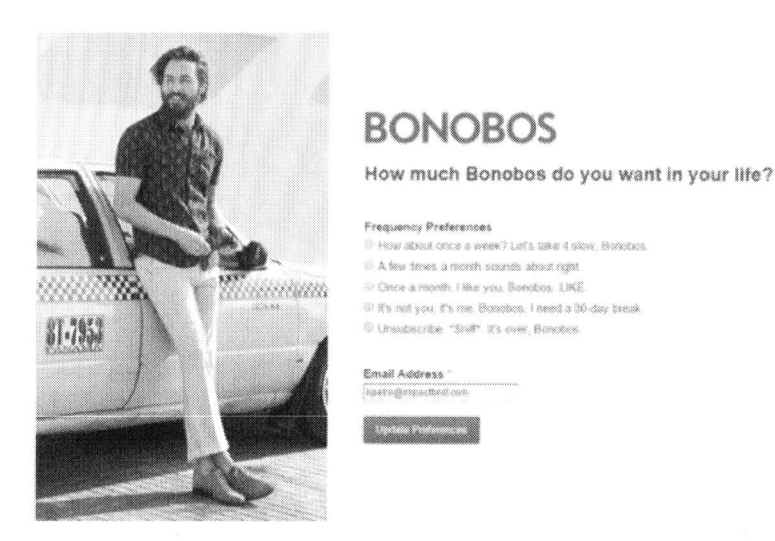

Giving customers the ability to manage the frequency with which you send information about your business can reduce unsubscription rates.

Coming Soon Landing Page

As you keep searching for your customers, you improve your products or create new products. To keep your customers updated on your business, you can create a coming soon page.

It's a good way to notify your customers of new products or services you're about to introduce to the market. Here's an example from shufflehound.com before their site was fully launched:

Chapter 2: Landing Pages

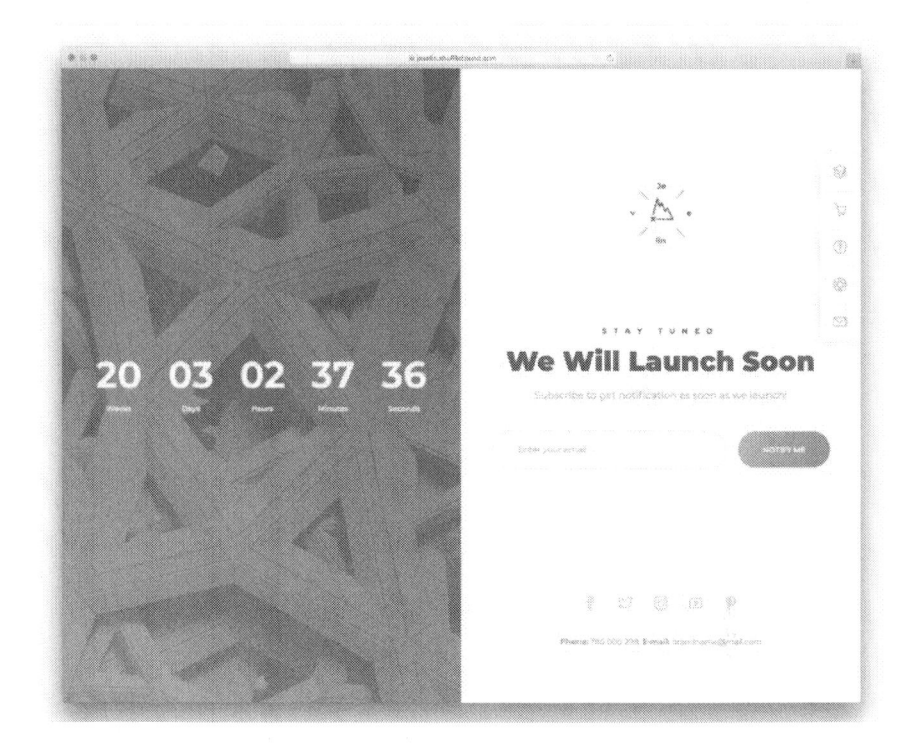

Click-Through Landing Page

This type of landing page is most common in the SaaS business. Clients need to trust your business or software before they'll buy it.

Most SaaS businesses have a page like this one to offer a trial period to their target customers. The customer can use the services free of charge for some time. If they like the services, they can purchase or subscribe to the business.

Here's an example of a click-through page from the Sprout Social website:

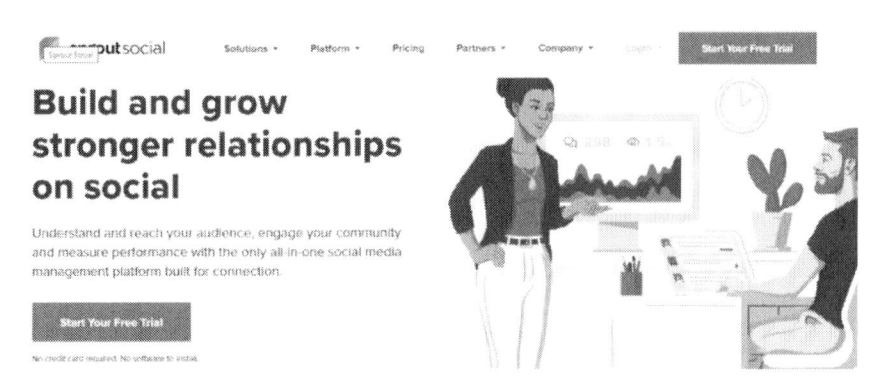

You can also link a click-through page to another page to help the customer fill in the billing details to pay for the software once the trial period is over.

Landing Page Metrics to Measure

Every landing page you create is part of a strategic plan to accomplish your business goals.

To determine how the pages are supporting your goals, it's essential to measure their performance. Here are some landing page metrics you can measure.

Conversion Rate

You need to keep track of how many potential customers convert and which landing page they're converting from.

A high conversion rate indicates that your landing pages are more effective. Research by [Databox shows a 26% average conversion rate](#) for landing pages.

Chapter 2: Landing Pages

What's your average landing page conversion rate?

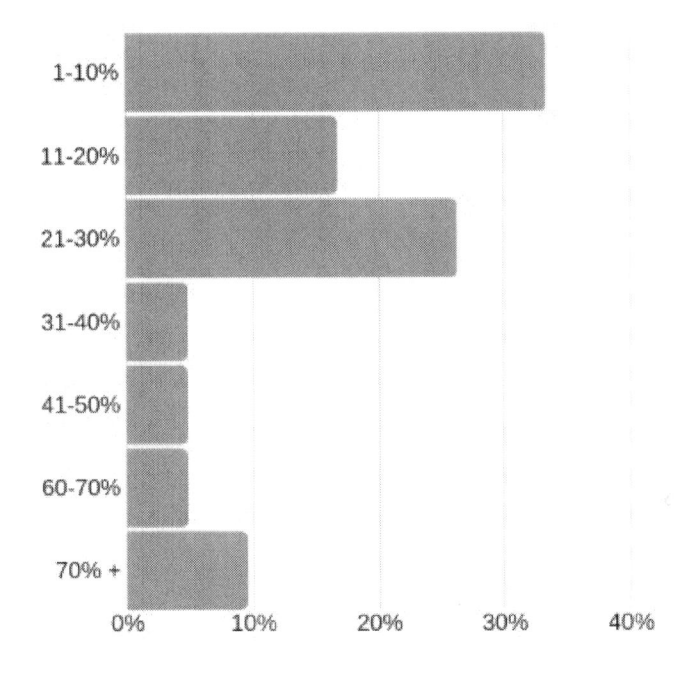

Range	
1-10%	~32%
11-20%	~20%
21-30%	~27%
31-40%	~4%
41-50%	~3%
60-70%	~3%
70% +	~5%

Average of all responses was 26%

databox

Bounce Rate

This is the percentage of visitors who leave your website without clicking to visit any page other than the one they initially landed on.

A high bounce rate is a clear indicator that your potential customers are not engaging with your pages. Several factors can contribute to a high bounce rate:

    Low-quality page content
    Slow loading
    Bad user experience
    Unresponsiveness

A study by RocketFuel shows that most websites have a bounce rate of between 26% and 70%.

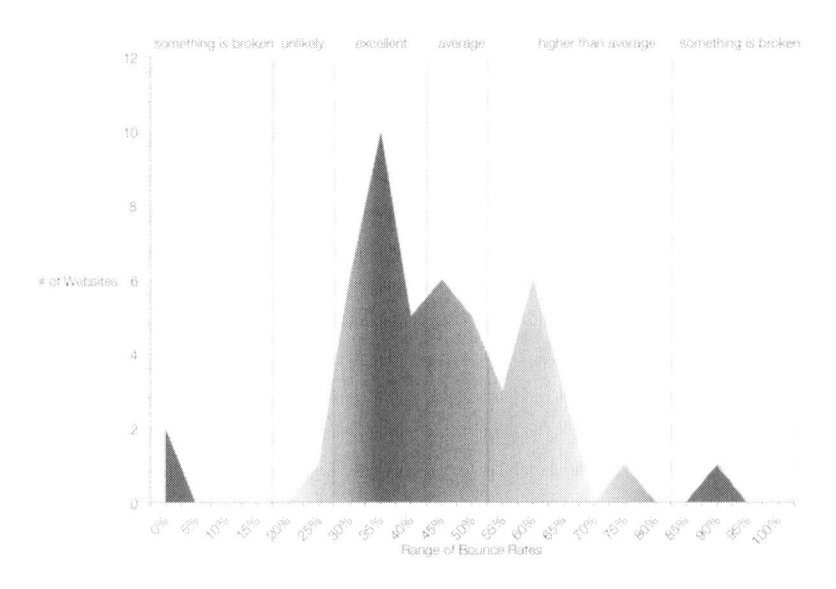

On the websites that fall outside these ranges, some aspect of the landing pages is broken or poorly executed.

Time Spent

If your potential clients spend more time on a particular landing page of your website, that page is effectively engaging them. It likely provides the information they want and educates them about your business products or services and how you can help them solve their problems.

When visitors leave your site shortly after they land on it, that's a sign that they didn't get what they wanted.

Readers engage more with images, so include images that link to your products or services on your landing pages. A great demo video can do even better to engage potential clients with your website.

Number of Subscribers

To conduct email marketing campaigns, you have to collect your potential clients' emails.

If the number of subscribers to your email list is rising every day, it shows that your landing pages are collecting subscriber emails. On the other hand, for example, if you're using an e-book as a lead magnet for your subscribers and the number of subscribers is low, you may want to switch to another lead magnet on your landing page.

Chapter 2: Landing Pages

Something like case studies, checklists, or infographics can make great lead magnets to draw subscribers. What kind of information are your potential clients interested in?

Content Shares

Potential clients are always searching for high-quality content that will help them overcome their challenges.

If they find that your landing pages offer such content, they'll share it on their social media sites to increase engagement. If your content has a high number of shares, likes, and comments, your potential readers love it and enjoy engaging with it. This increases brand awareness and search engine ranking, letting you reach lots of potential clients who may convert into clients.

Traffic Sources

Tracking down the sources of traffic for each of your landing pages can help you ensure that your landing pages attract the right audience.

Your traffic wouldn't do you any good if visitors aren't converting into clients. You can't achieve your business goals if you don't attract the right target market. You need your target clients to engage and convert.

A report by MarketingCharts shows that 57% of B2B marketers struggle to find leads that engage with their brand.

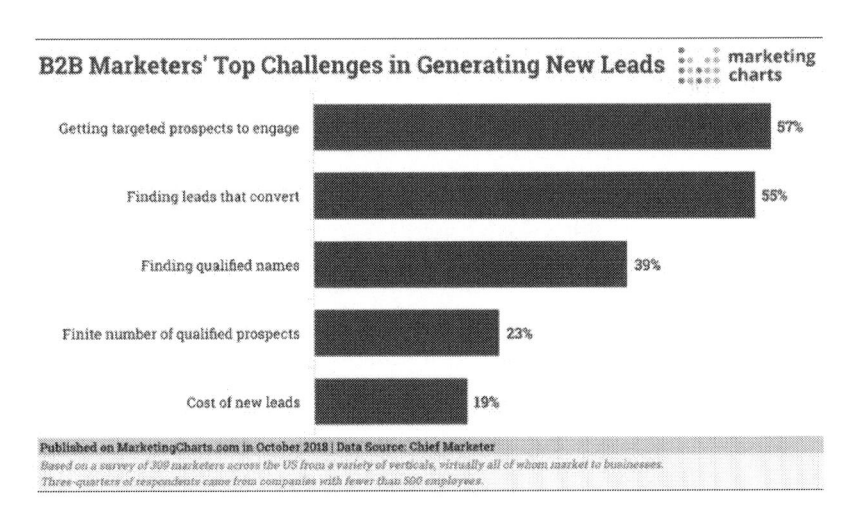

B2B Marketers' Top Challenges in Generating New Leads — marketing charts

Challenge	%
Getting targeted prospects to engage	57%
Finding leads that convert	55%
Finding qualified names	39%
Finite number of qualified prospects	23%
Cost of new leads	19%

Published on MarketingCharts.com in October 2018 | Data Source: Chief Marketer
Based on a survey of 309 marketers across the US from a variety of verticals, virtually all of whom market to businesses. Three-quarters of respondents came from companies with fewer than 500 employees.

Optimize the content on your different landing pages for search engines. Ensure that it provides your target client with the information they need about your products or services.

You can use social media channels to link your landing pages to your website to increase traffic. A Smart Insights report shows that these channels have a 1.81% referral conversion rate.

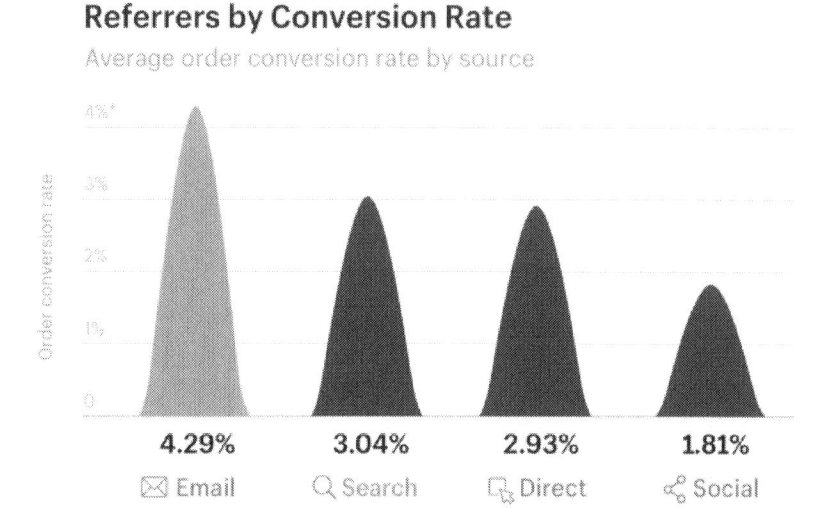

Referrers by Conversion Rate
Average order conversion rate by source

4.29%	3.04%	2.93%	1.81%
✉ Email	🔍 Search	🖱 Direct	⤳ Social

Form Abandonment Rate

You walk your potential clients through the sales cycle, and at the last stage of the cycle, some fill the cart but abandon it without making a purchase.

Clients hate long, complicated checkout processes. Research by Statista shows that 30% of potential buyers abandon their cart if they have to re-enter their credit card information.

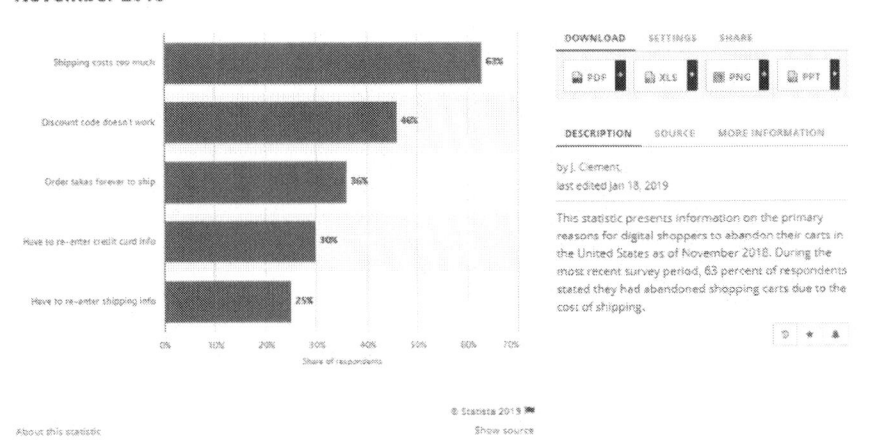

Primary reason for digital shoppers in the United States to abandon their carts as of November 2018

Your checkout process should be simple and shouldn't demand too much information from potential buyers.

Click-Through Rate for CTAs

Your CTAs are important for your business progress. A high click-through rate on your landing pages shows that leads are taking action and converting, which is a great step toward your business's success.

Organic Traffic

Remember, you've optimized your landing pages with target keywords. It's good to get high traffic from potential clients searching for content with the target keywords.

These results will direct leads to your landing pages that contain those keywords and increase their chances of converting. You can also measure traffic from social media, referrals, and pay-per-click traffic sources.

Return Visitors

If potential clients like your landing page content, product, or services offered, they'll return to your website. This is a great metric for measuring engagement with your landing pages. When you notice your leads revisiting your pages, it makes it easy to convince them and convert them into customers.

If they're already customers, it will be easy to retain them and keep generating revenue from their repeat purchases.

Form Submissions

A high form-submissions rate shows that target leads are liking your product or service offering and want to engage more with it. High engagement leads to an increase in conversion rates. The same applies to email subscriptions.

When you see more and more people joining your email list, that means they love your content and want updates on your content and product offers. You can persuade these people to become clients.

Essentials of a Perfect Landing Page

Here we list some must-have features that can help you get better results from your landing pages.

Headline

Your landing page must have an attractive headline to capture the attention of potential clients. It should include words that are meaningful to your target audience.

These words should focus on customer pain points. The ConvertKit Masterclass landing page is a good example:

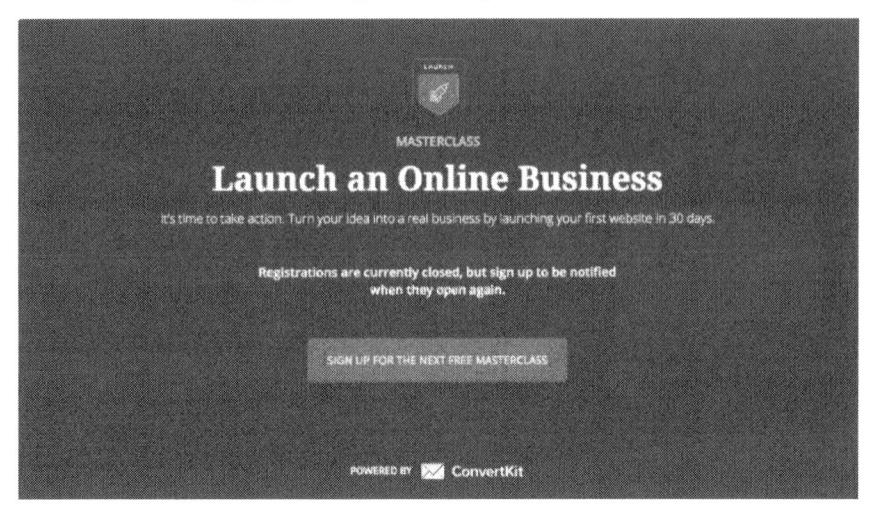

If, for instance, a potential client is searching for an online class about how to launch an online business, this headline will capture their attention. You can also include subheadings that help reinforce your message.

Brief Offer Description

You'll need to explain what your offer includes and why potential clients should care about it. The text should inspire demand in your reader.

For example, here's the brief description for the ConvertKit Masterclass headline above:

> ☑ Feeling stuck in your career path?
>
> ☑ Ready to make a change in your life?
>
> ☑ Dream of starting your own business, but not sure how to make that happen?
>
> So many creators sit on a great idea for too long while they wait for their circumstances to change or because they're too afraid to make a move. The *"Once this happens, I'll finally be able to...."* mentality doesn't usually pan out like you had hoped, and we all know fear can be a crippling roadblock.
>
> If these sound familiar, you're wasting valuable daylight waiting around for something that never comes around. That sure thing and that confidence you seek have to start by putting in the hard work yourself.
>
> It's time to stop waiting for your circumstances to change. It's time to take action. It's time to start building your business today.

Here's a more detailed description of the Masterclass:

What you get with Launch an Online Business Masterclass

Daily lessons
During our month together, you'll take part in course lessons each day of the week, Monday through Thursday. We've created these lessons to be simple and actionable steps to help you build on what you learned and created each day until you're able to hit publish on your website.

Weekly live trainings
Every Friday you'll hear from a ConvertKit team member on your topic for the week. These live trainings will be your chance to deep dive into the topic with an expert for more information and Q&A's.

Support from likeminded business creators like yourself
Not only will you hear from creators on the ConvertKit team throughout the month, you'll also be a part of a Facebook Community group with other students going through the masterclass. This amazing group of people will be your support system, advice-givers, source of encouragement, and helpful problem-solvers throughout your business-building process. And you never know- you just might meet your future mastermind partners in this group too.

A viable business, fully built website, and actionable plan to grow your audience
At the end of the month, you'll be all set to launch your business into the world. We're going to help you fully develop your business vision, create all the necessary pieces of content, and put together a promotional plan that is sure to set your business up for success.

Plus 30 days of ConvertKit for FREE
And of course this Masterclass will include a free 30-day trial of ConvertKit too! You didn't think we'd teach you how to use our product and then not give you a chance to try out for yourself, right?

REGISTER FOR THE FREE MASTERCLASS

And here's a description of the content of the Masterclass, divided into four different weeks. It shows the potential student what they'll learn each week.

The Masterclass Content

WEEK ONE
The Mission, Vision, and Why

- Why are you starting a business?
- What are the mission and core values of your business idea?
- What is the three to five year vision for your business? Who will it impact?

WEEK TWO
Building a Platform

- Renting vs. owning your content: The importance of building a website and email list
- Step by step website development
- Getting your email marketing set up with your ConvertKit account

WEEK THREE
Creating Your Launch Content

- Outlining your opt-in incentives and first sequence autoresponder
- Writing three key blog posts so you have content to launch with
- How to develop your about page and homepage content

WEEK FOUR
Launch Time

- Setting up and executing your promotion plans
- Hitting publish on your website and blog posts
- How to develop your email list over time with opt-ins and content upgrades

Information Capture Form

You need your potential clients' information to nurture them through the buyer stages. This begins with your target client taking action after reading your landing page information.

Your form shouldn't demand in-depth details from potential customers because they hate that.

Here's an example of this form for the above ConvertKit Masterclass landing page:

It's time to take action on your business. Are you ready?

If you're done with excuses, waiting around, and putting off your big ideas, we're here to help you make it happen. And guess what? We're offering up this masterclass for no charge at all. That's right- you can take Launch an Online Business Masterclass for FREE!

We want to make sure nothing stands in your way of building the business of your dreams. So if you're ready to make it happen, we're here to be your guides.

This masterclass registration has closed, sign up to be notified when registration opens again.

First Name

Email Address

SIGN UP FOR THE FREE MASTERCLASS

Images or Videos

This helps create a great first impression and attract potential clients. One example is found on the Airbnb website:

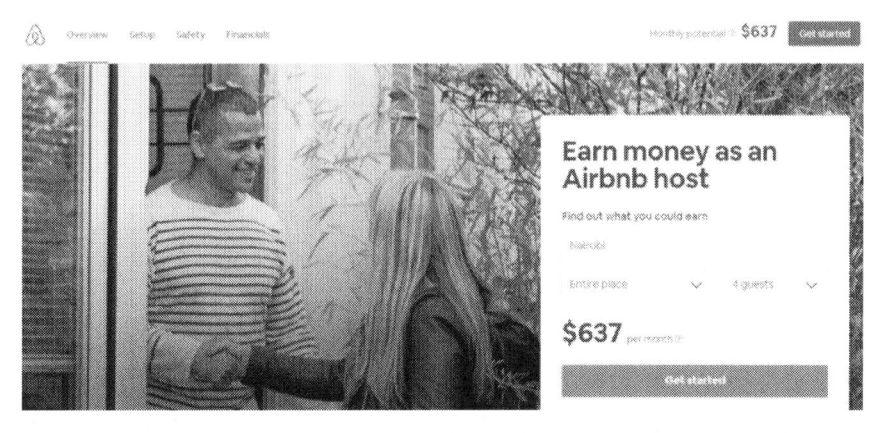

For instance, the welcoming picture shown here gives the potential client a sense of connection to the brand that makes it easy to engage with.

Chapter 2: Landing Pages

The psychology of color can help you create impressive images for your landing pages. Different colors influence consumer decisions differently.

Colors Influence on Consumer Decision

Image source: https://neilpatel.com/blog/the-psychology-of-color-how-to-use-colors-to-increase-conversion-rate/

Also, men and women tend to have different color preferences.

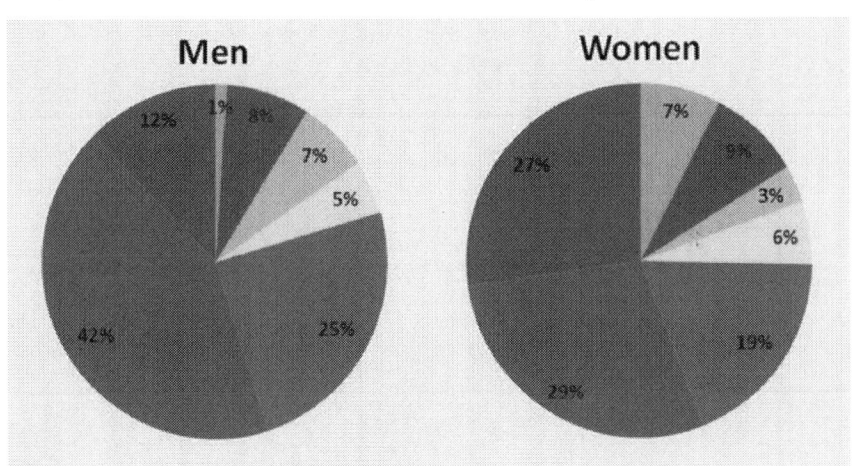

Image source: https://neilpatel.com/blog/the-psychology-of-color-how-to-use-colors-to-increase-conversion-rate/

Men's and women's favorite colors

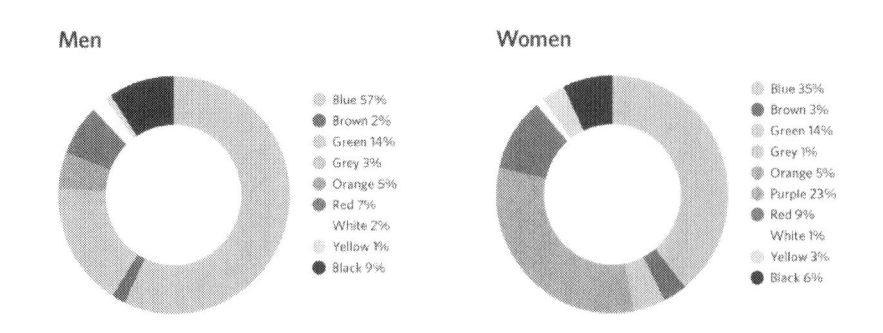

Men

- Blue 57%
- Brown 2%
- Green 14%
- Grey 3%
- Orange 5%
- Red 7%
- White 2%
- Yellow 1%
- Black 9%

Women

- Blue 35%
- Brown 3%
- Green 14%
- Grey 1%
- Orange 5%
- Purple 23%
- Red 9%
- White 1%
- Yellow 3%
- Black 6%

Image source: https://www.helpscout.com/blog/psychology-of-color/

Use colors that are attractive and engaging to your target audience, factoring in the color preferences of your potential clients based on their gender.

Different colors also trigger different emotions that affect the customer's purchasing potential in various ways.

YELLOW — OPTIMISTIC AND YOUTHFUL, OFTEN USED TO GRAB ATTENTION OF WINDOW SHOPPERS

RED — ENERGY, INCREASES HEART RATE, CREATES URGENCY, OFTEN SEEN IN CLEARANCE SALES

BLUE — CREATES THE SENSATIONAL OF TRUST AND SECURITY, OFTEN SEEN WITH BANKS AND BUSINESSES

GREEN — ASSOCIATED WITH WEALTHY, THE EASIEST COLOR FOR THE EYES TO PROCESS, USED TO RELAX IN STORES

ORANGE — AGGRESSIVE, CREATES A CALL TO ACTION: SUBSCRIBE, BUY, OR SELL

PINK — ROMANTIC AND FEMININE, USED TO MARKET PRODUCTS TO WOMAN AND YOUNG GIRLS

BLACK — POWERFUL AND SLEEK, USED TO MARKET LUXURY PRODUCTS

PURPLE — IS USED TO SOOTHE & CALM, OFTEN SEEN IN BEAUTY OR ANTI-AGING PRODUCTS

Chapter 2: Landing Pages

Image source: https://www.helpscout.com/blog/psychology-of-color/

Image source: https://thelogocompany.net/blog/infographics/psychology-color-logo-design/

Videos are more engaging and draw your leads' attention to your business brand.

Here's an example of a convincing video on one of the Outbrain website's landing pages.

Potential clients are more likely to remember video content than text-based content and videos are very persuasive.

Mobile-Friendly Content

Unresponsive websites can prevent your business from achieving its marketing goals. If your potential clients can't access your website on their mobile devices, they'll turn to your competitors.

Research by Statista projects that mobile users will reach 2.87 billion in 2020.

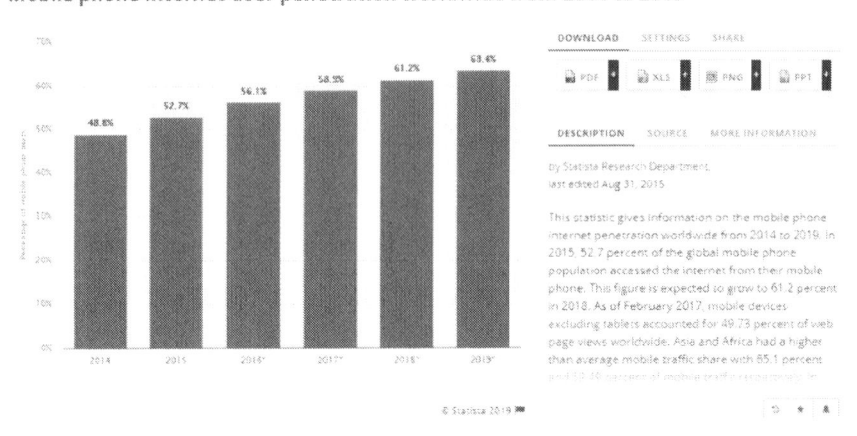

People are using mobile devices more than ever. Ensure that your landing pages are mobile-friendly. Customers should be able to load your page content quickly on their smartphones.

Social Sharing Buttons

You need to use all the methods you can to increase your brand awareness and attract, engage, and convert leads. One great way is to include sharing buttons on your pages. We like the way Hootsuite does it here:

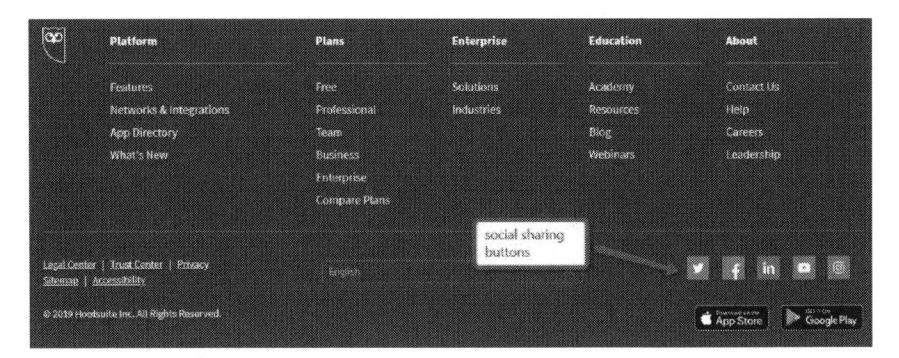

If a potential client finds your pages attractive, they can share that information on their social accounts with the simple click of a button. And if you make it easy, they'll be more likely to do so.

Search Engine Optimization

You want your page to rank high in search engine results so you can get your business in front of more eyes, right?

You have to optimize your content to increase your rankings. Run a keyword search and use those keywords within your content.

One great site that can help you with keyword searches is Ubersuggest.

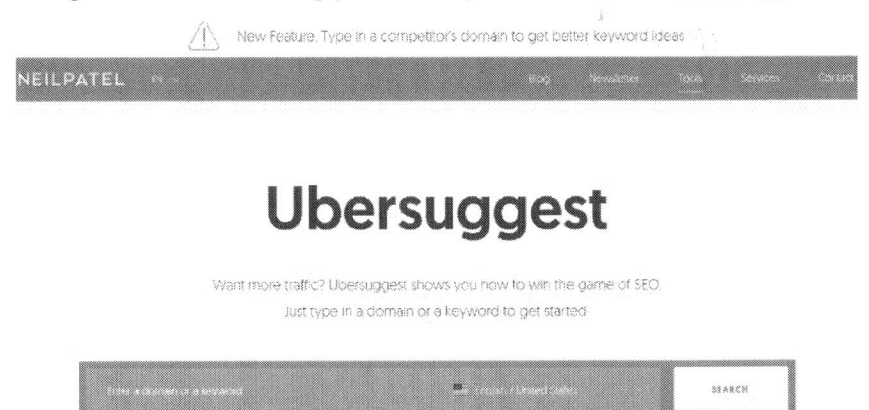

Here are more options for tools that can help with keyword searches. Once you find the right keywords, include them in your landing page headline.

You can also use your main keywords in your meta tag description, page title, and URL.

Remember to include secondary keywords within the content of your landing pages. This site can help you generate those keywords: http://lsigraph.com.

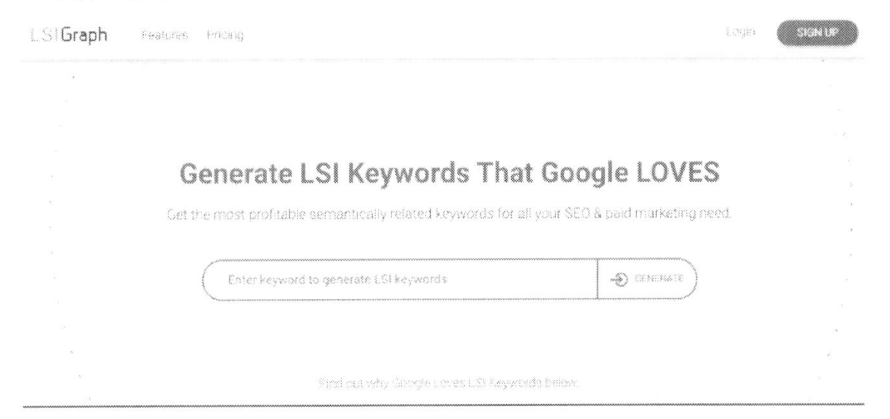

For more information about SEO, review "SEO Tips" in chapter 1.

Customer Testimonials

Through these are not a must for every landing page you create, they can help further your marketing plans.

Potential clients trust businesses other people have used and benefited from. Here's an example from the Muck Rack landing page:

Here's what our customers say about us

"Reading Muck Rack Alert emails is a daily requirement for me. They keep me up-to-date on the topics that matter most to me."

Mark Cuban
Owner of the Dallas Mavericks, investor, entrepreneur

"I use Muck Rack on a daily basis. From the alerts in my inbox to check for stories we're quoted in, to building quality media lists and seeing what stories are being read by the reporters I follow. Muck Rack is a great tool to get my work-life in order. I love this product."

Izzy Santa
Consumer Technology Association

"Getting the full spectrum around the issues that journalists are talking about, especially the issues we care about, helps us understand when is the best time to interact with a journalist...it's so interesting...to see the impact of the articles on social through Muck Rack."

Sebastian Majewski
Bill & Melinda Gates Foundation

"When you become a Muck Rack customer, you truly create an extension of your communications team."

Rachel Klinkatsis
Prologis

> "Muck Rack is a user-friendly media database. Where other tools are clunky, Muck Rack is intuitive and fast. I love that the platform is integrated with Twitter, and is more up-to-date than other databases I've used."
>
> Jacqui Wimberly
> Small Girls PR

> "Muck Rack is the map, compass and GPS for navigating the ever evolving media and journalist landscape. Truly without them, as a PR practitioner, I would be lost."
>
> Matt Prince
> Taco Bell

> "Muck Rack has helped my team and me meet new people, avert potential crises, strengthen relationships, and understand how journalists are responding to our news."
>
> Sandy Pell
> Head of Corporate Communications, Vidyard

You can also ask your customers to leave reviews for your services or products. Research by BrightLocal shows that 25% of potential clients trust reviews if they come from multiple clients.

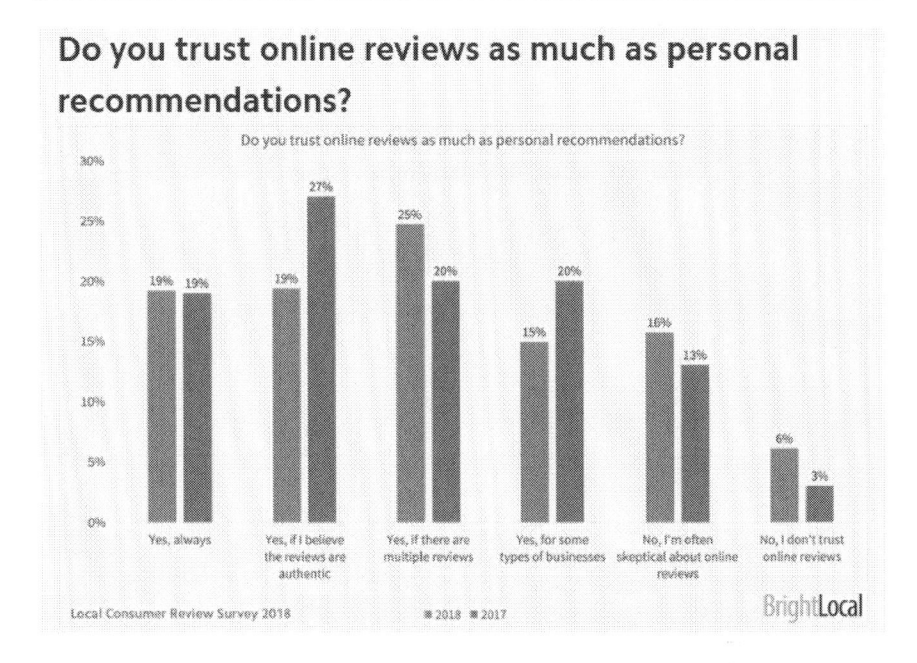

Do you trust online reviews as much as personal recommendations?

Do you trust online reviews as much as personal recommendations?

	Yes, always	Yes, if I believe the reviews are authentic	Yes, if there are multiple reviews	Yes, for some types of businesses	No, I'm often skeptical about online reviews	No, I don't trust online reviews
2018	19%	27%	19%	15%	16%	6%
2017	19%	25%	20%	20%	13%	3%

Local Consumer Review Survey 2018 — BrightLocal

A Single CTA

The end goal of your landing page preparation and marketing is to inspire your target customer to take action. To make it easy for them, limit your calls-to-action to just one per page. This will reduce confusion and make it easy for visitors to take the desired action on your page.

Here's an example of the Econsultancy training landing page. Throughout the page, they provide case studies, testimonials from past clients, and information about the types of training they conduct.

All these aim to build trust and encourage potential clients to take one action: sign up for the training.

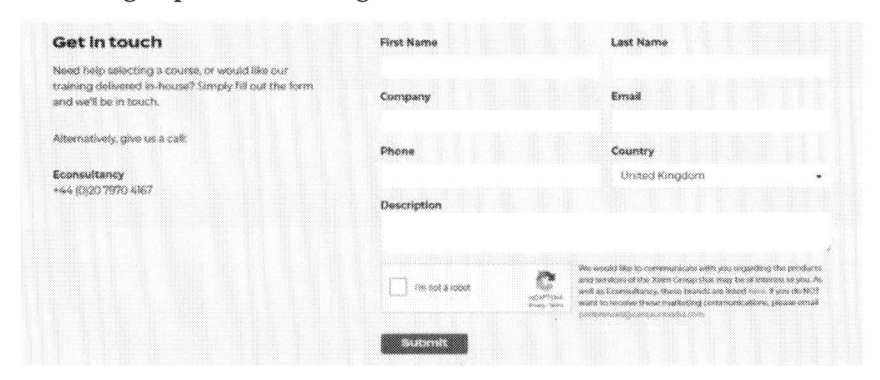

If the business used several CTAs, it would likely confuse the prospects about what action to take and send them away to consider the services of their competitors.

A Unique Selling Proposition

You're offering a product or service to your customers. Effective landing pages should display a unique selling value for your offer.

Let your potential customers know why they should take your offer instead of your competitor's. Create compelling copy for your ad that engages with your leads' emotions.

Help your customers see why your products or services are the best for them and can solve their problems.

A Simple Contact Method

You may have a great offer that attracts leads to your business. However, if they find it hard to contact you, they'll leave and do business with your competitors.

You should provide several different ways for target clients to contact you in case they have questions or need clarification.

A Tight Focus

You want your leads to engage with your brand and take action. One great way to help them accomplish this is by reducing anything on your page that can be a distraction.

Include content that helps your leads build trust with your brand, benefit from product offers, and take action.

Pop-ups are one annoying distraction that can affect your landing page conversions. Keep your landing page information simple and easy to understand.

Including white space and bullet points can enhance the flow of your information and make it easy for readers to understand and consume your landing page content.

Besides eliminating distractions, you can also focus the content to elicit a particular response. For example, consider using words that trigger specific emotions and motivate readers to act.

Chapter 2: Landing Pages

These Emotions Make People Click on Things

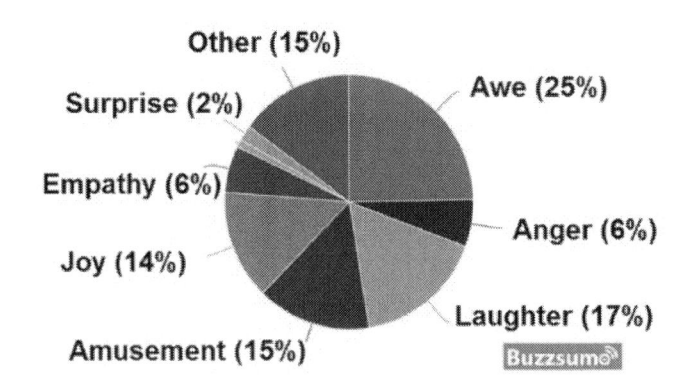

- Other (15%)
- Awe (25%)
- Surprise (2%)
- Empathy (6%)
- Anger (6%)
- Joy (14%)
- Laughter (17%)
- Amusement (15%)

Buzzsumo

Tools for Creating Landing Pages

You now know the essentials of your landing page and you're ready to get started. Here are some tools that can help you successfully accomplish page creation.

Instapage

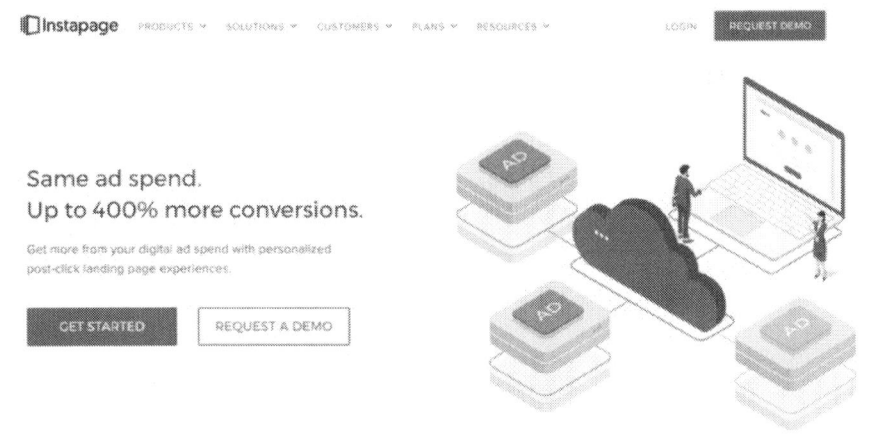

Same ad spend. Up to 400% more conversions.

Get more from your digital ad spend with personalized post-click landing page experiences.

GET STARTED   REQUEST A DEMO

This tool helps you create exceptional landing pages that are mobile-responsive. Here's the tool's pricing model:

Business	Enterprise
Everything you need to start building a/o optimizing post-click experiences for higher conversions.	The advanced features and services needed to scale your advertising operation and maximize ROI.
$149	Customized
✓ Postclick Score™	✓ Postclick Score™
✓ AdMap™	✓ AdMap™
✓ #1 Landing Page Builder	✓ #1 Landing Page Builder
✓ Thor Render Engine™ (Speed Boost)	✓ Thor Render Engine™ (Speed Boost)
✓ Instablocks™	✓ Instablocks™
✓ Multi-Step Forms	✓ Multi-Step Forms
✓ Server Side A/B Testing	✓ Server Side A/B Testing
✓ Heatmaps	✓ Heatmaps
✓ Conversion Analytics	✓ Conversion Analytics
✓ Dynamic Text Replacement	✓ Dynamic Text Replacement
✓ Zapier Integration	✓ Zapier Integration
✓ Salesforce Integration	✓ Salesforce Integration
✓ Marketo Integration	✓ Marketo Integration
✓ HubSpot Integration	✓ HubSpot Integration
✓ SSL Encryption	✓ SSL Encryption
✓ GDPR Compliance	✓ GDPR Compliance
✓ Page Redirects	✓ Page Redirects
✓ Google Single Sign On (SSO)	✓ Google Single Sign On (SSO)
	✓ Enterprise SSO (Okta & OneLogin)
	✓ 1:1 Ad to Page Personalization
	✓ Real-Time Visual Collaboration
	✓ Editable Global Blocks
	✓ AMP Pages & Experiences
	✓ Direct Lead Bypass
	✓ Audit Logs
	✓ Audit Logs
	✓ Guaranteed Uptime Enterprise SLA
	✓ Ad Spend Conversion Attribution
	✓ Page Migration Services
	✓ Dedicated Launch Specialist
	✓ Customer Success Manager
	✓ Custom Feature Implementation
SIGN UP	CONTACT SALES

Subscribe to the pricing model that suits your business. Once you start using the software, you can download the Instapage WordPress plugin to sync your landing pages to your website.

Chapter 2: Landing Pages

Launchrock

This is a great tool, especially if you're working on a "coming soon" page. These pages suit start-ups launching their products or website. You simply choose a template and edit it to achieve the desired look. Here's its pricing plan:

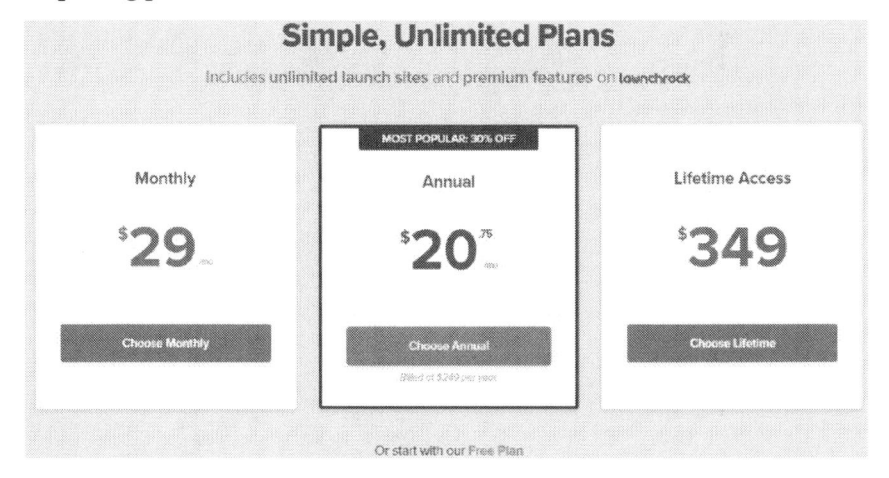

Five Second Tests

You need feedback from potential customers and existing customers to help improve your landing pages. This tool helps you get that feedback.

Five second tests

Optimize the clarity of your designs by measuring first impressions and recall.

What are they?

Five second tests are a method of user research that help you measure what information users take away and what impression they get within the first five seconds of viewing a design. They're commonly used to test whether web pages are effectively communicating their intended message.

You give participants five seconds to view a landing page, and then they answer questions related to the page. The test gives you data about how to improve your landing pages' first impressions among potential clients.

LeadPages

This tool has unique features to help you create amazing landing pages for your business website. It offers a variety of different templates you can select from, but not all the templates are free. Here are some examples:

Chapter 2: Landing Pages

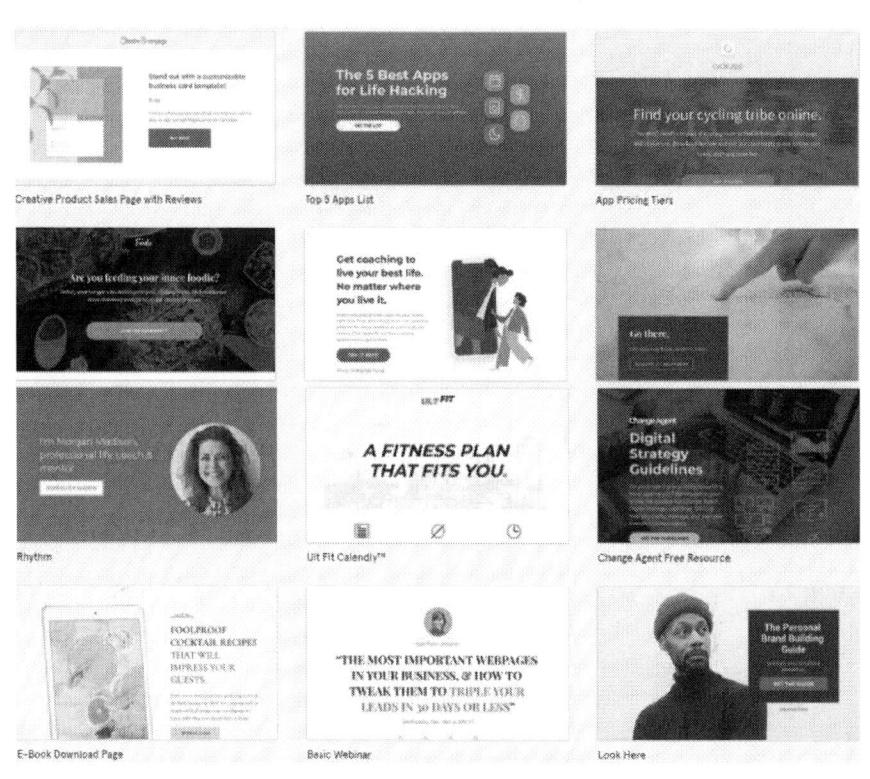

Creative Product Sales Page with Reviews	Top 5 Apps List	App Pricing Tiers
Rhythm	Ult Fit Calendly™	Change Agent Free Resource
E-Book Download Page	Basic Webinar	Look Here

And here's the LeadPages pricing structure:

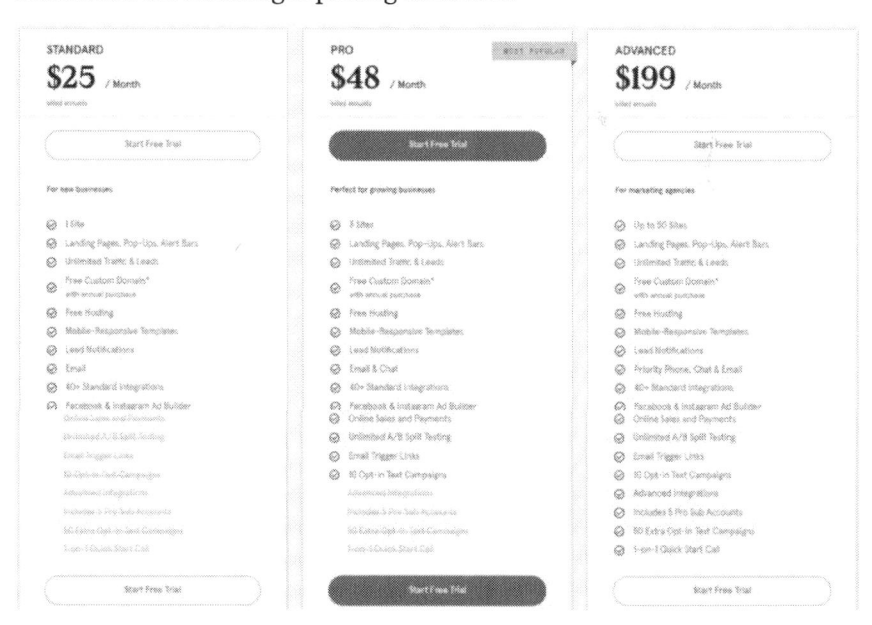

STANDARD — $25 / Month
billed annually

Start Free Trial

For new businesses:
- 1 Site
- Landing Pages, Pop-Ups, Alert Bars
- Unlimited Traffic & Leads
- Free Custom Domain* with annual purchase
- Free Hosting
- Mobile-Responsive Templates
- Lead Notifications
- Email
- 40+ Standard Integrations
- Facebook & Instagram Ad Builder
- Online Sales and Payments
- Unlimited A/B Split Testing
- Email Trigger Links
- 10 Opt-in Text Campaigns
- Advanced Integrations
- Includes 5 Pro Sub Accounts
- 50 Extra Opt-in Text Campaigns
- 1-on-1 Quick Start Call

Start Free Trial

PRO — $48 / Month — MOST POPULAR
billed annually

Start Free Trial

Perfect for growing businesses:
- 3 Sites
- Landing Pages, Pop-Ups, Alert Bars
- Unlimited Traffic & Leads
- Free Custom Domain* with annual purchase
- Free Hosting
- Mobile-Responsive Templates
- Lead Notifications
- Email & Chat
- 40+ Standard Integrations
- Facebook & Instagram Ad Builder
- Online Sales and Payments
- Unlimited A/B Split Testing
- Email Trigger Links
- 10 Opt-in Text Campaigns
- Advanced Integrations
- Includes 5 Pro Sub Accounts
- 50 Extra Opt-in Text Campaigns
- 1-on-1 Quick Start Call

Start Free Trial

ADVANCED — $199 / Month
billed annually

Start Free Trial

For marketing agencies:
- Up to 50 Sites
- Landing Pages, Pop-Ups, Alert Bars
- Unlimited Traffic & Leads
- Free Custom Domain* with annual purchase
- Free Hosting
- Mobile-Responsive Templates
- Lead Notifications
- Priority Phone, Chat & Email
- 40+ Standard Integrations
- Facebook & Instagram Ad Builder
- Online Sales and Payments
- Unlimited A/B Split Testing
- Email Trigger Links
- 10 Opt-in Text Campaigns
- Advanced Integrations
- Includes 5 Pro Sub Accounts
- 50 Extra Opt-in Text Campaigns
- 1-on-1 Quick Start Call

Start Free Trial

Unbounce

This tool helps you create landing pages with beautiful designs. It offers an assortment of templates and an easy drag-and-drop builder.

You can customize the templates to create the exact landing pages you want. The tool features a number of designs to suit your market niche, as shown here:

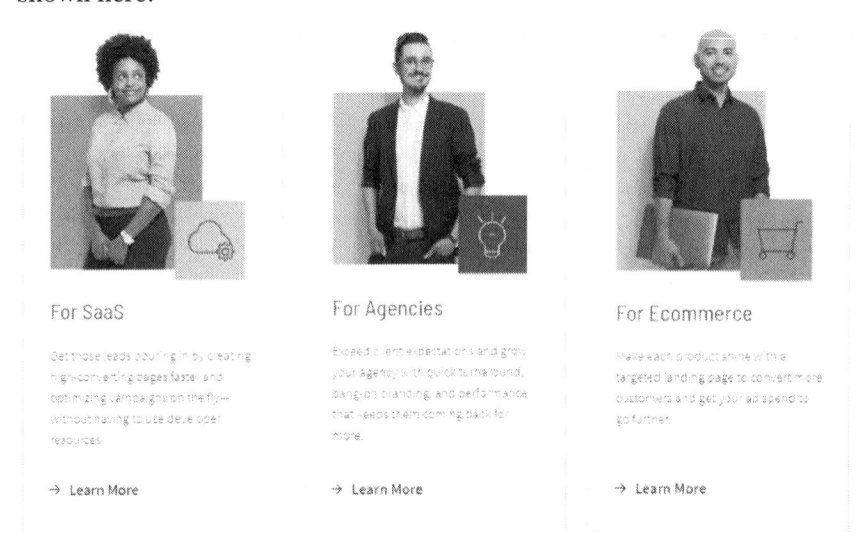

Chapter 2: Landing Pages

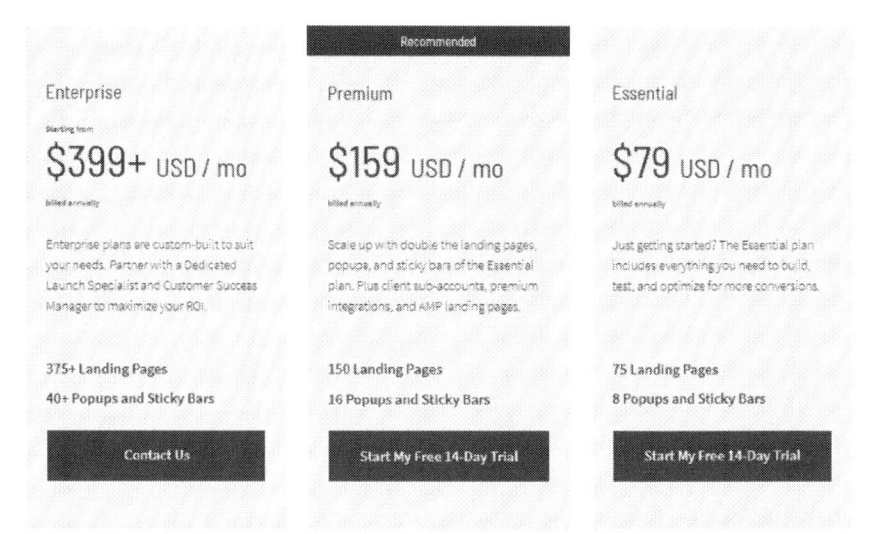

Here are Unbounce's prices for its different software packages:

	Recommended	
Enterprise	Premium	Essential
Starting from		
$399+ USD / mo	**$159** USD / mo	**$79** USD / mo
billed annually	billed annually	billed annually
Enterprise plans are custom-built to suit your needs. Partner with a Dedicated Launch Specialist and Customer Success Manager to maximize your ROI.	Scale up with double the landing pages, popups, and sticky bars of the Essential plan. Plus client sub-accounts, premium integrations, and AMP landing pages.	Just getting started? The Essential plan includes everything you need to build, test, and optimize for more conversions.
375+ Landing Pages	150 Landing Pages	75 Landing Pages
40+ Popups and Sticky Bars	16 Popups and Sticky Bars	8 Popups and Sticky Bars
Contact Us	Start My Free 14-Day Trial	Start My Free 14-Day Trial

The tool helps you create responsive landing pages that load rapidly on mobile devices. This is a great way to attract and capture leads as most potential customers use mobile devices to search for services or products.

You can also use the tool to conduct A/B testing for your landing page and optimize the pages with the highest conversions.

Here we display some of the Unbounce templates you can use:

O-SaaS

A theme that's designed to show off your SaaS product. There's plenty of contrast, space for key benefits, a pricing grid, and more.

→ VIEW THIS TEMPLATE

O-Consultancy

Perfect for consulting businesses, this lead gen page includes a longer form for capturing detailed info from your prospects.

→ VIEW THIS TEMPLATE

O-Book

Create a high-converting home for your next ebook with this bold theme. Offer your visitors a sneak peek at what's inside and close the deal with reader testimonials.

→ VIEW THIS TEMPLATE

For SaaS

Get those leads pouring in by creating high-converting pages faster and optimizing campaigns on the fly—without having to use developer resources.

→ Learn More

For Agencies

Exceed client expectations and grow your agency with quick turnaround, bang-on branding, and performance that keeps them coming back for more.

→ Learn More

For Ecommerce

Make each product shine with a targeted landing page to convert more customers and get your ad spend to go further.

→ Learn More

Chapter 2: Landing Pages

Getting Started-Lead Generation

A simple lead-capture page with clearly laid-out sections for benefits, and even a customizable conversion-focused form.

→ VIEW THIS TEMPLATE

MODA

Influenced by Unbounce customer Indochino's high-converting design, this template works for any business with a few customizations.

→ VIEW THIS TEMPLATE

ALLHËR

Designed for real estate companies, this template allows for plenty of space to show off imagery and benefits of your customers' dream homes.

→ VIEW THIS TEMPLATE

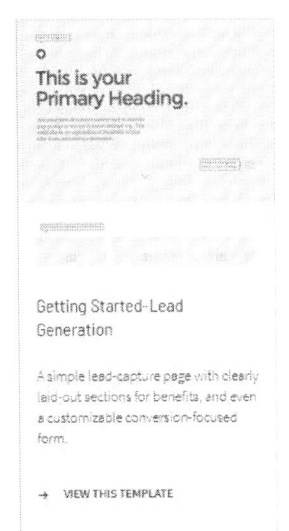

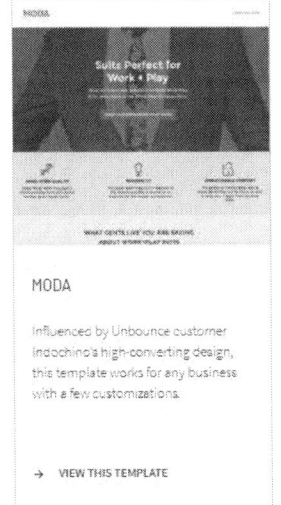

UserTesting

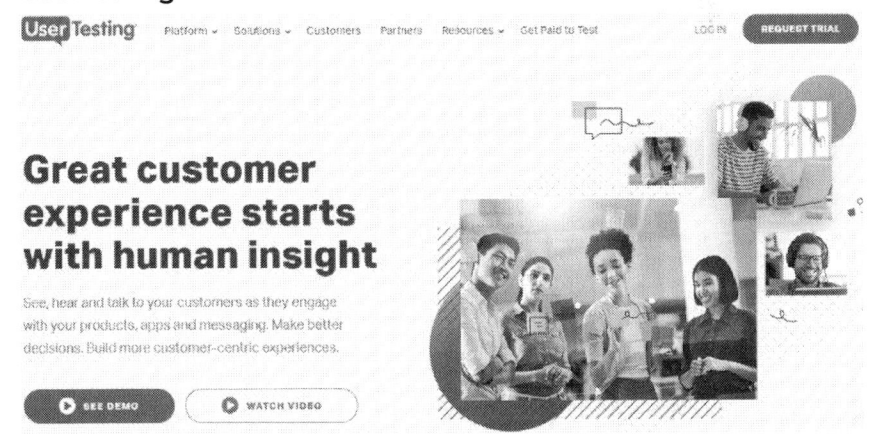

Glowing reviews of your landing pages can increase your conversion rates. The UserTesting tool records audio as users interact with your pages.

It records their feedback, which you can use to improve your landing pages, build trust, and increase conversions.

Here's how the tool works:

How it works

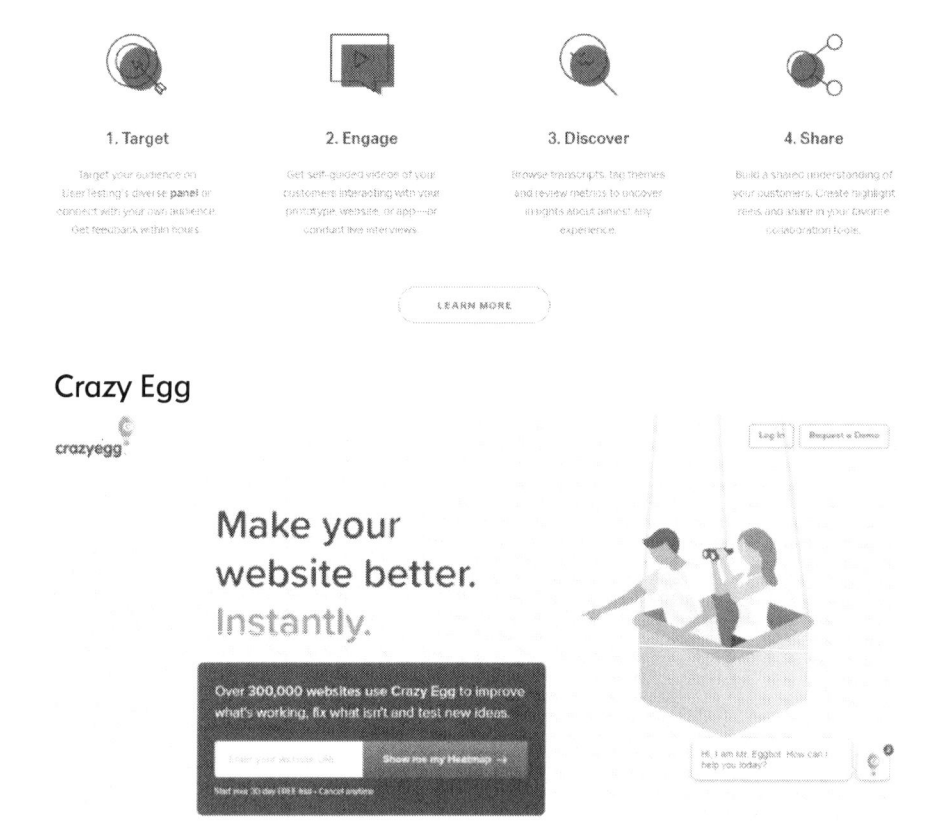

1. Target
Target your audience on UserTesting's diverse panel or connect with your own audience. Get feedback within hours.

2. Engage
Get self-guided videos of your customers interacting with your prototype, website, or app—or conduct live interviews.

3. Discover
Browse transcripts, tag themes and review metrics to uncover insights about any experience.

4. Share
Build a shared understanding of your customers. Create highlight reels and share in your favorite collaboration tools.

LEARN MORE

Crazy Egg

You can use this tool to find out what potential clients are doing on your landing pages. View data about user engagement and decide what to improve.

The data you collect from tracking visitor activity can let you create better services or products.

Below is the CrazyEgg pricing model:

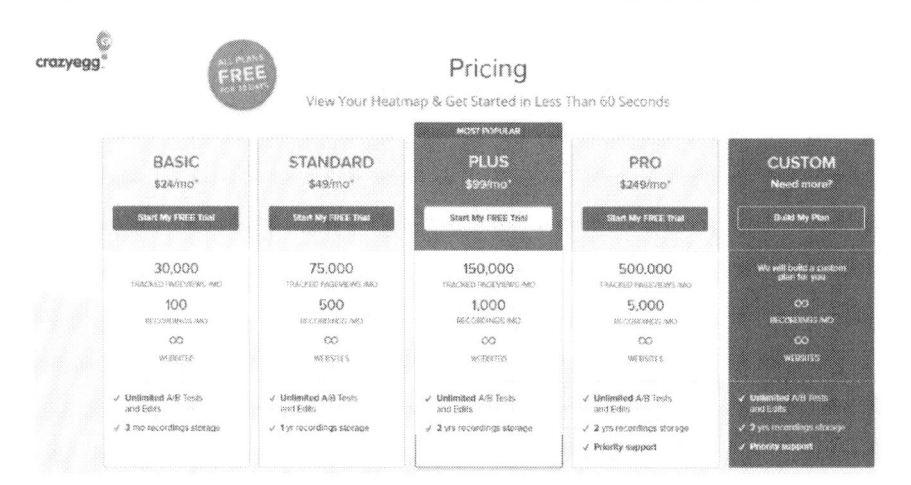

Olark

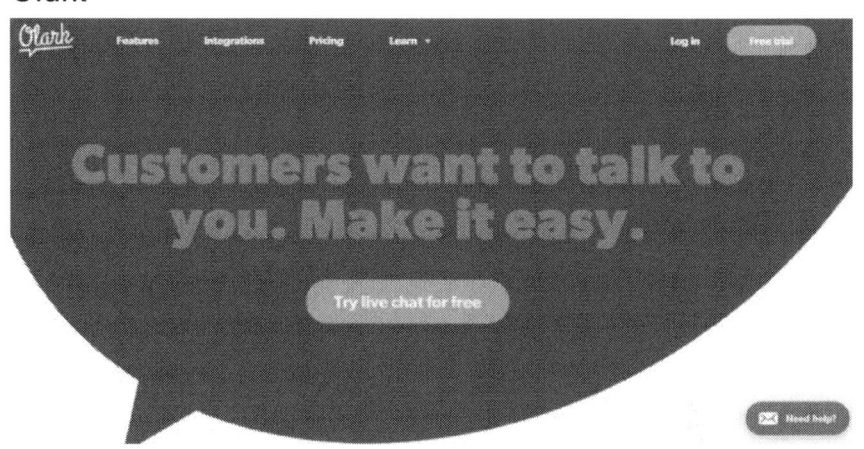

Your customers or prospects may have many questions as they browse your landing pages. You can use the Olark tool, live chat software, to answer these questions.

It appears as a small chat widget at the bottom of your pages and expands when a visitor clicks on it.

Here's how it looks:

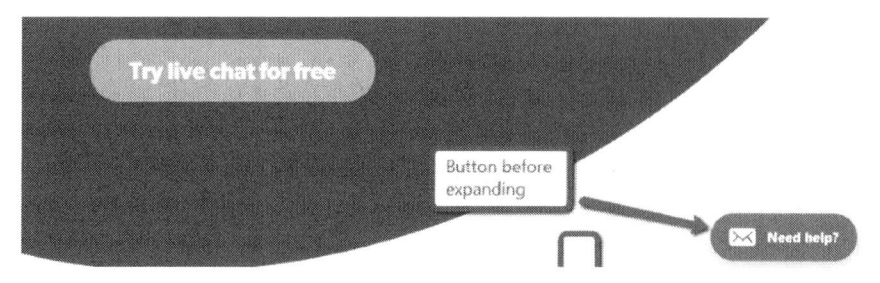

And here's how it looks after expanding:

This live chat answers questions or provides information to target customers as they interact with the page to teach them about your business and how you can help them.

Questions from your potential clients can help you improve your landing pages and the way you reach out to your target clients.

The Olark live chat tool is compatible with several software programs that you can choose from to build your brand awareness and attract and build trust with potential customers. Visit the website for its pricing plan.

Optimizely

To improve your website and landing pages' effectiveness, you need to do a split test.

Optimizely helps you conduct landing page A/B tests to improve your marketing and engage your customers. You can check out its pricing model to see if it suits your marketing plans.

UsersThink

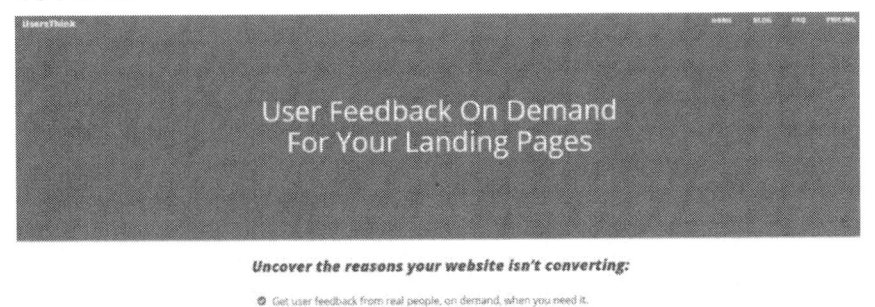

User Feedback On Demand For Your Landing Pages

Uncover the reasons your website isn't converting:

- Get user feedback from real people, on demand, when you need it.
- Learn what works, what doesn't, and how to improve your landing pages with UsersThink.
- No setup, no hassles, results within 24 hours.

Feedback plays a vital role in improving your customer experience. Do you need real people to provide feedback for your landing pages and help you improve them?

If so, you should give UsersThink software a try. Through this tool, real people will guide you with their feedback on what works or doesn't work on your pages. Here's the cost of this tool:

Stop guessing what's wrong with your landing page, and learn what people *really* think.

One-Time Landing Page Feedback:

Business	Professional	Bootstrap
$99	**$69**	**$39**
18 Users	12 Users	6 Users
No Setup	No Setup	No Setup
In 24 Hours	In 24 Hours	In 24 Hours
Get Feedback From 18 Users Right Now »	Get Feedback From 12 Users Right Now »	Get Feedback From 6 Users Right Now »

Now that you've learned all about landing pages and their importance to customers' impressions of your brand, let's explore ads.

Chapter 3: Creating Ads

Once you've started an online business, you have to market it to attract leads and convert them into clients. There are different ways businesses market their products or services.

In this chapter, we'll focus on advertising: how to design great ads that will help achieve your business goals.

Businesses create ads for many purposes. In this chapter, we'll start by listing the reasons businesses create ads.

Objectives of Using Ads

Lead Generation

You need to nurture and convert leads into clients for your business. One way to acquire these leads is by creating ads that target their pain points.

Statistics from the CMI show that 84% of brands use paid channels to attract leads to their brand.

Reasons Why Agency Content Marketers Use Paid Methods to Distribute Content

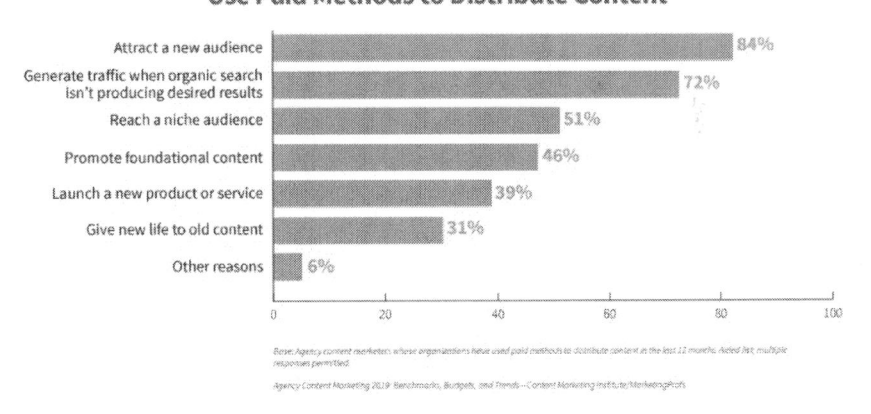

Reason	Percentage
Attract a new audience	84%
Generate traffic when organic search isn't producing desired results	72%
Reach a niche audience	51%
Promote foundational content	46%
Launch a new product or service	39%
Give new life to old content	31%
Other reasons	6%

Base: Agency content marketers whose organizations have used paid methods to distribute content in the last 12 months. Aided list; multiple responses permitted.

Agency Content Marketing 2019: Benchmarks, Budgets, and Trends—Content Marketing Institute/MarketingProfs

Businesses create ads and include CTAs to capture leads' information, which they can use to nurture them down the sales funnel.

Once you have the leads' information, you can add them to your email marketing list for nurturing.

Increase Conversions

You don't want just any leads, but leads who will convert into clients for your business. One objective of your advertising is to increase your business's conversions and sales.

Research by eMarketer shows that US brands will spend a collective $166.67 billion on mobile ads by the year 2023.

US Digital Ad Spending on Select Channels, 2019-2023
billions

	2019	2020	2021	2022	2023
Mobile*	$99.21	$120.37	$138.43	$152.93	$166.67
Desktop/laptop**	$23.20	$22.03	$23.04	$22.34	$21.04
Connected TV***	$6.94	$8.88	$10.81	$12.49	$14.12

Note: *includes advertising that appears on mobile phones, tablets and mobile internet-connected devices; **includes advertising that appears on desktop and laptop computers and other nonmobile internet-connected devices; ***includes advertising that appears on connected TV (CTV) devices
Source: eMarketer, Oct 2019

250079   www.eMarketer.com

This shows that brands are investing heavily in ads to increase conversions. A business using Google Ads can make up to $2 in revenue when they spend $1 on their ads.

Introduce a New Product or Service

Brands keep developing new and better products or services to help solve clients' pain points. As a marketing method, brands can use ads to advertise their new products to the target market. Product ads increase the chances of generating a sale.

Research by SparkCentral shows that 26% of clicks on an ad result in a sale.

Chapter 3: Creating Ads

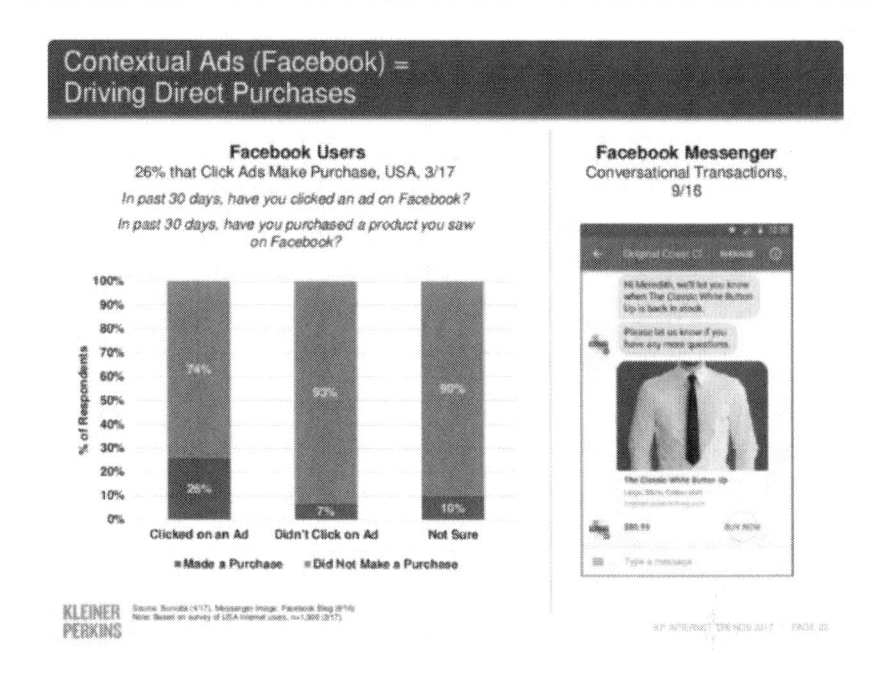

Contextual Ads (Facebook) = Driving Direct Purchases

Facebook Users — 26% that Click Ads Make Purchase, USA, 3/17

In past 30 days, have you clicked an ad on Facebook?
In past 30 days, have you purchased a product you saw on Facebook?

	Clicked on an Ad	Didn't Click on Ad	Not Sure
Made a Purchase	74%	7%	10%
Did Not Make a Purchase	26%	93%	90%

Facebook Messenger — Conversational Transactions, 9/16

KLEINER PERKINS

If potential clients click on an ad for a newly introduced product, there's a high chance that some will become clients.

Retain Existing Customers

You have business competitors and they're all competing for the same clients. You don't want to get a client today, then lose them to your competitor tomorrow, right? Your retained customers are more likely to spend money on your business and give you a high customer lifetime value.

That's why you need ads: to keep your clients engaged with your brand. Ads help keep your customers informed about your business and what it can do to help address their challenges.

Engagement and Traffic

Leads have to engage with a brand and build trust with it before they agree to do business. Ads help brands engage potential clients with the business, develop a relationship with them, and convert them into clients.

Advertising your business also increases website traffic so more potential clients can know about your products and services. Boosting web traffic is the main challenge brands face in their business marketing.

What are your company's top marketing challenges?

Challenge	Percentage
Generating traffic and leads	63%
Proving the ROI of our marketing activities	40%
Securing enough budget	28%
Identifying the right technologies for our needs	26%
Managing our website	26%
Targeting content for an international audience	21%
Training our team	19%
Hiring top talent	16%
Finding an executive sponsor	7%

STATE of INBOUND

With the right ads, you can draw target clients to your business and easily nurture and convert them.

Increase Brand Awareness

You may have awesome products or services that help solve your target clients' challenges. However, if the target market doesn't know about you or your business, the chances of growing the business are low.

Ads help you increase your brand awareness so more potential clients know about your products or services.

It also helps inform your potential clients of what your brand is all about. Your brand awareness across social media can inspire customers to buy your products.

A study by Marketing Charts shows that 37% of shoppers say brands on social media inspire their purchase decisions.

Chapter 3: Creating Ads

Online Media Used for Purchase Inspiration

marketing charts

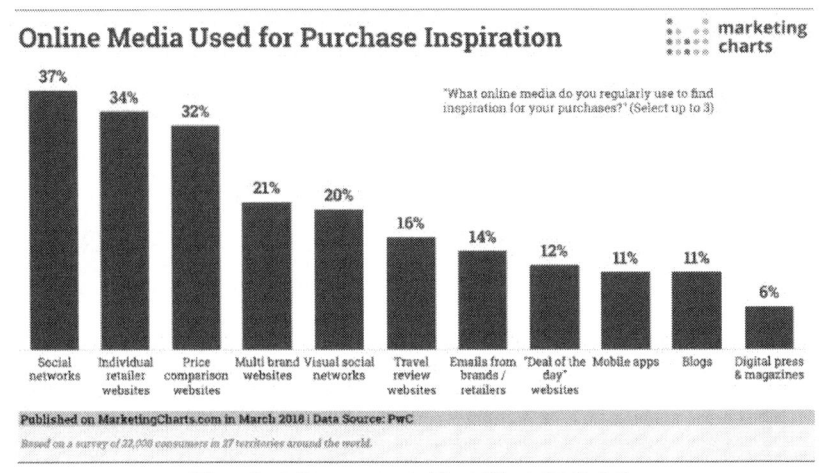

"What online media do you regularly use to find inspiration for your purchases?" (Select up to 3)

Category	%
Social networks	37%
Individual retailer websites	34%
Price comparison websites	32%
Multi brand websites	21%
Visual social networks	20%
Travel review websites	16%
Emails from brands / retailers	14%
"Deal of the day" websites	12%
Mobile apps	11%
Blogs	11%
Digital press & magazines	6%

Published on MarketingCharts.com in March 2018 | Data Source: PwC
Based on a survey of 22,000 consumers in 27 territories around the world.

Online media used by consumers around the world for purchase inspiration.

Improve Your Brand's Image

When you advertise your business, it sends a clear signal to your customers that you're ready to do business. It also notifies competitors that you're there to offer the best solutions to your clients' problems.

With a great image in the industry, you can attract potential customers' attention to your business brand.

Here's an example of a SEMrush Facebook ad:

> SEMrush
> Sponsored
>
> Take your content marketing to the next level with SEMrush Content Marketing Platform. Have a free trial!
>
> [image of SEMrush ad: "EMPOWER YOUR CONTENT MARKETING WITH DATA"]
>
> SEMRUSH.COM
> **Free SEMrush Content Marketing Platform Trial**
> All-Encompassing Approach to Content Marketing How do you provide value to your audience through a unique content experience? How do you develop or improve your content s...
>
> [Learn More]

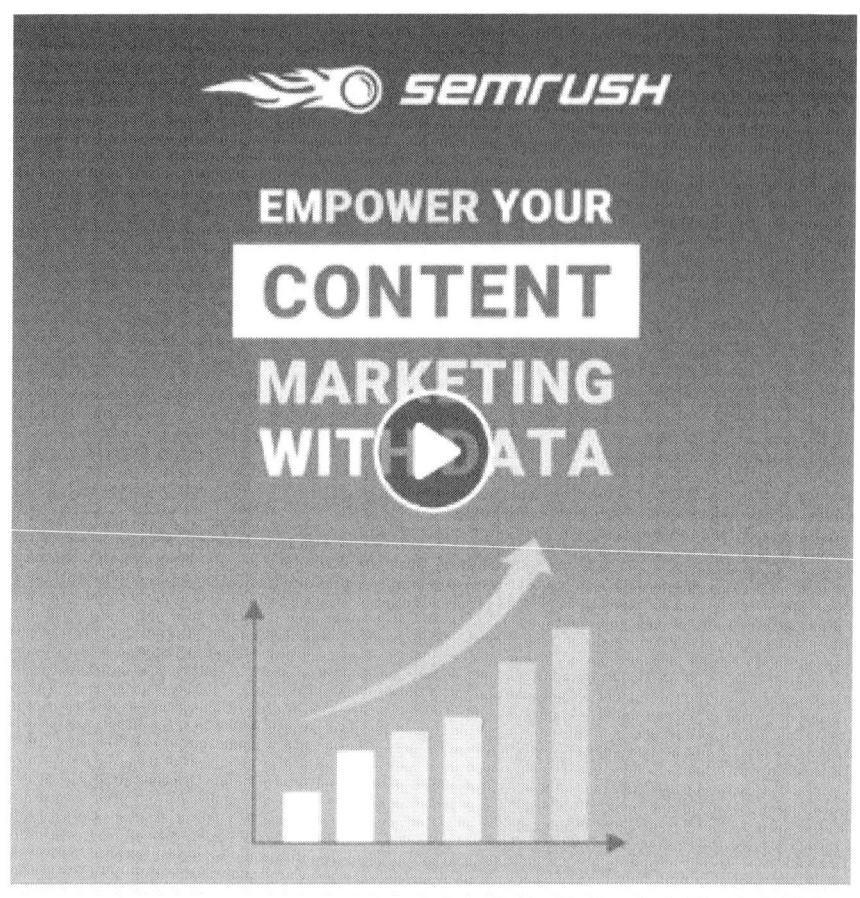

If you're just browsing through Facebook and come across this ad, it can attract you to learn more about how to up your content marketing game.

Keep Customers Updated

Businesses undergo changes each day to better their services or products.

Great advertisements help keep customers updated about new ways your company can meet their needs.

Promote Video Views

You create videos to draw your potential customers to your brand. Ads help you get these videos in front of your leads and engage them.

When leads see interesting and educational videos, they make a connection with the brand. This makes it easy for the business to win their trust, nurture them, and convert them into customers. Videos are becoming more popular and effective in marketing than ever before.

Research by Wix, compiled by Omnicore Agency, predicts that videos will account for 50% of all searches by 2020.

Voice search quick stats

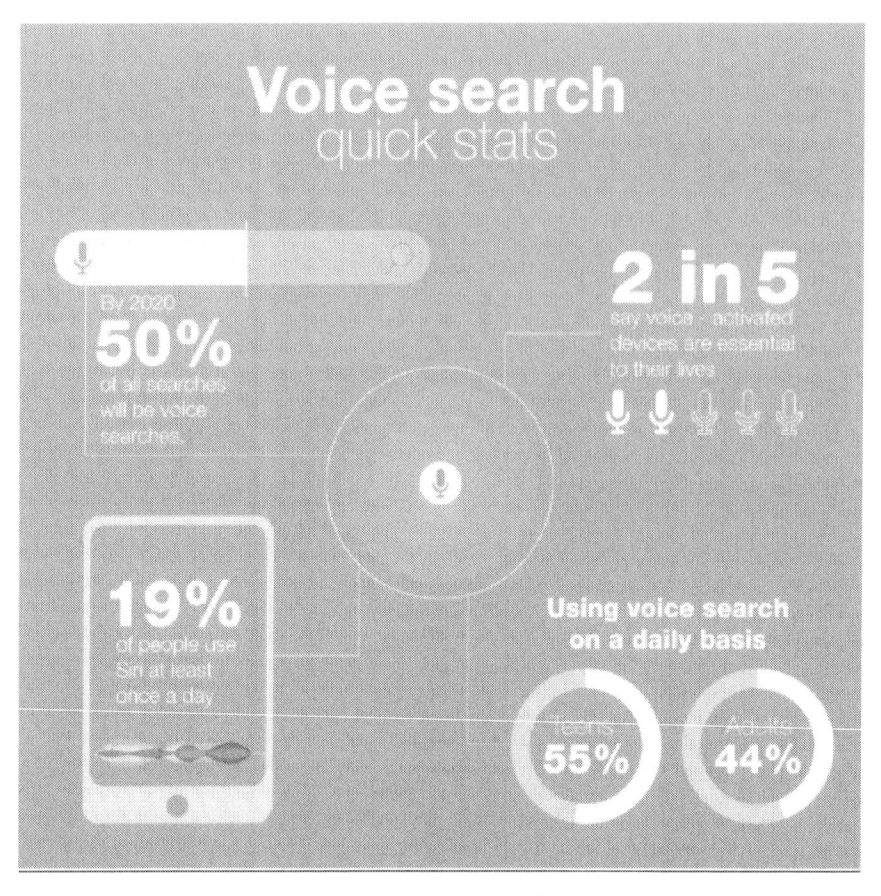

By 2020 **50%** of all searches will be voice searches.

2 in 5 say voice-activated devices are essential to their lives

19% of people use Siri at least once a day

Using voice search on a daily basis
Teens **55%** Adults **44%**

If you use videos to market your brand and advertise it compellingly, you can generate a ton of leads that more easily convert into clients and increase sales and revenue.

Types of Advertising

Digital Advertisement

Technological innovations have introduced new and different ways for a brand to reach out to its target clients.

Through online marketing, brands can point to their business and attract leads. Some websites have ads within their pages to help promote their own business or other brands' products. Google has a great service, Google Adwords, that helps brands advertise their business online.

With Google Adwords, you can use keywords to attract your target clients to your brand and increase search engine rankings for your website. For instance, when you target potential clients by using beauty products as keywords on Google Adwords, clients' searches for these terms will lead them to your website.

You can also use Google Adsense to host adverts on your website that will attract leads to your business. Google matches the ads with the type of content you post on your site.

Social Media Ads

Brands can use social media to advertise their services or products and generate leads. Creating different ads for different social media sites is a good way to attract leads to your business.

One smart method of placing ads on social media is by using ads retargeting. You can segregate groups of target clients who visited your website but didn't take any action. Retargeting ads help you place pixels and send target ads to attract potential clients as they browse through other websites on the internet.

If you employ retargeting, be sure to target potential clients based on the actions they take on your site.

Similarly, brands can also use the sponsored ads option. A report by CMI shows that 79% of marketers use sponsored content on social sites to promote their business.

Types of Paid Content Distribution Methods Agency Marketers Use

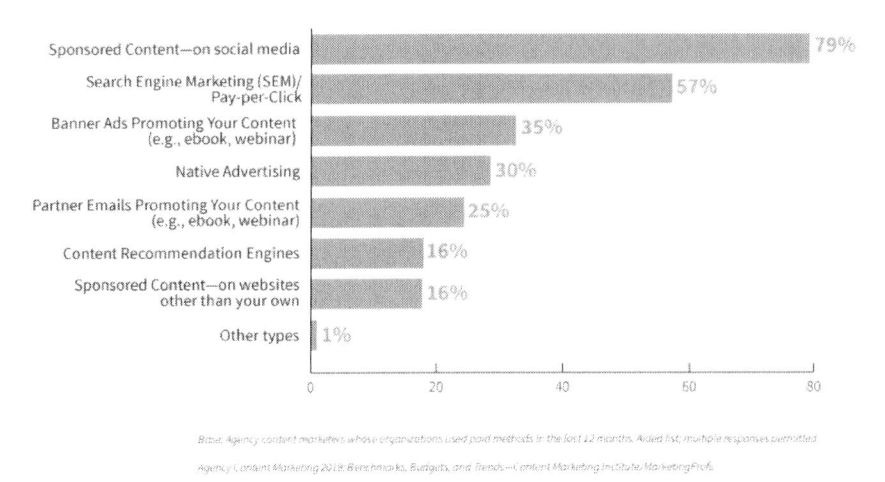

Method	Percentage
Sponsored Content—on social media	79%
Search Engine Marketing (SEM)/Pay-per-Click	57%
Banner Ads Promoting Your Content (e.g., ebook, webinar)	35%
Native Advertising	30%
Partner Emails Promoting Your Content (e.g., ebook, webinar)	25%
Content Recommendation Engines	16%
Sponsored Content—on websites other than your own	16%
Other types	1%

Base: Agency content marketers whose organizations used paid methods in the last 12 months. Aided list; multiple responses permitted.

Agency Content Marketing 2018: Benchmarks, Budgets, and Trends—Content Marketing Institute/MarketingProfs

However, the brand has to pay for the placement of this ad on social media sites. Here's an example:

Leadfeeder
Sponsored

We've compiled 61 B2B lead generation strategies for 2019. Stay ahead of the curve.

LEADFEEDER.COM
61 B2B Lead Generation Strategies For 2019   Learn More

You can also place ads on other social sites like Linkedin, Twitter, and Instagram.

To post ads on LinkedIn, create a business page and place your ads there, or place them within your social feeds. Here's an example of such an ad:

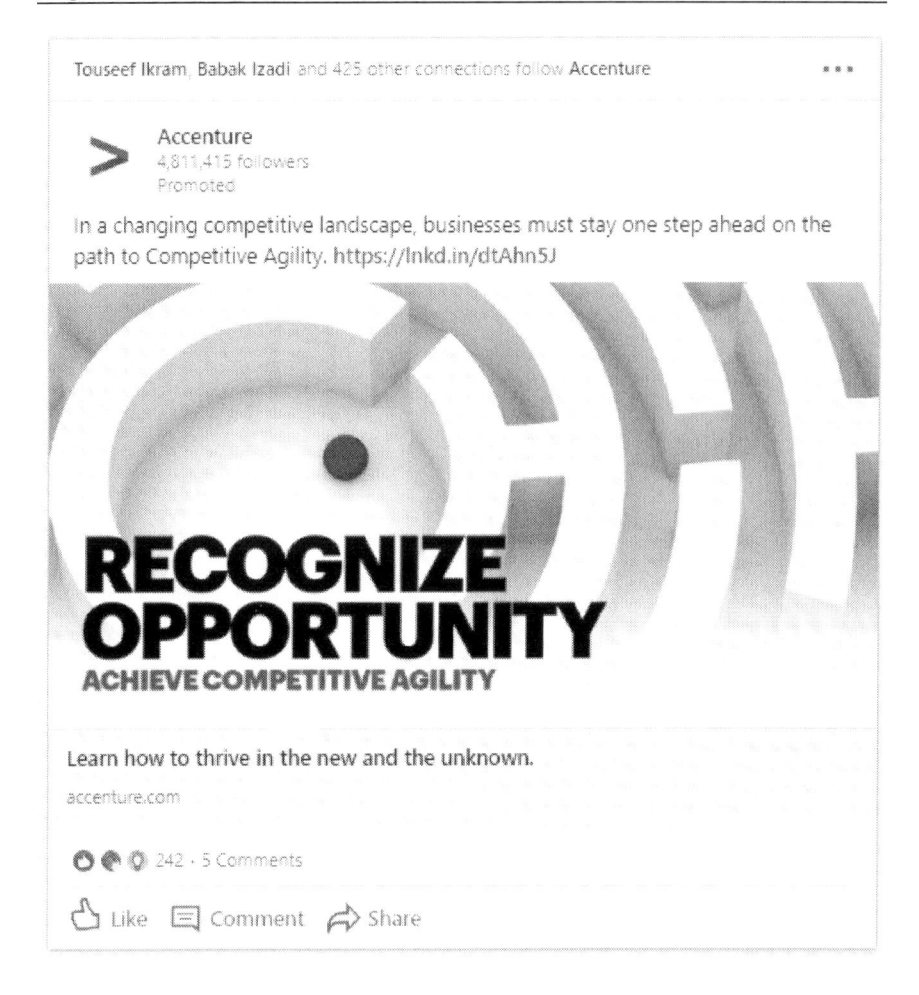

Video Ads

Videos are the most effective ways brands can reach out to their target customers. Target leads are more likely to click ads with videos compared to text-based ads.

Brands can create short video ads based on the objectives they want to achieve for the target clients. The attention span of the reader in this digital age is reducing rapidly.

Chapter 3: Creating Ads

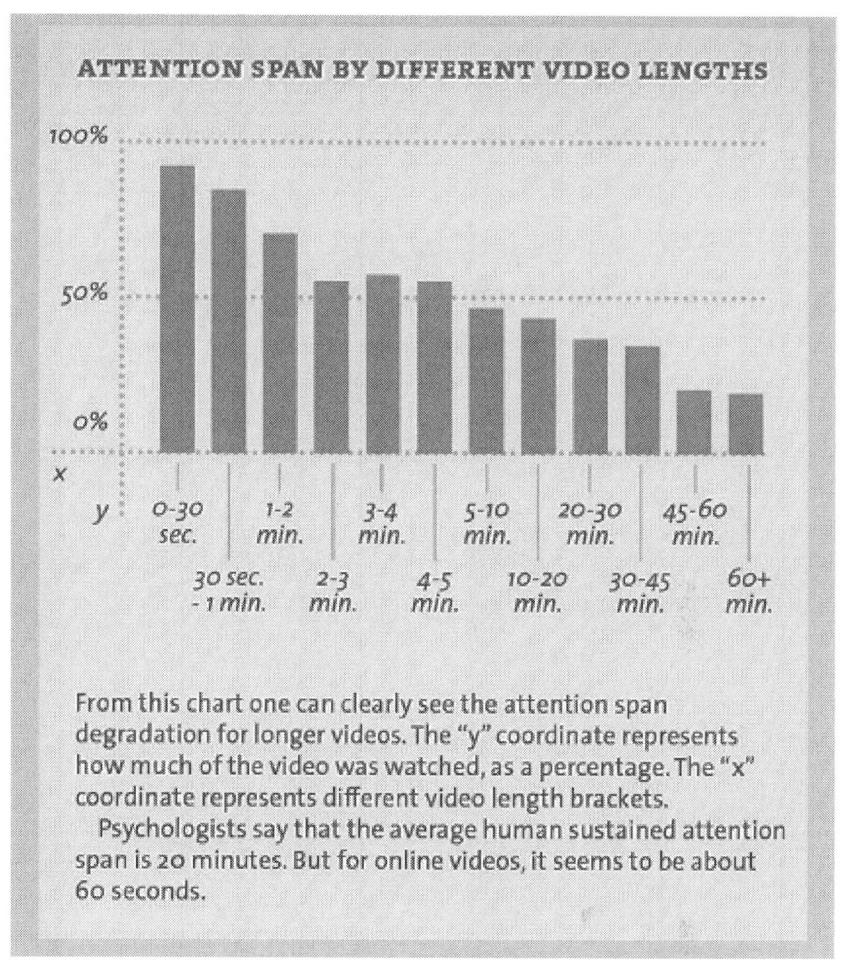

ATTENTION SPAN BY DIFFERENT VIDEO LENGTHS

[Bar chart showing attention span percentages decreasing across video length brackets: 0-30 sec, 30 sec - 1 min, 1-2 min, 2-3 min, 3-4 min, 4-5 min, 5-10 min, 10-20 min, 20-30 min, 30-45 min, 45-60 min, 60+ min. Y-axis: 0% to 100%.]

From this chart one can clearly see the attention span degradation for longer videos. The "y" coordinate represents how much of the video was watched, as a percentage. The "x" coordinate represents different video length brackets.

Psychologists say that the average human sustained attention span is 20 minutes. But for online videos, it seems to be about 60 seconds.

Image source: https://gisteo.com/60-second-explainer-videos/

If you make your video ads to be within 30 seconds they will have high engagement.

Radio and Podcast Ads

This is another type of ad in the market. Brands can use radio to communicate to their potential customers about their services and how they can help with clients' difficulties.

Podcasts are becoming a popular setting for ads. A report by Statista shows that more brands are spending on podcast ads to reach customers.

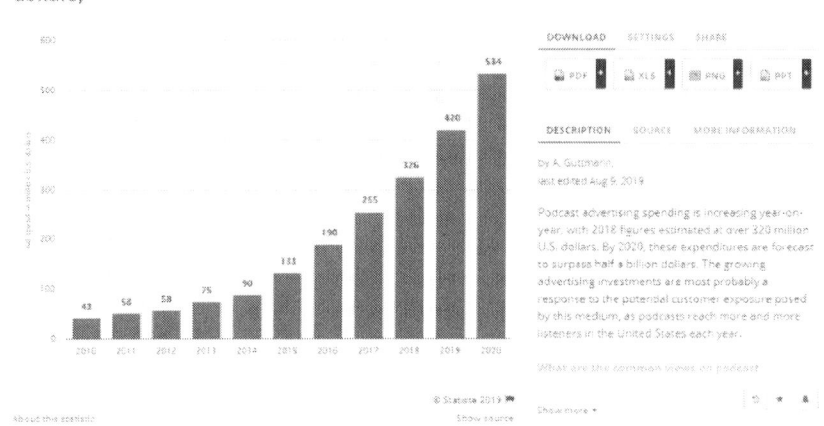

Podcast advertising spending in the United States from 2010 to 2020 (in million U.S. dollars)

With more potential customers using mobile devices, podcast ads can reach countless potential clients and engage them. Businesses also still value radio advertisements to promote their offerings.

Research by Statista projects that radio ad spending will reach $18.4 billion by 2023.

Radio advertising spending in the United States in 2019 and 2023 (in billion U.S. dollars)

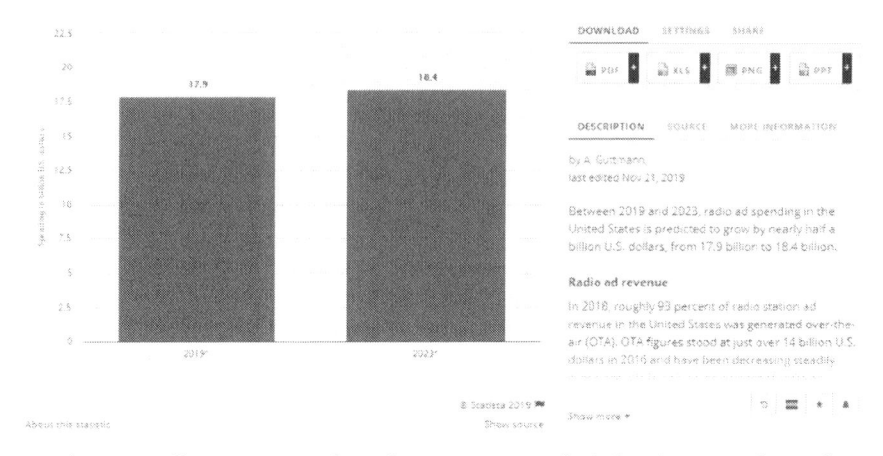

Marketers still invest in radio ads to promote their business and reach a wider target market for their products or services.

Outdoor Ads

Brands use this type of ad to reach their target clients if they can't easily reach them online. One great way to attract your target market with this type of advertising is through billboards.

Here's an example of a billboard used to promote the Toyota RAV4 Hybrid model:

The 10-story billboard couldn't be ignored. Gawkers immediately went to social media.

Fly posters and other types of posters are also categorized as outdoor advertising.

Print Media Ads

Some businesses use newspapers and magazines to promote their business. Though it's a more traditional approach, it's still a valid form of advertising.

You can target magazines in your market niche and place your business ads there. If you're in the beauty industry, here are some magazines you can read and place your ads in.

If the magazines are popular, placing ads in them can be effective for generating leads. You can place your ads in weekly, monthly, or quarterly published magazines.

Product Placement Ads

Have you ever noticed, for example, a movie character driving a certain kind of car? Businesses can promote their branded products or services within the context of video productions such as movies or shows to attract a large audience to their brand.

TV Advertising

Television has a long history as a popular setting for promoting brands to potential customers. Companies create short videos and commercials, which are aired at intervals during and between TV shows.

The most effective TV ads air during the most popular shows and during shows that are related to the product they promote.

A report by Statista shows that TV ads account for 6.8 billion in online advertising in the US.

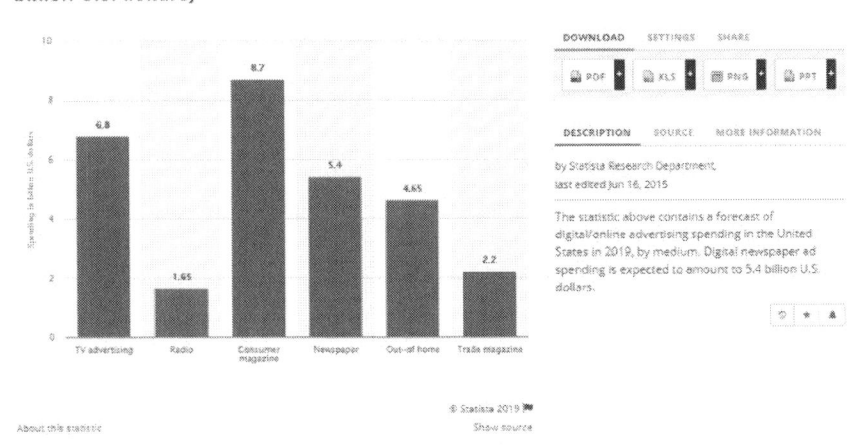

Online/digital advertising spending in the United States in 2019, by medium (in billion U.S. dollars)

How to Get Ideas for Your Ad Copy

To effectively achieve your marketing objectives for your ad, you have to create an attractive ad.

But, you may be asking yourself, how can I get ideas to help me create stunning ads? Don't worry! We're here to help. Here are some tips for coming up with fantastic ideas.

Ask Your Team

Two heads are better than one. You can ask your marketing team to help you come up with ideas for amazing and attractive ads.

Read Business/Marketing News

The marketing world is changing and so is the way customers interact with brands. Reading business and marketing news can keep you on the cutting edge when it comes to reaching your target clients.

Pay Attention to Online Advertising Sites

Since these sites help brands advertise their services or products, you can learn a lot by looking at the copy they publish.

This will give you ideas for how to create your own ad copy. One example of a site to explore is ClassifiedAds.com.

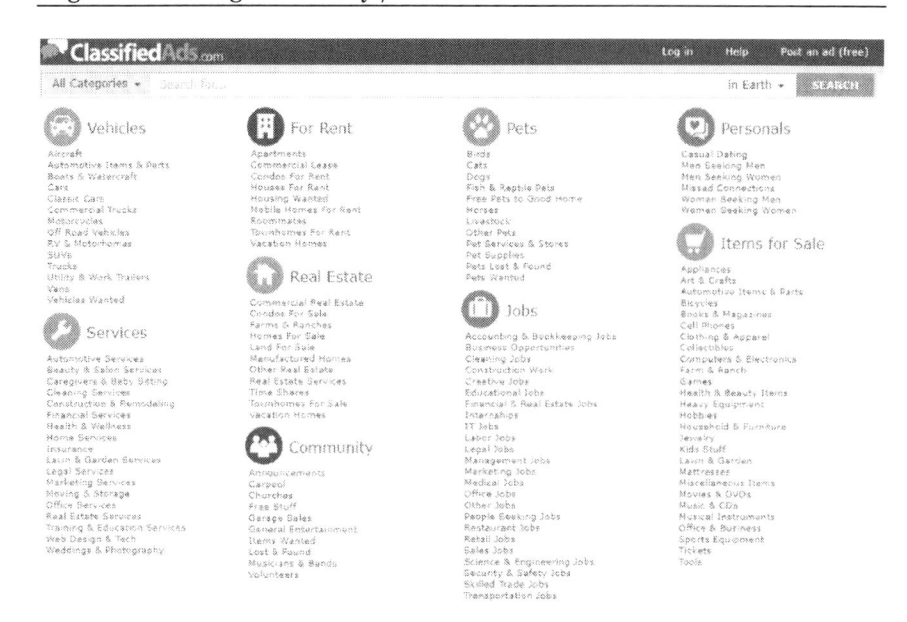

You can open the ads in your market niche and check them out. For example, I opened a commercial real estate ad under the real estate category, and this is what I found:

Chapter 3: Creating Ads

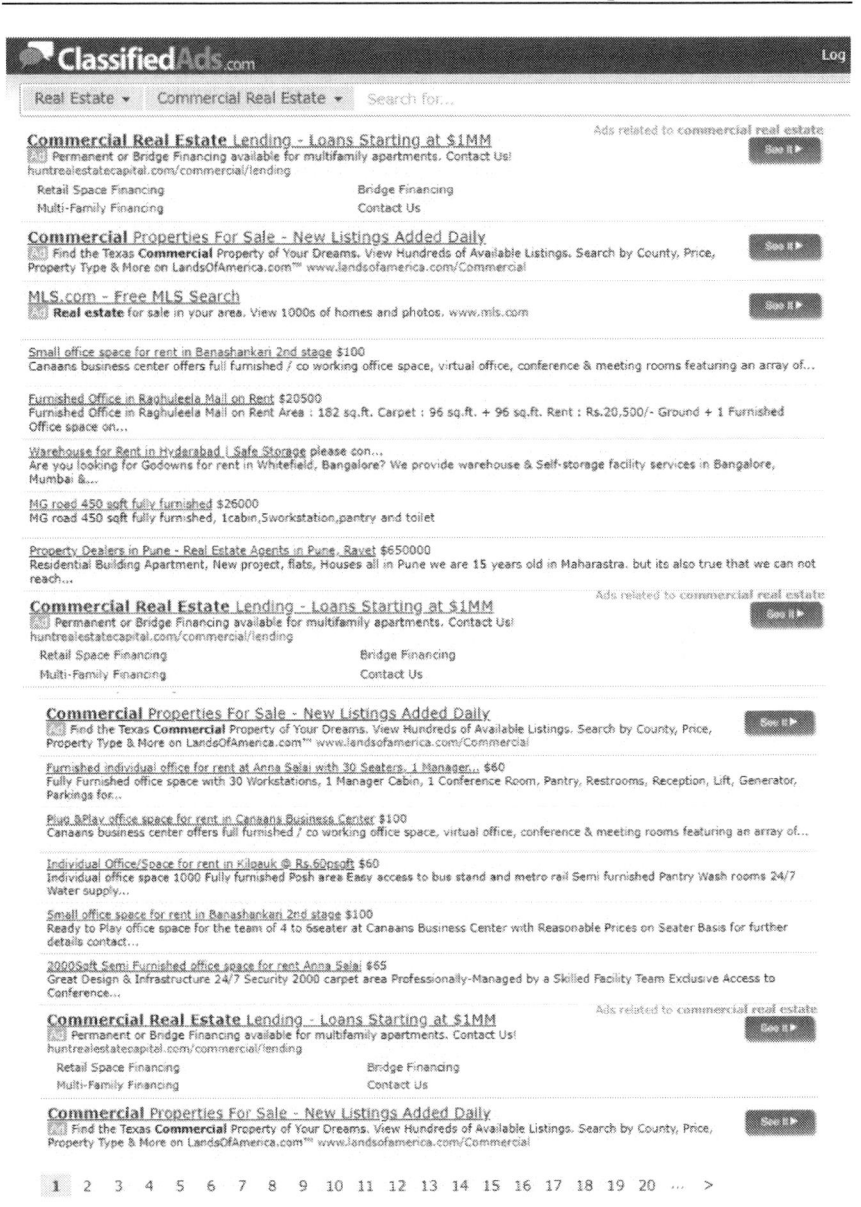

Here are a few other advertising sites you can check out to get an idea of the kinds of ads you should create based on your target niche market.

Watch Competitor Ads

Since your competitors offer services or products within the same niche and target the same clients you do, they can give you some ideas.

Check out the types of ad copy your competitors create to gather insights about how to create your own ads. Just make sure you don't copy the ads exactly as they are. Simply use them for inspiration as you create your own dynamite ads.

Review Your Keywords

You've been marketing your business for some time and know the types of keywords that rank well. Review these keywords and use the best-performing ones in your ads.

This will help rank your ads on search engines and draw traffic to your brand.

Listen to Customers

You'll know the best ways to attract leads to your business with ads based on what potential customers say about their pain points. You can listen to your current clients for ideas about how to write your ads. For example, what positive things do customers say about your business?

Alternatively, survey potential customers to learn about their interests. The headline of your ad can feature words that touch on the pain points mentioned by potential customers in your survey. This is an excellent way to catch your prospects' attention.

How to Write Ad Copy That Sells

Now that you know how to gather ideas for your ads, let's look at how to actually create amazing ads that will progress your company toward your business objectives.

Research Your Target Market

Before you start writing your ad, do thorough research on your target market. Understand your potential customers and the pains they're experiencing.

Your research will also help you learn more about the types of ads your competitors create so you can outcompete them.

Be Interesting and Direct

The human attention span is very short. Create copy that's short and direct. Get right to the point.

If you're creating an ad for a setting that does well with longer copy, ensure that it stays interesting to keep readers engaged throughout.

Catch readers' attention by including visuals that match your ad copy. You can use images of the product you offer.

Craft a Captivating Headline

Your headlines can make or break your ads. When writing headlines, aim for short, attractive, and engaging.

Also, include keywords that relate to your target clients' problems. I ran a simple search for the keyword *rental houses*, and this is what I got:

> Need to Rent Your **House** Out? - Rent Your Property Stress-Free [AD]
> www.allpropertymanagement.com | Report Ad
> We Work Hard to Find the Best Property Managers so You Don't Have To. Get 5 Free Quotes. Review Results of Top Local Property Managers. Compare, Select & Chat. It's Just That Easy
>
> Single Family Home/Condo
> Need a Property Manager to Operate Your Rental? Get 5 Free...
>
> Commercial Properties
> Find Professional Property Mgrs. Specialized in Commercial Props.
>
> Why Hire a Property Mgr?
> There Are at Least 10 Reason to Hire a Professional. Learn Why.
>
> Association Management
> Property Managers Specializing in Working w/ HOA & Condo...

Your headline should focus on the benefits your clients can get by using your business. For example, the above ad headline tells potential customers that they'll deal with less stress, which is a common concern for landlords.

Since you're not the only business in the market, your headline needs to offer a unique selling proposition. Give your potential clients a reason to do business with you rather than your competitors. You can include brief statistics and data to back up your arguments.

Another effective tactic is to include questions in your ad headline that spur your potential customers to respond to your ad. The above example also employs this trick.

Conduct A/B Testing

The only way you can measure the performance of your ads on the market is by running an A/B test. Create a variety of ads with different headlines and place them strategically.

As needed, adjust the body text, headlines, and CTAs to see which ones best convince potential clients to use your services.

As you perform the split testing, ensure that all the ads lead potential clients to land on the same page. If you direct them to different pages, it will be hard to measure the conversions.

Here are some tools to help with A/B testing:

Adobe Target

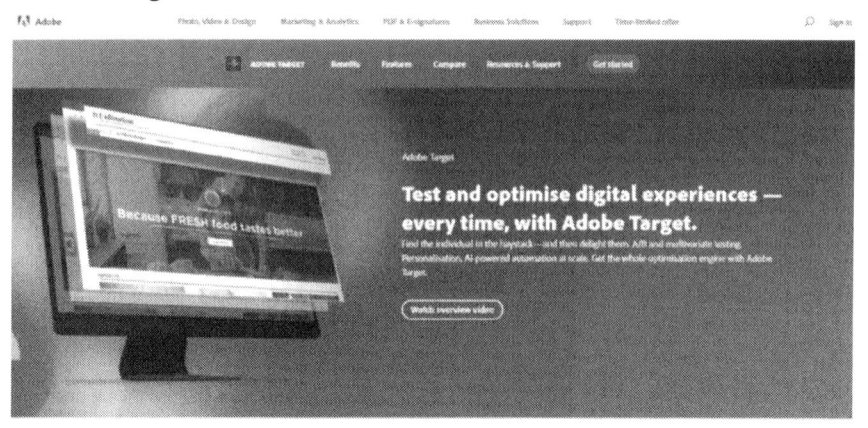

This tool offers recommendations based on data collected from customers. It provides both automated and mobile app personalization to improve your marketing process.

Here are some of the benefits you can get from this tool:

Chapter 3: Creating Ads

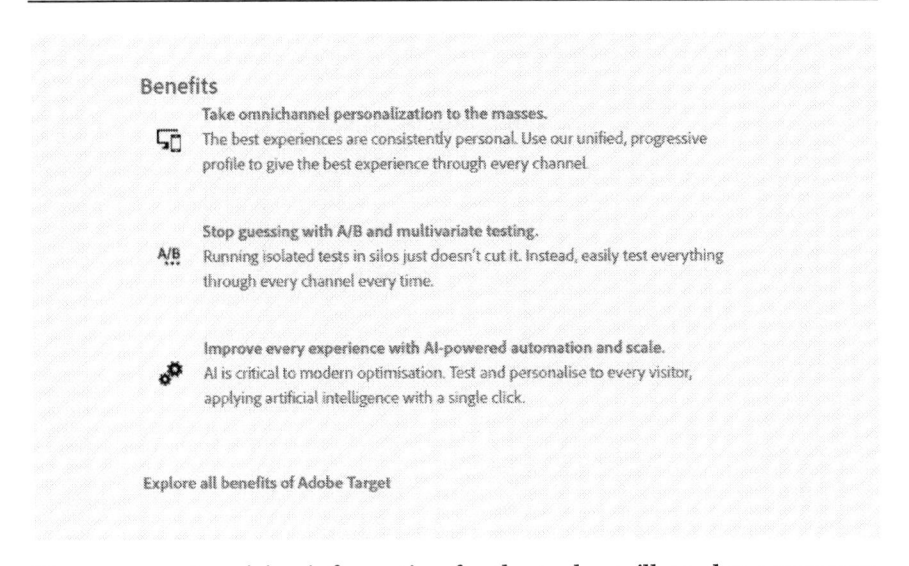

Benefits

Take omnichannel personalization to the masses.
The best experiences are consistently personal. Use our unified, progressive profile to give the best experience through every channel.

Stop guessing with A/B and multivariate testing.
Running isolated tests in silos just doesn't cut it. Instead, easily test everything through every channel every time.

Improve every experience with AI-powered automation and scale.
AI is critical to modern optimisation. Test and personalise to every visitor, applying artificial intelligence with a single click.

Explore all benefits of Adobe Target

To see accurate pricing information for the tool, you'll need to enter your location.

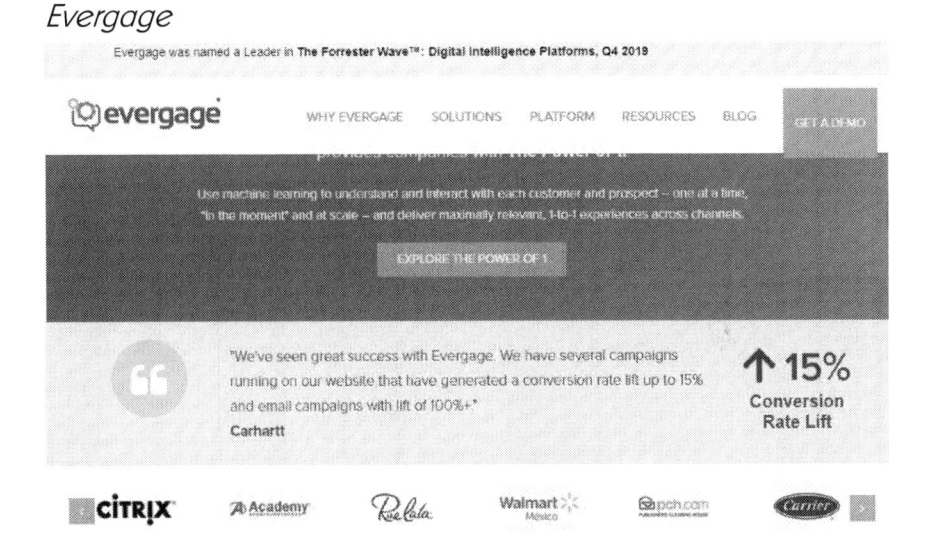

Evergage

Evergage was named a Leader in The Forrester Wave™: Digital Intelligence Platforms, Q4 2019

Use machine learning to understand and interact with each customer and prospect – one at a time, "in the moment" and at scale – and deliver maximally relevant, 1-to-1 experiences across channels.

EXPLORE THE POWER OF 1

"We've seen great success with Evergage. We have several campaigns running on our website that have generated a conversion rate lift up to 15% and email campaigns with lift of 100%+."
Carhartt

↑ 15%
Conversion Rate Lift

This tool is powered by machine learning that helps provide the best experience with your split-test tools. You can create unique experiences for your customers to build more trust and engagement.

These experiences can be shared across multiple channels to increase user engagement with your brand's products or services.

Optimizely

This is a great experimentation tool to help your brand engage and convert leads.

It has several price plans to suit different types of brands and provide the best growth results.

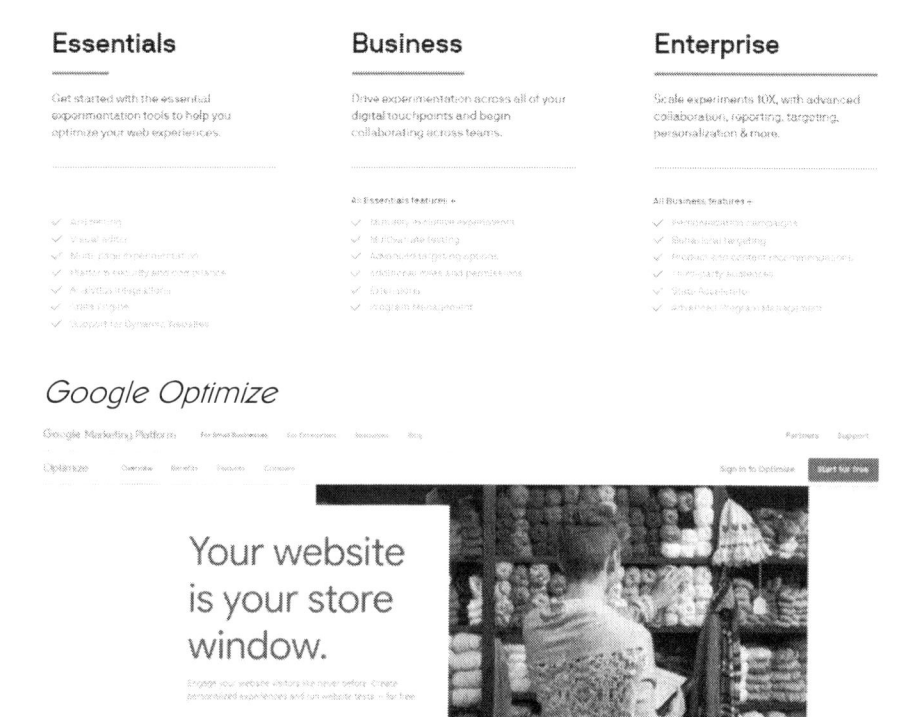

Google Optimize

To effectively use this tool, ensure that you have someone who knows how to set tracking for your data. If you're a big brand with many teams, Google Analytics 360 is the best choice for you.

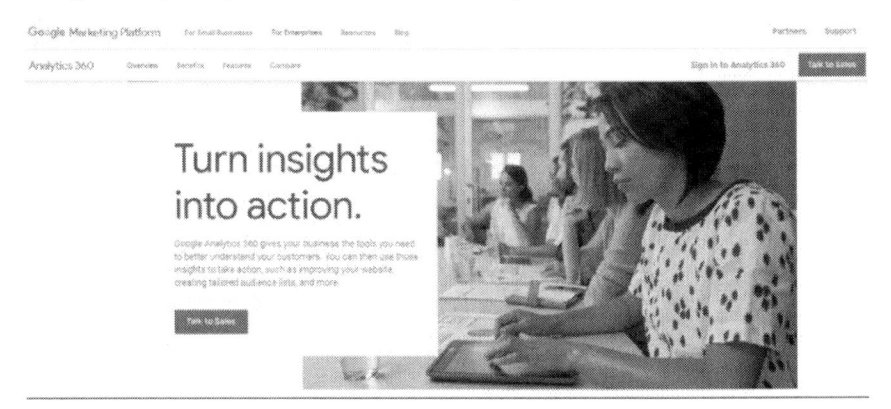

AB Tasty

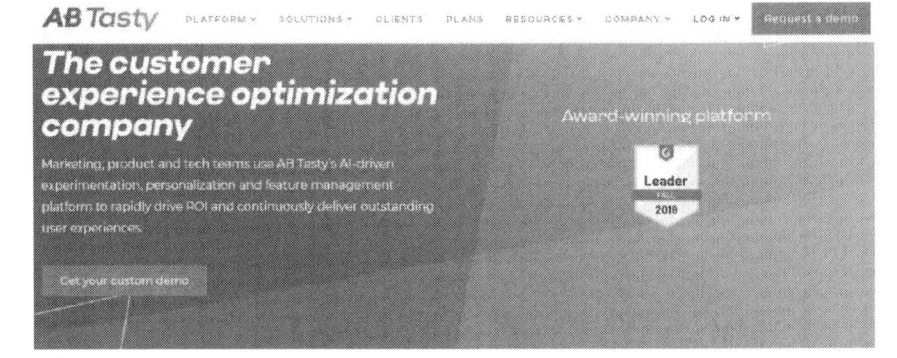

This tool includes amazing features for your A/B split testing. You can use its funnel-testing feature to see how your target customers experiment with the customer data from different pages on your business website.

It also has a drag-and-drop editor that makes the whole process of split testing easy.

Nelio A/B Testing

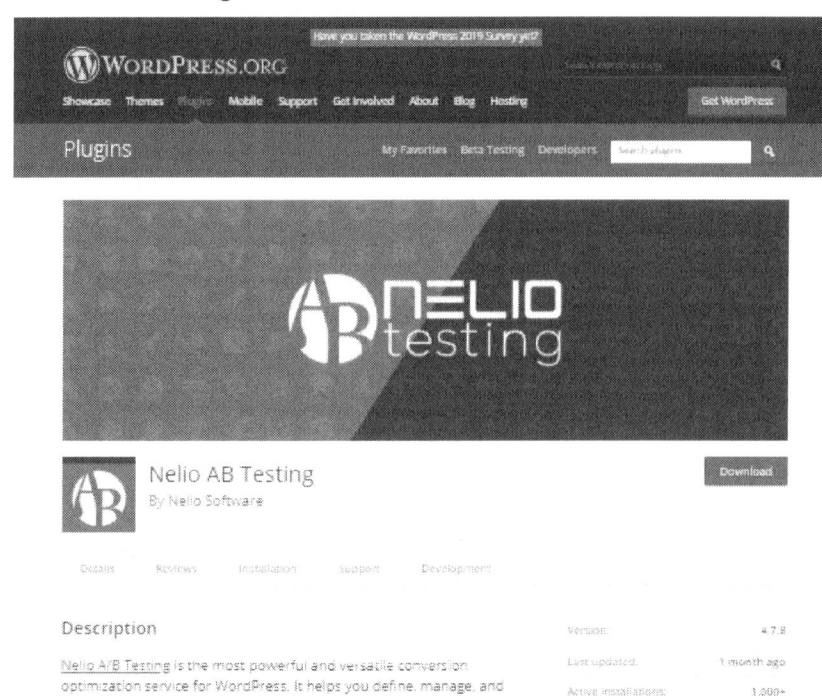

This is a great WordPress plugin that helps you optimize your copies to attract leads and increase business conversions. You can also use the plugin to test widgets.

Chapter 3: Creating Ads

Apptimize

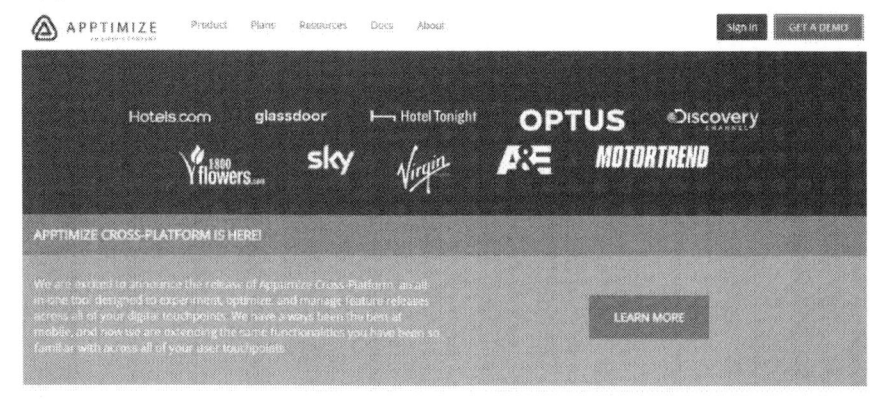

This split-test tool is suitable for mobile-centric businesses. You can easily run new experiences with this tool. Here are the Apptimize plans:

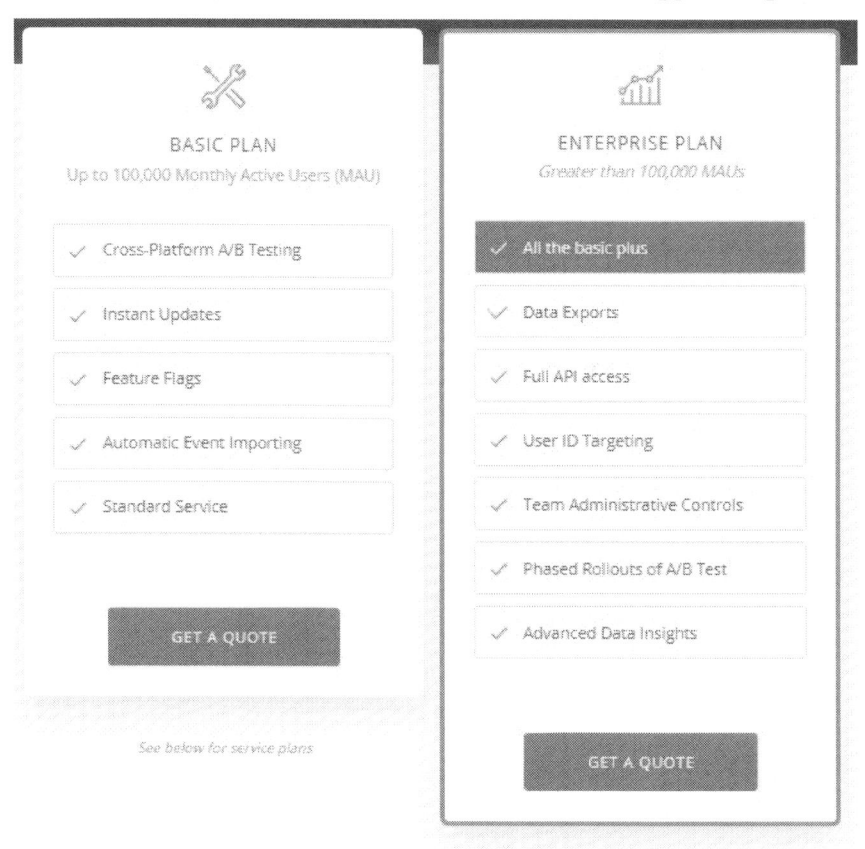

And here are its service plans:

SERVICE PLANS

Feature	Standard	Silver	Gold
Email Support (9AM-5PM Pacific Time; Response by next business day)	✓	✓	✓
Technical Documentation	✓	✓	✓
Dedicated Customer Success Manager		✓	✓
Implementation and Onboarding		✓	✓
Technical Integration Services			✓
Dedicated Slack Channel			✓
Multi-day onsite training led by mobile strategists and forward deployed engineers			✓
Emergency Escalation Process with Guaranteed 2-hour Response Time for Tier 1 Issues			✓
Telephone Support			✓

Chapter 3: Creating Ads

Leadformly

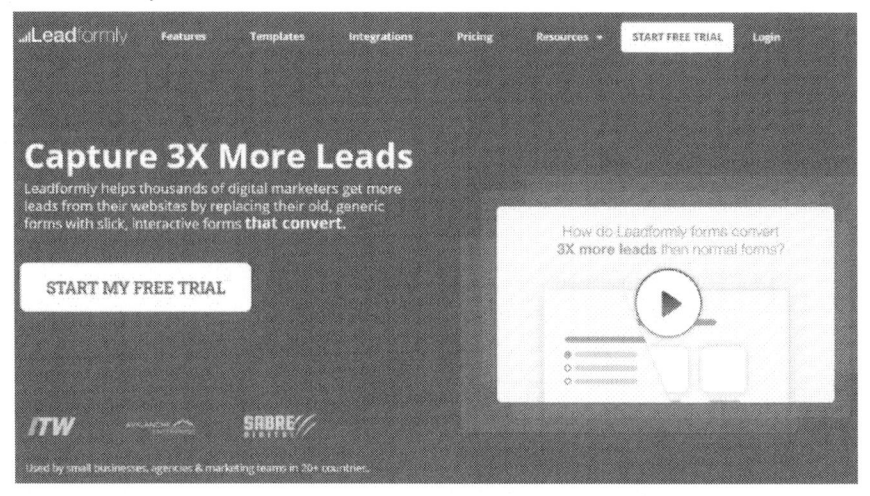

This tool provides in-depth analytics that some other tools don't. It supplies insights into business owners with great split-testing features.

You can also integrate the tool with other platforms. Here are some of the compatible platforms you can use:

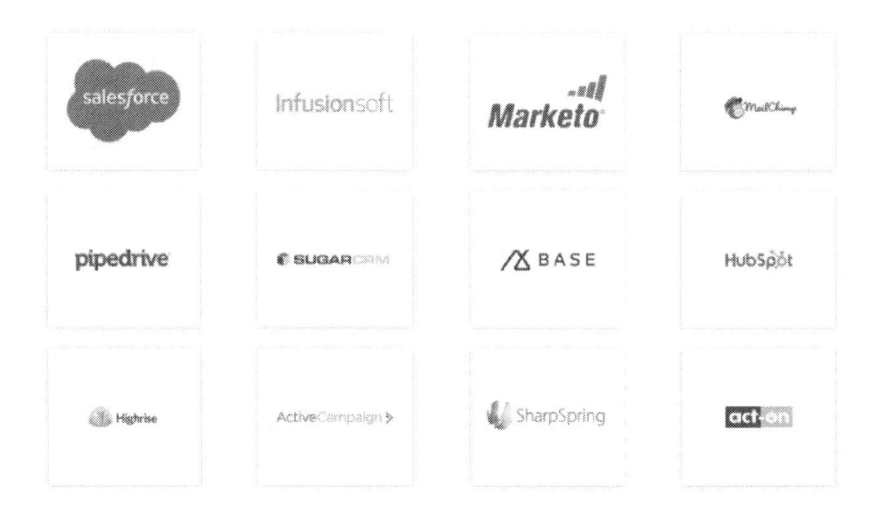

And here are even more integrations for the Leadformly tool:

More Leadformly integrations powered by Zapier

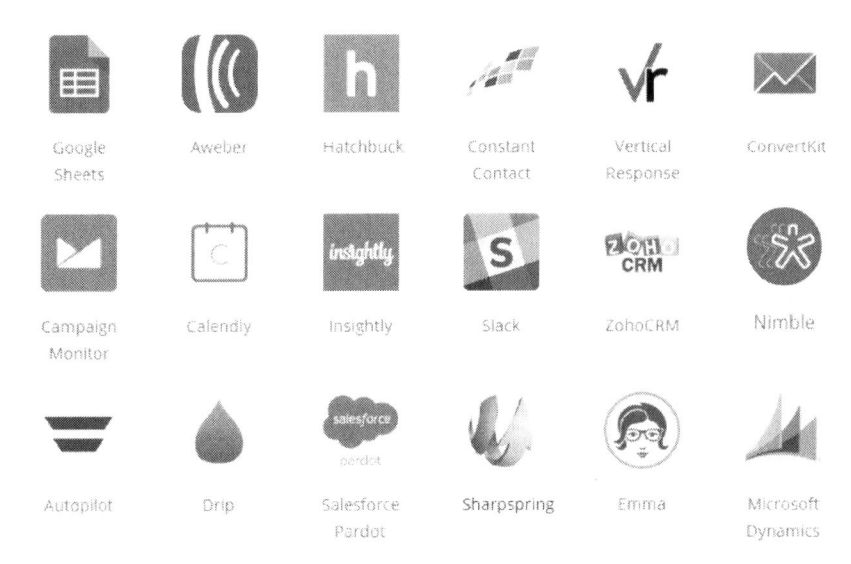

Google Sheets	Aweber	Hatchbuck	Constant Contact	Vertical Response	ConvertKit
Campaign Monitor	Calendly	Insightly	Slack	ZohoCRM	Nimble
Autopilot	Drip	Salesforce Pardot	Sharpspring	Emma	Microsoft Dynamics

Tips to Improve Your Ad Performance

You don't just need to create ads. You need ads that will convert your target readers into customers. Ad performance in search engine results is of utmost importance.

Worldwide desktop market share of leading search engines from January 2010 to July 2019

Since Google is responsible for nearly 90% of all search market share, understanding how to streamline your ads for Google's search engine is vital. Here are some tips you can apply to increase the performance of your ads.

Optimize for Mobile

Many potential clients use mobile devices to search for products or services. If they can't access your ads on a mobile device, you lose a chance to convert them into clients.

A report by Expanded Ramblings shows that 70% of potential customers call a business directly from Google Search. If that potential client can't reach you on mobile, you lose a great chance to convert them.

Use Local Advertisement

You want to target all the potential clients who use your services or products. As a marketer, you must target local clients and use keywords that will attract them to your business.

If target clients see that your business is within their local range, they'll visit it and probably make some purchases if they love your products. To increase local searches, use extensions with a map thumbnail.

A report by HubSpot shows that the top priority for 69% of companies is to convert leads into clients.

Marketers prioritize converting leads into customers

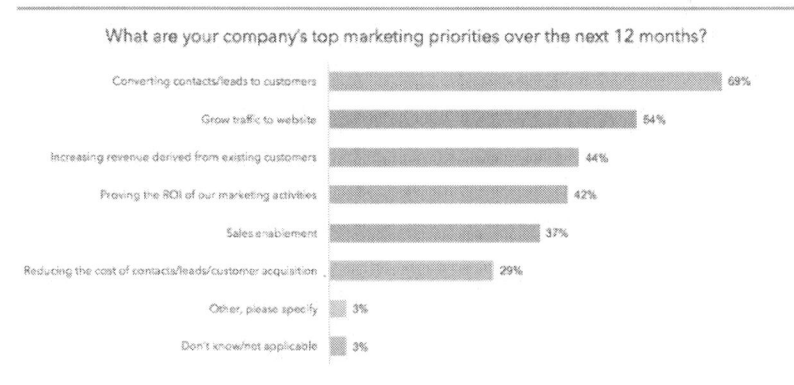

What are your company's top marketing priorities over the next 12 months?

Priority	%
Converting contacts/leads to customers	69%
Grow traffic to website	54%
Increasing revenue derived from existing customers	44%
Proving the ROI of our marketing activities	42%
Sales enablement	37%
Reducing the cost of contacts/leads/customer acquisition	29%
Other, please specify	3%
Don't know/not applicable	3%

HubSpot Research

Brands that deploy local advertisements for their business can accomplish this top priority and increase engagement and conversion.

Include Keywords for SEO

You need your ad to reach as many leads as possible, right? That means you need to carefully select keywords that will attract potential clients. See chapter 2, "Essentials of a Perfect Landing Page: Search Engine Optimization" for tools that can help you find effective keywords.

Be Timely

Cost-per-action (CPA) campaign ads are more effective when the target customer is online.

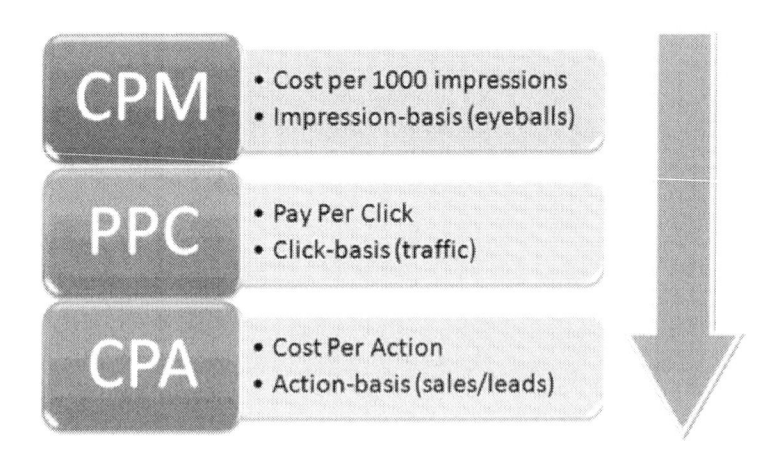

CPM
- Cost per 1000 impressions
- Impression-basis (eyeballs)

PPC
- Pay Per Click
- Click-basis (traffic)

CPA
- Cost Per Action
- Action-basis (sales/leads)

Showing ads at the right time helps catch the attention of leads, engage them, and convert them. Promote your ads when your target leads are active on the internet.

Use Google Display Network

This tool can easily help you find the right audience for your ads. It generates 180 billion impressions per month from internet users all over the world.

It has great targeting options to show your message to potential clients. You can create responsive ads that match the publisher's site. You can also create and upload ads with images that catch the attention of your leads.

The tool lets you create engaging ads, such as video ads on Youtube, to draw leads in.

Position Ads Wisely

You may have a great and attractive ad, but the performance and returns from the ads depend on where you place them. Ads that are placed at the top of the page perform better.

Research by AccuraCast shows that ads placed at the top of the Google results page have a click-through rate of 8%.

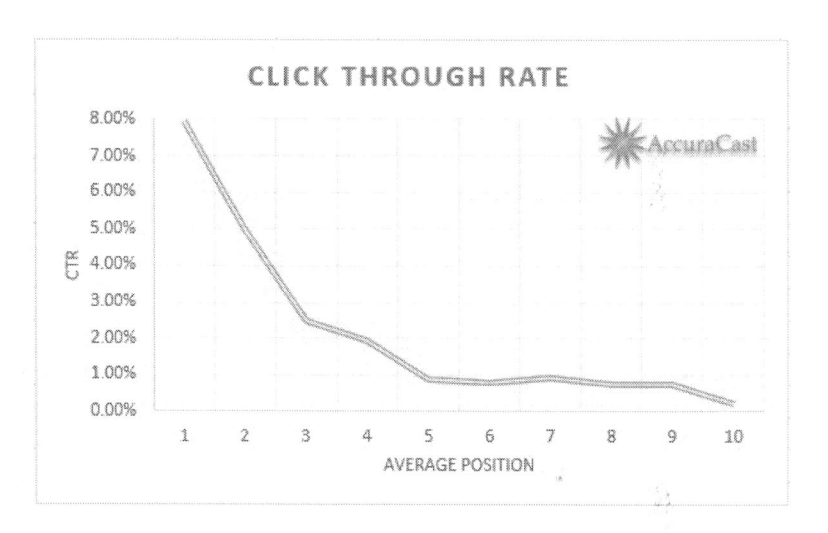

Click Through Rate chart by AccuraCast showing CTR vs Average Position (1-10), with CTR starting near 8% at position 1 and decreasing to near 0% at position 10.

Add Clear and Compelling CTAs

The end goal for your ads is for the target client to take action and make a purchase, right? Use compelling calls-to-action that will motivate leads to act after they see your ads.

Since you've developed a buyer persona for your target market, you'll create CTAs that match that buyer persona and help drive leads to respond.

Colors can also be useful when crafting your CTA. See chapter 2, "Essentials of a Perfect Landing Page: Images or Videos" for more about the psychology of color.

Ad Metrics to Measure

If you can't measure it, you can't evaluate it. So here are some metrics that can indicate your ads' performance and help you evaluate their returns on your investment.

Traffic Results

Remember, you optimized your ads with target keywords. The traffic can come from different sources. Paid search traffic comes from ads at the top of the Google search engine results.

Here's an example I got after searching "best travel places."

> Discover Reno Tahoe - What Would You Like to Do? [AD]
> www.visitrenotahoe.com Report Ad
> This place - more than any other - rewards those who heed its call.
>
> 30 World's Best Places to Visit | U.S. News Travel
> https://travel.usnews.com/rankings/worlds-best-vacations/
> World's Best Places to Visit Paris. Every day, the magnetic City of Light draws visitors who travel from around... Rome. When you visit the Eternal City, prepare to cross a few must-see attractions... Tahiti. Travel to this island - the largest in French Polynesia - if you've been dreaming...
>
> Best in Travel - The best places to visit in 2020 - Lonely Planet
> https://www.lonelyplanet.com/best-in-travel
> What are the best destinations to visit in 2020? Lonely Planet's travel experts reveal all...

You can also generate traffic from ads on your social accounts like Facebook, Twitter, Instagram, and LinkedIn. You can get direct or referral traffic to your website.

Evaluate and measure the traffic from your ads on different marketing channels. High and recurring traffic shows that your ads are performing well.

Bounce Rate

This metric can help you understand how leads interact with your landing pages after clicking on your ad. A high bounce rate shows that the content you've posted on your pages isn't suitable for your audience.

Your ads link to your website landing pages. If the bounce rate is high, it shows that either your ads are not attracting target clients or customers aren't finding what they want on your website. Your website should contain only high-quality content that tells your readers what they need to know. This will motivate readers to engage with your business and take action.

It can also mean that they got all the information they needed from the first page they encountered on your website. You may need to incorporate a new CTA or other components on your landing page that attracts readers to another part of your site, keeping them around a bit longer. A high bounce rate can affect your conversions. Here are some [ways to reduce bounce rates](#).

Conversion Rate

You're creating an ad so you can attract potential customers to your business and sell them your products. To evaluate the performance of your ads, evaluate the conversions you get from them.

That will help you know whether your ads are effective or not. High conversion rates show that the ad is attracting and convincing people to use your products or services.

You can divide conversions into micro and macro categories. Micro conversions are the small actions leads take toward purchasing your products or services. These can be joining your email list or signing up for your blog updates or newsletter. Macro conversions include the target client's purchase of your product or service.

Cost per Action

This gives you corrective views of actions your leads take based on your ads. If, for instance, you have a cost-per-action of 50 cents, then you'll generate actions for your ads at that rate.

This metric helps you manage your ads more effectively. With a lower CPA, you can control more conversions from your ads.

Cost per Conversion

This metric will help you plan the cost of your conversions and manage it well. Here's the formula for calculating this metric:

$$CPC = \frac{\text{Total Cost}}{\text{Total No. of Conversions}}$$

Return on Ad Investment

Since you're in business, you don't just want to create ads randomly. You need to measure the returns you're getting from your investment in your ads.

Keep tracking your conversions and sales that result from your ads and calculate your ROI from each one. If you're not making much profit from an advertisement, consider improving the ad component of your marketing strategy.

Click-Through Rate

Click-Through Rate (CTR) Formula

Calculate how frequently people click on an ad or link

$$\text{CTR (Click-Through Rate)} = \left(\frac{\text{Total Measured Clicks}}{\text{Total Measured Impressions}}\right) \times 100$$

*Click-Through Rate is expressed as a percentage, so for ease of use x100 is added to the above equation.

What does it mean?
Total Measured Clicks: The total amount of clicks on an ad (which were counted by a server).
Total Measured Impressions: Number of times something (such as an ad or webpage) was loaded on a page (and counted by a server). For emails you could replace Impressions with Opens.

theonlineadvertisingguide.com — TOAG

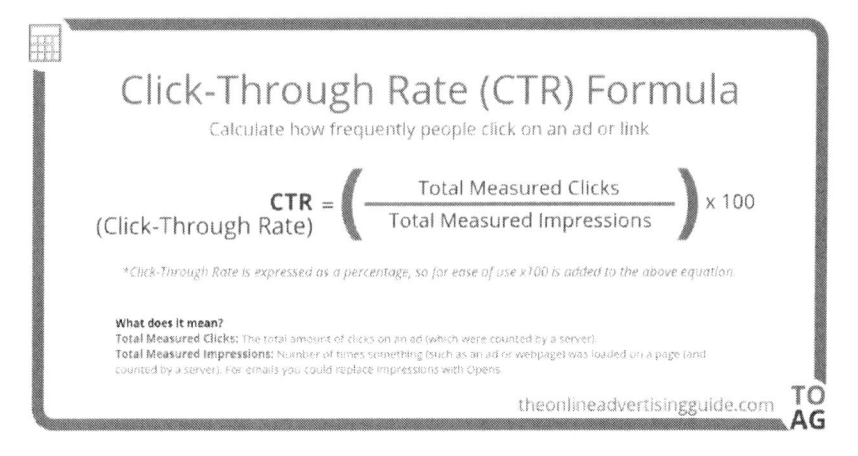

You can measure the clicks that direct your target clients to your landing pages. This metric is also important for determining your Google Ads' quality scores.

Average Cost per Acquisition

As the name suggests, this is the cost you pay to acquire one lead from your ads. Below is how the metric is calculated.

The metric is calculated by dividing the total costs of customer acquisition with the customer conversions from your ads.

Here's a simple calculation for this metric. Let's say, for instance, you have two conversions from your ads.

If one cost you $4 and the other $1, then the average cost per acquisition is $2.50.

Customer Lifetime Value

Your ads can be a great source to help you acquire clients. You can evaluate the customer lifetime value of clients you get through your advertising. Here's a simple formula for the metric:

$$\text{LTV} = \text{Average transaction} + \text{Annual purchase frequency} + \text{Expected years of relationship}$$

Alternatively, you can use this formula to calculate it:

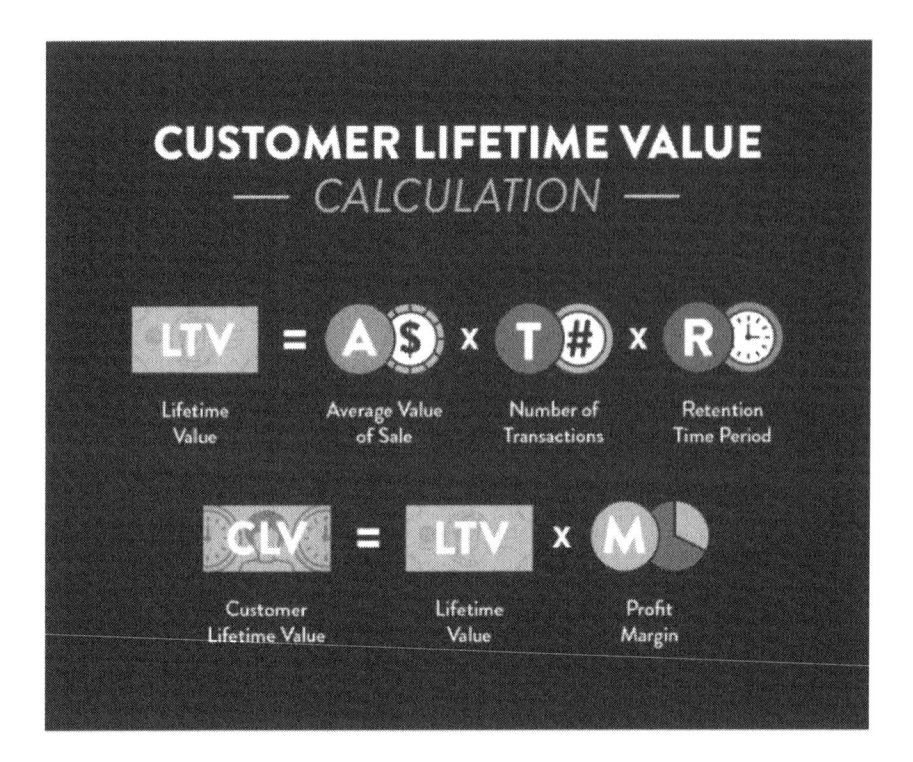

CUSTOMER LIFETIME VALUE CALCULATION

LTV = A$ × T# × R🕐

Lifetime Value — Average Value of Sale — Number of Transactions — Retention Time Period

CLV = LTV × M

Customer Lifetime Value — Lifetime Value — Profit Margin

Conversion Rate by Marketing Channel

You need to know which marketing channels lead to high conversions for your ads. Measure the lead conversion rate for each channel and compare them.

Maximize the number of ads you distribute on the channels that work best for you to increase conversions and generate sales and ROI.

Tools for Ad Creation

Know that you know the metrics that indicate successful ads, here are some tools you can use to create attractive ads.

Grammarly

grammarly
Great Writing, Simplified
Compose clear, mistake-free writing that makes the right impression with Grammarly's writing assistant.

Your competitors want the same clients you do. A key way to ensure that you don't rule your company out is by aiming for the highest-quality content.

You don't want grammar or spelling mistakes to distract readers from the messages in your ads. You can copy and paste your ad copy into a word processing program that's compatible with Grammarly, such as Microsoft Word, to check for grammar or other kinds of errors before publishing it.

Zapier

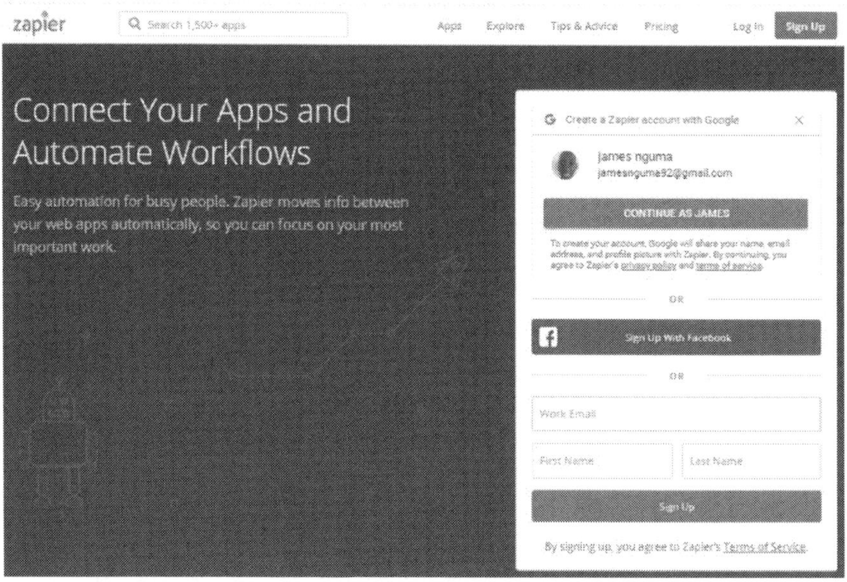
zapier
Search 1,500+ apps
Apps
Explore
Tips & Advice
Pricing
Log In
Sign Up
Connect Your Apps and Automate Workflows
Easy automation for busy people. Zapier moves info between your web apps automatically, so you can focus on your most important work.
Create a Zapier account with Google
james nguma
jamesnguma92@gmail.com
CONTINUE AS JAMES
OR
Sign Up With Facebook
OR
Work Email
First Name
Last Name
Sign Up
By signing up, you agree to Zapier's Terms of Service.

Different parts of your marketing process require different tools. Zapier helps you integrate these tools into your system so you can run your ads in an effective way. All the apps shown here can integrate with this tool:

Chapter 3: Creating Ads

Google Sheets	Gmail	Slack	Google Calendar	Mailchimp
Trello	Facebook Lead Ads	Twitter	Google Drive	Facebook Pages
Typeform	ActiveCampaign	Airtable	ClickFunnels	Google Forms
HubSpot	Pipedrive	Asana	Gravity Forms	Calendly
HubSpot CRM	Google Contacts	Instagram	Salesforce	Stripe

YouTube	Dropbox	Discord	WordPress	Acuity Scheduling
Todoist	Shopify	Twilio	Infusionsoft by Keap	Evernote
Pinterest	WooCommerce	ManyChat	Microsoft Office 365	JotForm
Wufoo	Eventbrite	Google Tasks	QuickBooks Online	Microsoft Excel
Microsoft Outlook	Zoho CRM	Squarespace	Intercom	Zendesk

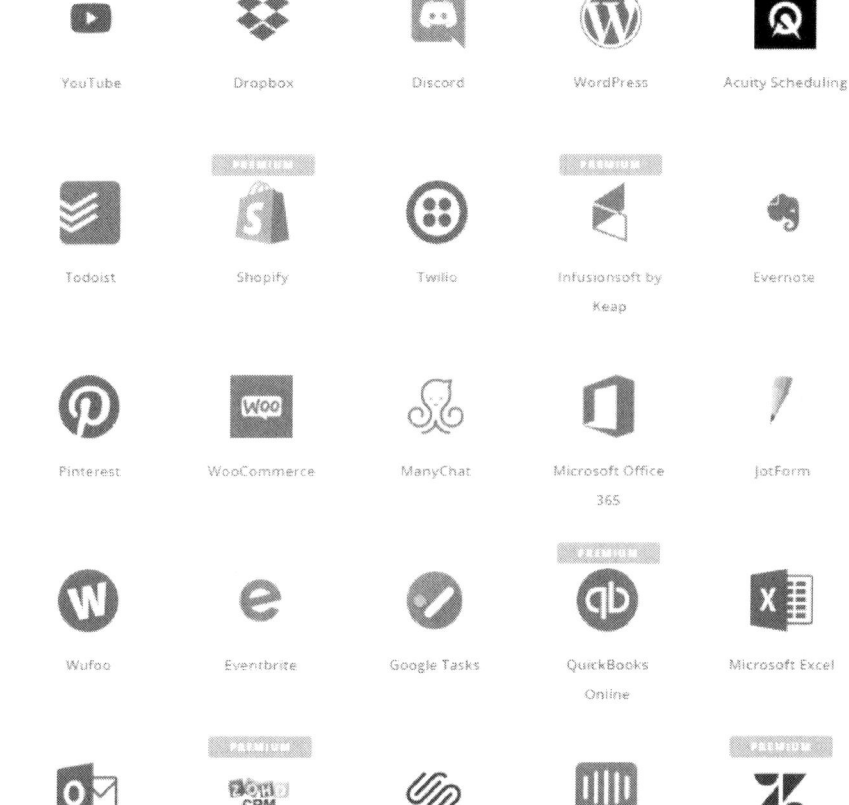

Chapter 3: Creating Ads

Google Docs	ConvertKit	Podio	LinkedIn		SurveyMonkey
Toggl	Xero	Unbounce	Zoom		Wunderlist
GitHub	Teachable	Webflow	Cognito Forms		Kajabi
ScheduleOnce	Freshdesk	Constant Contact	MailerLite		Wave
Smartsheet	PayPal	ClickSend SMS	Sendinblue		Jira Software Cloud

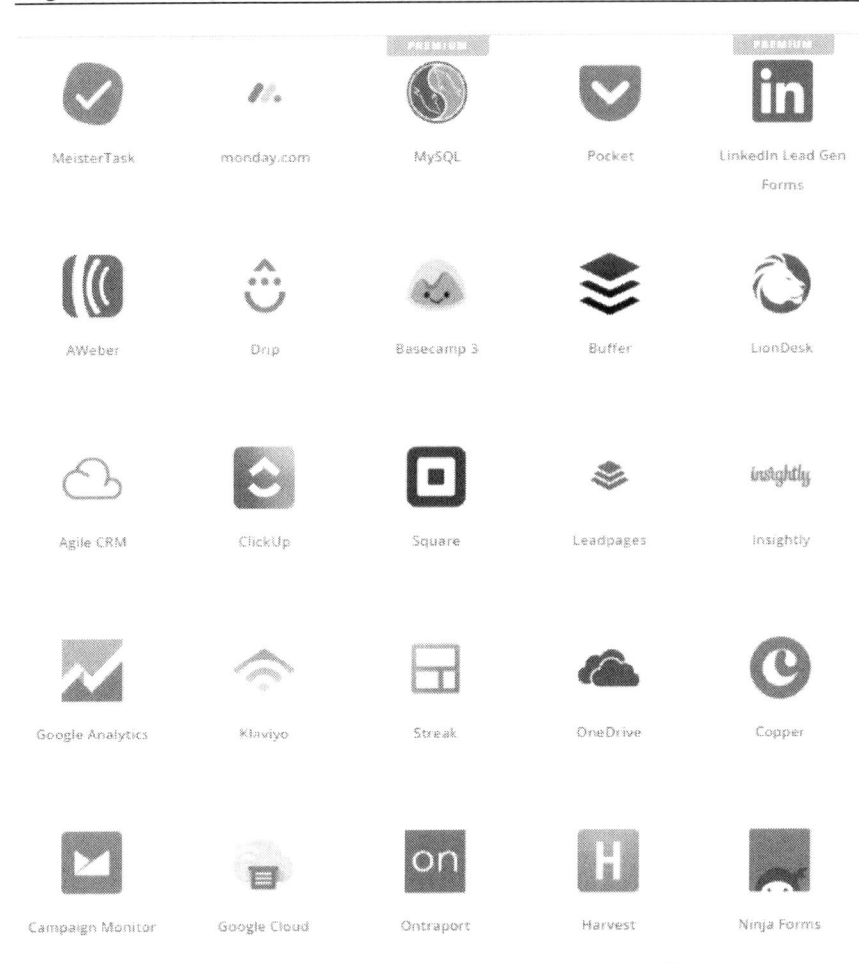

MeisterTask	monday.com	MySQL	Pocket	LinkedIn Lead Gen Forms
AWeber	Drip	Basecamp 3	Buffer	LionDesk
Agile CRM	ClickUp	Square	Leadpages	Insightly
Google Analytics	Klaviyo	Streak	OneDrive	Copper
Campaign Monitor	Google Cloud	Ontraport	Harvest	Ninja Forms

With these integrations, you can manage your ads well, increase your brand awareness, and convert leads into customers.

AdEspresso

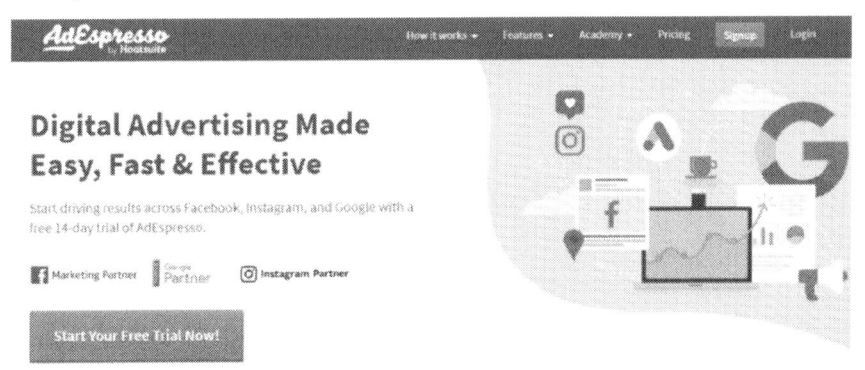

Digital Advertising Made Easy, Fast & Effective

Start driving results across Facebook, Instagram, and Google with a free 14-day trial of AdEspresso.

Start Your Free Trial Now!

Chapter 3: Creating Ads

This tool helps you create multiple ad campaigns on Facebook, Google Ads, and Instagram.

Create Campaigns Across 3 Channels in Minutes

AdEspresso supports Facebook, Instagram and Google Ads campaign creation. Utilize AdEspresso's user-friendly interface to create and manage your campaigns in minutes instead of hours.

Start Your Free Trial Now!

You can install the Pixel Caffeine WordPress plugin.

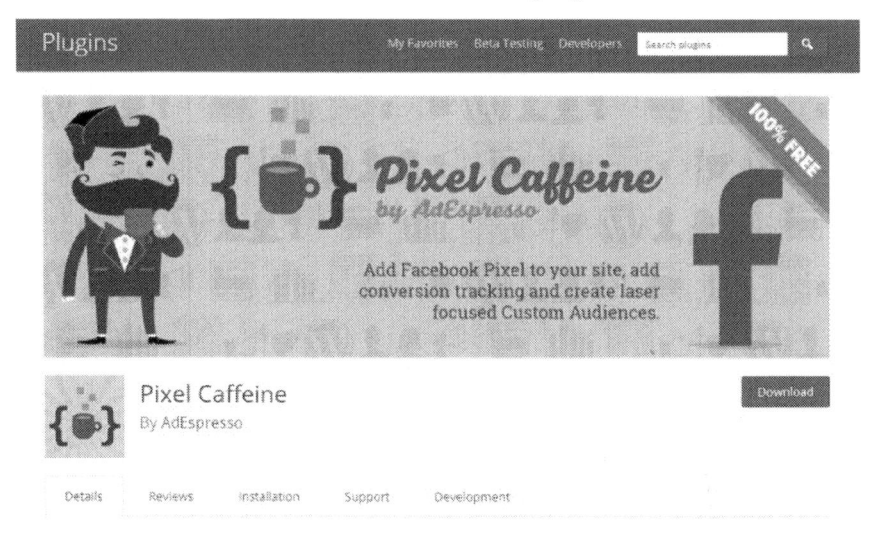

Pixel Caffeine
By AdEspresso

Add Facebook Pixel to your site, add conversion tracking and create laser focused Custom Audiences.

The plugin helps you manage your Facebook product catalog. It can also help you add tracking events and create a customized audience for your brand.

Here's the pricing model for the tool:

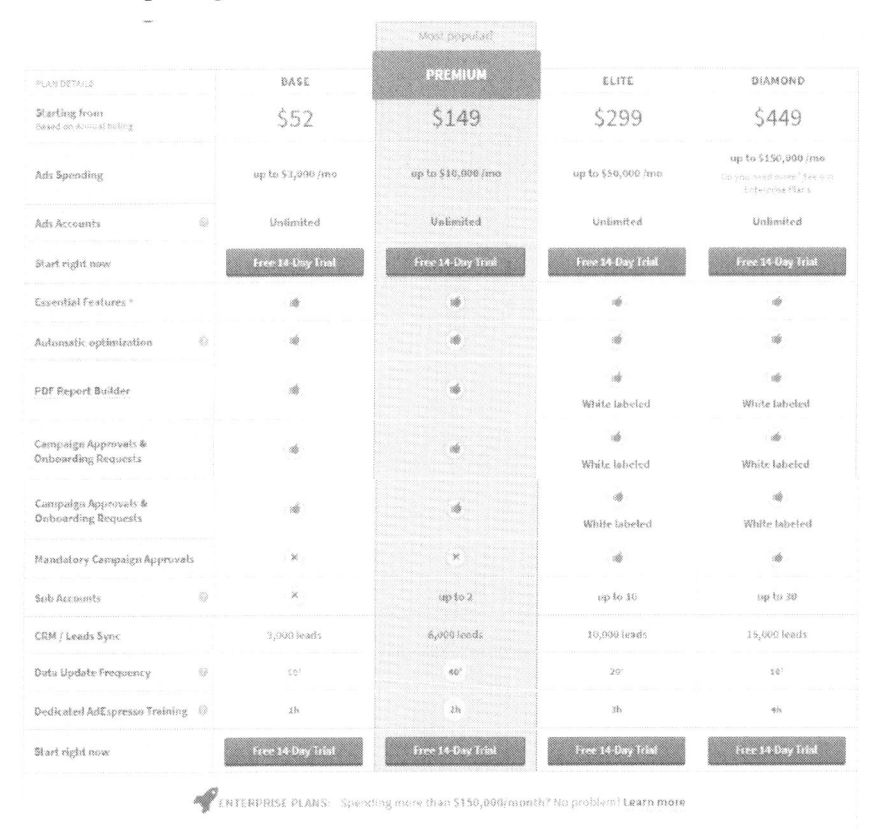

PLAN DETAILS	BASE	PREMIUM (Most popular)	ELITE	DIAMOND
Starting from (Based on Annual Billing)	$52	$149	$299	$449
Ads Spending	up to $3,000 /mo	up to $10,000 /mo	up to $50,000 /mo	up to $150,000 /mo (Do you need more? See our Enterprise Plans)
Ads Accounts	Unlimited	Unlimited	Unlimited	Unlimited
Start right now	Free 14-Day Trial	Free 14-Day Trial	Free 14-Day Trial	Free 14-Day Trial
Essential Features	✓	✓	✓	✓
Automatic optimization	✓	✓	✓	✓
PDF Report Builder	✓	✓	✓ White labeled	✓ White labeled
Campaign Approvals & Onboarding Requests	✓	✓	✓ White labeled	✓ White labeled
Campaign Approvals & Onboarding Requests	✓	✓	✓ White labeled	✓ White labeled
Mandatory Campaign Approvals	✗	✗	✓	✓
Sub Accounts	✗	up to 2	up to 10	up to 30
CRM / Leads Sync	3,000 leads	8,000 leads	10,000 leads	15,000 leads
Data Update Frequency	60'	40'	20'	10'
Dedicated AdEspresso Training	1h	2h	3h	4h
Start right now	Free 14-Day Trial	Free 14-Day Trial	Free 14-Day Trial	Free 14-Day Trial

🚀 ENTERPRISE PLANS: Spending more than $150,000/month? No problem! Learn more

SEMrush

Chapter 3: Creating Ads

SEMrush offers myriad features that help you manage and plan your ads in the right way. It gives you insight into what to invest and how to carry on your marketing campaigns.

Check out the SEMrush website to see how it works and how its features can help you run your ads. Here's the SEMrush pricing model:

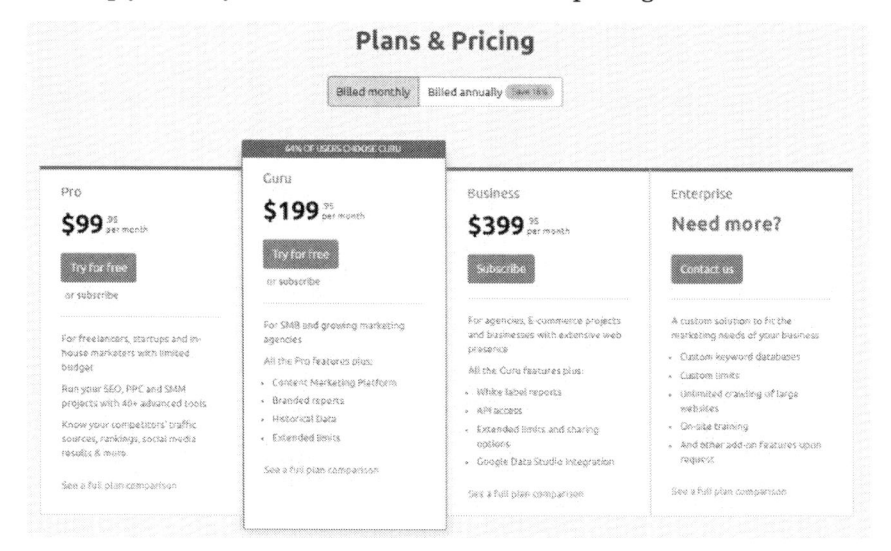

SpyFu

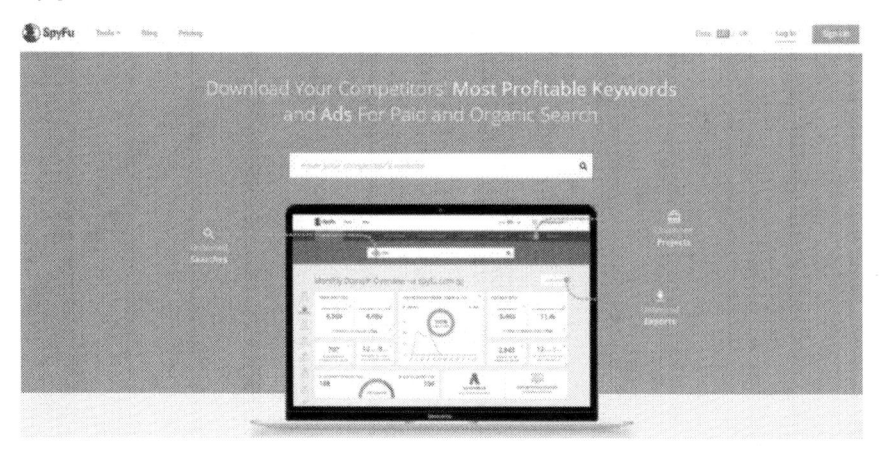

You can use this tool to learn more about your competitors' marketing activities.

You can know which keywords they use and how effective they are in their marketing campaigns. The tool can also help you identify the top-performing keywords and their ROI.

It will tell you the cost per click for the keywords your competitors use, and this can give you insight into how you should plan your ads.

Here's the SpyFu pricing structure:

Canva

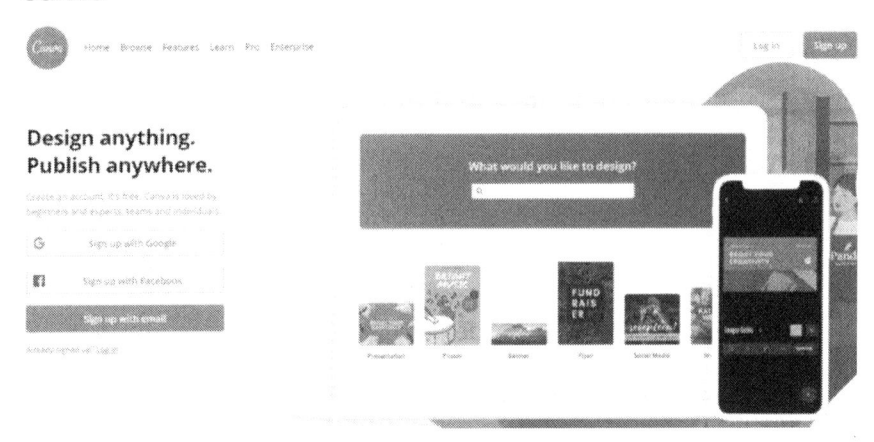

To make your ads attractive and engaging, you need a great design. Canva provides exceptional designs. It has free templates to choose from when creating your ads.

You can also integrate the tool with other platforms to make the work easier. Here are some of these sites:

Chapter 3: Creating Ads

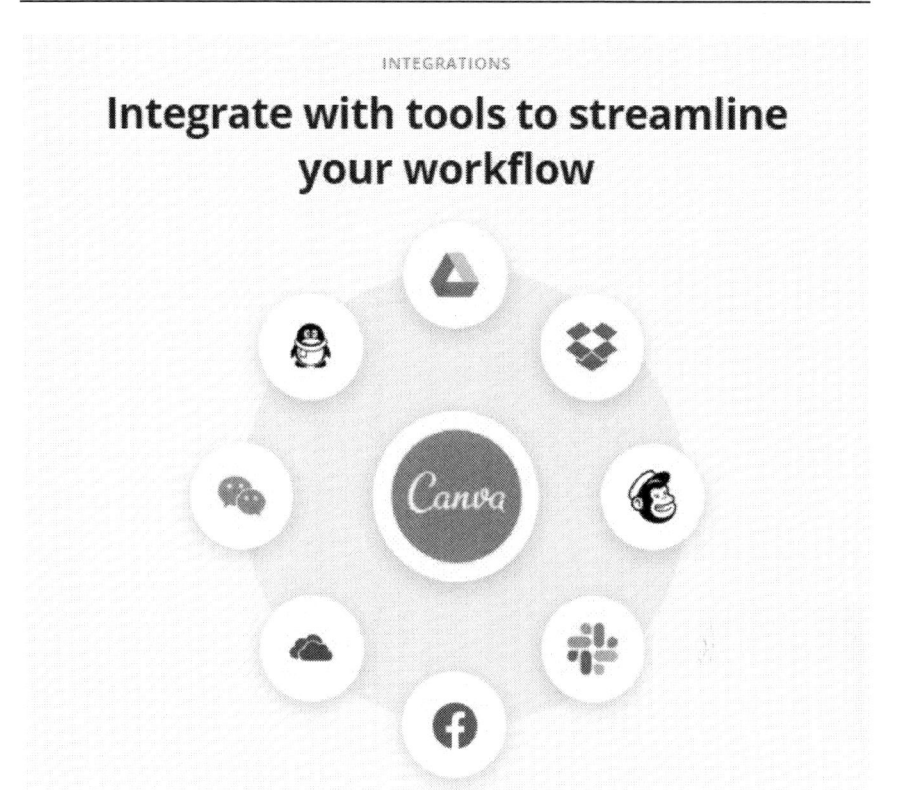

INTEGRATIONS

Integrate with tools to streamline your workflow

Google URL Builder

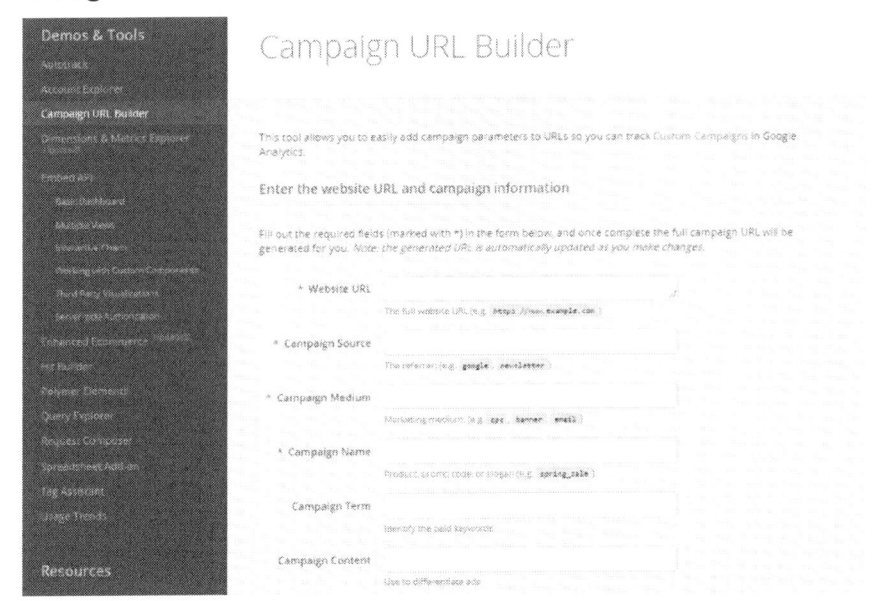

Sometimes you get dark traffic, meaning you can't account for its origin or measure it.

With Google URL Builder, you can add your campaign parameters to your URL to track everything that occurs within the ad links. This enables you to keep tabs on every source of traffic, data, and information.

AdStage

Chapter 3: Creating Ads

With AdStage, you can optimize your AdWords campaigns to reach more target clients. The tool can optimize your ad campaigns on multiple channels like Twitter, LinkedIn, and Facebook.

You can automate and integrate it with different platforms as shown here:

Looking for integrations? We've got you covered.

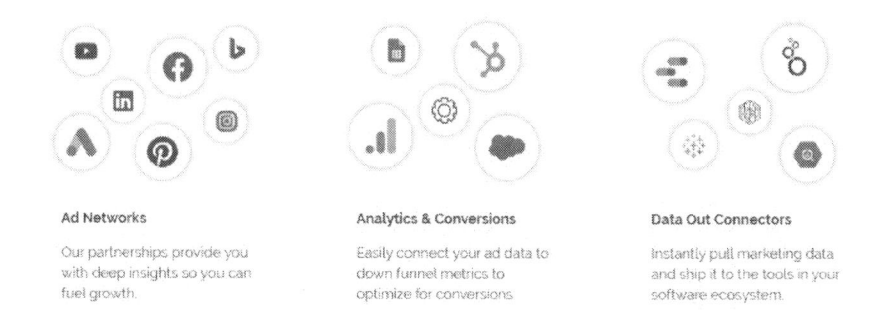

Ad Networks	Analytics & Conversions	Data Out Connectors
Our partnerships provide you with deep insights so you can fuel growth.	Easily connect your ad data to down funnel metrics to optimize for conversions.	Instantly pull marketing data and ship it to the tools in your software ecosystem.

And here is its pricing structure:

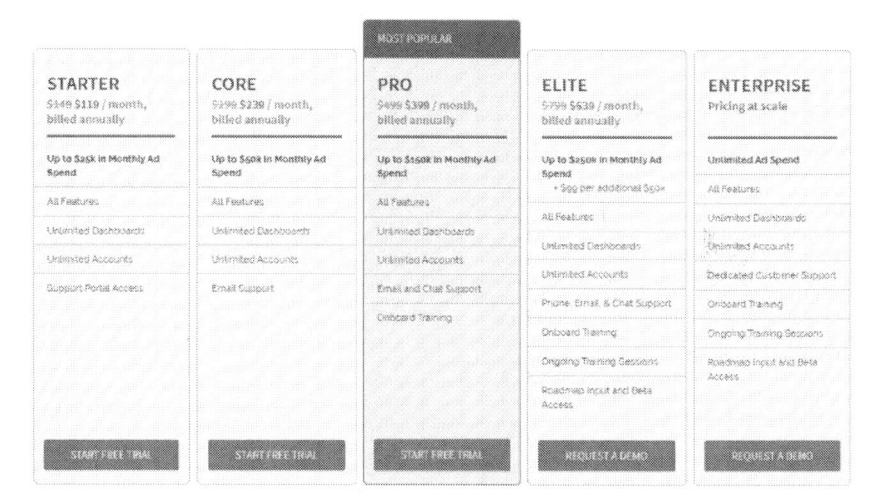

STARTER	CORE	PRO	ELITE	ENTERPRISE
$149 $119 / month, billed annually	$299 $239 / month, billed annually	$499 $399 / month, billed annually	$799 $639 / month, billed annually	Pricing at scale
Up to $25k in Monthly Ad Spend	Up to $50k in Monthly Ad Spend	Up to $150k in Monthly Ad Spend	Up to $250k in Monthly Ad Spend + $99 per additional $50k	Unlimited Ad Spend
All Features	All Features	All Features	All Features	All Features
Unlimited Dashboards	Unlimited Dashboards	Unlimited Dashboards	Unlimited Dashboards	Unlimited Dashboards
Unlimited Accounts	Unlimited Accounts	Unlimited Accounts	Unlimited Accounts	Unlimited Accounts
Support Portal Access	Email Support	Email and Chat Support	Phone, Email, & Chat Support	Dedicated Customer Support
		Onboard Training	Onboard Training	Onboard Training
			Ongoing Training Sessions	Ongoing Training Sessions
			Roadmap Input and Beta Access	Roadmap Input and Beta Access
START FREE TRIAL	START FREE TRIAL	START FREE TRIAL	REQUEST A DEMO	REQUEST A DEMO

What to Know Before Getting into Advertising

Not Every Channel Will Work for You

There are different advertising channels on the market. So if certain marketing channels let's say Twitter doesn't work for you don't force it. Concentrate your efforts on channels that work and spend more on them.

Search for Free Marketing Opportunities

You're in business and a business needs to make profits. As you start your ad campaigns, look for free sites first and use them.

Even though most of them have limited features, they can help you run your ads. You can supplement them with paid ads as you continue growing your business.

Focus on the Profits

When measuring your ad metrics, focus on those that help you grow your business and increase your ROI.

You'll generate higher income from your ads by focusing on how to create better ones that generate more leads and increase conversions.

Be Patient

It can take some time to see results from your ads. You're not going to get results overnight. Be patient and keep improving your ad performance to determine what works best for your brand.

Features of the Updated Facebook Ads Manager

Great businesses keep inventing new and better ways to serve their customers. Here are some of the new and improved updates to the Facebook Ads Manager.

Chapter 3: Creating Ads

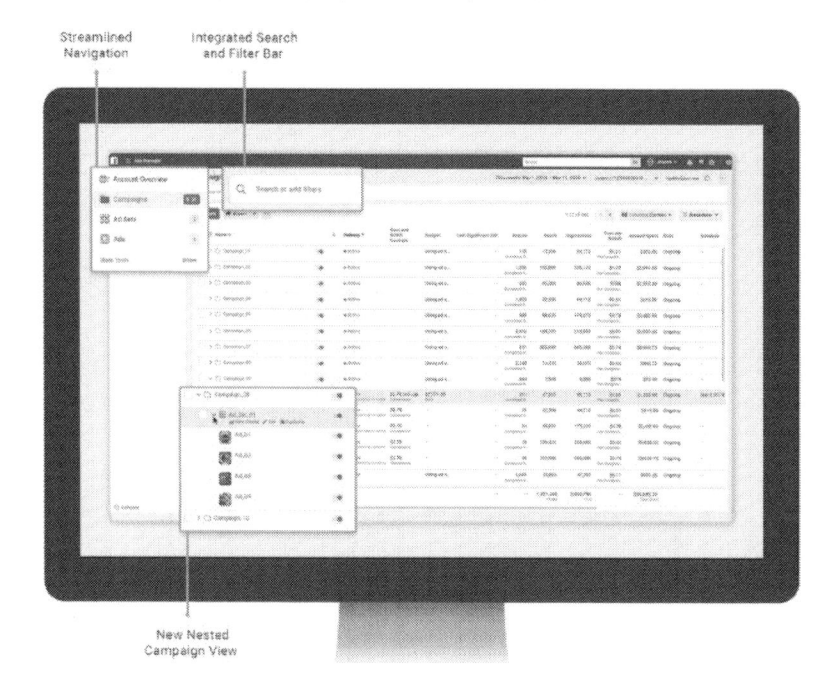

Improved Ads Manager Experience

Streamlined Navigation

Integrated Search and Filter Bar

New Nested Campaign View

New Learning Phase Insights

This improvement affects the account overview of the manager. With it, you'll be able to look at the ad set and budget spent for the previous two weeks and the percentage of the conversions of the ad.

Visit the Facebook for Business site to learn more about this update.

Performance Warnings

This update notifies you about the past, present, and predicted performance of your ads. It will give you recommendations that can help you run your ads effectively. You can see the recommendations during the process of setting up the ad or in the performance warning section of the ads account manager.

Customized Ad Creation Process

Your main goal in creating ads is to reach the target market, engage them with your business, and convert them into clients.

Ads Manager is introducing asset customization for ads. With this new feature, it's easy to customize your ads in different ways for placement on your ad channel. It lets you optimize your ads to increase engagement with target customers. You can also use it to maximize messages, traffic, and conversions.

Ad Preview Experience

As the name suggests, this feature helps you preview the way your ads will look when you place them. It highlights how your target readers will view and interact with your ads once they're published.

Using this feature makes it easy to customize your ads and take care of any errors that appear during the process of creation because you can see how the ads will look after placement.

New Features of Google Ads

Google has introduced improved features to help marketers reach out to their target clients in more effective ways. Here are some of these features.

Responsive Search Ads

Headlines matter a lot as a component of your ad copy. You can write 15 different headlines with this feature and add four descriptions of your ads.

After you've created the ads, Google will run different headlines through its machine learning algorithm. This will help it determine which ads perform best based on the ad copy, the keywords you've used, and the target market.

Automatic Bumper Machine

With its expertise in machine learning, Google has decided to use the bumper machine to create interesting six-second video ads.

You can edit the video ads after creating them to adjust factors such as soundtrack and colors.

The Reinvention of Google Shopping

Brands and individual business owners have been using Google shopping for a long time to search for and market products. However, the latest update has added more features.

Brands can include personal recommendations for products they want as well as ads.

Deep Linking in Apps

You can now link and track conversions with mobile apps that have deep linking.

> *Your app users will be taken directly from your Search, Display and Shopping ads directly to the relevant page in your mobile app if they have your app already installed. That means your customers will be able to complete their desired action—buy something, book a trip or order food delivery—in a way that's optimized for the destination that drives the highest value for your brand."*

This tool can help you with deep linking to your apps. You can visit the website's pricing page to find out more about its pricing structure.

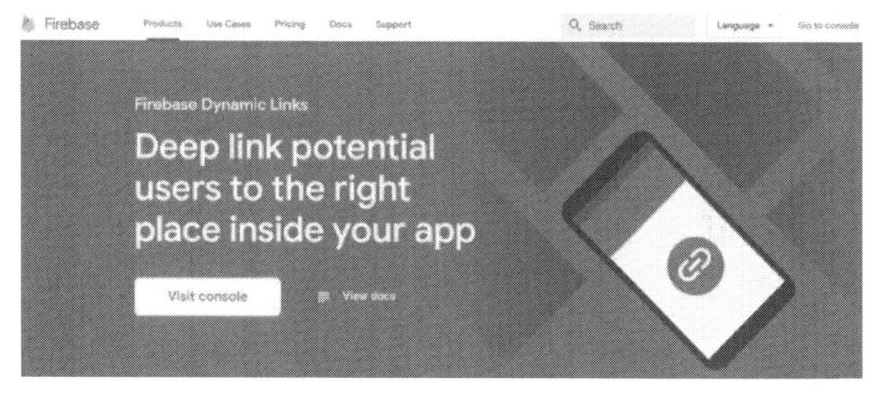

The links you create will direct users to your apps if they've installed them. The ads will support both universal and app links, which will match with the operating system of the user's mobile phone.

You can integrate Firebase with Google Analytics to simplify the tracking process and share lead conversion data with tools like Google Ads.

CTA Extension for Video Ads

Video is becoming more popular than ever and brands are using it more often to advertise their businesses and engage leads. Research by Wistia shows that short videos perform better.

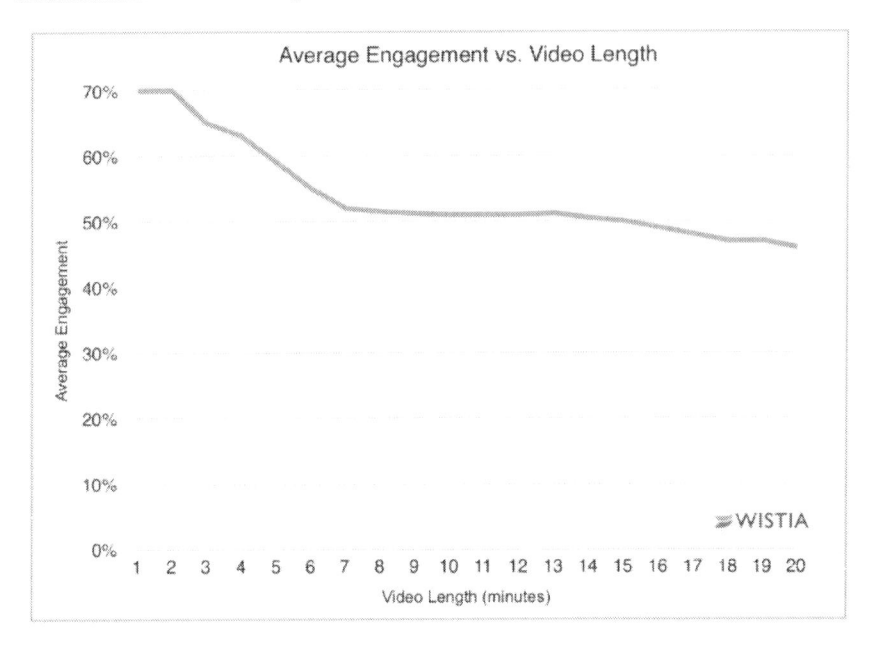

Google seems to have known this better than anyone. They've included video extensions on TrueView with calls-to-action for video viewers as they watch the videos.

Viewers don't have to watch the whole ad video if they don't want to since there's an option available to skip the ad. Here's an example:

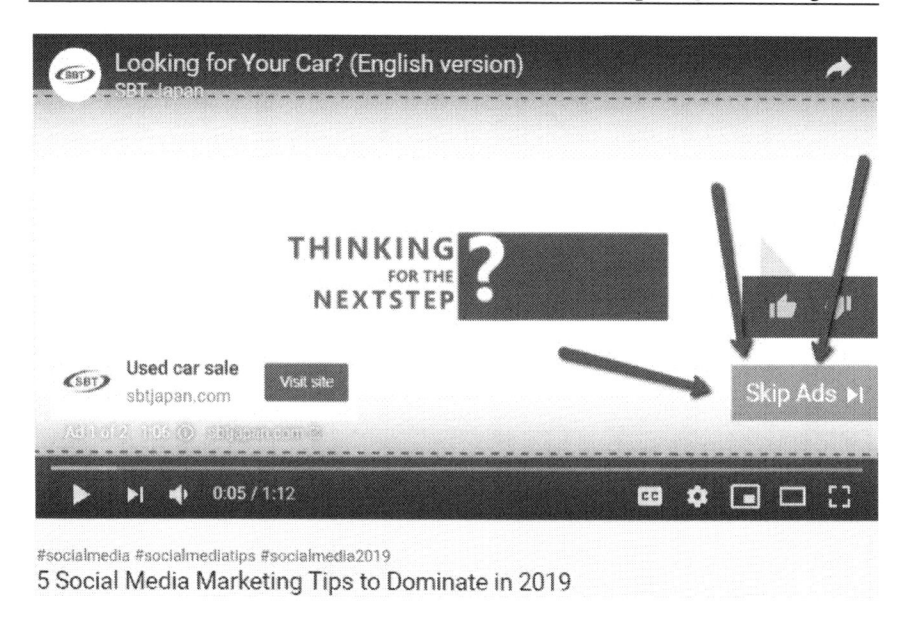

YouTube Masthead for TV

Google is launching a YouTube masthead for TV screens. This is the result of some successful testing campaigns.

Advertisers can use this tool to reach their target market when potential customers watch TV. This will be made possible with the YouTube app's incorporation into TV and will make it easy for brands to advertise their services to potential customers when they open the app on their TV screen. If the viewers are using compatible devices, the masthead will autoplay and let them watch videos after a few seconds.

Marketers can purchase the YouTube masthead on the basis of a cost per thousand impressions.

This feature will help increase brand awareness and reach a large number of target customers because most people like to watch videos.

That concludes our discussion of ads and how best to use them. Read on to learn about how to generate B2B leads.

Chapter 4: B2B Sales

As a marketer, you need to generate sales and grow your business ROI. In this chapter, we'll talk more about business-to-business (B2B) sales and how to attract leads to your business, convert them, and generate more sales and business growth.

To start, B2B is the process through which one business reaches out to another to sell them their goods or services.

Unlike the process through which brands reach out to end consumers, this type of marketing is a long process and requires brands to build trust with each other before they do business.

Every business starts with lead generation. In the same way, we'll start with the best ways for brands to generate leads for their business.

How to Generate B2B Leads

Here, we'll list a few methods you can use to attract other businesses and generate leads for your business.

Engage Prospects on Social Media

Social media is one of the major platforms where you can find leads. Research by Emarsys shows that there are 3.2 billion users on social media each day.

Daily Active Social Media Users — Oberlo

3.2 billion social media users — which equates to about **42% of the population.**
(Emarsys, 2019)

Out of this huge number, many can turn out to be customers for your brand. Posting helpful information and offering your services on these social media sites can be a great way to attract these potential clients to your brand.

For instance, research conducted by the Pew Research Center shows that most Americans use Facebook and YouTube.

Majority of Americans now use Facebook, YouTube

% of U.S. adults who say they use the following social media sites online or on their cellphone

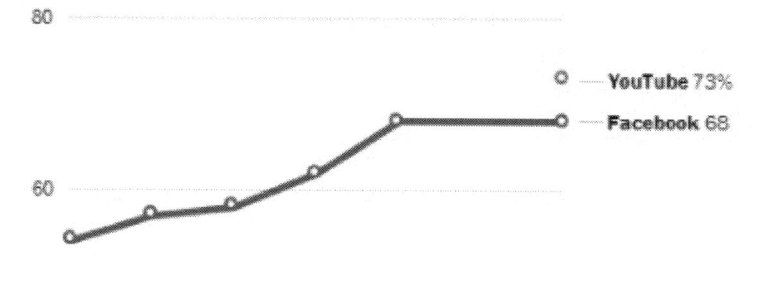

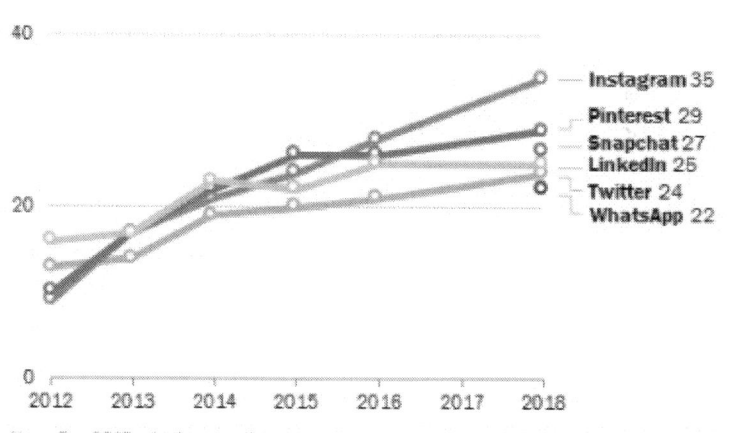

- YouTube 73%
- Facebook 68
- Instagram 35
- Pinterest 29
- Snapchat 27
- LinkedIn 25
- Twitter 24
- WhatsApp 22

Note: Pre-2018 telephone poll data is not available for YouTube, Snapchat or WhatsApp.
Source: Survey conducted Jan. 3-10, 2018. Trend data from previous Pew Research Center surveys.
"Social Media Use in 2018"

PEW RESEARCH CENTER

With data from this research, you can use these sites to target most of your leads. You can then engage them, build more trust, nurture them, and convert them into clients.

Knowing how often and when your target clients visit these sites on a daily basis can also help you attract them. You can plan to engage them when they're active on these sites.

For instance, 51% of Facebook users visit the site several times per day.

A majority of Facebook, Snapchat and Instagram users visit these platforms on a daily basis

Among U.S. adults who say they use ___, the % who use each site ...

	Several times a day	About once a day	Less often	NET Daily
Facebook	51%	23%	26%	74%
Snapchat	49	14	36	63
Instagram	38	22	39	60
Twitter	26	20	53	46
YouTube	29	17	55	45

Note: Respondents who did not give answer are not shown. "Less often" category includes users who visit these sites a few times a week, every few weeks or less often.
Source: Survey conducted Jan. 3-10, 2018.
"Social Media Use in 2018"

PEW RESEARCH CENTER

You can attract and target these prospects easily since they're on these sites most of the time.

Many potential clients use different social sites. For instance, 90% of LinkedIn users also use Facebook.

Substantial 'reciprocity' across major social media platforms
% of ___ users who also ...

	Use Twitter	Use Instagram	Use Facebook	Use Snapchat	Use YouTube	Use WhatsApp	Use Pinterest	Use LinkedIn
Twitter	–	73%	90%	54%	95%	35%	49%	50%
Instagram	50	–	91	60	95	35	47	41
Facebook	32	47	–	35	87	27	37	33
Snapchat	48	77	89	–	95	33	44	37
YouTube	31	45	81	35	–	28	36	32
WhatsApp	38	55	85	40	92	–	33	40
Pinterest	41	56	89	41	92	25	–	42
LinkedIn	47	57	90	40	94	35	49	–

Source: Survey conducted Jan. 3-10, 2018.
"Social Media Use in 2018"
PEW RESEARCH CENTER

90% of LinkedIn users also use Facebook

Don't focus all your attention on one social site. Use several sites to promote brand awareness and then engage leads as you build more trust with them.

Ensure that the content you post to social media sites is engaging and educational for the target customer. Interact with potential customers and try to solve their pain points.

Be Active in Groups and Forums

Groups, forums, and online communities are plentiful, and joining them gives you an opportunity to be helpful. Remember, most of your target clients will join these groups in search of a solution to their pain points.

Once you're in a group, be active. Ask and answer questions within the platform. This will help show your thought leadership skills to potential clients.

For example, join some LinkedIn groups and use them to attract leads to your business by being useful and helpful to group members.

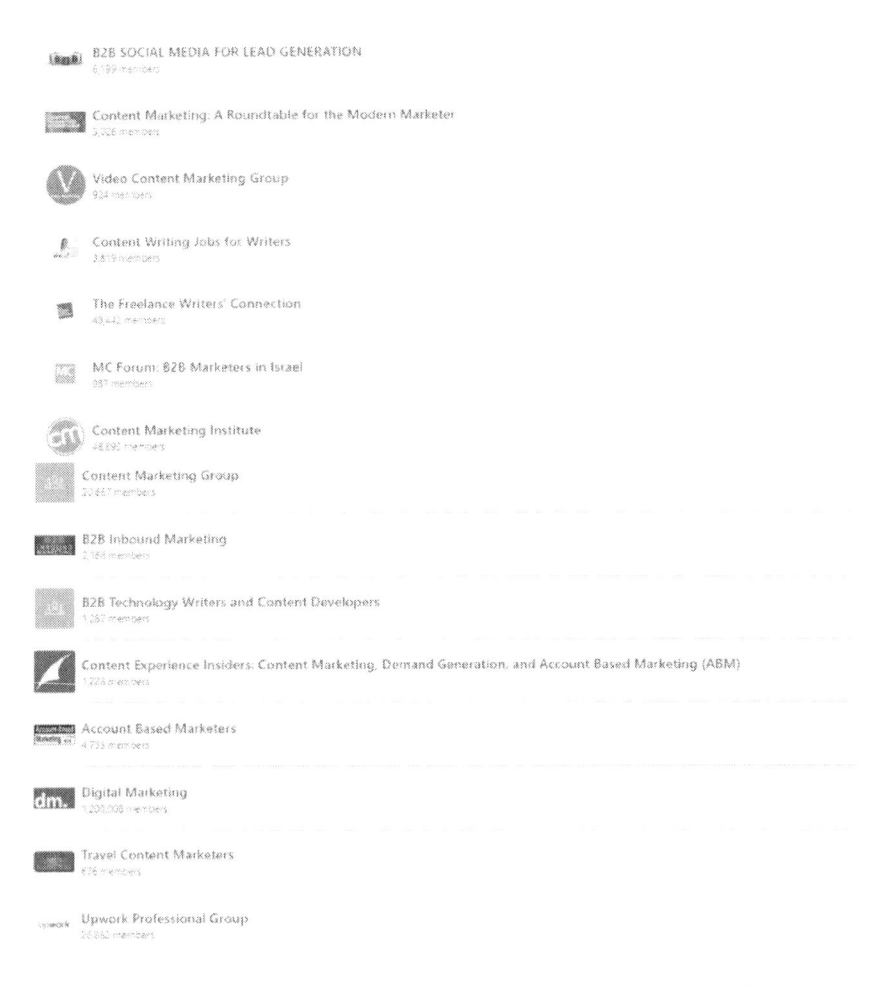

- B2B SOCIAL MEDIA FOR LEAD GENERATION
  6,199 members
- Content Marketing: A Roundtable for the Modern Marketer
  5,028 members
- Video Content Marketing Group
  934 members
- Content Writing Jobs for Writers
  3,819 members
- The Freelance Writers' Connection
  43,442 members
- MC Forum: B2B Marketers in Israel
  387 members
- Content Marketing Institute
  48,692 members
- Content Marketing Group
  20,667 members
- B2B Inbound Marketing
  2,188 members
- B2B Technology Writers and Content Developers
  1,267 members
- Content Experience Insiders: Content Marketing, Demand Generation, and Account Based Marketing (ABM)
  1,228 members
- Account Based Marketers
  4,733 members
- Digital Marketing
  1,205,008 members
- Travel Content Marketers
  636 members
- Upwork Professional Group
  26,882 members

Post relevant, interesting questions to the groups you join. Other great sites where you can be active and contribute are Quora and inbound.org.

Get Testimonials and Online Reviews

Brands and individual customers trust and prefer to do business with brands others have used and liked. Many marketers have taken advantage of this fact to attract leads to their brands.

EMERGING TRENDS

37% of B2B marketers are using marketing automation to generate leads.

49% of B2B marketers are heavily engaged in mobile marketing for generating leads.

71% of B2B marketers are using content marketing to generate leads.

88% of B2B marketers said case studies were effective.

89% of B2B marketers said customer testimonials were effective.

Customer testimonials & case studies were cited as the most effective B2B content marketing tactics

Research by Bright Local shows that 27% of potential clients read online reviews before they engage brands.

Do you read online reviews for businesses?

Do you read online reviews for businesses?

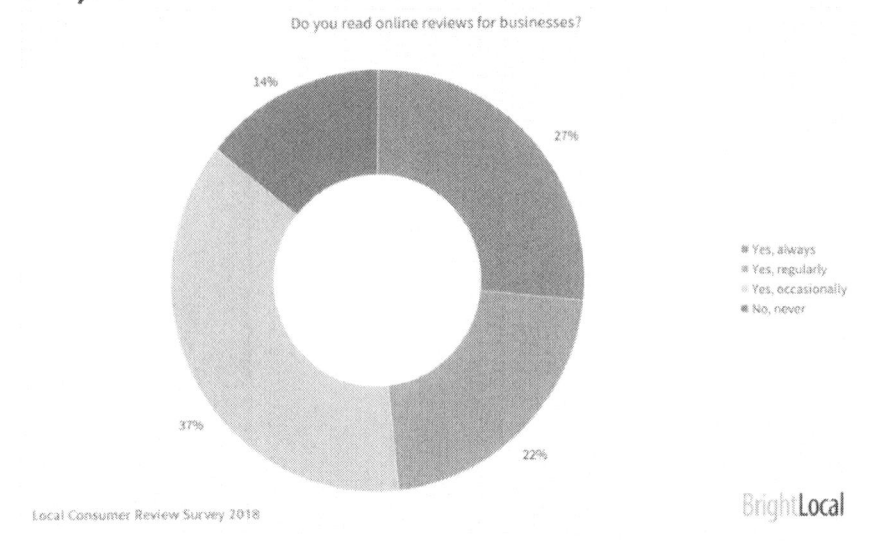

- 14% — Yes, always
- 27% — Yes, regularly
- 22% — Yes, occasionally
- 37% — No, never

Local Consumer Review Survey 2018 — BrightLocal

If your previous clients liked your brand, services, or products, they'll leave positive reviews. These will show potential clients that your business offers great services or products and is worth engaging with.

In the same way, testimonials play a vital role in your lead generation. Ask your past clients to post about their experiences with your company on your website.

Here's an example of testimonials from Buffer customers:

Chapter 4: B2B Sales

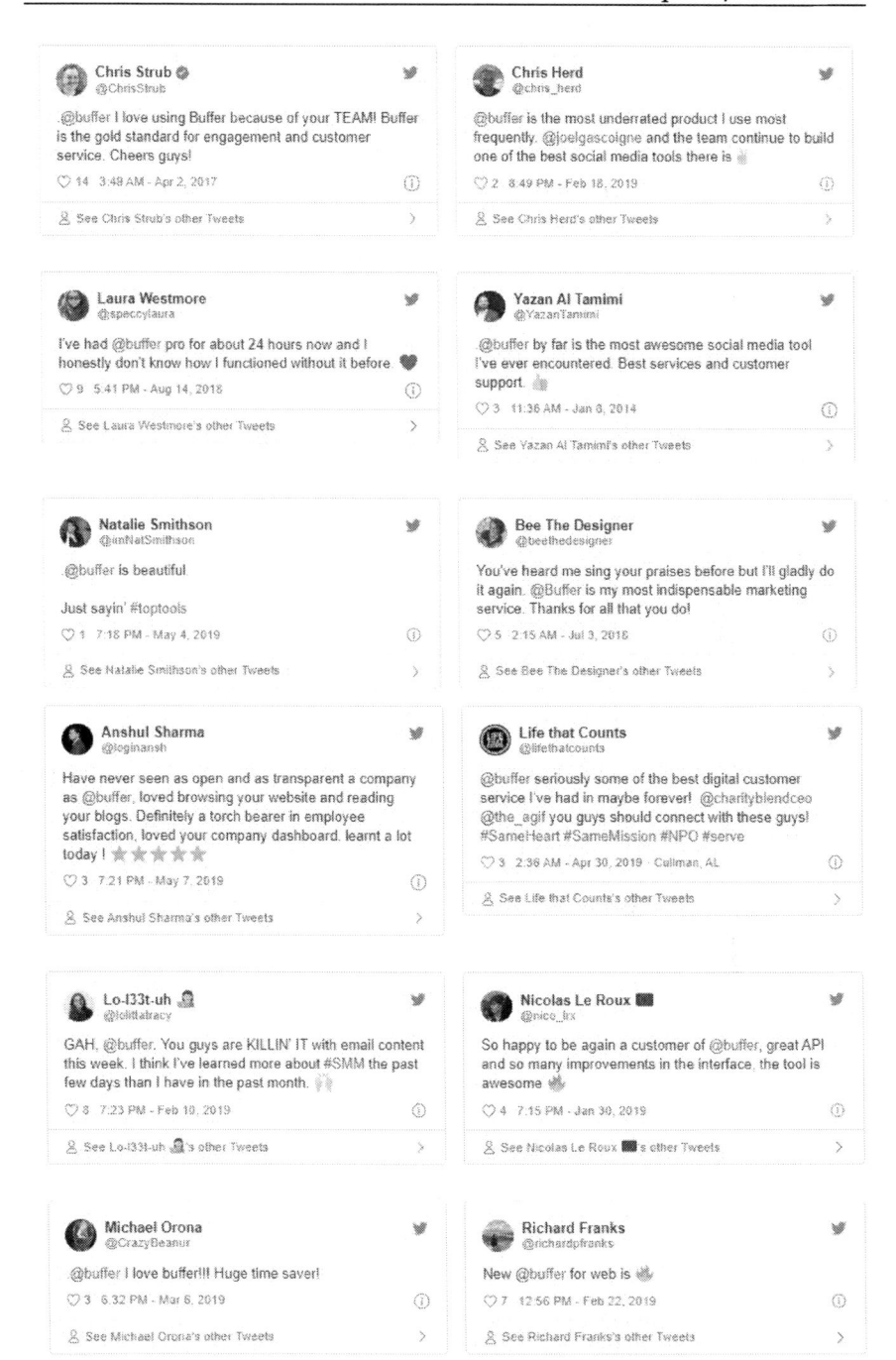

Chris Strub ✓
@ChrisStrub

.@buffer I love using Buffer because of your TEAM! Buffer is the gold standard for engagement and customer service. Cheers guys!

♡ 14   3:49 AM - Apr 2, 2017

See Chris Strub's other Tweets

Chris Herd
@chris_herd

@buffer is the most underrated product I use most frequently. @joelgascoigne and the team continue to build one of the best social media tools there is

♡ 2   8:49 PM - Feb 18, 2019

See Chris Herd's other Tweets

Laura Westmore
@speccylaura

I've had @buffer pro for about 24 hours now and I honestly don't know how I functioned without it before.

♡ 9   5:41 PM - Aug 14, 2018

See Laura Westmore's other Tweets

Yazan Al Tamimi
@YazanTamimi

.@buffer by far is the most awesome social media tool I've ever encountered. Best services and customer support.

♡ 3   11:36 AM - Jan 6, 2014

See Yazan Al Tamimi's other Tweets

Natalie Smithson
@imNatSmithson

.@buffer is beautiful.

Just sayin' #toptools

♡ 1   7:18 PM - May 4, 2019

See Natalie Smithson's other Tweets

Bee The Designer
@beethedesigner

You've heard me sing your praises before but I'll gladly do it again. @Buffer is my most indispensable marketing service. Thanks for all that you do!

♡ 5   2:15 AM - Jul 3, 2018

See Bee The Designer's other Tweets

Anshul Sharma
@loginansh

Have never seen as open and as transparent a company as @buffer, loved browsing your website and reading your blogs. Definitely a torch bearer in employee satisfaction, loved your company dashboard. learnt a lot today ! ★★★★★

♡ 3   7:21 PM - May 7, 2019

See Anshul Sharma's other Tweets

Life that Counts
@lifethatcounts

@buffer seriously some of the best digital customer service I've had in maybe forever! @charityblendceo @the_agif you guys should connect with these guys! #SameHeart #SameMission #NPO #serve

♡ 3   2:36 AM - Apr 30, 2019 · Cullman, AL

See Life that Counts's other Tweets

Lo-l33t-uh
@lolittabracy

GAH, @buffer. You guys are KILLIN' IT with email content this week. I think I've learned more about #SMM the past few days than I have in the past month.

♡ 8   7:23 PM - Feb 19, 2019

See Lo-l33t-uh's other Tweets

Nicolas Le Roux
@nico_lrx

So happy to be again a customer of @buffer, great API and so many improvements in the interface, the tool is awesome

♡ 4   7:15 PM - Jan 30, 2019

See Nicolas Le Roux's other Tweets

Michael Orona
@CrazyBeanur

.@buffer I love buffer!!! Huge time saver!

♡ 3   6:32 PM - Mar 6, 2019

See Michael Orona's other Tweets

Richard Franks
@richardpfranks

New @buffer for web is

♡ 7   12:56 PM - Feb 22, 2019

See Richard Franks's other Tweets

When clients talk about how your brand helped them, it shows that they loved your business and advocates your brand to other target customers.

Case studies also play a major role in lead generation. They offer more detail than testimonials and give prospects a chance to see how your company might work in a specific situation or solve a particular problem.

Here are some examples of case studies for the Voy Media brand.

Use Lead Magnets

In the previous chapter, we talked about lead magnets and gave some examples. You need to grow your email list to be able to nurture leads as you build trust.

Lead magnets are great for acquiring your target customers' contact information. This chart shows some of the many different types of lead magnets you can use to attract leads and grow your email list:

Chapter 4: B2B Sales

LEAD MAGNETS

	CONTENT BAIT	WIDGETS	QUIZES	LIVE DEMOS	WEBINARS	FREE TRIALS	CONTESTS	SPECIAL OFFERS
TARGET AUDIENCE	B2C, B2B	B2C, B2B	B2C, B2B (rare)	B2B	B2C	B2C, B2B	B2C, B2B	B2C, B2B
CUSTOMER CONCERN	Lack of information, wants to learn	Wants to compare but not ready to buy	Boredom, curiosity	Looking for product information	Lack of information, wants to learn	Wants to compare but not ready to buy	Boredom, desire	Price concerns
YOUR SOLUTION	Education	Custom offer	Amusement	Personal approach	Data, education	Product trial	Prizes	Coupon, gift, etc.

Image source: https://www.semrush.com/blog/8-types-of-lead-magnets-for-your-website/

Use the right type of lead magnet to draw the attention of each of your target customers. This will be easy once you have your buyer persona and know exactly the kind of clients you want to target.

You can also use lead magnets to attract a customer to the next stage of their buying journey.

Awareness Stage → **Consideration Stage** → **Decision Stage**

Prospect is experiencing and expressing symptoms of a problem or opportunity. Is doing educational research to more clearly understand, frame, and give a name to their problem.

Prospect has now clearly defined and given a name to their problem or opportunity. Is committed to researching and understanding all of the available approaches and/or methods to solving the defined problem or opportunity.

Prospect has now decided on their solution strategy, method, or approach. Is compiling a long list of all available vendors and products in their given solution strategy. Is researching to whittle the long list down to a short list and ultimately make a final purchase decision.

201

For example, case studies are the most effective lead magnets if you're looking to attract leads to the last stage of the buying journey.

In addition to lead magnets, brands can use gated content to get contact information from the target clients. You can offer valuable information that can help your target clients in return for personal data like their business, name, and email address.

Ensure that your gated content is worth the personal information you ask of your target clients. If it isn't, they won't see the need to exchange their valuable information for the content you give them.

Use Your Blog to Attract Leads

Every potential client who conducts a Google search does so because they're looking for a solution to a problem. To attract quality leads to your business, you must have the answer to the challenges that your potential clients face.

Create high-quality content that educates the target customer about how to solve their pain points. Offer all the information your target clients need.

A report by the CMI shows that 77% of agencies create in-depth content for their business marketing.

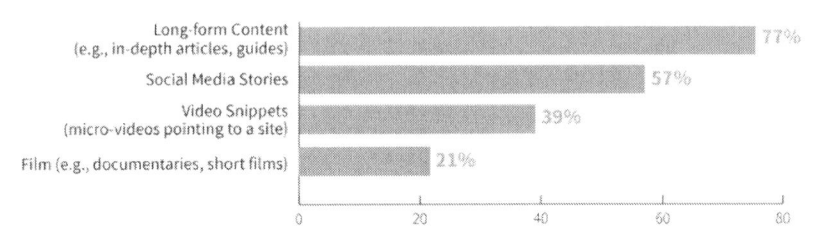

Agency Content Marketers' Use or Development of Select Types of Content in the Last 12 Months

Content Type	Percentage
Long-form Content (e.g., in-depth articles, guides)	77%
Social Media Stories	57%
Video Snippets (micro-videos pointing to a site)	39%
Film (e.g., documentaries, short films)	21%

Base: Agency content marketers. Aided list, multiple responses permitted.
Agency Content Marketing 2019: Benchmarks, Budgets, and Trends—Content Marketing Institute/MarketingProfs

Your content can include links, images, screenshots, or videos that help the target customer consume it. Include lots of white space for ease of reading.

This will build more trust with target customers who visit your blog page and engage them, besides helping you build a reputation as a thought leader in your market niche.

The CMI also reports that 60% of marketers have generated more leads by creating high-quality content for their website.

Goals Agency Marketers Have Achieved by Using Content Marketing Successfully in Last 12 Months

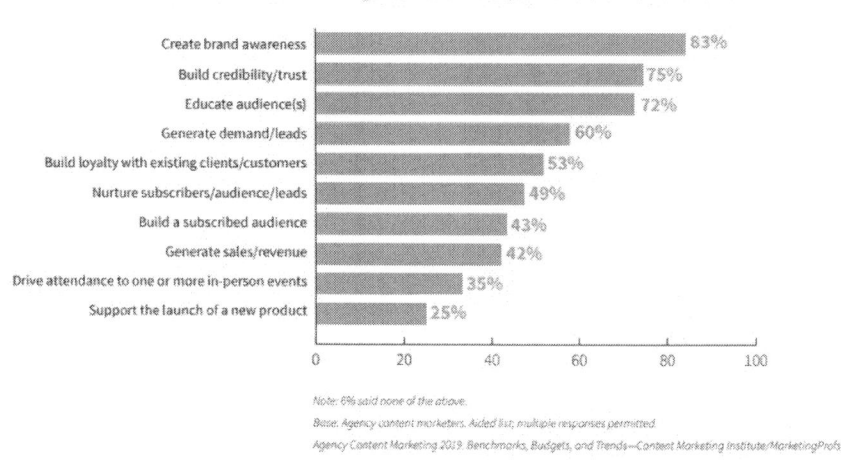

Goal	Percentage
Create brand awareness	83%
Build credibility/trust	75%
Educate audience(s)	72%
Generate demand/leads	60%
Build loyalty with existing clients/customers	53%
Nurture subscribers/audience/leads	49%
Build a subscribed audience	43%
Generate sales/revenue	42%
Drive attendance to one or more in-person events	35%
Support the launch of a new product	25%

Note: 6% said none of the above.
Base: Agency content marketers. Aided list; multiple responses permitted.
Agency Content Marketing 2019: Benchmarks, Budgets, and Trends—Content Marketing Institute/MarketingProfs

If your brand still isn't producing engaging, educational, and informative content, then look for someone to help you produce it.

Interact with your readers in the comment section of your blog posts. This will help you understand their pain points and come up with better and more advanced ways to solve their problems.

Also, get readers to subscribe to your blog for updates every time you publish new content and keep them educated with fresh content. This will keep them engaged with your website as you continue offering new high-quality content.

Use CTAs in Your Marketing

You want your content's readers to take action as soon as they've read your content. There's no better way to motivate them to do that than by including compelling CTAs in your content.

For example, you can leave an awesome call-to-action at the end of your blog page to encourage your readers to subscribe to your newsletter.

Here are some examples of CTAs in a blog post from the OptinMonster website:

12 Proven Ways to Convert Abandoning Visitors into Subscribers

Over 70% of visitors who abandon your website will never return!

Learn how to unlock the highest conversion revenue from each of your website visitors!

DOWNLOAD NOW

Add a Comment

We're glad you have chosen to leave a comment. Please keep in mind that all comments are moderated according to our **privacy policy**, and all links are nofollow. Do NOT use keywords in the name field. Let's have a personal and meaningful conversation.

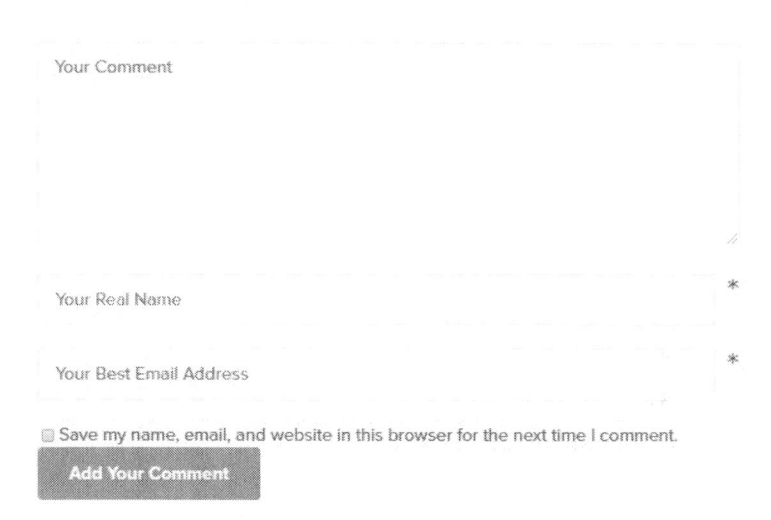

> Your Comment
>
> Your Real Name *
>
> Your Best Email Address *
>
> ☐ Save my name, email, and website in this browser for the next time I comment.
>
> **Add Your Comment**

If a reader is interested, they can take action and download the e-book, subscribe to blog updates or both. Either way, the business will get the contact details of the potential client and use them to nurture the leads into clients.

Ensure that your calls-to-action are clear to make it easy for readers to respond.

Research by the CMI shows that [63% of marketers use clear CTAs](#) to guide their readers as they nurture them through the sales cycle.

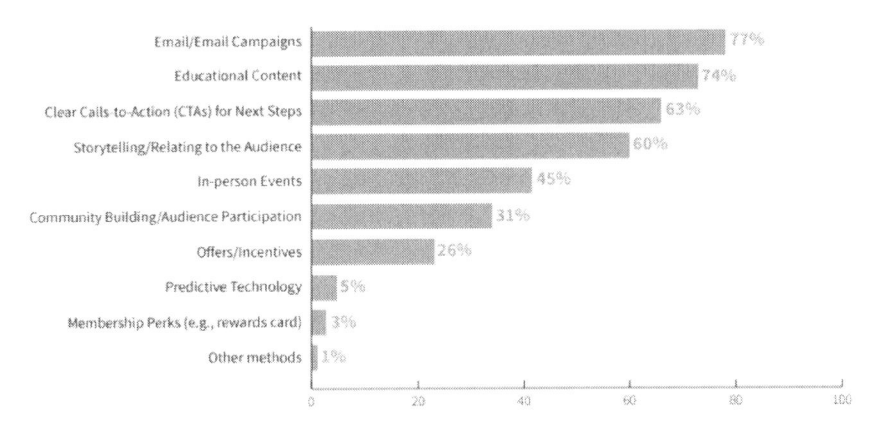

Content Marketing Methods Agency Marketers Use to Nurture Their Audience

Method	Percentage
Email/Email Campaigns	77%
Educational Content	74%
Clear Calls-to-Action (CTAs) for Next Steps	63%
Storytelling/Relating to the Audience	60%
In-person Events	45%
Community Building/Audience Participation	31%
Offers/Incentives	26%
Predictive Technology	5%
Membership Perks (e.g., rewards card)	3%
Other methods	1%

Base: Agency content marketers whose organizations nurture their audience. Aided list; multiple responses permitted.
Agency Content Marketing 2019: Benchmarks, Budgets, and Trends – Content Marketing Institute/MarketingProfs

Live Chat Customer Support

Sometimes potential clients visit your website but get confused as they navigate it and need immediate help. A live chat on the website can be a convenient source of guidance for the readers and help engage them.

If buyers can message a business as they interact with it, their trust grows and it's more likely they'll do business together. Live chat also makes it easy to capture your target clients' details.

The Internet Trends report by Mary Meeker shows that 60% of brands would like to provide easy access to online support channels to improve customer care.

Chapter 4: B2B Sales

INTERNET TRENDS 2018

Social Media =
Can Provide Opportunity to Improve Customer Service...

104 people clipped this slide

If you could choose two things for organizations to improve in customer service, what would they be? (Select two), 8/16

- Easier Access to Online Support Channels: 60%
- Faster Agent Response Times: 53%
- Consistent Customer Experience Across Channels: 29%
- Faster Access to Live Support: 21%

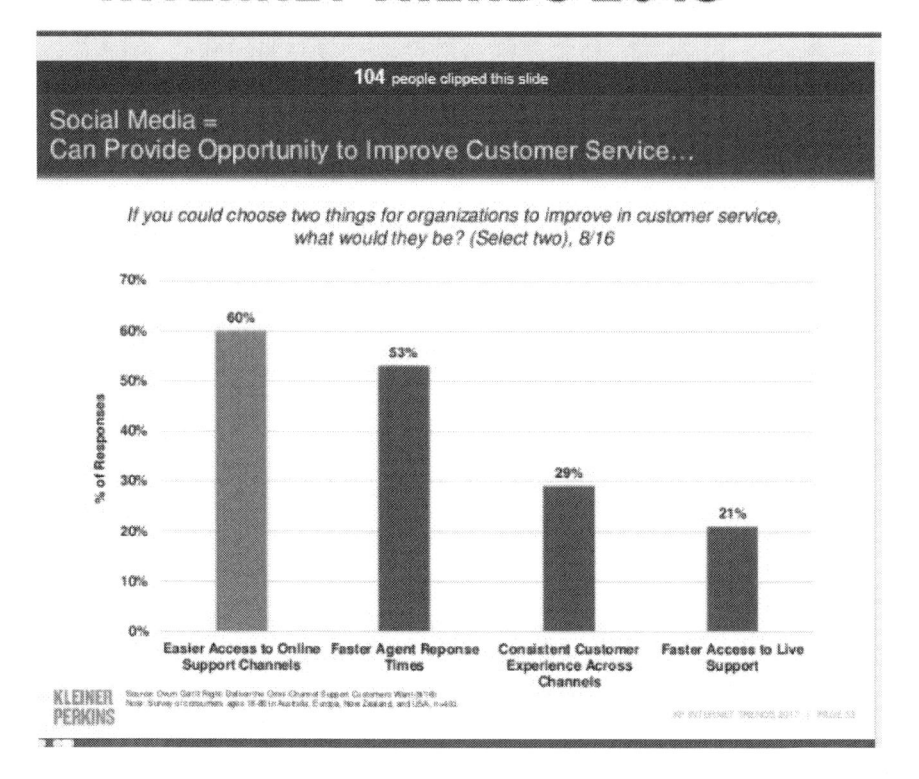

KLEINER PERKINS

Google and Facebook Ads

In the previous chapter on creating ads, we discussed how you can use ads to raise brand awareness among your customers.

Create keyword-targeted ads and post them on Google to help draw traffic to your website. For example, I ran a keyword search for "kids shoes," and here's what I got:

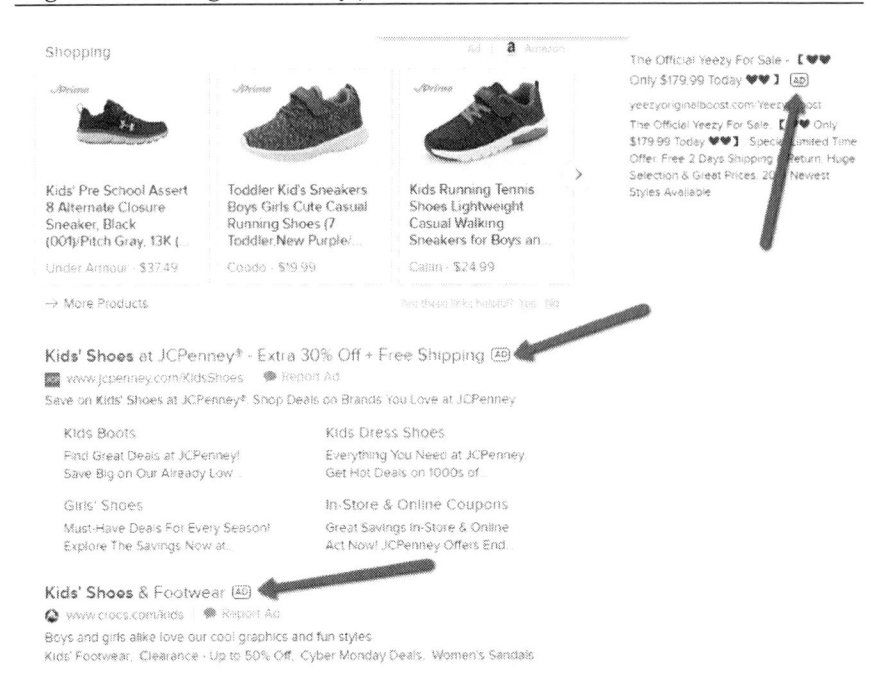

If a potential client is searching for shoes for their kids and types these keywords into the search engine, they'll be directed to those websites. This is how you attract leads to your business and engage them with your brand.

Create Laser-Focused Landing Pages

In chapter 2, we discussed the different types of landing pages and why they matter. Landing pages are also a great way to draw leads to your B2B brand.

When creating your landing pages, ensure that they're laser-focused on what you want to teach the customer. The actions you want customers to take the moment they land on the website should also be easy to discern.

Each of your landing pages should have a single CTA to keep the lead engaged and avoid confusing them about what they should do on that page. For example, on this website, the owner offers online courses, like cold email training. Here's the CTA on the site's landing page with the courses.

KILLER COLD EMAILING – A marketing course for freelance writing beginners who want to make their first $1,000 and beyond!

My premium marketing course for writers who are ready to create a full-time freelance writing business! This is best suited for beginners or more intermediate-level writers who aren't getting the results/clients they want from their marketing.

In this course, you'll learn how to:

- Choose a profitable freelance writing niche
- Set up a website/portfolio that sells
- Cold email and pitch your way to your first $1,000 freelance writing. EVEN IF you have no experience

Here are some **student results:**

"Just from 1 tiny change this course suggested. I'm bringing in an additional revenue every month!" – Abby

"One client paid me $1,200 for a single (feature-style) blog post." – Tara

"After changing my cold-emailing strategy and LinkedIn profile, I was able to attract and write for three high-paying clients all over $1,200 for each project the second week since enrolling in the course." – Krystal

Click here to learn more, and enroll for instant access!

>> The call-to-action button

Besides the single CTA per page, ensure that your website is mobile-responsive and target clients can access it effortlessly on their smartphones.

Create Webinars

You can use webinars to reach out to your target clients and promote your brand.

A report by the CMI shows that 43% of B2B brands use webinars to generate leads.

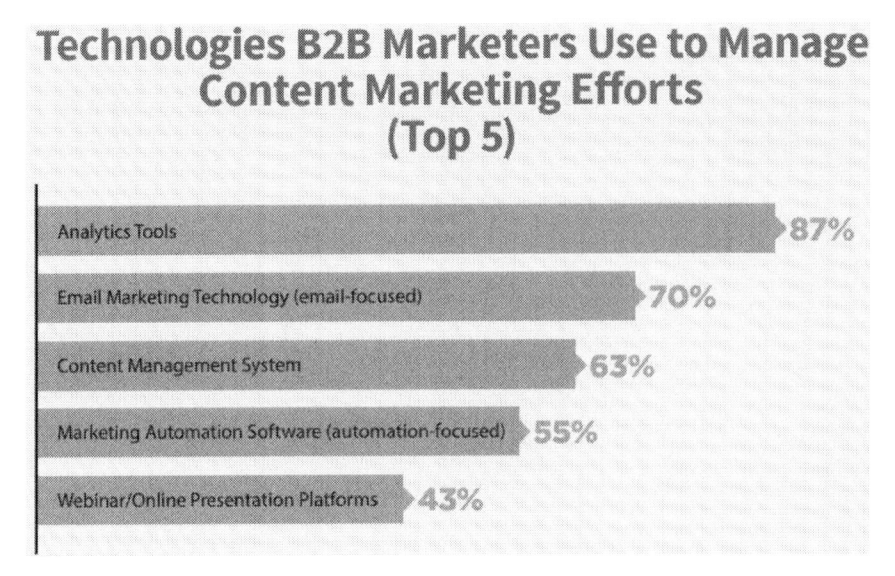

Technologies B2B Marketers Use to Manage Content Marketing Efforts (Top 5)

Technology	Percentage
Analytics Tools	87%
Email Marketing Technology (email-focused)	70%
Content Management System	63%
Marketing Automation Software (automation-focused)	55%
Webinar/Online Presentation Platforms	43%

This indicates that webinars can be a great source of leads for your business. Before you start preparing for the webinar, do thorough research to identify the main pain points of your target clients.

Create webinars that aim at giving insights to these target clients about how to resolve those difficulties. Present your webinar on a topic that interests and educates the target clients.

To increase signups for the webinar, consider a joint webinar presentation: collaborate with another business that offers the same services you do. Here's an example of a joint presentation:

Chapter 4: B2B Sales

LIVE TRAINING: THE THREE-STEP SYSTEM TO AUTOMATE YOUR MARKETING - AND FIND YOUR FIRST 10,000 READERS

Claim My Spot Now!

February 11 — **THURSDAY FEBRUARY 11th** at 3pm EST, 8pm GMT

Time left until session starts...
0 DAYS | 0 HOURS | 0 MINUTES | 0 SECONDS

Presented by **NICK STEPHENSON** And **DAVID SITEMAN GARLAND**

YOUR LIVE TRAINING WILL COVER:

- The Three-Step Formula You can use to Automate Your Audience Building
- How to Explode your Platform and Mailing List with Free List-Building Strategies
- The Four Reasons why people don't buy - and What you can do about it

Then you can tap into the other business's email list to grow the number of webinar subscribers and get more contact details for leads.

To achieve a high number of lead signups, remember to promote your webinar to your potential clients. You can use your website, social media sites, and communities to accomplish this. You can also send your email subscribers information about the webinar event and ask your social media connections to share it.

Choose the best day to actively promote your webinar. A BrightTALK report that was compiled by Smart Insights shows that Wednesday is the best day for webinar promotion.

Sunday	2%
Monday	21%
Tuesday	22%
Wednesday	23%
Thursday	19%
Friday	11%
Saturday	2%

It's essential to choose the right webinar platform for your presentation. You need to record your webinar using high-quality sound and images.

Choose a platform that supports both recording and replay features. This will help you send the webinar to the people on your email list and engage them even after the event is over. You can also send a link to the webinar to target clients who missed the live event to engage them.

Since most of your leads use mobile devices for their searches, ensure that the webinar platform is mobile-friendly.

B2B Sales Metrics to Track

To measure business growth, you need to track metrics that help you evaluate your business's progress. In this section, we'll talk about some of the most helpful metrics.

Customer Lifetime Value

Once you convert a lead, you can track how many sales you get from that particular client over a lifetime.

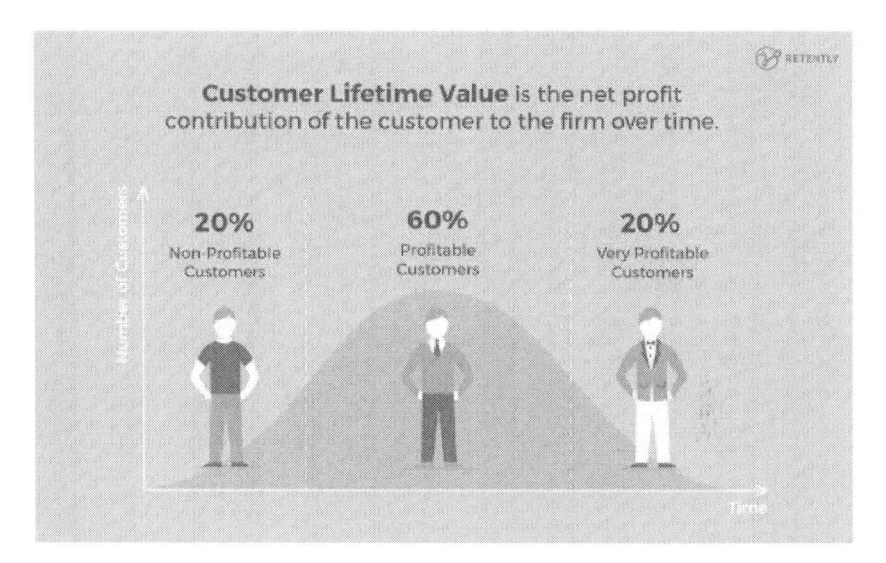

Customer Lifetime Value is the net profit contribution of the customer to the firm over time.

20%	60%	20%
Non-Profitable Customers	Profitable Customers	Very Profitable Customers

This means the customer will make repeat purchases of your products or services. Tracking repeat purchases is helpful when you want to evaluate how much a single customer brings to your business over a span of time.

You can use Net Promoter Score software to measure your customers' loyalty triggers and maximize them to draw more clients to make repeat purchases.

> **Net Promoter® Score (NPS®) is one of the most common customer experience metrics used by companies around the world. With Qualtrics' NPS software you get a simple, flexible and powerful platform to engage your customers.**
>
> **With Net Promoter® Score you can:**
>
> + Segment customers by loyalty
> + Identify unsatisfied and at-risk customers
> + Optimize around a single customer metric
> + Benchmark against industry and competitor scores
> + Uncover customer loyalty drivers
> + Monitor improvements in products, services and across the entire customer journey

Alongside this metric, you should track your customer serving cost. If it costs too much to serve your customers every time they make a repeat purchase, it won't do your business any good. You'll suffer losses even if a customer buys from your business again and again.

Lead Sources

You're not going to get all your leads from one marketing channel. As a marketer, you must track down your lead sources. Optimize channels that bring in more qualified leads at a low cost.

Video marketing is one of the most popular sources for leads. A report by the State of Inbound shows that more brands are including videos in their marketing.

Chapter 4: B2B Sales

STATE of INBOUND

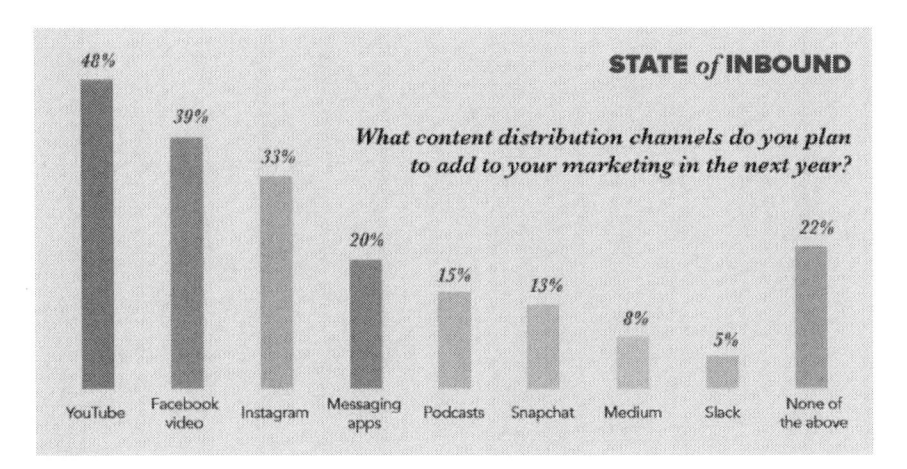

What content distribution channels do you plan to add to your marketing in the next year?

Channel	%
YouTube	48%
Facebook video	39%
Instagram	33%
Messaging apps	20%
Podcasts	15%
Snapchat	13%
Medium	8%
Slack	5%
None of the above	22%

When you search for leads, focus on sources that are hotbeds of potential customers for your specific brand. For example, LinkedIn is the leading source for B2B leads.

Average Sales Cycle

Measuring this metric helps shorten your cycle. You need to evaluate the time it takes from a customer's initial engagement with your business until you convert them to a client.

This metric helps you to creatively devise ways to shorten the cycle and engage more leads with your business brand. It also tells you how efficient your sales operations are to your customers.

Tracking your sales cycle and lead conversion helps you plan the best ways to achieve your business revenue goals and grow your business faster.

Conversion Rates

Your ultimate goal for your branding and marketing is to acquire leads who can convert into clients and buy your services or products.

That's why this metric is key. You need to know how many leads are converting into clients. You can track whether they convert the first time they visit your website or during a repeat visit.

This helps you know how to provide more value to keep the leads coming to your website and convert them. Here's an example of a conversion rate funnel for e-commerce brands.

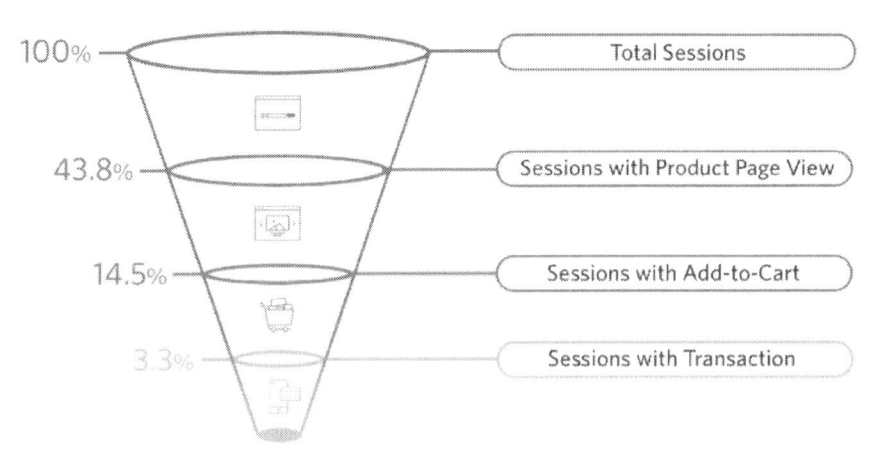

```
100%  ─────── Total Sessions
43.8% ─────── Sessions with Product Page View
14.5% ─────── Sessions with Add-to-Cart
3.3%  ─────── Sessions with Transaction
```

Converting leads to customers is a top priority for brands, according to HubSpot research, so effectively tracking this metric is fundamental to success.

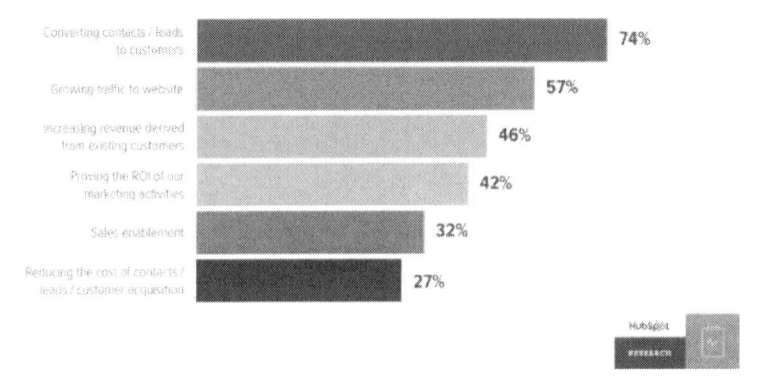

What are your company's top marketing priorities over the next 12 months?

Priority	%
Converting contacts / leads to customers	74%
Growing traffic to website	57%
Increasing revenue derived from existing customers	46%
Proving the ROI of our marketing activities	42%
Sales enablement	32%
Reducing the cost of contacts / leads / customer acquisition	27%

HubSpot Research

Monthly Recurring Revenue

If you're in the SaaS business, your customers will use your services by subscribing on either a monthly or yearly basis.

For example, here's the Voy Media pricing model:

Chapter 4: B2B Sales

STANDARD	GROWTH	PRO	ENTERPRISE
If your advertising is $1,000 - $19,999 a month	If your advertising is $20,000 - $49,999 a month	If your advertising is $50,000 - $500k/month	If your advertising is $500k - $1M/month
Free Account Setup	Free Account Setup	Free Account Setup	Free Account Setup
$0 Setup Fee	$0 Setup Fee	$0 Setup Fee	$0 Setup Fee
Full Service Facebook & Instagram Ads	Full Service Facebook & Instagram Ads	Full Service Facebook & Instagram Ads	Full Service Facebook & Instagram Ads
Facebook & Audience Network Retargeting	Facebook & Audience Network Retargeting	Facebook & Audience Network Retargeting	Facebook & Audience Network Retargeting
Dedicated Account Manager	Dedicated Account Manager	Dedicated Account Manager	Dedicated Account Strategist, Creative Designer
1 on 1 Strategy Consultations	1 on 1 Strategy Consultations	1 on 1 Strategy Consultations	1 on 1 Strategy Consultations
Return on Ad Spend Tracking	Return on Ad Spend Tracking	Return on Ad Spend Tracking	Return on Ad Spend Tracking
Real Time Analytics	Real Time Analytics	Real Time Analytics	Real Time Analytics
Email, Skype, Phone Contact	Email, Skype, Phone Contact	Email, Skype, Phone Contact	Access to Personal Phone
Bi-weekly Reporting	Bi-weekly Reporting	On Demand Reporting	On Demand Reporting
PER MONTH $2K or 20% of Ad Budget, the greater	PER MONTH 15% of Ad Budget	PER MONTH 10% of Ad Budget	PER MONTH 9% of Ad Budget
CHOOSE PLAN	CHOOSE PLAN	CHOOSE PLAN	CHOOSE PLAN

With this pricing model, tracking the monthly revenue you get from your customers can help you make a plan to achieve your marketing goals. You should set lead conversion targets to grow your recurring monthly income to the level of your goals.

Number of Closed Deals

Many leads enter your sales cycle, but not all of them convert into customers. With this metric, you can calculate the total number of leads that convert out of those that entered your sales cycle.

Deals closed = (number of closed deals / total) × 100

If the percentage of closed deals is low, you'll need to monitor where your leads are disappearing from your sales cycle. Once you've determined what's making them drop out, solve those problems to increase your conversion rate.

Customer Acquisition Costs

Your business will incur expenses in the process of acquiring a customer. It costs <u>five times more to acquire a new customer</u> than to retain an existing one.

If you're spending more on the process of acquiring a new customer than the customer is spending on your business, you need to change your marketing strategy.

With this metric, you can measure how expensive your marketing process is and come up with strategic plans to acquire more customers at reduced costs.

Customer Net Worth

Loyal customers are hard to get and, as a brand, you'll retain them only by valuing them and giving them the best you can.

This metric is the difference between the lifetime value the customer brings to your business and the total costs you incurred in the process of acquiring the customer. You can express this value as the ratio of CLV: CAC (customer lifetime value to customer acquisition cost).

This metric helps you plan your business's strategic growth based on the return on investment from the customer. It also helps you spot the most loyal customers who spend heavily on your business so you can give them better service to solve their problems.

How to Improve Lead Conversion

You now know the metrics you can use to monitor your B2B sales. However, the most important thing is to convert as many leads as possible into clients for your business, right?

You need to come up with a strategic plan to improve lead conversion rates. Here are some effective tactics.

Start Lead Scoring to Access and Qualify Leads

You don't just want leads to take action on your business, but action that can lead them to convert into clients. Therefore, you need to assign your leads scores based on the activities they perform on your site. This approach can keep you from wasting time, money, and energy on leads that are less likely to convert.

Chapter 4: B2B Sales

For instance, you can give your leads points if they

- Open your emails
- Like your content
- Comment on your content
- Share your content
- Subscribe to your newsletters

You can then set a score target at which you'll consider them marketing-qualified leads (MQLs) for your brand. Once they qualify, you can be more confident that your efforts will lead to conversions.

The Marketo lead scoring process is a good example of how lead scoring works:

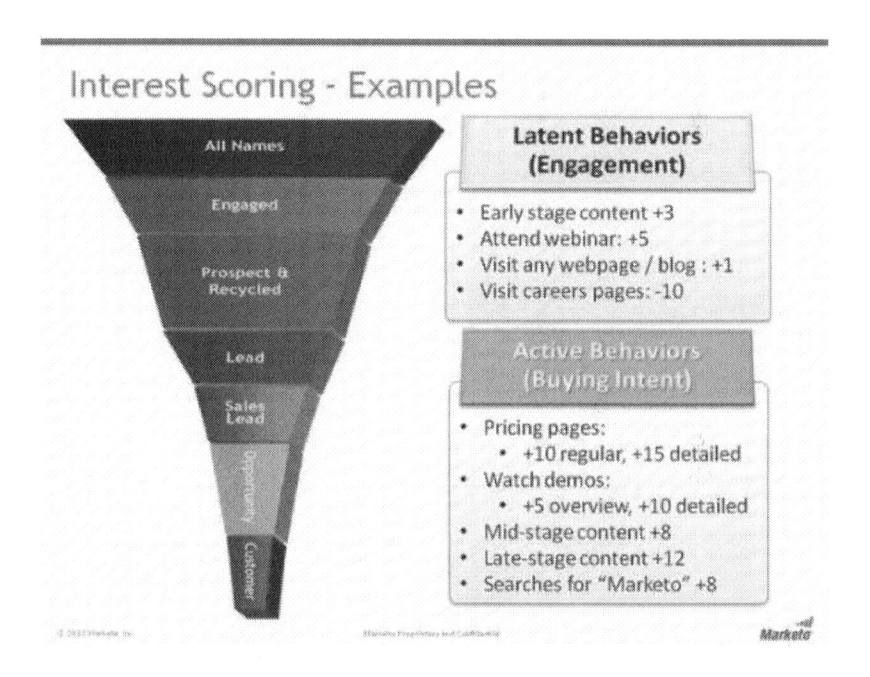

Interest Scoring - Examples

Latent Behaviors (Engagement)
- Early stage content +3
- Attend webinar: +5
- Visit any webpage / blog : +1
- Visit careers pages: -10

Active Behaviors (Buying Intent)
- Pricing pages:
  - +10 regular, +15 detailed
- Watch demos:
  - +5 overview, +10 detailed
- Mid-stage content +8
- Late-stage content +12
- Searches for "Marketo" +8

Follow a Documented Content Marketing Strategy

Your readers and potential clients want to receive fresh, original content from you on a regular basis. As a business marketer, you need to have a documented strategy for producing and promoting your content.

Some brands that use this method have seen great results from it. A report by the CMI shows that 42% of organizations have a documented content marketing strategy.

Proportion of Agency Marketers With a Content Marketing Strategy

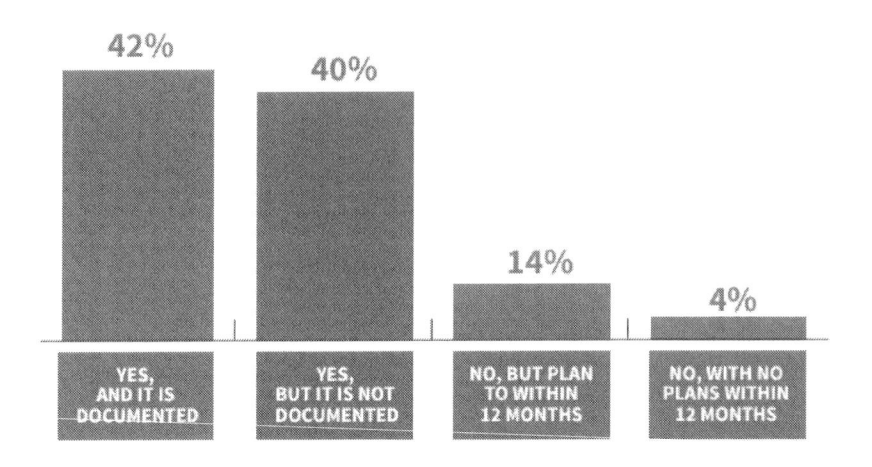

Category	Percentage
YES, AND IT IS DOCUMENTED	42%
YES, BUT IT IS NOT DOCUMENTED	40%
NO, BUT PLAN TO WITHIN 12 MONTHS	14%
NO, WITH NO PLANS WITHIN 12 MONTHS	4%

Base: Agency content marketers; aided list.

Agency Content Marketing 2019. Benchmarks, Budgets, and Trends—Content Marketing Institute/MarketingProfs

A documented strategy offers a range of advantages to improve your brand growth and lead conversion rate.

Benefits of a Documented Agency Content Marketing Strategy

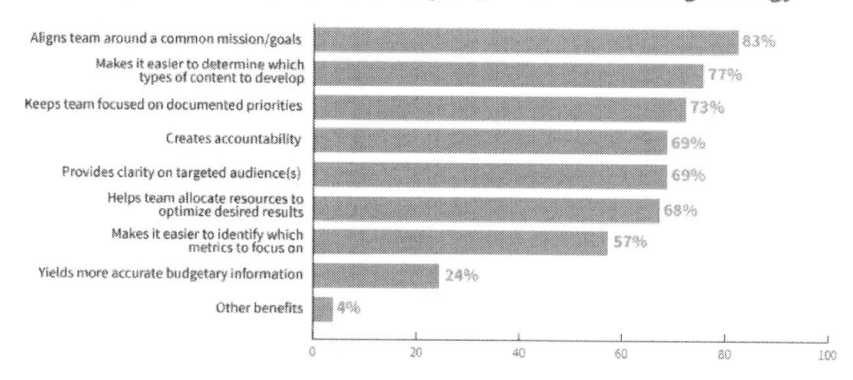

Benefit	%
Aligns team around a common mission/goals	83%
Makes it easier to determine which types of content to develop	77%
Keeps team focused on documented priorities	73%
Creates accountability	69%
Provides clarity on targeted audience(s)	69%
Helps team allocate resources to optimize desired results	68%
Makes it easier to identify which metrics to focus on	57%
Yields more accurate budgetary information	24%
Other benefits	4%

Base: Agency content marketers who have a documented content marketing strategy. Aided list; multiple responses permitted.

Agency Content Marketing 2019: Benchmarks, Budgets, and Trends—Content Marketing Institute/MarketingProfs

For instance, once you determine the right kind of content to create, you'll attract more target leads to your brand. Since you offer high-quality content, you'll engage them and become a thought leader. They'll trust you more and be more likely to convert and use your products or services.

Use Email Marketing Software

Once you get your leads' contact information, you need to nurture them through the sales cycle. One great way is to use email marketing.

Streamlining the process and track your progress toward lead conversion is simple with email marketing software. Research by the CMI shows that 73% of marketers use email marketing software as part of their lead nurturing campaigns.

Types of Technologies Agency Marketers Use to Assist With the Management of Content Marketing Efforts

Technology	Percentage
Analytics Tools	83%
Social Media Publishing/Analytics	82%
Email Marketing Software	73%
Content Creation/Optimization	65%
Content Management System (CMS)	62%
Workflow/Project Management/Editorial Calendaring	57%
Marketing Automation System	39%
Content Syndication/Promotional Tools	28%
Integrated Content Marketing Platform (CMP)	15%
Chatbots	12%
Artificial Intelligence (AI)	1%

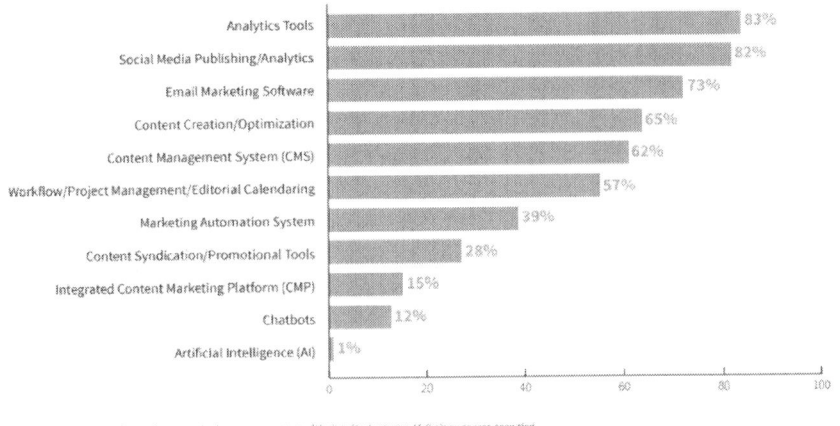

Base: Agency content marketers whose organizations use one or more of the listed technologies. Multiple responses permitted.

Agency Content Marketing 2019: Benchmarks, Budgets, and Trends—Content Marketing Institute/MarketingProfs

Also, integrate your CRM with other marketing automation software to boost the effectiveness of your lead generation and nurturing campaigns.

Have a mobile-friendly website

Many leads judge your business by the professionalism of your website. Ensure that your site is easy to navigate and mobile-friendly.

Consider using accelerated mobile pages (AMPs), which load faster on mobile devices. Your web design should be responsive and beautiful to catch the attention of your readers.

Remember, more and more website traffic comes from mobile devices every year, as shown in Statista research.

Chapter 4: B2B Sales

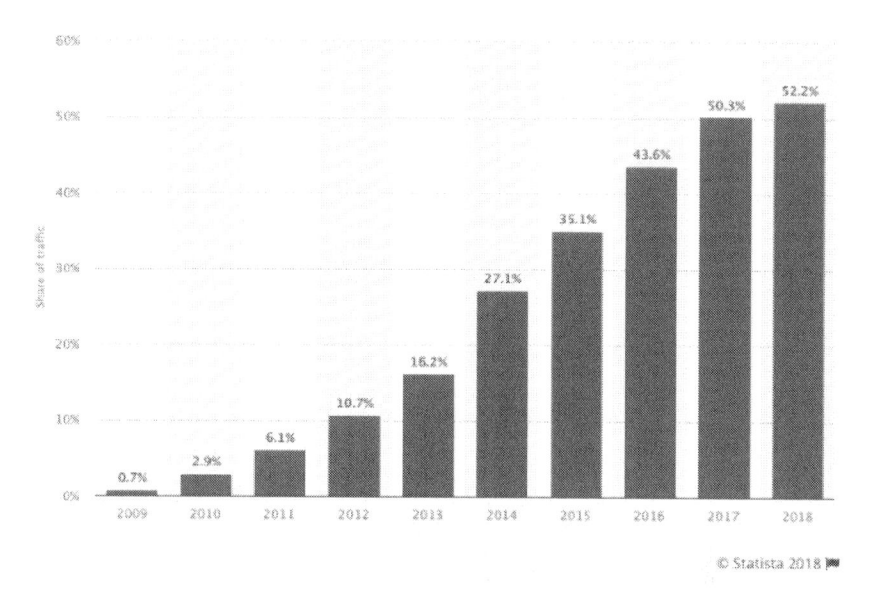

Year	Share of traffic
2009	0.7%
2010	2.9%
2011	6.1%
2012	10.7%
2013	16.2%
2014	27.1%
2015	35.1%
2016	43.6%
2017	50.3%
2018	52.2%

© Statista 2018

Avoid incorporating pop-ups that can distract your target client as they browse your site. Your landing page content should be prominent and simple, with a clear call-to-action for your target clients.

Test and Optimize Your CTA

Want your readers to take action and buy something from your brand? Then you need to keep testing your calls-to-action to see what works well, and then optimize them.

This will lead to more target clients to act, which can result in sales. Use attractive colors that will invite your leads to respond to your CTAs. For more about how the right colors can influence your prospective clients, see chapter 2, "Essentials of a Perfect Landing Page: Images and Videos."

Watch Your Competitors

Other brands are offering the same services or products as you and targeting the same clients you want. You can research them to see how they market their business, engage leads, and convert them. This will give you insight into your own business growth. Implement tips you learn from them, but don't copy them.

Visit the websites of your competitors and check out the type of content they produce. Also, study their website design and social media engagement. You'll get a glimpse of how they interact with their target customers and how you, too, can interact with them to promote trust and engagement.

Produce Video Content

Video marketing is increasingly popular online. Many potential customers now consume more video content than any other type of content.

Research by the CMI shows that 72% of marketers use video content to market their business.

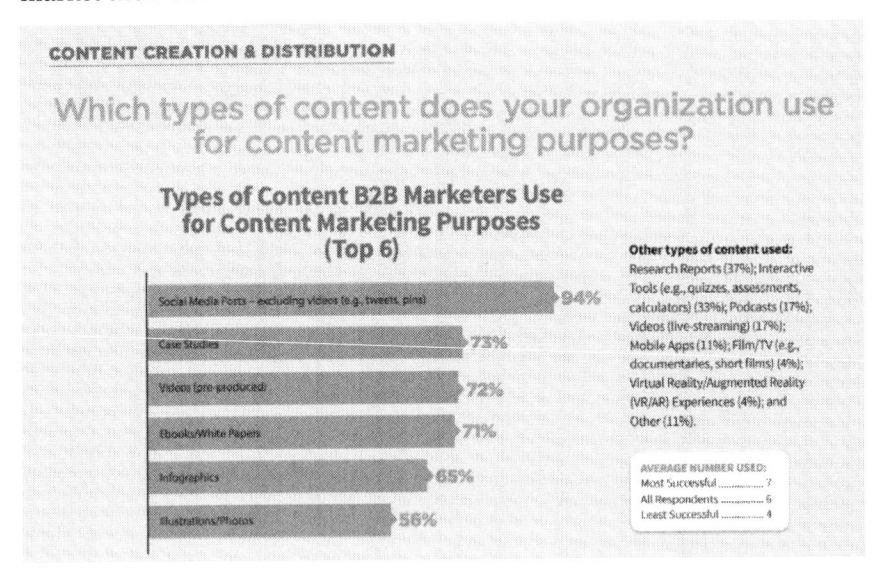

CONTENT CREATION & DISTRIBUTION

Which types of content does your organization use for content marketing purposes?

Types of Content B2B Marketers Use for Content Marketing Purposes (Top 6)

- Social Media Posts – excluding videos (e.g. tweets, pins) — 94%
- Case Studies — 73%
- Videos (pre-produced) — 72%
- Ebooks/White Papers — 71%
- Infographics — 65%
- Illustrations/Photos — 56%

Other types of content used: Research Reports (37%); Interactive Tools (e.g., quizzes, assessments, calculators) (33%); Podcasts (17%); Videos (live-streaming) (17%); Mobile Apps (11%); Film/TV (e.g., documentaries, short films) (4%); Virtual Reality/Augmented Reality (VR/AR) Experiences (4%); and Other (11%).

AVERAGE NUMBER USED:
Most Successful 7
All Respondents 6
Least Successful 4

Since your primary goal is to engage leads and convert them, you need to create video content. For instance, you can create a demo video to explain how your products work to your potential customers.

You can also create video content that explains how to use your products or services with in-depth insights that can effectively solve their pains.

Here are some examples from the Shopify website:

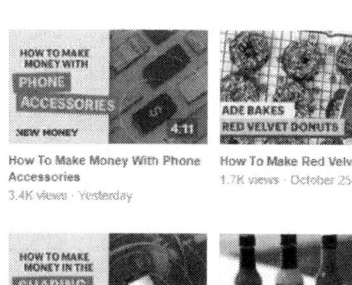

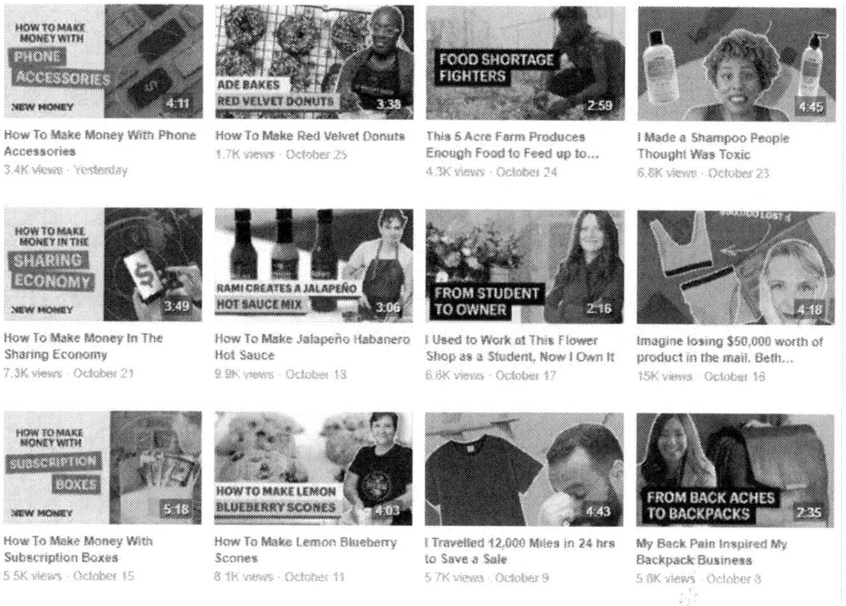

Chapter 4: B2B Sales

Another good approach is to ask your past clients to participate in video testimonials. Your target customers will find it easy to listen to and watch testimonials from these past clients, which will build more trust and increase the chances of conversion.

Among the many different types of videos you can create to market your business, consider these:

- Explanation videos
- How-to videos
- Product demonstration videos
- Launch videos
- Customer testimonials

Any type you produce can help move your target clients down the sales funnel.

By giving potential customers what they want, you'll increase your lead conversions and bring more clients to your business.

Nurture Your Leads

The buyer journey for B2B customers can be long and complicated. If you don't guide your potential clients and nurture them along the buyer journey, they'll lose interest and start looking into your competitors.

Provide in-depth, entertaining, and educational content that will illuminate your business better and demonstrate how it can help them get rid of their pain points.

Nurturing your leads in the right way will build more trust and increase conversions. For instance, personalizing each email you send your leads shows them you care about them. It means you've taken time to research them and their business and to devise a helpful strategy.

According to Marketo research, 96% of leads who visit your website are not ready to buy. The way you present your business to your leads and nurture them will determine whether they convert into customers or leave your business.

A report by Ascend2 shows that the most important lead generation strategy objective for 71% of brands is to convert leads into customers.

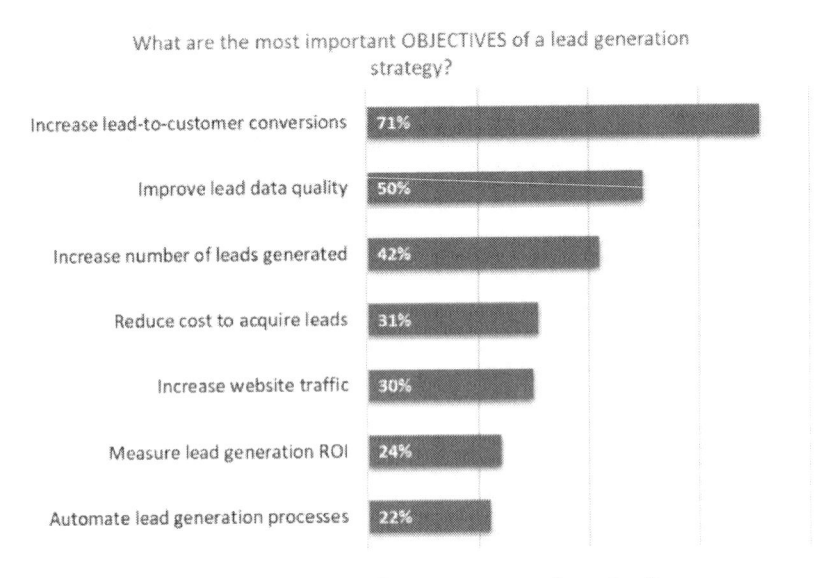

What are the most important OBJECTIVES of a lead generation strategy?

Objective	Percentage
Increase lead-to-customer conversions	71%
Improve lead data quality	50%
Increase number of leads generated	42%
Reduce cost to acquire leads	31%
Increase website traffic	30%
Measure lead generation ROI	24%
Automate lead generation processes	22%

Ascend2

Lead Generation to Increase Conversions Survey
Ascend2 and Research Partners, August 2017

At the same time, the report shows that less than half are "very successful" at achieving that goal.

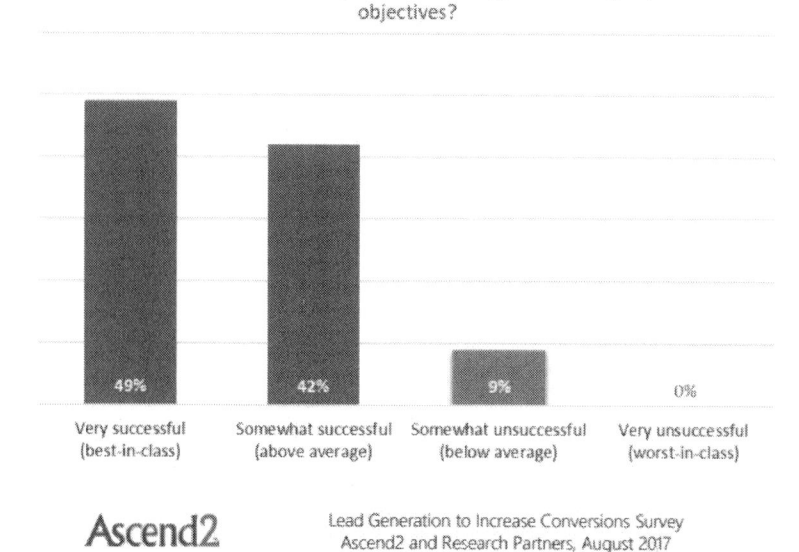

How SUCCESSFUL is a lead generation strategy at achieving important objectives?

Very successful (best-in-class)	Somewhat successful (above average)	Somewhat unsuccessful (below average)	Very unsuccessful (worst-in-class)
49%	42%	9%	0%

Ascend2 — Lead Generation to Increase Conversions Survey
Ascend2 and Research Partners, August 2017

Brands have to convince their leads to use of their services or products. That's why, among B2B brands, 53% of sales cycles are long and involve influencers who try to help build trust with leads.

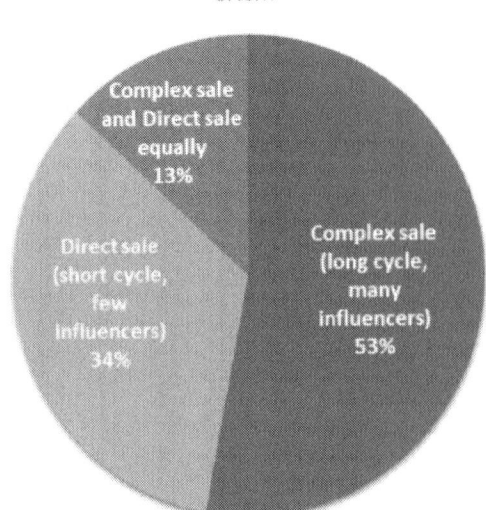

Which best describes the type of SALES CYCLE encountered most often?

- Complex sale and Direct sale equally: 13%
- Direct sale (short cycle, few influencers): 34%
- Complex sale (long cycle, many influencers): 53%

Ascend2 — Lead Generation to Increase Conversions Survey, Ascend2 and Research Partners, August 2017

Tools to Increase B2B Sales

Running an online business can be hard, especially when you're just starting out and need to increase brand awareness to generate more leads and sales.

These tools can be integral to your lead generation, marketing, lead conversion, and sales.

Gong

You need to use all the possible means to ensure that your leads take action and convert into clients, right?

Gong software is the answer. It enables you to collect your customer insights to find ways to deliver value. These insights lead to closing more deals with your leads.

The business team can make decisions based on real insights from customers rather than just team members' opinions. This leads to better ways to solve pain points and convert leads.

To simplify the collection of these insights, integrate the software with your various marketing channels.

You can visit the Gong website and fill out a form to request pricing details. It requires very little information:

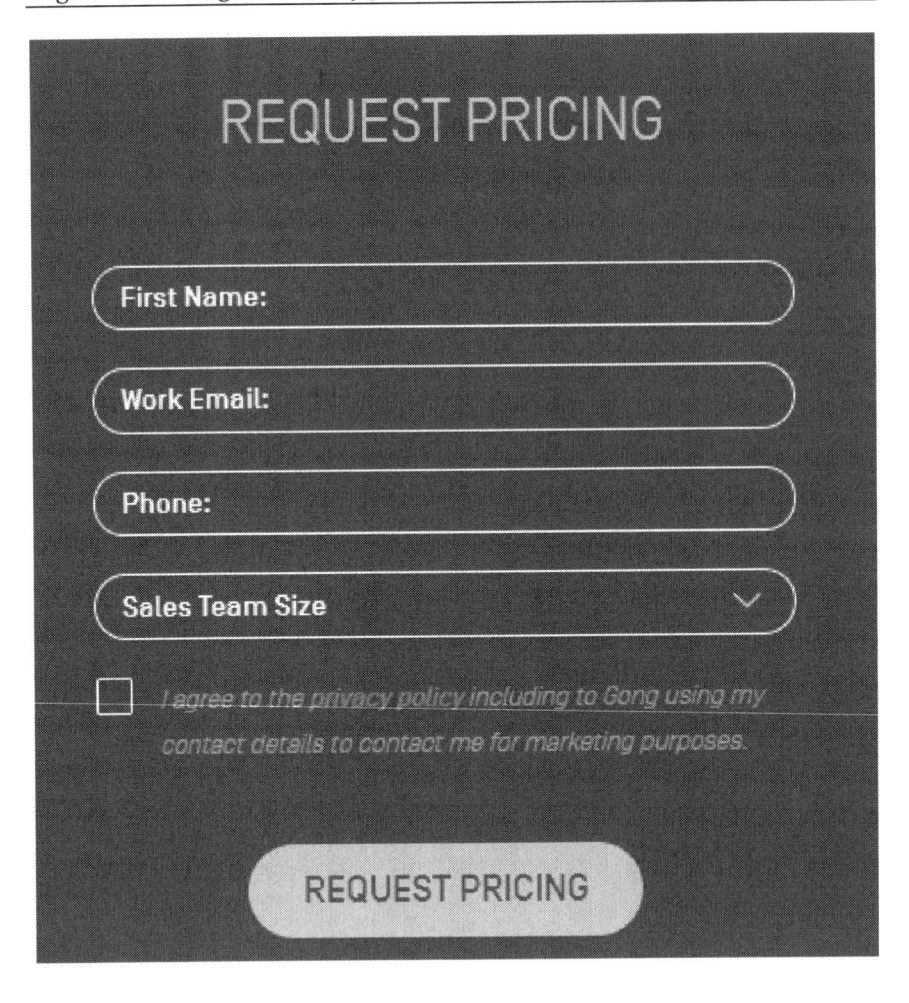

Zendesk

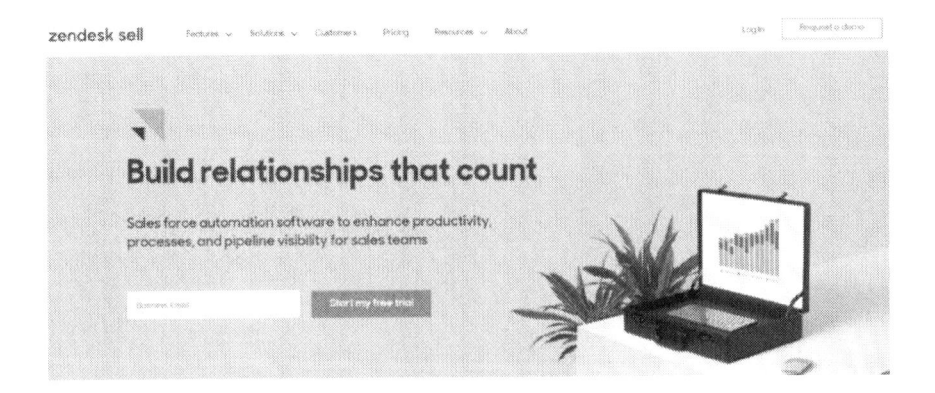

You need to keep track of your leads' progress through the sales cycle. This tool helps you manage your customer relationships.

It lets you easily track all communications with your customers and potential customers and keep improving your lead nurturing process to increase conversions.

Here are some of the features of this great marketing tool:

All-In-One Sales Platform

Sell
Manage your sales process and customer relationships.

Communicate
Get smarter, more seamless communication tools.

Integrate
Sync your data and tools to Sell easily with our API.

Prospect
Prospecting suite with lead discovery and enrichment.

Implement & Integrate

Success
Trust our expert, in-house implementation team.

Marketplace
Explore our integrations and sync your sales tools.

You can integrate a number of other tools with this software to help run your business and increase conversions and sales.

LinkedIn Sales Navigator

Linkedin is the best platform for any B2B brand looking to increase brand awareness, generate more leads, and bolster sales.

Most of the B2B leads you to want to reach and convert into customers are using LinkedIn. A Sumo report shows that a large share of traffic from social sites to blogs and websites comes from LinkedIn.

LINKEDIN DRIVES MORE TRAFFIC TO B2B BLOGS & SITES

90% of the social traffic was driven by the big three networks, with half of it coming from LinkedIn

You can take advantage of this great channel and use its Sales Navigator tool to grow your B2B sales. Here are some things the tool can help with:

Target	Understand	Engage
Find the right people and companies faster	Keep track of key lead and company changes.	Reach and engage with prospects

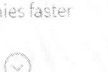

Chapter 4: B2B Sales

Here's the pricing for the Sales Navigator tool:

You can visit the website and learn more about the pricing structure and features of every single Sales Navigator plan.

Crystal

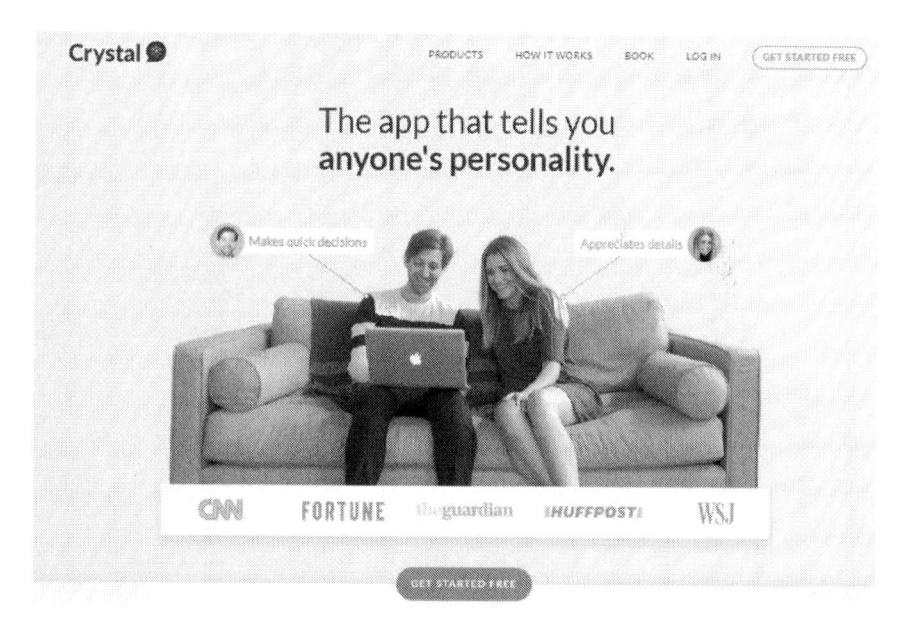

Different leads have different personalities that affect their buying decisions and the brands they choose. With this tool, you can analyze the personality of your target customers and create content that suits them.

For instance, some of your potential clients will require in-depth information about your business before they'll buy from you. Others will just need to see testimonials from past clients to be convinced.

Some will take longer to make decisions, while others have a rapid decision-making process. Knowing the personality of each of your leads will help you understand how to nurture them into esteemed customers for your business.

LeadSquared

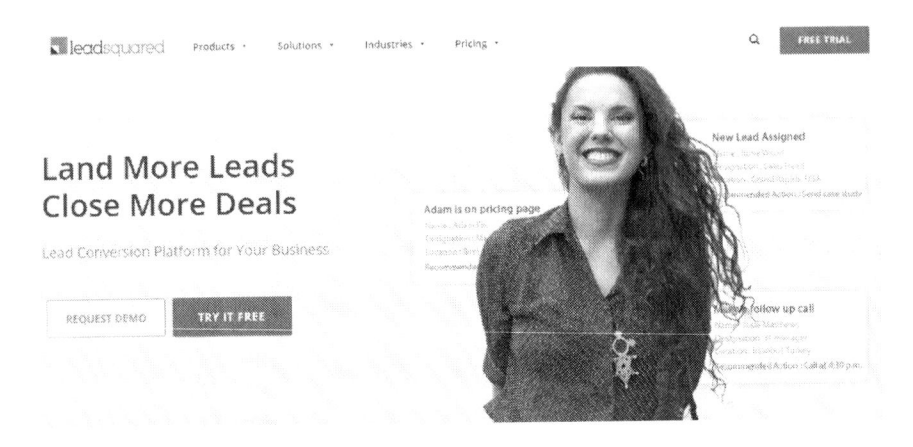

If you want to increase your lead generation, nurture your leads, and land more business deals, this tool can offer some substantial assistance.

The tool easily captures leads from different sources and draws them to your business. You can analyze the performance of your leads as you nurture them smoothly through the buyer journey stages, earn their trust, and close deals with them.

This tool integrates with many different platforms.

Chapter 4: B2B Sales

Leadfeeder

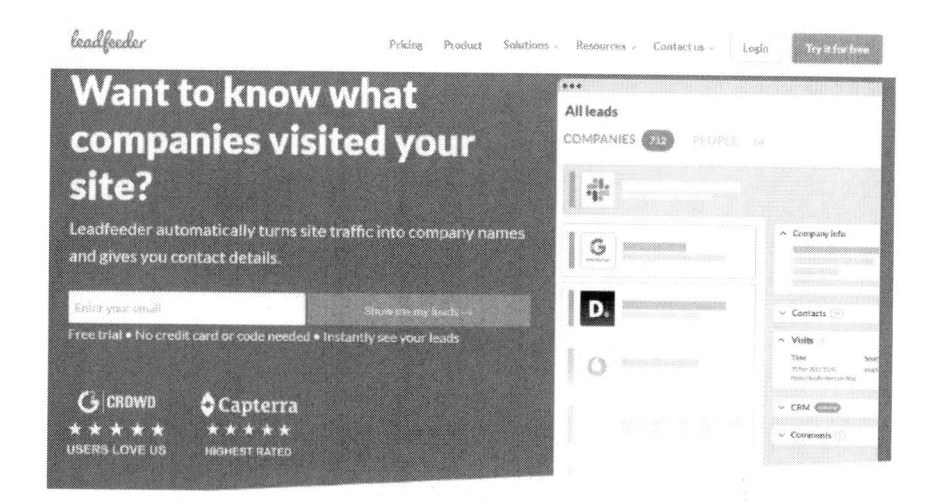

Most potential clients start searching for a solution online. Because you've optimized your website and social media accounts, most of these leads will find your website.

However, some will leave your site the moment they land on it. With Leadfeeder, you can get the contact details of these leads and follow up to nurture them.

The tool helps you track all your website visitors so you can gather data about their pain points and find the best way to help them.

Here's the tool's pricing model:

LITE

A basic version of Leadfeeder with limited features that shows the last 7 days worth of leads only

$0 /month

Sign up

Always free

PREMIUM

All features. Start with a Premium trial and if you do nothing you will be downgraded to Lite after 2 weeks

from $53 /month

Start your free trial

No credit card required

How we calculate the price

And here are the details for the two pricing models:

	LITE	PREMIUM
Unlimited users	✓	✓
Data retention	Last 7 days	Unlimited
Number of leads	Max 100 leads	Up to unlimited (Depends on price tier.)
Company details	✓	✓
Contacts database		✓
Custom feeds		✓
Custom feeds		✓
Visit details		✓
CRM integrations		✓
Dedicated customer success manager		✓
Powerful filtering		✓
Collaboration tools		✓
Imported lists		✓

Close

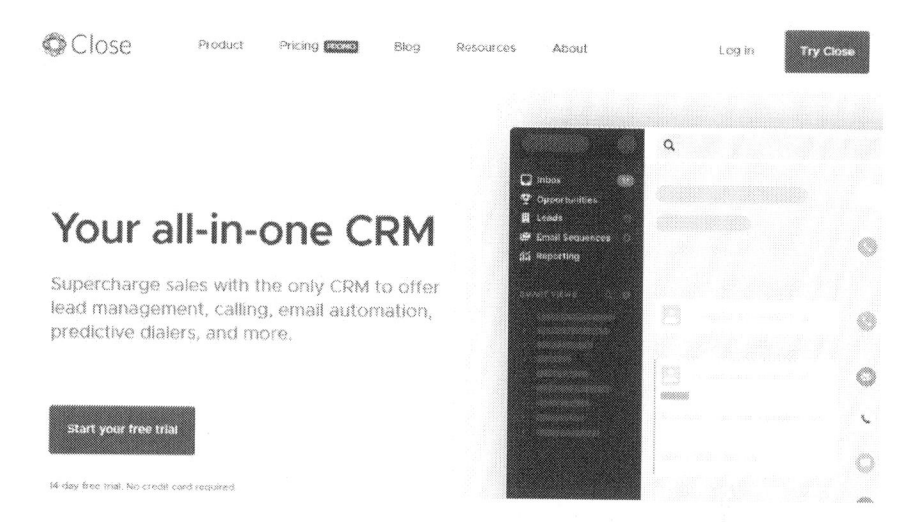

Your all-in-one CRM

Supercharge sales with the only CRM to offer lead management, calling, email automation, predictive dialers, and more.

If you're running a SaaS business, then you need a well-organized CRM. Effectively managing your business operations makes it easy to engage with potential customers and convince them to use your services or products.

Here are some of the platforms you can integrate with this tool:

Zapier	**Help Scout**	**Zendesk**
Connect to 1,000+ apps	Customer Messaging	Customer Messaging
Intercom	**Drift**	**PandaDoc**
Customer Engagement	Conversation Marketing	Document Automation
Get Accept	**Slack**	**99Inbound**
Document Automation	Messaging Platform	Form Builder

Chapter 4: B2B Sales

Cardin	**LeadFuze**	**LinkMatch**
Lead Generation	Lead Generation	Lead Generation
HubSpot	**Marketo**	**Mailchimp**
Marketing Automation	Marketing Automation	Email Marketing
Unbounce	**Facebook Ad Leads**	**Gong**
Landing Page Builder	Marketing	Call Analytics
Plecto	**Google Sheets**	**CommissionApp**
Analytics	Spreadsheet	Commission Calculation
Process Street	**Retool**	**Stitch**
Workflow Management	Custom App Builder	Data Replication ETL

You can effortlessly manage your lead nurturing process and build trust with your target clients that can lead to more conversions and sales.

Here's the pricing model for this software:

Close more deals faster, for *even* less

Get a modern CRM with built-in email and calling at an unbeatable value.

STARTER	BASIC	PROFESSIONAL	BUSINESS
The best all-in-one sales starter kit for 1-3 person teams	Scale up your sales outreach efforts with a single tool	Automate outreach with built-in Email Sequences and Power Dialer	The ultimate all-in-one CRM and sales productivity solution
$35	$65	$76 / $95	$116 / $145
per user per month	per user per month	per user per month	per user per month
Try for free	Try for free	Try for free	Try for free

Clickfunnels

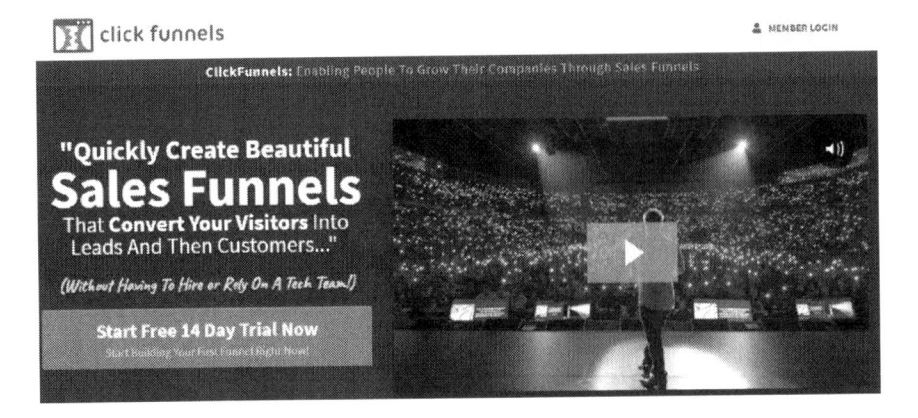

"Quickly Create Beautiful Sales Funnels That **Convert Your Visitors** Into Leads And Then Customers..."

Acquiring clients for B2B business is a long, complicated process. You need a great tool to help you create and organize your sales funnel.

You can efficiently direct your leads through the nurturing process without any confusion, which makes them more likely to convert and use your business's products or services.

Generate leads for your business using the great tools this software provides. The beautiful pages you design will help you sell your business to your target clients.

Here's the pricing model for this tool:

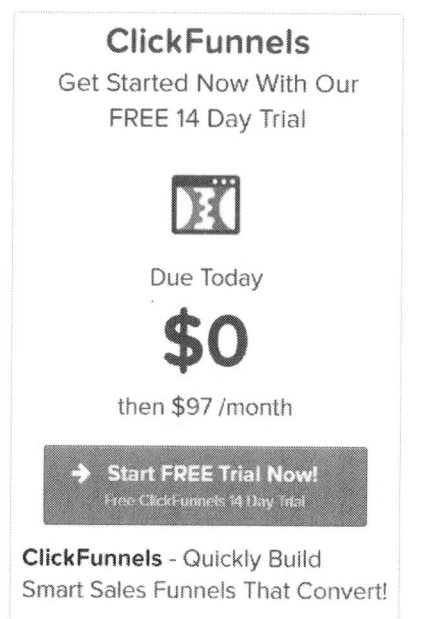

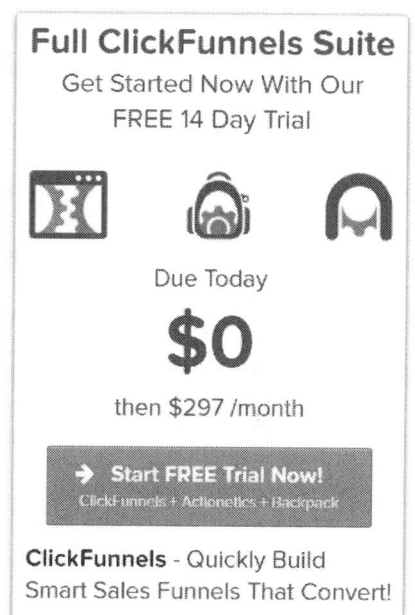

ClickFunnels	Full ClickFunnels Suite
Get Started Now With Our FREE 14 Day Trial	Get Started Now With Our FREE 14 Day Trial
Due Today	Due Today
$0	**$0**
then $97 /month	then $297 /month
→ Start FREE Trial Now! Free ClickFunnels 14 Day Trial	→ Start FREE Trial Now! ClickFunnels + Actionetics + Backpack
ClickFunnels - Quickly Build Smart Sales Funnels That Convert!	**ClickFunnels** - Quickly Build Smart Sales Funnels That Convert!

Best B2B Sales Books to Read

Knowledge is power. The online world changes each day, and marketers need to have the right knowledge to adapt to these changes.

Customer demands are ever-changing, too. If your business doesn't keep up with market trends, it will be difficult to serve your clients and satisfy their pain points.

To stay updated with fresh knowledge and grow your business, here are some books you can read.

Eat Their Lunch by Anthony Iannarino

You're constantly reaching out to potential buyers in hopes of converting them into clients. That means you need to learn how to beat your competitors in your market niche and win those clients.

This book will teach you how to acquire your competitors' clients and offer them your products or services to solve their challenges.

Conversations That Win the Complex Sale by Erik Peterson and Tim Riesterer

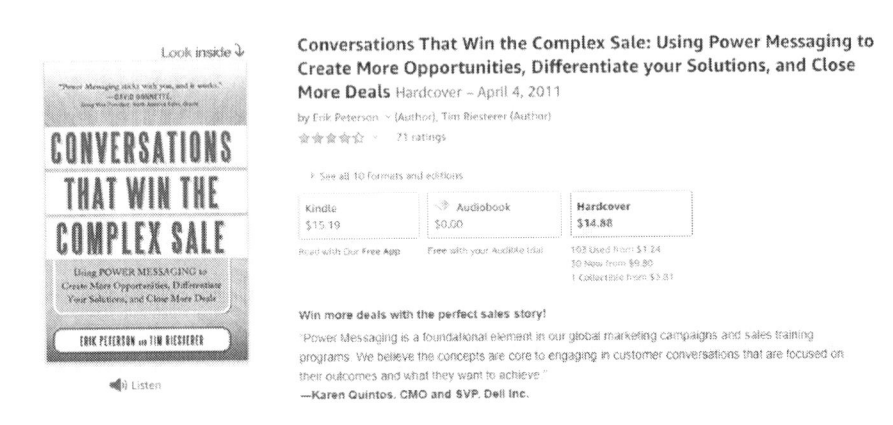

Sales stories can play a vital role in engaging and converting leads into customers.

By reading this book, you'll learn how to write messages and copy that close more deals for your brands and double your sales. Peterson will teach you how to create first impressions with your leads and draw their attention to your business. You'll become an expert on engaging your leads with great conversations that lead to further engagement and lead conversion.

High-Profit Prospecting by Mark Hunter

Technology advancements have brought lots of changes to the online business world. This book will give you in-depth knowledge of how you can leverage and use these digital changes to grow your business.

You'll learn how to engage leads on social media, optimize your website, and create a unique brand voice to beat your competitors.

Then you'll cover how to prospect the right way, manage your sales pipeline, and increase your lead conversions, business sales, and revenue.

Sales Differentiation by Lee B. Salz

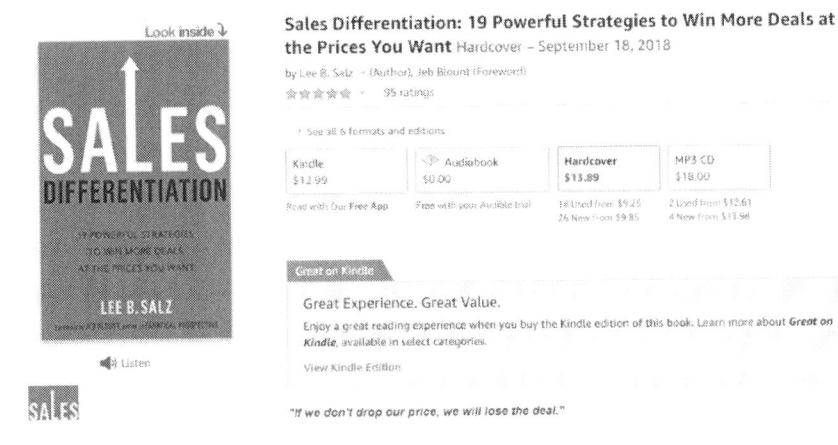

You've set your price target for acquiring leads to your business, and it seems you're not acquiring leads.

This book will show you how to win great deals for your business within your price margins. You'll learn how to differentiate your business from your competitors and win more deals.

Sales Manifesto by Jeffrey Gitomer

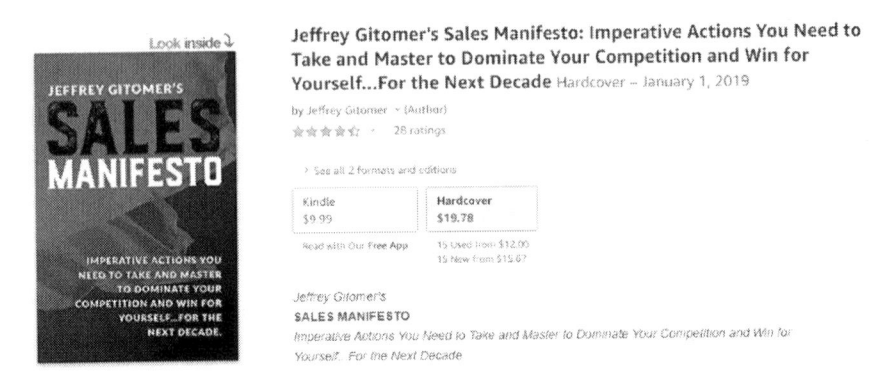

There will always be competitors in your business niche, so you need a superior marketing strategy to stay ahead of them.

This book shows you how to build long-term relationships with your target clients. You can keep these customers for the long haul and enjoy repeat revenue.

Chapter 4: B2B Sales

You'll also learn about the marketing elements you can use to increase your profits and grow your business.

Deep Work: Rules for Focused Success in a Distracted World by Cal Newport

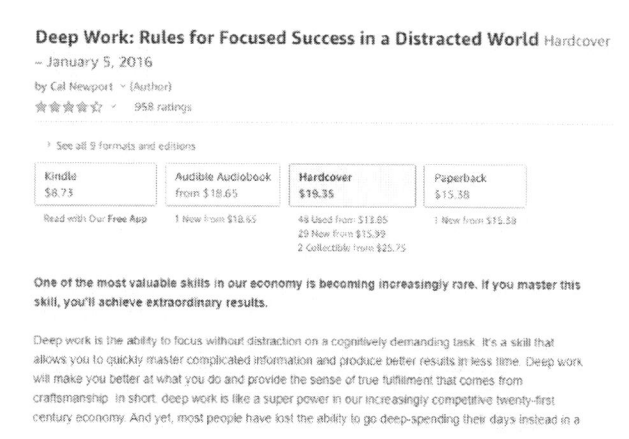

The online world is full of distractions that can affect your ability to market your brand to your target audience. You'll learn how to focus on your goals and give your best to achieve business growth.

The Challenger Sale: Taking Control of the Customer Conversation by Matthew Dixon and Brent Adamson

The research presented in this book shows that every sales rep has one of these five profiles:

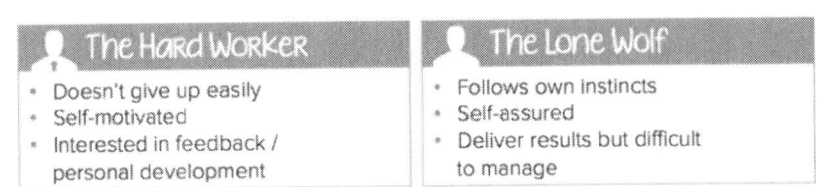

The Hard Worker
- Doesn't give up easily
- Self-motivated
- Interested in feedback / personal development

The Lone Wolf
- Follows own instincts
- Self-assured
- Deliver results but difficult to manage

The Relationship Builder
- Classic consultative rep
- Builds advocates internally
- Creates relationships with prospects

The Challenger
- Different view of the world
- Loves to debate / pushes customer
- Strong understanding of customer's business

The Problem Solver
- Highly detail-oriented
- Reliable responds to stakeholders
- Ensures all problems are solved

Based on your profile, this book will teach you how to reach your target market, engage them, and take control of the conversation. This gives you the upper hand of knowing more about your customers and providing the best solutions to their challenges.

The book will provide you with knowledge and skills that can help you become a challenger and build a great business empire.

Amp Up Your Sales by Andy Paul

Amp Up Your Sales: Powerful Strategies That Move Customers to Make Fast, Favorable Decisions Paperback – November 26, 2014

by Andy Paul (Author)

40 ratings

> See all 6 formats and editions

Kindle	Audiobook	Paperback
$9.99	$0.00	$10.93
Read with Our Free App	Free with your Audible trial	17 Used from $1.27 8 New from $5.87

Customers today are overloaded with information and overwhelmed by options. The truth is, product value is so high across the competition that any kind of meaningful product differentiation—at least in the customers' eyes—has all but disappeared. Therefore, between not recognizing product differences, combined with not having any time to spare to investigate what they don't know, the difference maker for many decision makers... is you! The salesperson who is always responsive and completely focused on value will, more times than not, be the one who will stand out from the crowd and get the sale. Combining leading-edge research with a vast amount of field experience, Amp Up Your Sales will show anyone how to become the trusted sales professional who consistently wins new business. Readers will learn how to: · Maximize the value of their selling· Accelerate responsiveness to build trust and credibility·

It can take a lot of effort to convince B2B customers to use your services or products. You need a strategy that gets your target clients to make decisions fast about using your brand to solve their pain points.

To effectively accomplish this, you need to provide value to your target customers. This book will guide you on how to up your marketing strategies to win leads to your business.

You'll learn how to build credibility with new potential customers and win them over.

Read on for an expert course in using Facebook and Instagram to market your business.

Chapter 5: Facebook Advertising

Suppose you have an online business and you're wondering whether you can advertise the business on Facebook. Are you worried about the ROI for your advertising and how it will affect business growth?

Well, don't worry. This chapter will give you all the insight you need to start advertising on Facebook. To start, let's explore why you need to use Facebook for effective brand advertising.

Reasons to Advertise on Facebook

Suitable for Clients in Different Niches

You can use Facebook to reach clients in different niches and industries, such as B2B, B2C, and SaaS. As one of the most popular social sites, with 2.45 billion users, it's a great setting for increasing brand awareness. Facebook has tons of target clients for your business and you can reach them and promote your business to them on the site. This makes it easy to market your brand to a wide variety of customers.

Customers Are Easy to Reach

Facebook is a great place where customers hang out. Research by Statista shows that Facebook has 2.45 billion active users.

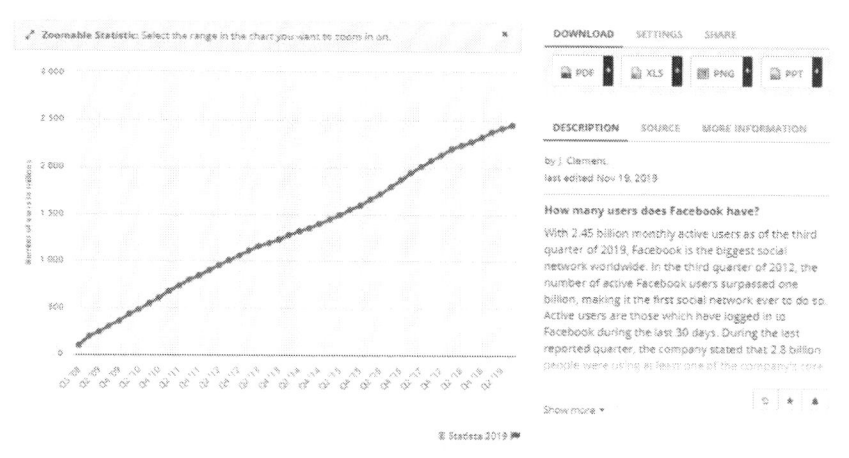

This shows that most of your potential customers probably spend time on Facebook. If you put your brand in front of these target clients by using Facebook Ads to market your business, it will be easy to attract more clients.

Another study by Oberlo shows that Facebook is the leading social media site, reaching 60.6% of internet users.

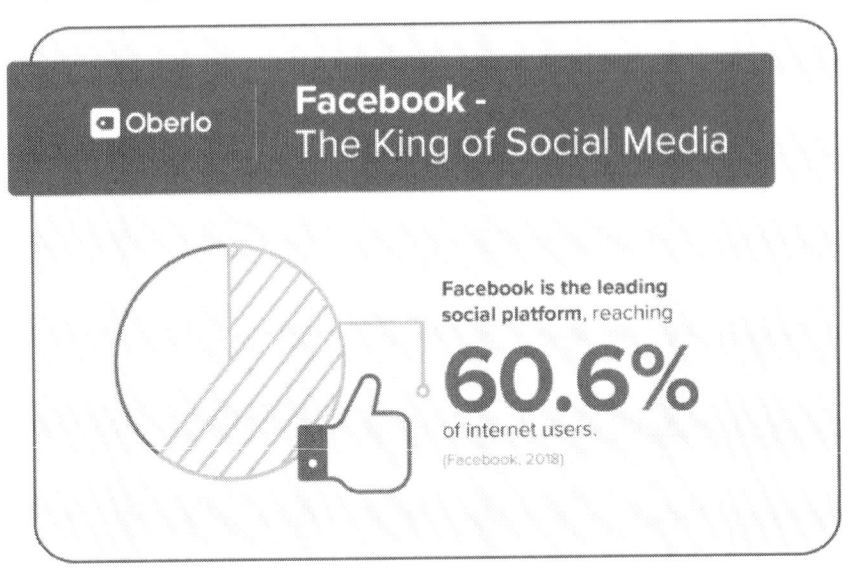

Oberlo

Facebook - The King of Social Media

Facebook is the leading social platform, reaching

60.6%

of internet users.

(Facebook, 2018)

Brands can use this opportunity to formulate ways of attracting these leads and converting them into customers.

Facebook users spend an average of 58 minutes per visit, and most users visit the site multiple times a day.

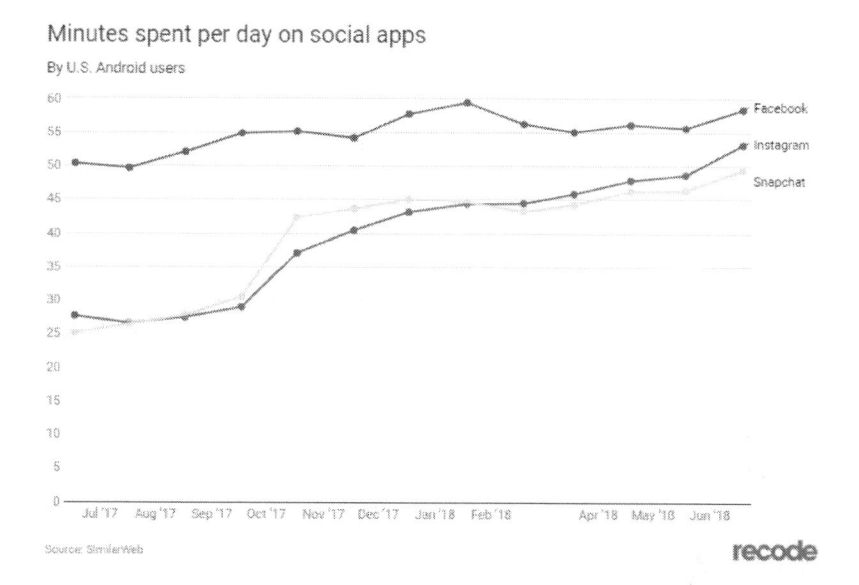

Minutes spent per day on social apps
By U.S. Android users

Source: SimilarWeb — recode

Since most of your potential customers spend time on Facebook, your brand can reach out to them and engage them there.

Company Pages Increase Brand Awareness

Many customers like to do business with brands they know and trust. To gain this trust from potential clients, you can create a business page and reach out to them through the page. Here's the Voy Media Facebook page:

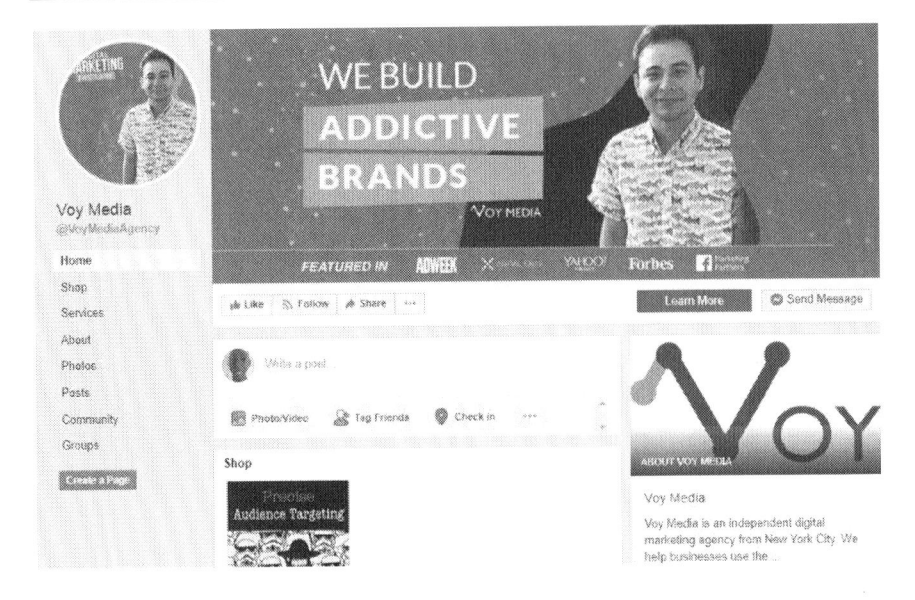

Through pages like these, you can reach out to prospective clients, engage them, and convert them into clients.

Include a link that will lead target clients to your business website. Once the target clients land there, they can learn more about your services and how to use them. You can notify your target market about your new products and how these will help them address their concerns.

Through Facebook Ads, many people will discover your business and engage with it, increasing your conversion rates.

Keeps You Ahead of Competitors

You have competitors who are searching for the same potential customers you want. Facebook advertising is a smart way to stay ahead of your competitors' game and win more clients to your brand.

When done well, Facebook advertising is an amazing way to build trust with the target market, generate traffic for your website, and increase your lead conversion and sales.

With Facebook, you can target your competitors' followers and win them to your business. Research what your competitors are doing and improve your lead generation process to generate more leads to your brand.

Easy to Remarket to Previous Target Clients

In the process of marketing your business, you interact with target clients, but some don't convert into clients. Using Facebook advertising makes it easy to reach these target clients and remarket your brand. Since they're already familiar with your business's products and services, converting them into clients is easier.

More Affordable

Marketing your brand through Facebook is less expensive compared to other marketing channels brands use to reach their target clients.

For instance, here's the cost of Facebook Ads compared to the cost of other marketing channels:

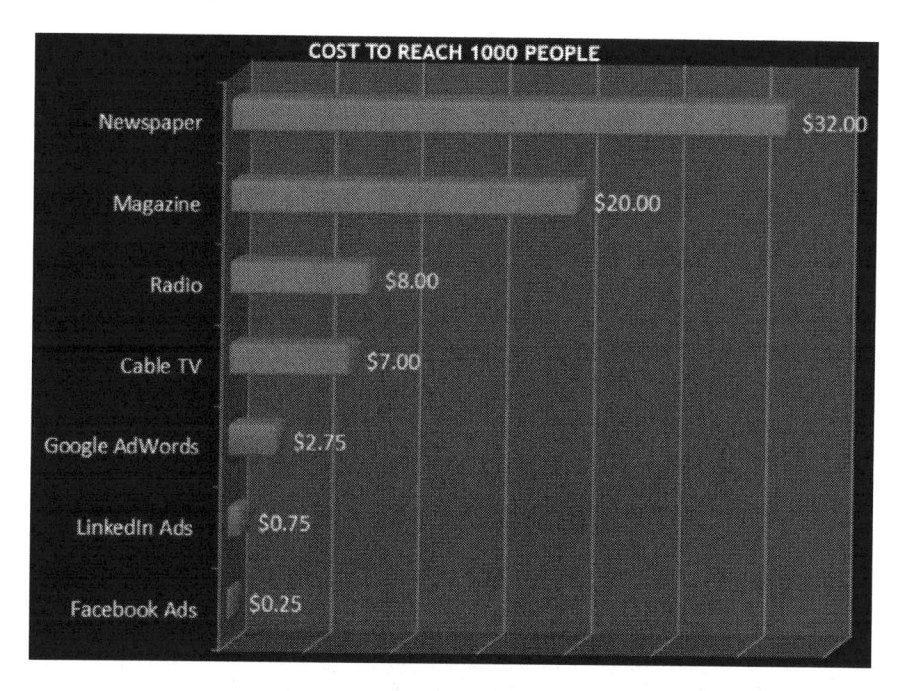

COST TO REACH 1000 PEOPLE

Newspaper	$32.00
Magazine	$20.00
Radio	$8.00
Cable TV	$7.00
Google AdWords	$2.75
LinkedIn Ads	$0.75
Facebook Ads	$0.25

The chart makes it clear that a brand can easily run Facebook ads and reach a high number of potential clients on a small budget.

Taking advantage of Facebook can help you minimize your marketing expenses and increase your ROI because it empowers you to reach more leads. This will increase the number of lead conversions and sales for your business.

Increases User Engagement

Online business is a trust-building process. You need to win the trust of your potential clients before you can sell them your products or services. One great way to accomplish this is to promote your brand through Facebook Ads.

Target clients are easy to reach, and you can tell them about your business and the solutions you offer. Ads direct your target clients to your business website, where they can learn more.

All this is a trust-building journey to bring your customers closer to home and engage them with your business.

Provides Analytics Reports on Your Ad Performance

"You can't improve it if you can't measure it." That's how the saying goes. To increase your marketing efforts and improve them, you need to gauge their performance.

One advantage of Facebook Ads is that you get a report that shows you what's working and what isn't.

When should you use Ads Manager?

Use Ads Manager if you want to:

- Quickly duplicate your ads, ad sets and advertising campaigns.
- Edit all your ad settings, such as targeting and budget, from one place.
- See all of the metrics that matter to you in one consolidated view.
- Analyse results and make informed changes to your ads and campaigns.
- Customise your graphs and tables to see the metrics that are most important to you.

If you need to manage Pages, accounts and user access in addition to ads, consider using Business Manager.

The data makes it easy to tweak your marketing by telling you which ads to optimize to boost brand awareness and lead generation.

You'll have all the analytics you need in your Ads Manager account. This simplifies your advertising work since you'll only use ads that perform better to market your business.

Types of Facebook Ads

There are different types of ads you can publish on Facebook to market and advertise your business. However, the choice among these ads depends on what you want to achieve with them.

Here are the objectives to consider as you create Facebook ads for your brand:

Awareness	Consideration	Conversion
Brand awareness	Traffic	Conversions
Reach	Engagement	Product catalog sales
	App installs	Store visits
	Video views	
	Lead generation	
	Messages	

These are some of the types of ads you can design to fit within your Facebook advertising.

Video Ads

Video has become a great way for brands to reach their target clients. Video marketing tends to generate a high social media ROI.

Social Media ROI

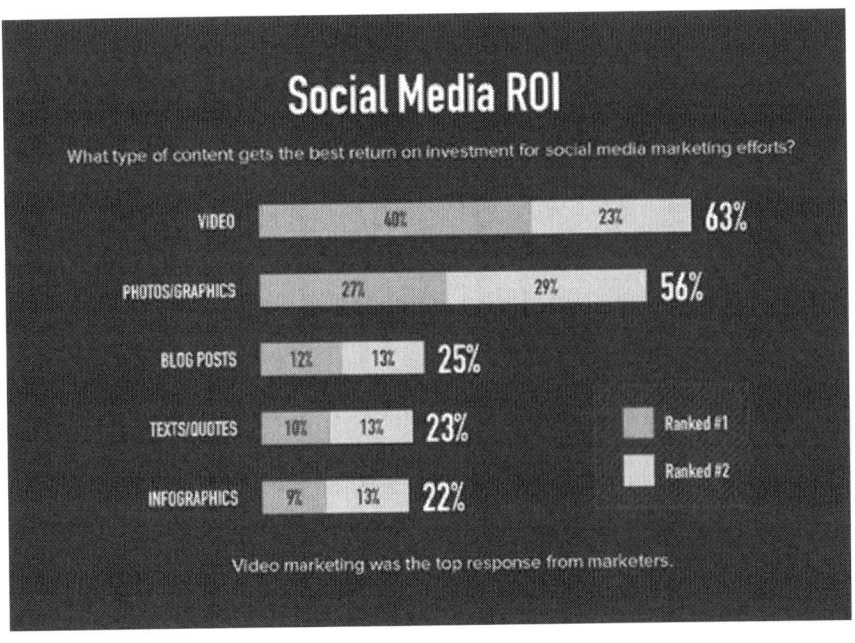

What type of content gets the best return on investment for social media marketing efforts?

Content Type	Ranked #1	Ranked #2	Total
VIDEO	40%	23%	63%
PHOTOS/GRAPHICS	27%	29%	56%
BLOG POSTS	12%	13%	25%
TEXTS/QUOTES	10%	13%	23%
INFOGRAPHICS	9%	13%	22%

Video marketing was the top response from marketers.

Many companies and individual business owners are now creating more video content to advertise their brand, products, and services to their customers through social media.

Potential customers prefer watching videos over reading text-based content. For example, here are some videos from Neil Patel's Facebook page that he uses to market his business.

Chapter 5: Facebook Advertising

Here are some more examples of Facebook Ads videos from Marketo.

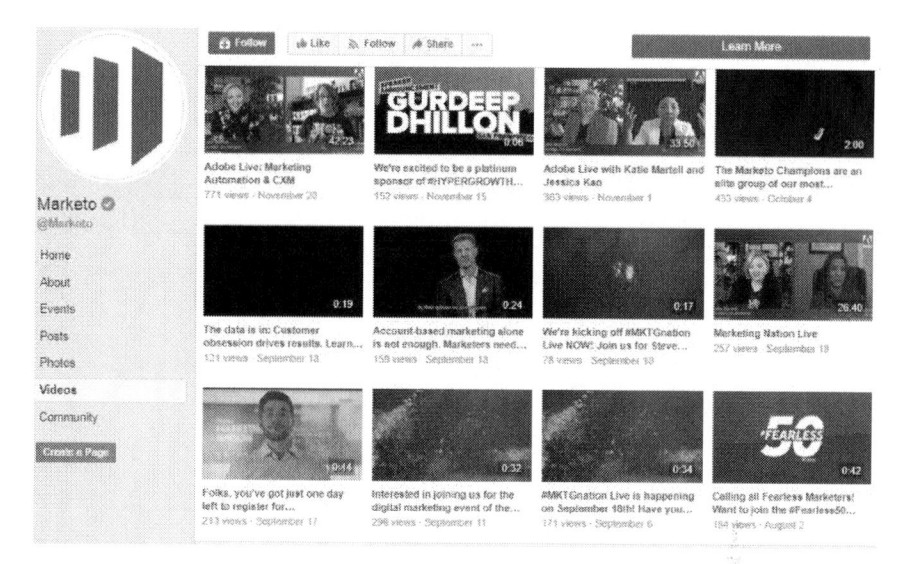

When creating ad videos, keep them attractive and short. Shorter videos increase engagement with leads and drive the target clients to take action.

Image Ads

In this type of ad, the business creates an image with a CTA that will entice the target customer to take action. Here's an example:

If you're a potential client and click the "learn more" button, you'll be directed to the main website of the business, where you can do something, like sign up for the email newsletter:

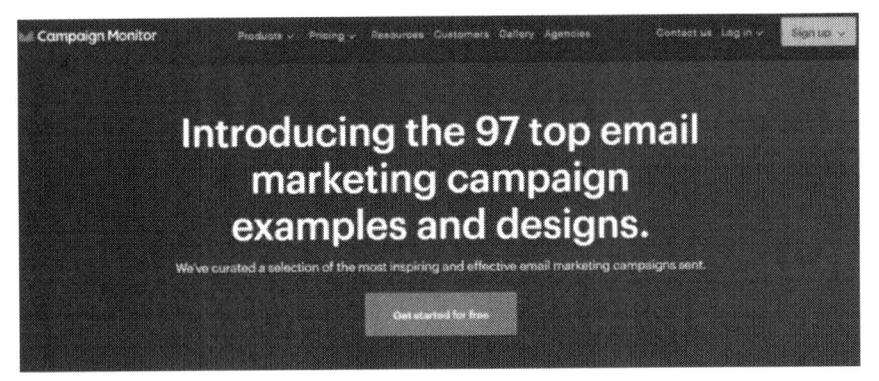

Here's another Facebook image ad with a CTA encouraging readers to take action:

Chapter 5: Facebook Advertising

MessageBird
Sponsored

Take control of your customer experience with WhatsApp Business API.
- Send automated notifications, alerts, and reminders.
- Have one-on-one customer support conversations.
- Protect your clients' accounts with 2FA.
All with one flexible API.

WhatsApp Business API
Improve your customer experience

MESSAGEBIRD.COM
Does your CEO know about this?　　Sign Up

Be sure to use attractive images that impress the target audience and draw them in.

Slideshow Ads

As the name suggests, these are like videos, but made up of a series of still images.

You can also include photos and texts to reinforce the ad's message to the audience. Here's an example of a Facebook slideshow ad:

Each slideshow should be short and designed to accomplish a specific objective in your marketing process.

As a marketer, ensure that you create your slideshow ads so that they engage and attract the target audience to your brand.

Carousel Ads

In this type of ad, brands can display different images with calls-to-action to inspire target clients to take action after viewing the ads.

Gayle Getaways Travel and Tours
June 27

Discover CENTRAL VISAYAS

Here's another example of a carousel ad on Facebook:

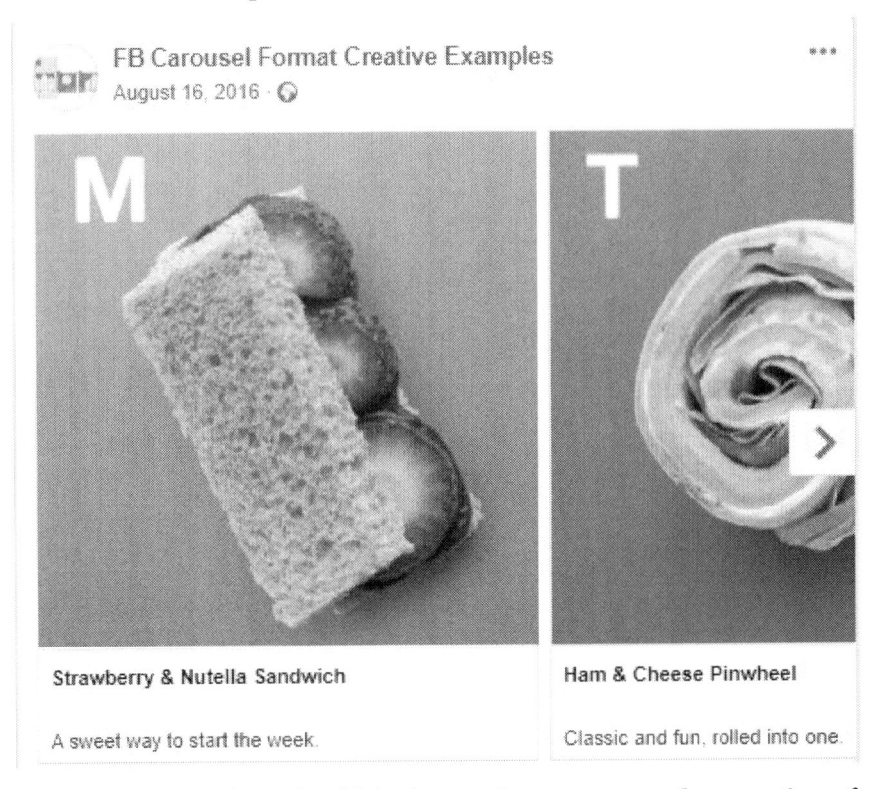

FB Carousel Format Creative Examples
August 16, 2016

Strawberry & Nutella Sandwich
A sweet way to start the week.

Ham & Cheese Pinwheel
Classic and fun, rolled into one.

Your images or videos should be interesting to capture the attention of potential clients. Include a clear CTA so target clients know exactly how to take action after watching or viewing your ad.

Lead Ads

You want to engage your target clients so you can draw them to your business and nurture them. Lead ads can help you generate leads. Create ads with CTAs to collect email addresses for your target clients.

You can use email marketing techniques to nurture the leads through the sales cycle and convert them into clients.

Dynamic Ads

When it comes to online marketing, your target clients have different degrees of attraction to your brand and what you offer. Some are highly attracted to your products and that makes it easy for you to sell to them.

Others need more nurturing and want you to educate them about what you offer and why they need it.

Dynamic ads help you reach out to potential clients who have already expressed interest in your products. These ads adjust automatically to display content that's most suited to each individual user at their particular stage of the sales cycle.

Before running these types of ads, you need to know your target clients well and create highly attractive ads that impress and engage them based on the aspect of your business they've shown interest in.

Best Facebook Ads Metrics to Track

To achieve business success, you need to track the performance of your Facebook ads.

However, you might be wondering, what should I track to measure the performance of my ads and ensure increased lead generation, sales, and business ROI?

These are some of the metrics you can track to evaluate the performance of your Facebook ads.

Impressions

The target audience has to be impressed with your ads before they'll engage with them. It follows, then, that the number of impressions your ads have indicates the level of interest your target clients have in your brand.

If an ad has high impression rates, that means many target clients have shown interest in it and are ready to engage with your brand.

In relation to impressions, you can also track the cost-per-thousand-impressions (CPM) to gauge how much it will cost you to show your ads to your target audience 1,000 times.

Click Links

Measuring the number of clicks you get on your ad's CTA is a good way to test its performance. Every ad you create should include a call-to-action because you want the target clients to act.

You need to evaluate the actions target clients take in response to your ads. For example, in this ad, the owner intended to collect email addresses from target clients when they downloaded the free e-book:

![Diggity Marketing sponsored ad showing Free Download: Diggity's Evergreen Onsite SEO Guide with a Download button]

To evaluate the performance of your ad, you can estimate the number of signups you collected from e-book downloads.

If the number is high, then most of the target clients were interested in your ads.

Advertising Cost

This metric involves comparing your business marketing costs to the profits you earn through your ads. The cost of advertising your business through your Facebook ads will be based on either the CPC or CPM model.

Chapter 5: Facebook Advertising

If your advertising cost is higher than the return you're getting from your ads, you need to reevaluate your ad strategy.

Conversion Rates

One great metric to help evaluate how your Facebook advertising is doing is by tracking conversion rates.

Research from Wordstream shows a 9.21% lead conversion rate across different markets.

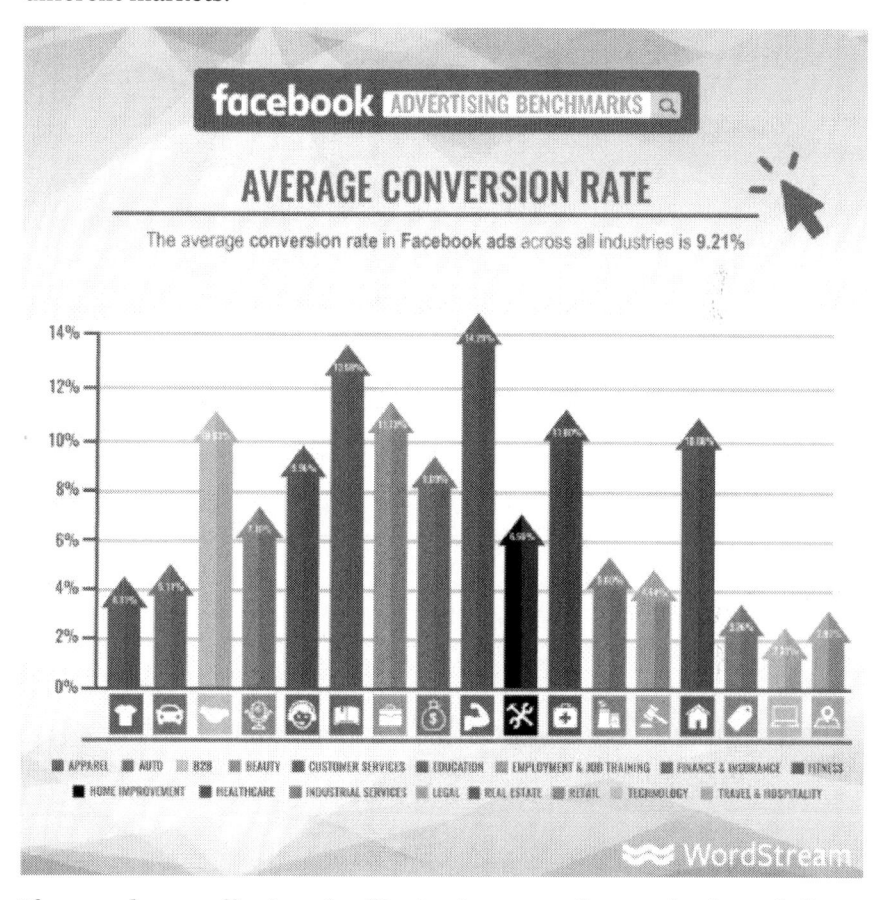

If your ads are effective, they'll win the trust of target leads and direct them to your landing pages to learn more about your services or products. From there, it's easy to convert the leads into clients. In the chapter 2, we described how to optimize landing pages. Follow that guidance to draw your target customers to take action with your business and convert.

Website Traffic

Your website is your online shop and you need to make as many leads aware of your business as possible to increase sales. Traffic to your site is a reliable indicator of your Facebook Ads performance.

You can evaluate the click-through rates to your website from your ads and the actions leads take on the site. Based on what you find, you can adjust the methods you use to draw traffic.

Research by Marketing Charts shows that social sites lead to an average of 2.7 sessions per visitor.

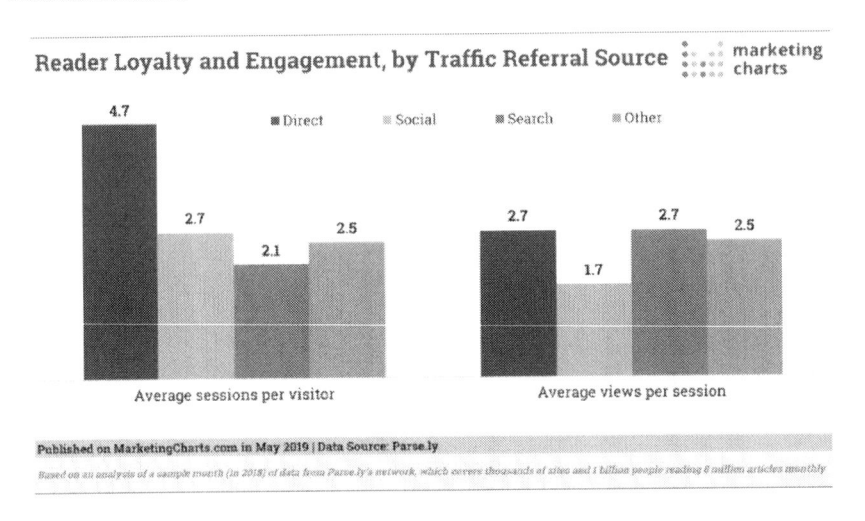

Reader Loyalty and Engagement, by Traffic Referral Source — marketing charts

■ Direct   ■ Social   ■ Search   ■ Other

Average sessions per visitor: 4.7, 2.7, 2.1, 2.5
Average views per session: 2.7, 1.7, 2.7, 2.5

Published on MarketingCharts.com in May 2019 | Data Source: Parse.ly
Based on an analysis of a sample month (in 2018) of data from Parse.ly's network, which covers thousands of sites and 1 billion people reading 8 million articles monthly

By counting these sessions, you can evaluate the traffic to your website from Facebook advertising and gauge its performance in your business marketing.

Another study by Marketing Charts showed that Facebook has a 19% referral rate, better than most social media sites, when it comes to generating website traffic for brands.

Social Media Traffic to Online Media Sites:
Percentage of Referrals Who Are Returning Visitors

marketing charts

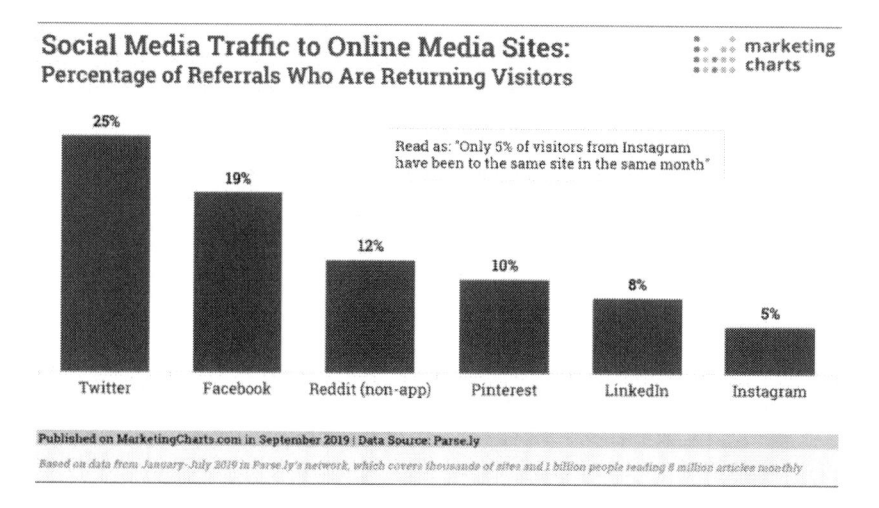

- Twitter: 25%
- Facebook: 19%
- Reddit (non-app): 12%
- Pinterest: 10%
- LinkedIn: 8%
- Instagram: 5%

Read as: "Only 5% of visitors from Instagram have been to the same site in the same month"

Published on MarketingCharts.com in September 2019 | Data Source: Parse.ly
Based on data from January-July 2019 in Parse.ly's network, which covers thousands of sites and 1 billion people reading 8 million articles monthly

Since Facebook has so many users who are potential clients for your brand, it can be easy to draw their attention to your website, and from there pursue them as potential clients.

User Engagement

It will take some time for your leads to make a purchase from your business once they've become familiar with your products or services.

They'll need to engage with your brand to see how your products or services will help them. You can evaluate user engagement with your brand through your Facebook ads.

Higher user engagement shows that your ads are performing better and drawing more engaged traffic to your business.

Tools for Facebook Advertising

An assortment of tools are out there to make growing your business through Facebook advertising easier. We share quite a few of them here.

Qwaya

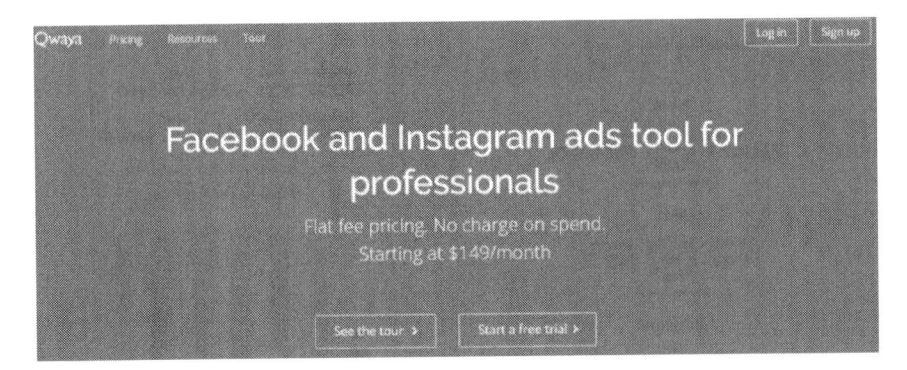

This is a great social media marketing tool for your brands. The tool specializes in Facebook advertising and provides all the software you need to run your Facebook Ads campaigns.

This makes it easy to manage your ads as you promote your brand and generate leads and sales. Here are some ways this software can assist with your marketing:

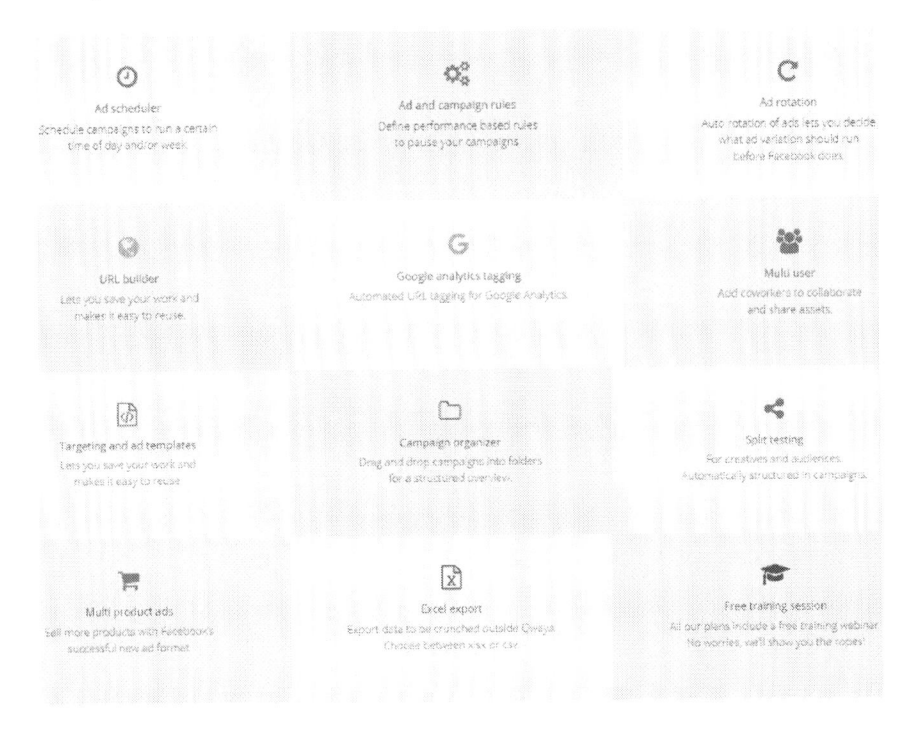

Chapter 5: Facebook Advertising

And here's the pricing model for the software:

Get your free trial!
No credit card required

Premium	Business	Agency
$149 per month	$249 per month	$349 per month
1 user	5 user	10 user
Unlimited ads	Unlimited ads	Unlimited ads
Unlimited Facebook users	Unlimited Facebook users	Unlimited Facebook users

Here's what some of the clients who have used Qwaya have to say:

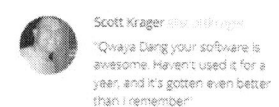

Marketing Partner

G2A   iChica   webprofits   ADMIRAL MARKETS

Scott Krager
"Qwaya Dang your software is awesome. Haven't used it for a year, and it's gotten even better than I remember"

Jay Deiboldt
"If you run FB ads and you're not using Qwaya you're doing it wrong."

Carl Sednaoui
"Running Facebook ads? You need to use Qwaya. Hands down best tool/customer support"

Facebook Ads ROI Calculator

You need to track your investments to see whether your marketing channels are helping you grow your business. This tool helps you calculate your Facebook Ads ROI so you can find opportunities for improvement.

This is what the calculator looks like:

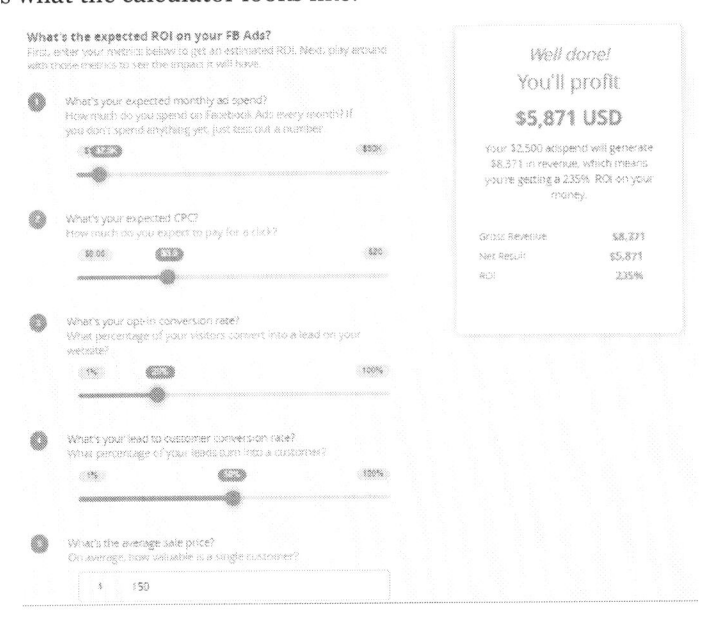

Chapter 5: Facebook Advertising

You can integrate this software with other apps and tools to make calculating your ROI easy. Here are some of these tools:

ActiveCampaign	ActiveDEMAND	AgileCRM	arpReach
autopilot	autorespond	AWeber	Bizzy
BombBomb	Campaign Monitor	click funnels	Constant Contact
ConvertKit	Customer.io	Drip	Elastic Email
emailcloudx	Email Octopus	emailONE	enormail

FLUTTERMAIL	Genoo	GetResponse	GetResponse 360
GoToWebinar	HubSpot	iContact	Infusionsoft
INTERCOM	interspire	JotForm	KLAVIYO
Klick Tipp	Mad Mimi	MailChimp	mailer lite
Mailer.one	mailplus	MailWizz EMA	MARKETHERO

Chapter 5: Facebook Advertising

These are some other solutions this software offers business marketers:

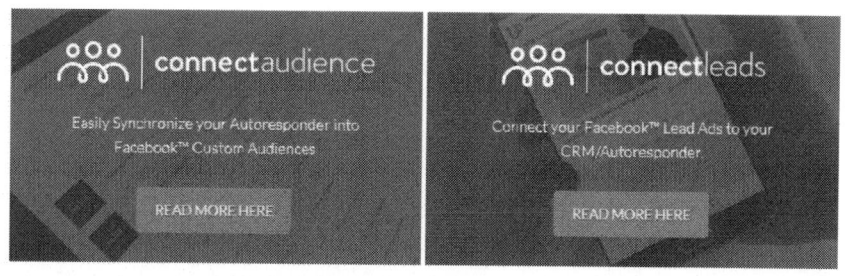

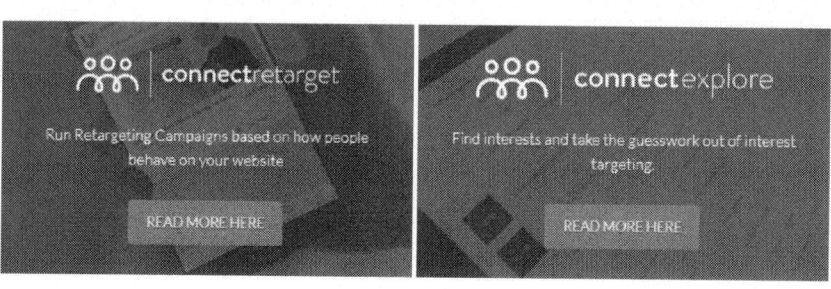

connectaudience
Easily Synchronize your Autoresponder into Facebook™ Custom Audiences
READ MORE HERE

connectleads
Connect your Facebook™ Lead Ads to your CRM/Autoresponder
READ MORE HERE

connectretarget
Run Retargeting Campaigns based on how people behave on your website
READ MORE HERE

connectexplore
Find interests and take the guesswork out of interest targeting.
READ MORE HERE

Driftrock

driftrock   AGENCY TOOLS   CASE STUDIES   PRODUCTS   INDUSTRIES   INTEGRATIONS   PRICING   BLOG   SIGN IN

Capture & Convert 3X more leads

The easiest way to acquire, optimise and convert leads from your digital marketing.

Google Partner   LinkedIn   Facebook Marketing Partner

GET STARTED

You need to draw leads to your business and engage them in your marketing process. This tool helps you do that. You can use it to streamline your lead generation campaigns.

Its range of products furthers your marketing goals as you reach out to your target clients, raise brand awareness, and earn the trust of your leads.

Here are tools you can integrate with Driftrock in your business marketing:

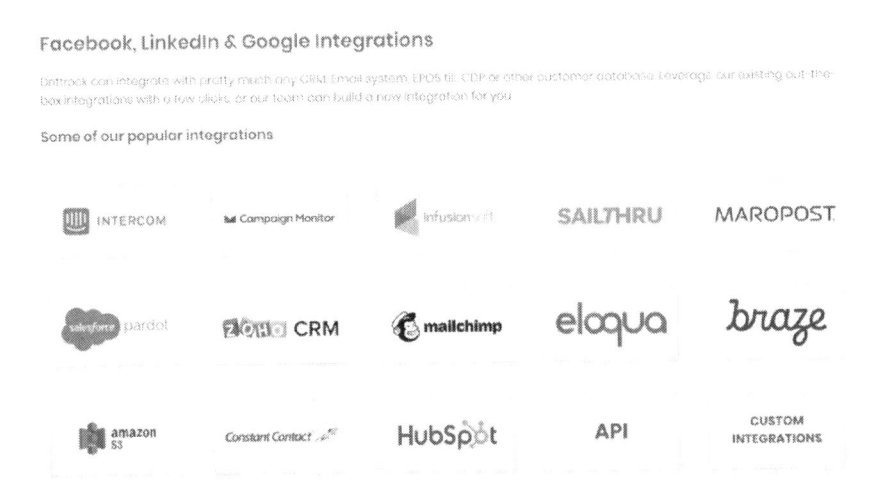

Facebook, LinkedIn & Google Integrations

Driftrock can integrate with pretty much any CRM, Email system, EPOS till, CDP or other customer database. Leverage our existing out-the-box integrations with a few clicks, or our team can build a new integration for you.

Some of our popular integrations

- INTERCOM
- Campaign Monitor
- Infusionsoft
- SAILTHRU
- MAROPOST
- salesforce pardot
- Zoho CRM
- mailchimp
- eloqua
- braze
- amazon S3
- Constant Contact
- HubSpot
- API
- CUSTOM INTEGRATIONS

You can visit Driftrock's website to learn more about its pricing model.

Connectio–Facebook Ads Keyword Search

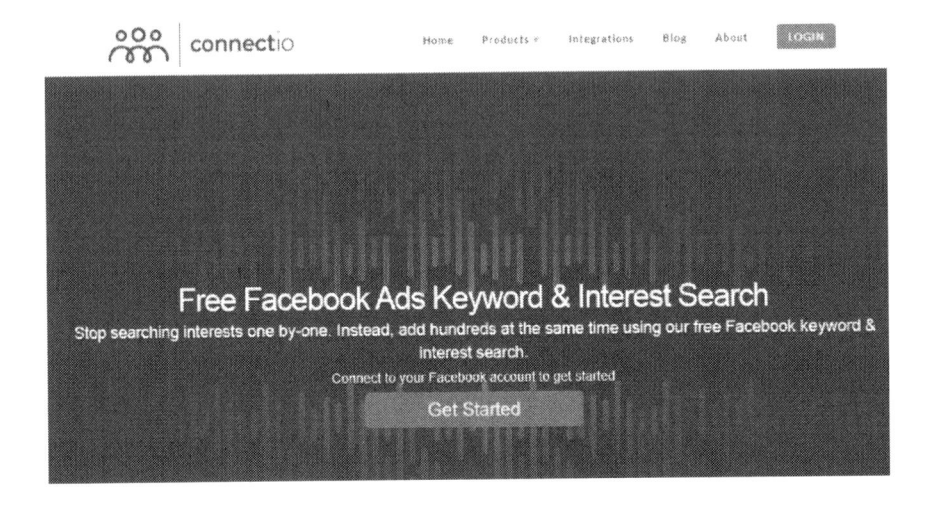

Free Facebook Ads Keyword & Interest Search

Stop searching interests one by-one. Instead, add hundreds at the same time using our free Facebook keyword & interest search.

Connect to your Facebook account to get started

Get Started

You need your ads to rank high on search engines if you want to attract your target clients. To ensure high rankings, you need to use the same keywords your target clients use when they're searching for solutions to their problems. This tool will help you come up with great keywords you can use in your ads so they'll earn high rankings.

Unsplash

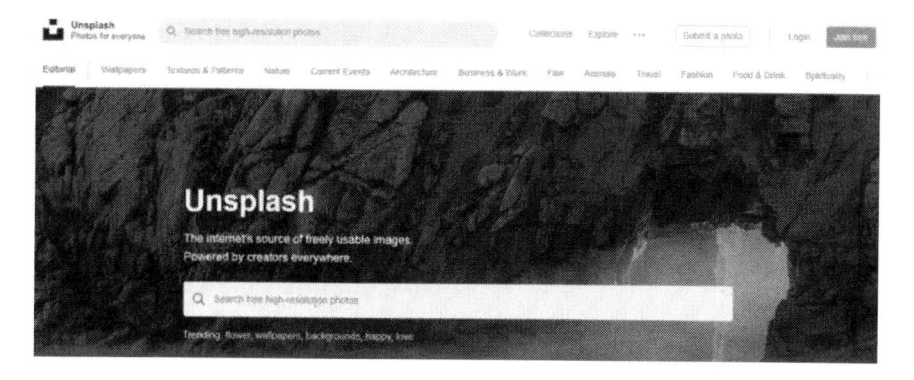

Your ads need beautifully designed images to attract your target clients. This tool offers a selection of different images you can use in your ads to improve their efficiency.

Pablo by Buffer

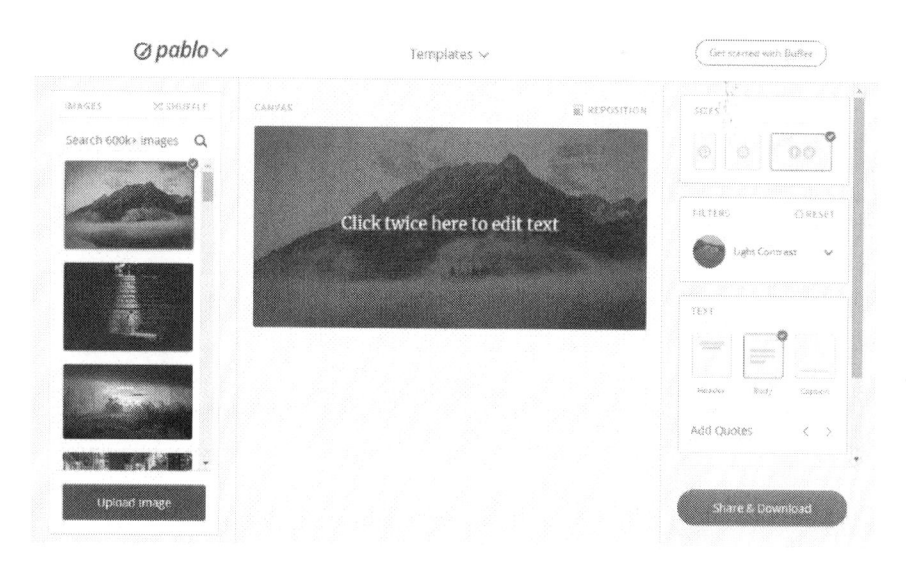

Sometimes you may need to create your own images for your ads. You can use this tool by Buffer Software to create stellar images or adapt other images to suit your taste.

It can also help you overlay social media quotes on your images and manage your social media accounts.

The app is free to use. Here are some of its amazing features:

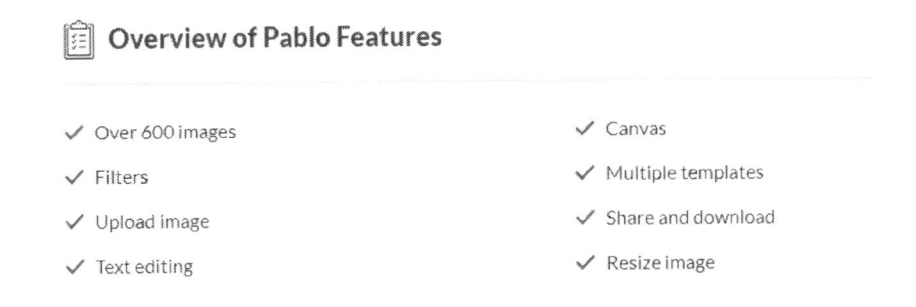

Overview of Pablo Features

- Over 600 images
- Filters
- Upload image
- Text editing

- Canvas
- Multiple templates
- Share and download
- Resize image

Hootsuite Ads

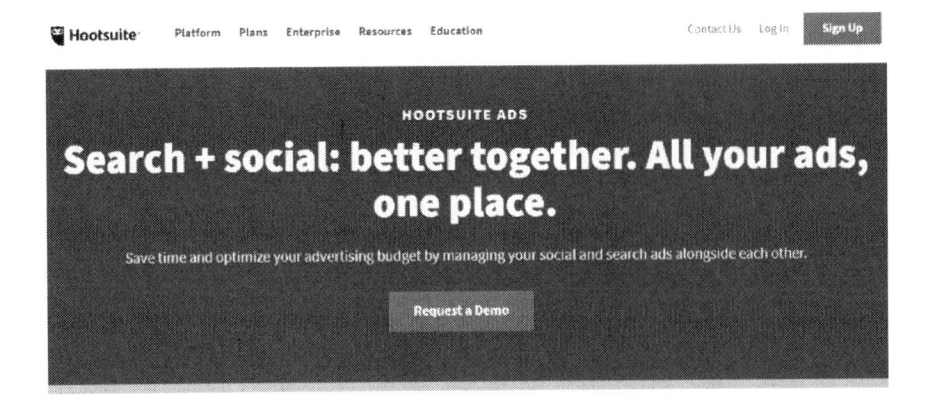

This is a great tool to help you expertly manage all your ads in one place. With it, you can create and test ads for social channels like Facebook and Instagram.

These are Hootsuite's core features:

Core features of the Hootsuite platform

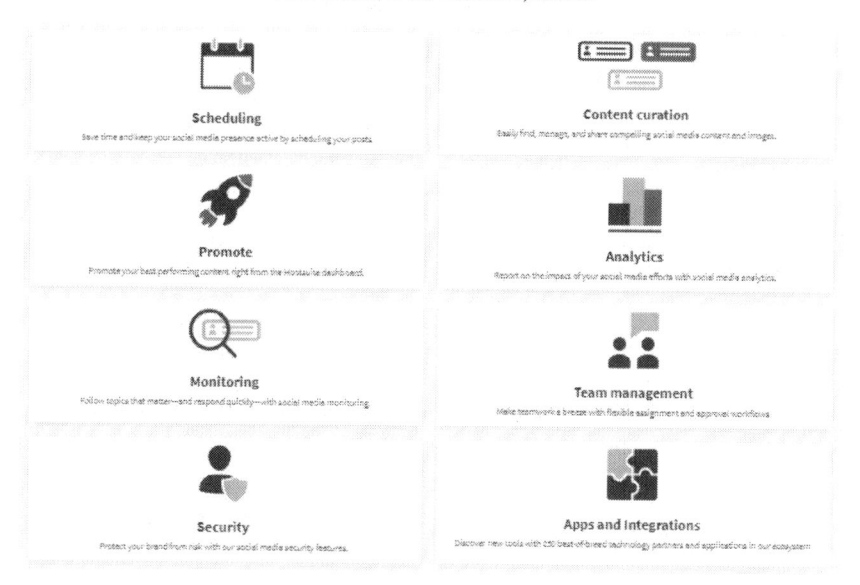

Scheduling — Save time and keep your social media presence active by scheduling your posts

Content curation — Easily find, manage, and share compelling social media content and images.

Promote — Promote your best performing content right from the Hootsuite dashboard.

Analytics — Report on the impact of your social media efforts with social media analytics.

Monitoring — Follow topics that matter—and respond quickly—with social media monitoring

Team management — Make teamwork a breeze with flexible assignment and approval workflows

Security — Protect your brand from risk with our social media security features.

Apps and Integrations — Discover new tools with 250 best-of-breed technology partners and applications in our ecosystem

And here's the tool's pricing plan:

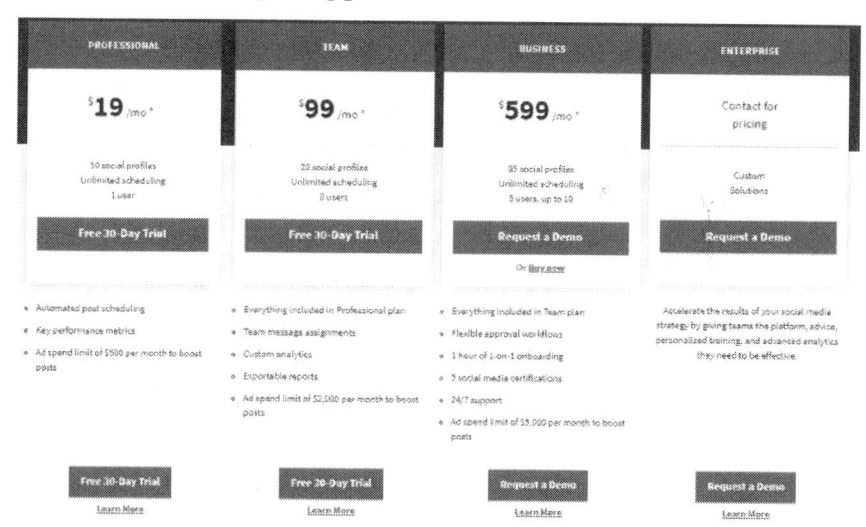

PROFESSIONAL	TEAM	BUSINESS	ENTERPRISE
$19/mo*	$99/mo*	$599/mo*	Contact for pricing
10 social profiles Unlimited scheduling 1 user	20 social profiles Unlimited scheduling 3 users	35 social profiles Unlimited scheduling 5 users, up to 10	Custom Solutions
Free 30-Day Trial	Free 30-Day Trial	Request a Demo Or Buy now	Request a Demo
• Automated post scheduling • Key performance metrics • Ad spend limit of $500 per month to boost posts	• Everything included in Professional plan • Team message assignments • Custom analytics • Exportable reports • Ad spend limit of $2,000 per month to boost posts	• Everything included in Team plan • Flexible approval workflows • 1 hour of 1-on-1 onboarding • 3 social media certifications • 24/7 support • Ad spend limit of $5,000 per month to boost posts	Accelerate the results of your social media strategy by giving teams the platform, advice, personalized training, and advanced analytics they need to be effective.
Free 30-Day Trial Learn More	Free 30-Day Trial Learn More	Request a Demo Learn More	Request a Demo Learn More

Wicked Reports

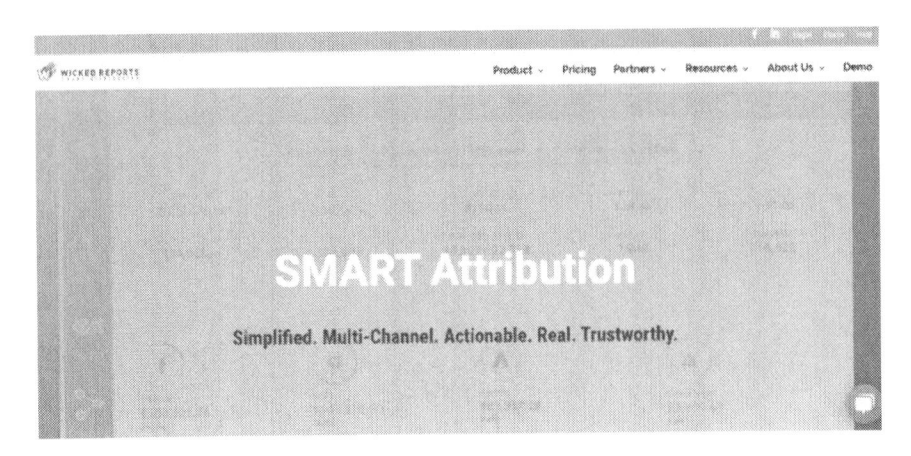

Every marketer needs to measure and track ad performance and the overall marketing process to evaluate business growth. The Wicked Reports tool is great for performance analysis.

Here are some other tools you can integrate with Wicked Reports software:

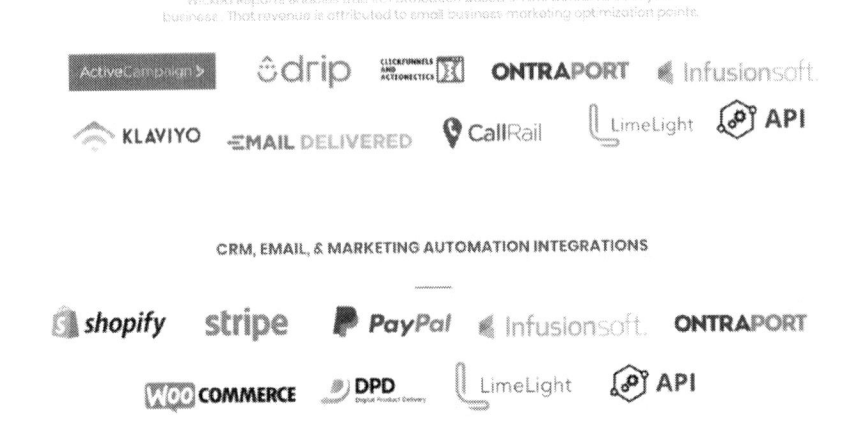

Chapter 5: Facebook Advertising

And here's the Wicked Reports pricing model:

Basic	Premium	Platinum
Independent Setup. Requires Native Integrations.	Some Live Support. Supports Native and Non-Native Integration.	Support Over 3 Months. For Complex Integrations.
$250	$750	$1500
• Unlimited Email Support • Tracking Verification Consult • Kickoff Call • Deep Dive Data Analysis Consult • 30/60/90 Account Health check-in • Weekly Account Oversight • Non-Native CRM Zap/HTTP Post Setup • Cart Zap/HTTP Post Setup • Historical Contact/Order Data Import • Email UTM Tagging Assistance • API Implementation Support • Google Tag Manager Setup • API Implementation Support • Assistance Configuring UTMs and tracking across all Emails, Ad Campaigns, and Social Profiles	• Unlimited Email Support • Tracking Verification Consult • Deep Dive Data Analysis Consult • 30/60/90 Account Health check-in • Non-Native CRM Zap/HTTP Post Setup • Weekly Account Oversight • Email UTM Tagging Assistance (Up to 40 Emails) • Kickoff Call • Cart Zap/HTTP Post Setup • Historical Contact/Order Data Import • API Implementation Support • Google Tag Manager Setup • API Implementation Support • Assistance Configuring UTMs and tracking across all Emails, Ad Campaigns, and Social Profiles	• Unlimited Email Support • Tracking Verification Consult • Kickoff Call • Deep Dive Data Analysis Consult • 30/60/90 Account Health check-in • Weekly Account Oversight During Initial Setup • Non-Native CRM Zap/HTTP Post Setup Assistance • Non-Native Cart Zap/HTTP Post Setup Assistance • Historical Contact/Order Data Import (One Time) • Email UTM Tagging Assistance (Up to 40 emails) • API Implementation Support • Google Tag Manager Setup Assistance • Guidance Configuring UTMs and tracking across all Emails, Ad Campaigns, and Social Profiles
Buy Now	Buy Now	Buy Now

AdRoll

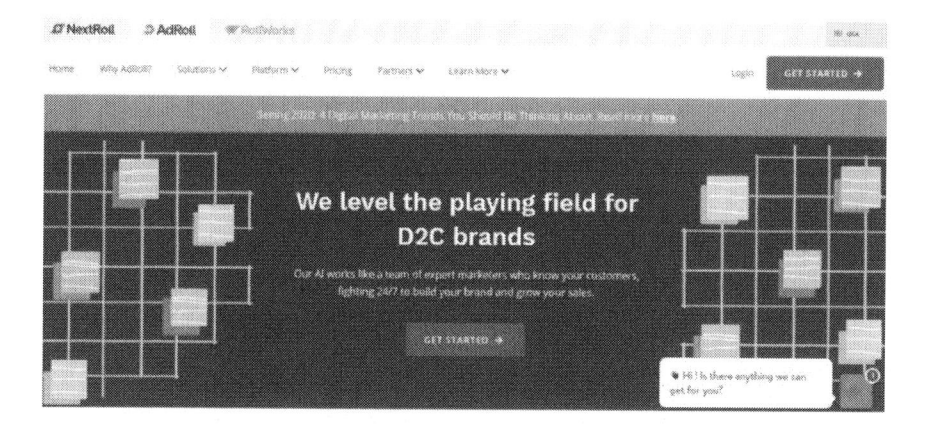

We level the playing field for D2C brands

Our AI works like a team of expert marketers who know your customers, fighting 24/7 to build your brand and grow your sales.

GET STARTED →

This software has amazing AI-driven tools to help you manage your ads, emails, and marketing strategies and grow your business.

With AdRoll, you can create memorable experiences across various marketing channels to bring awareness to your brand and attract leads to your business.

Here are some of the great features of this tool that help you unlock high ROI and business growth:

Unlock a higher ROI with AdRoll's features

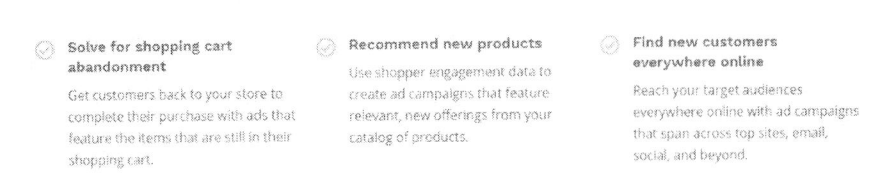

Solve for shopping cart abandonment
Get customers back to your store to complete their purchase with ads that feature the items that are still in their shopping cart.

Recommend new products
Use shopper engagement data to create ad campaigns that feature relevant, new offerings from your catalog of products.

Find new customers everywhere online
Reach your target audiences everywhere online with ad campaigns that span across top sites, email, social, and beyond.

There are also tons of different tools and software you can integrate with AdRoll to enhance your marketing process.

You can visit the AdRoll website to learn more about pricing for the software and its features.

Facebook Ads Manager

Chapter 5: Facebook Advertising

This tool gives you everything you need to create your Facebook ads. With its help, you can get insights about how to run your ads and also track how your ads perform on the market.

Ads Manager helps you find the best way to teach the target market about your brand and how it can help with their challenges. You can also learn about other brands in your niche and see the types of ads they create and how they perform on the market. That insight can help you create and run better ads.

In line with the increasing reliance on mobile devices, the tool also includes new mobile-friendly features. The Ads Manager app makes it easy to run mobile ads for your business.

AdStage

Your Marketing Data in One Platform

We're on a mission to make analytics easy!

Start Free Trial

AdStage helps great brands improve their decision-making processes. It provides insights and data that empower brands to make informed business management and marketing decisions. You can use the tool to automate and run your Facebook ads.

With AdStage, you can post ads on many ad network types to market your brand through different channels.

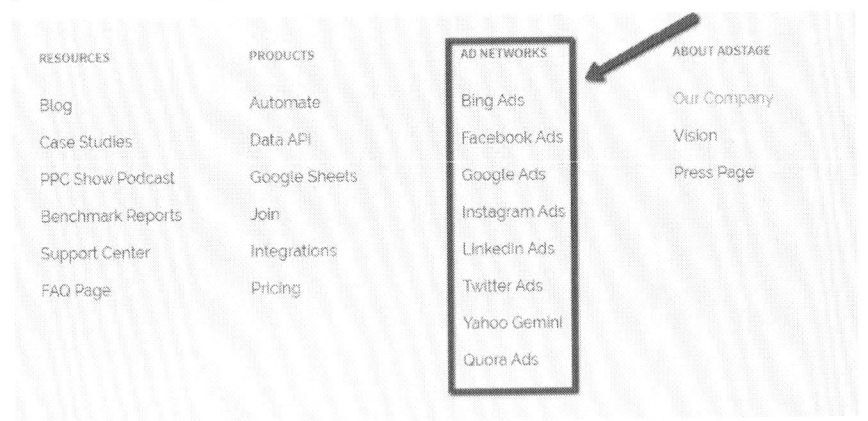

Visit the AdStage website to learn more about the different types of ads the tool runs and how you can use it to automate your marketing.

StitcherAds

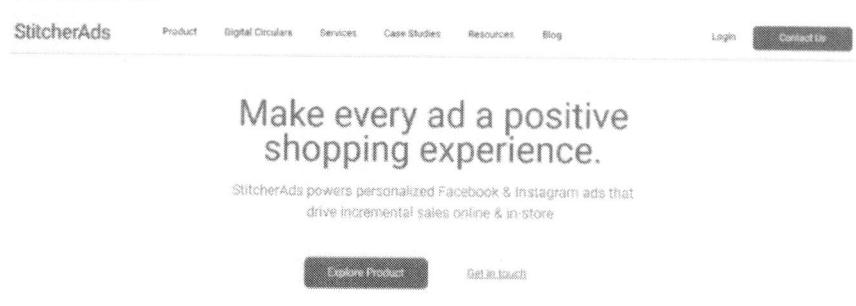

Make every ad a positive shopping experience.

This tool makes Facebook marketing easy by creating personalized ads.

It comes in handy to support and help you scale the performance of your Facebook and Instagram ads.

Here are some other tools you can integrate with StitcherAds:

Integrate the technology you need

Perfect Audience

With Perfect Audience, you have the power to control your retargeting advertising from one place for ease of management.

You can analyze your retargeting efforts in different channels to help improve your marketing efforts across these channels.

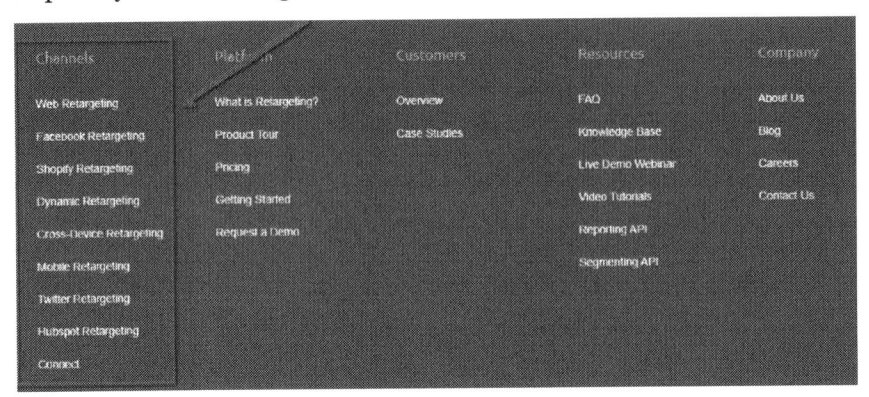

Visit the Perfect Audience website to see its pricing model and the services it offers.

Chapter 5: Facebook Advertising

Adphorus

Adphorus gives you insight into how to optimize your ads on Facebook to reach out to more target clients.

The tool is focused on travel marketing and draws on scientific research to help grow your travel brand. Here's how the travel marketing cycle looks:

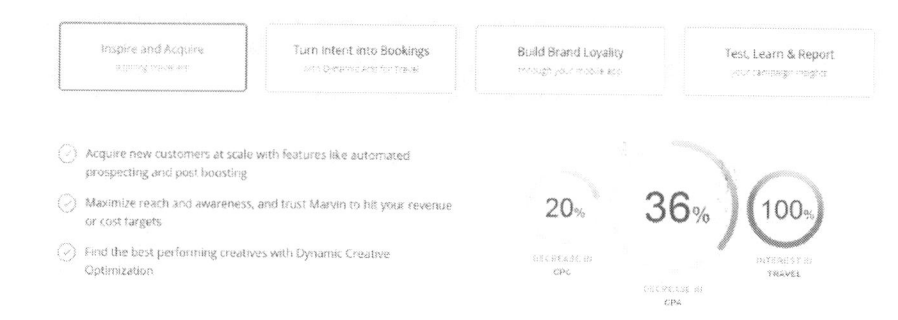

MakeMeReach

LEVEL-UP YOUR ONLINE ADVERTISING
Powerful Platform, Expert Team

This is an ad tech company that helps brands optimize their ads and raise brand awareness among the target customers.

The tool provides resources to help scale your marketing efforts and grow your business. You can manage all your ads from different marketing channels with ease on a single platform.

Here are some of the brands the company has partnered with to provide better services to its customers.

You can integrate the tool with other software and tools to make the most of your marketing strategy.

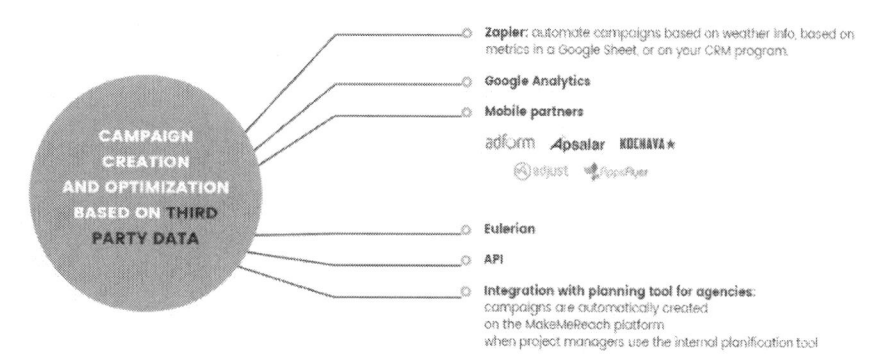

Chapter 5: Facebook Advertising

Advanced INTEGRATIONS

CAMPAIGN CREATION AND OPTIMIZATION BASED ON THIRD PARTY DATA

- **Zapier:** automate campaigns based on weather info, based on metrics in a Google Sheet, or on your CRM program.
- **Google Analytics**
- **Mobile partners**
  adform Apsalar KOCHAVA
  adjust AppsFlyer
- **Eulerian**
- **API**
- **Integration with planning tool for agencies:** campaigns are automatically created on the MakeMeReach platform when project managers use the internal planification tool

Learn more about the tool's pricing structure by visiting the website.

Smartly.io

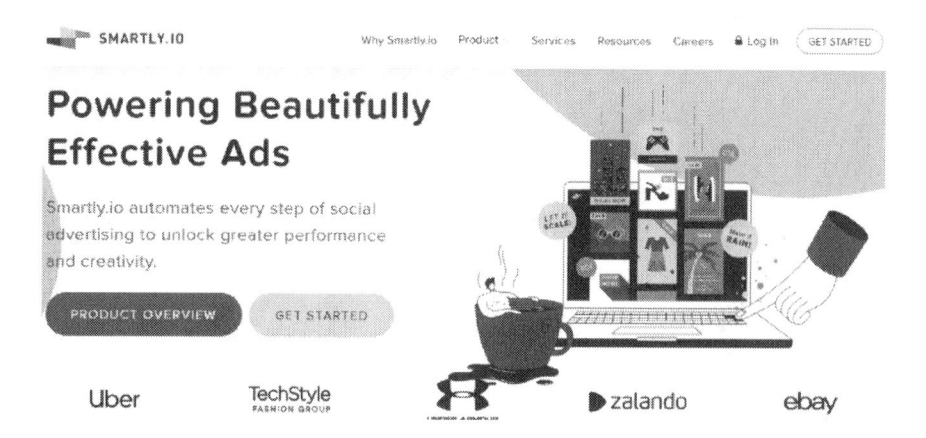

Powering Beautifully Effective Ads

Smartly.io automates every step of social advertising to unlock greater performance and creativity.

PRODUCT OVERVIEW   GET STARTED

Uber   TechStyle FASHION GROUP   zalando   ebay

Smartly can help you create beautiful ads and uses automation to scale them across different social sites and increase brand awareness.

You can leverage performance data to increase your business sales by optimizing ads that work.

Here's the pricing model for the tool:

Smartly.io Pricing

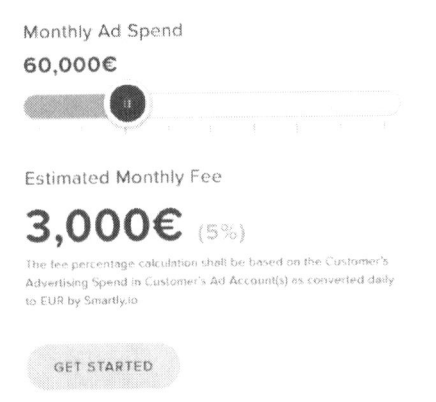

Monthly Ad Spend
60,000€

Spend Range	Fee
Less than 50k€	2,500€
50k€ - 100k€	5.0%
100k€ - 200k€	4.5%
200k€ - 350k€	4.0%
350k€ - 500k€	3.5%
More than 500k€	3.0%

Estimated Monthly Fee

3,000€ (5%)

The fee percentage calculation shall be based on the Customer's Advertising Spend in Customer's Ad Account(s) as converted daily to EUR by Smartly.io

GET STARTED

Sprinklr

Building a great brand requires learning more about your customers. By doing so, you can give your customers the best experience possible.

Remember, customer experience will soon be the most important aspect of customer satisfaction, even more than price and quality. That's why you need a great tool to help you manage your customer experiences.

Sprinklr can help. The tool makes managing your customer experiences as simple as you create more ads for your business. Customer experiences can help you understand how to create more focused ads that achieve your goals.

You can visit sprinklr.com to learn more about its services and pricing model.

Chapter 5: Facebook Advertising

Kenshoo

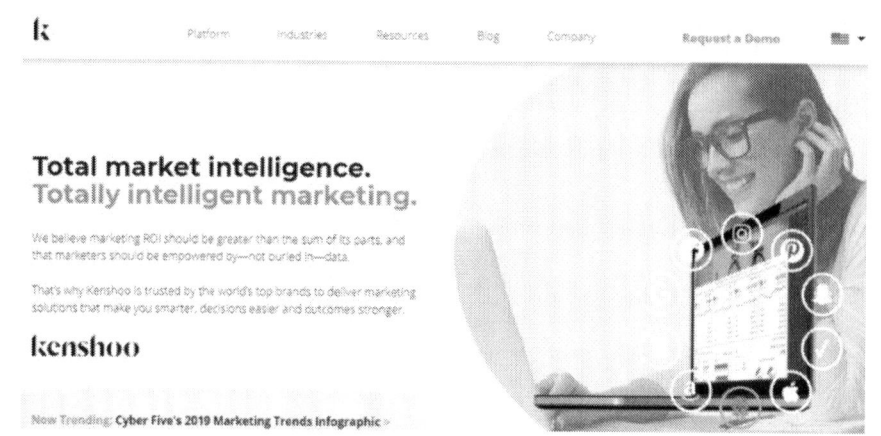

For a successful marketing campaign, you need to collect data from your customers or potential customers to grow and improve your business.

The data will help you understand your customers, their behaviors, and how to meet their needs. Kenshoo offers excellent marketing solutions to help brands grow their business through advertising.

It gives insights about customer data and how businesses can use that data to engage, build trust, and convert leads through advertising.

Visit the website to learn more about the tool and how to use it effectively to manage your Facebook ads.

Zalster

This is a great tool to help you optimize your Facebook ads with marketing automation. It reduces the workload of managing your ads and optimizes them for better results.

The tool is run by experts who are ready to assist you if you have questions about how it works. It also helps with cross-channel ad optimization to reach more target clients and increase conversion rates.

How to Start a Facebook Ads Campaign

Now that you have the tools you need to create outstanding Facebook ads, let's look at how to get your campaign started. Note that you'll need to have a Facebook page before you create your ads.

Visit Facebook Ads Manager

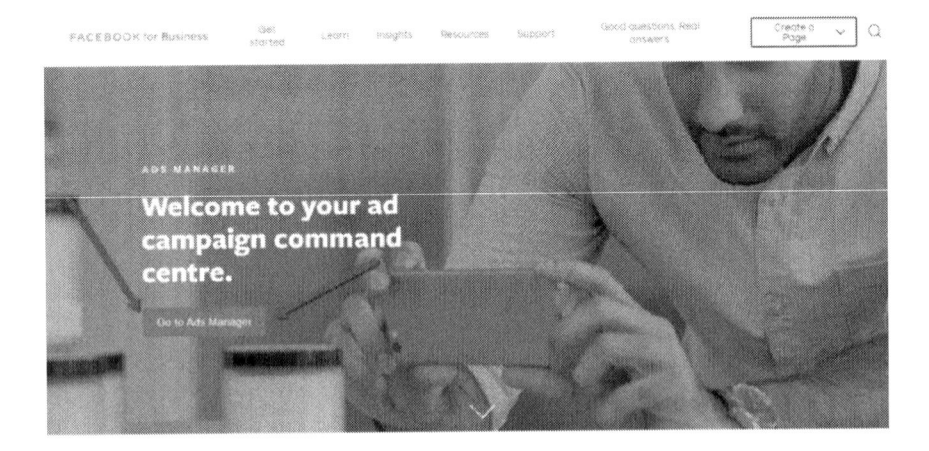

Create your own account. This will be the hub for creating and managing your ads.

Set Goals for Your Ads

Before you start on your ads, you need to understand why you're creating them. Choose an objective.

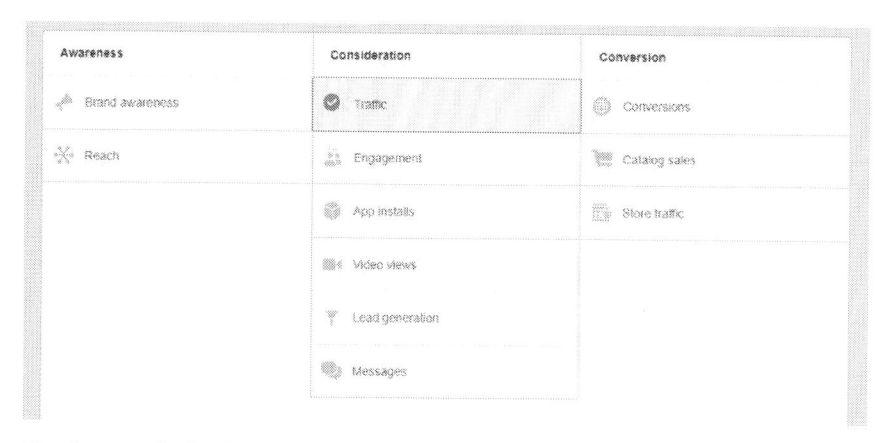

Awareness	Consideration	Conversion
Brand awareness	Traffic	Conversions
Reach	Engagement	Catalog sales
	App installs	Store traffic
	Video views	
	Lead generation	
	Messages	

Having goals laid out helps you create specific ads that ask potential clients to perform a specific action. You can also decide where you want your ads to drive your traffic.

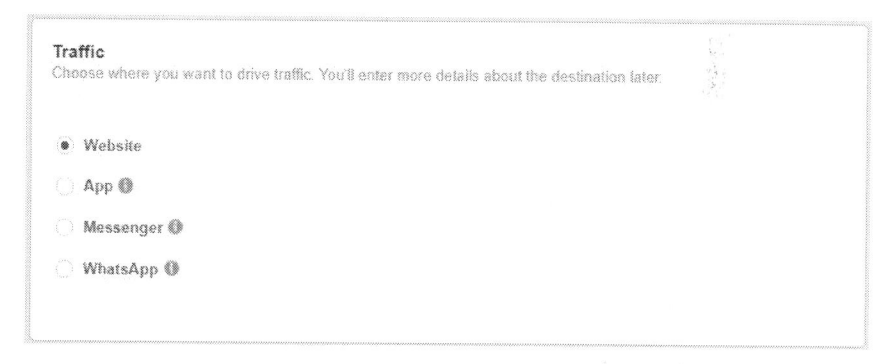

Traffic
Choose where you want to drive traffic. You'll enter more details about the destination later.

- Website
- App
- Messenger
- WhatsApp

Invesp's research shows that people spend different shares of their ad budget to accomplish different goals on Facebook.

AD SPEND SHARE BY GOALS

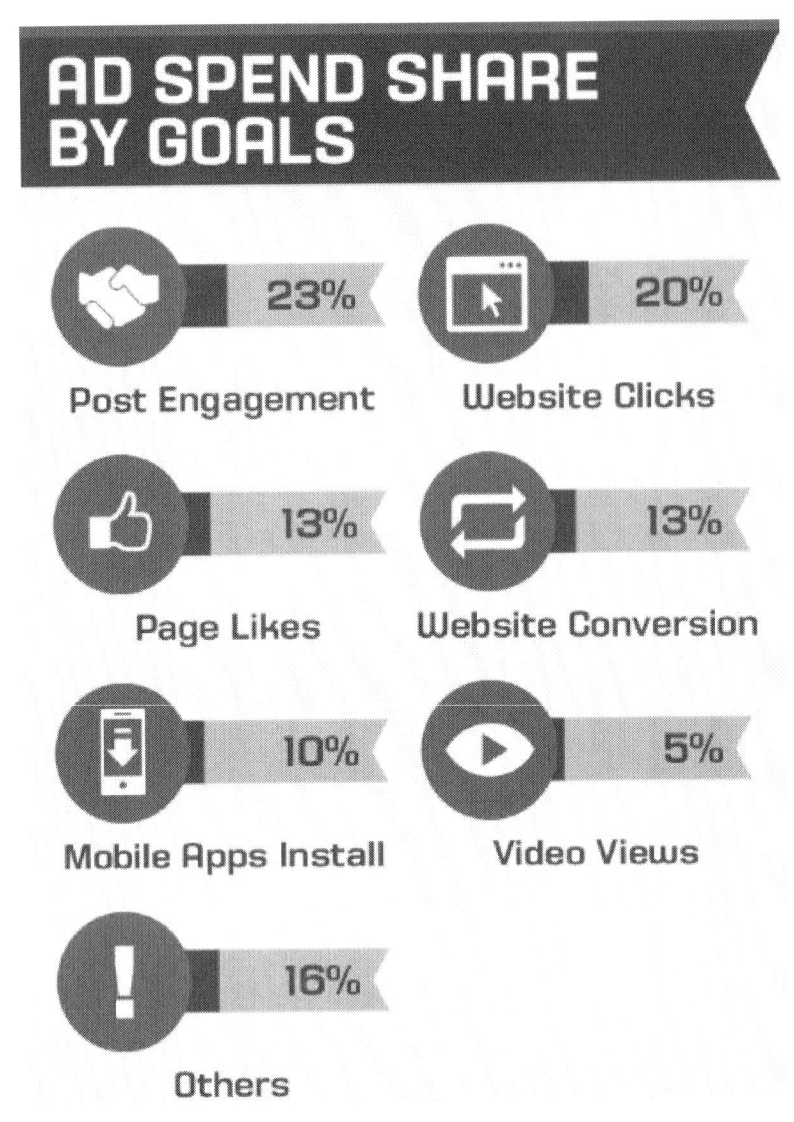

- 23% Post Engagement
- 20% Website Clicks
- 13% Page Likes
- 13% Website Conversion
- 10% Mobile Apps Install
- 5% Video Views
- 16% Others

This shows that prioritizing your goals can help you reach more target customers for your brand. It also makes it easy to track your ads' performance in relation to the goals you've set.

Choose Your Audience

Once you've created your Ads account and set your goals, you need to choose your audience.

Chapter 5: Facebook Advertising

There are many factors to consider in this step of the process. Your choices will be based on the target audience you want to reach and the objectives of your ads.

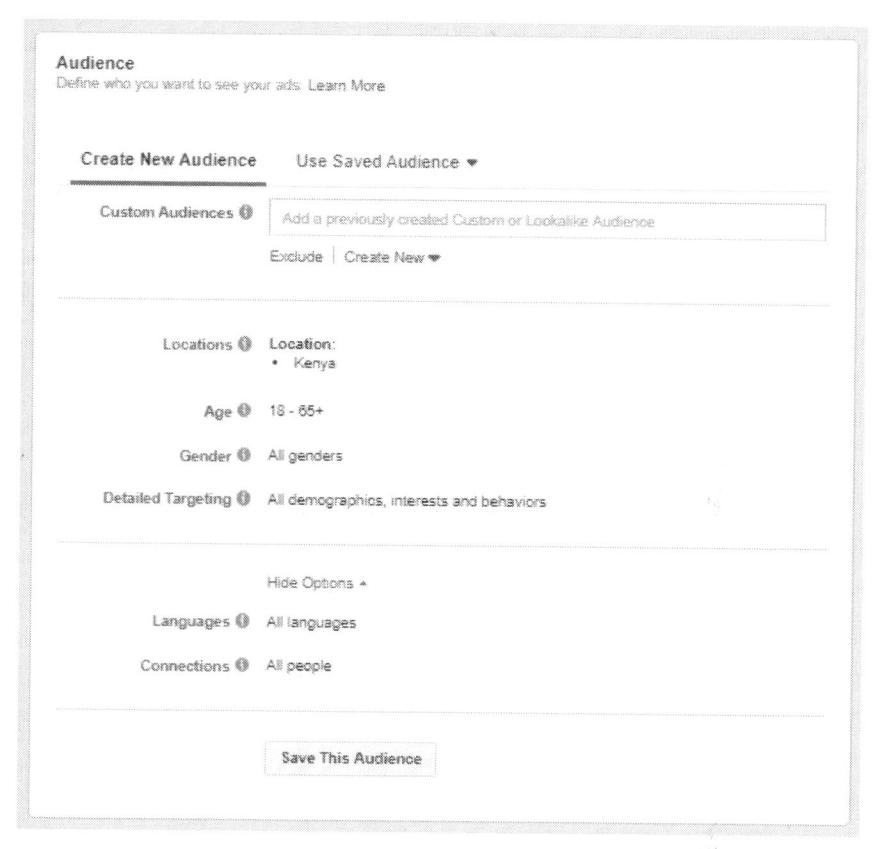

```
Audience
Define who you want to see your ads. Learn More

    Create New Audience      Use Saved Audience ▼

        Custom Audiences ❶   [ Add a previously created Custom or Lookalike Audience ]
                             Exclude | Create New ▼

              Locations ❶    Location:
                               • Kenya

                    Age ❶    18 - 65+

                 Gender ❶    All genders

      Detailed Targeting ❶   All demographics, interests and behaviors

                             Hide Options ▲

              Languages ❶    All languages

            Connections ❶    All people

                             [ Save This Audience ]
```

When you define who you want to see your ads, it's easy to reach the target market because they're likely already interested in your business and probably easier to convert into customers.

Set Your Ads Budget

At this stage of creating an Ads campaign, you set your target budget for your ads.

Optimization & Spending Controls
Define how much you'd like to spend, and when you'd like your ads to appear

Optimization for Ad Delivery: Link Clicks

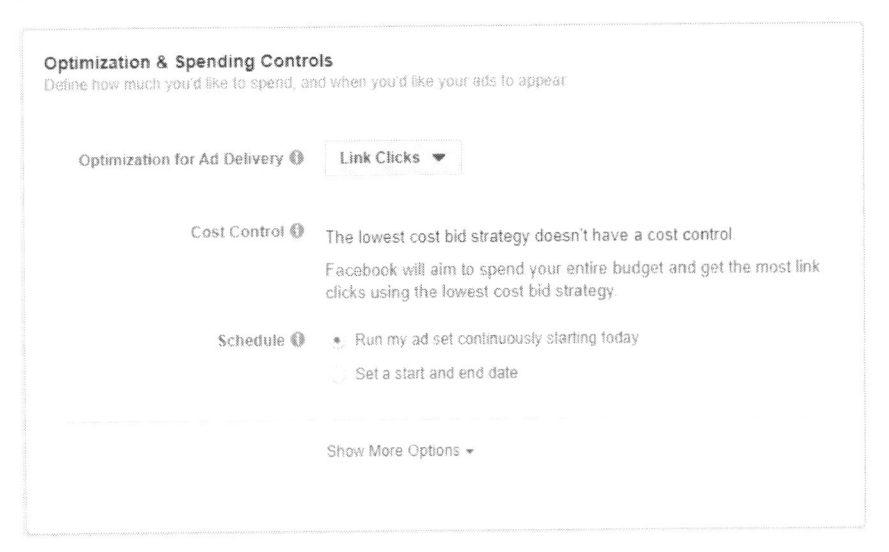

Cost Control: The lowest cost bid strategy doesn't have a cost control.
Facebook will aim to spend your entire budget and get the most link clicks using the lowest cost bid strategy.

Schedule:
- Run my ad set continuously starting today
- Set a start and end date

Show More Options

You can also set a schedule that lets you stay within your budget. You can then create your ads and plan the ad placements.

When creating your ads, you can set the type of format you want them to appear in.

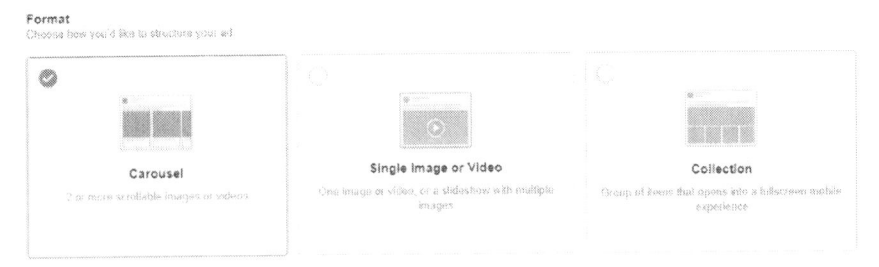

Format
Choose how you'd like to structure your ad

- **Carousel** — 2 or more scrollable images or videos
- **Single Image or Video** — One image or video, or a slideshow with multiple images
- **Collection** — Group of items that opens into a fullscreen mobile experience

You can also set the dimensions of your ads. These will depend on whether you're posting an image or video ads. For image ads, you'll choose from the options shown here:

● Image   ○ Video / Slideshow   Remove

[Select Image]

IMAGE SPECIFICATIONS

- Recommended image size: **1080 × 1080 pixels**
- Recommended image ratio: **1:1**
- To maximize ad delivery, use an image that contains **little or no overlaid text.** Learn More

For questions and more information, see the Facebook Ad Guidelines.

Headline (optional) ❶

[Write a short headline]

Description (optional) ❶

[Include additional details]

Website URL ❶

[http://www.example.com/page]

Build a URL Parameter

Here are the video ads dimension settings:

○ Image   ● Video / Slideshow   Remove

[Select Video]   [Create Slideshow]   [Use Templates]

VIDEO RECOMMENDATIONS:

- Recommended Length: **Up to 15 seconds**
- Recommended Aspect Ratio: **Vertical (4:5)**
  View aspect ratio specifications
- Sound: **Enabled with captions included**
- Thumbnails: **Dynamically selected**

VIDEO SPECIFICATIONS:

- Recommended format: **.mp4, .mov or .gif**
  View full list of supported formats
- **Required Lengths By Placement:**
  - Facebook: **240 minutes max**
  - In-Stream: **5 - 15 seconds**
  - Audience Network: **5 - 120 seconds**
  - Instagram Stories: **Up to 120 seconds**
  - Rewarded Video: **3 - 60 seconds**
- Resolution: **600px minimum width**
- File size: **Up to 4 GB max**

SLIDESHOW SPECIFICATIONS:

- Use high resolution images or a video file to create a slideshow
- Facebook and Instagram: 15 seconds max
- Slideshows will loop

For questions and more information, see the Facebook Ad Guidelines.

Headline (optional)

> Write a short headline

Description (optional)

> Include additional details

Website URL

> http://www.example.com/page

Build a URL Parameter

If you need to collect data and track your ad performance, you can include tracking settings to monitor how your ads are doing and learn how to improve them.

Tracking

Conversion Tracking

Facebook Pixel [Set Up]

App Events [Set Up]

Offline Events [Set Up]

URL Parameters (optional)

key1=value1&key2=value2

Build a URL Parameter

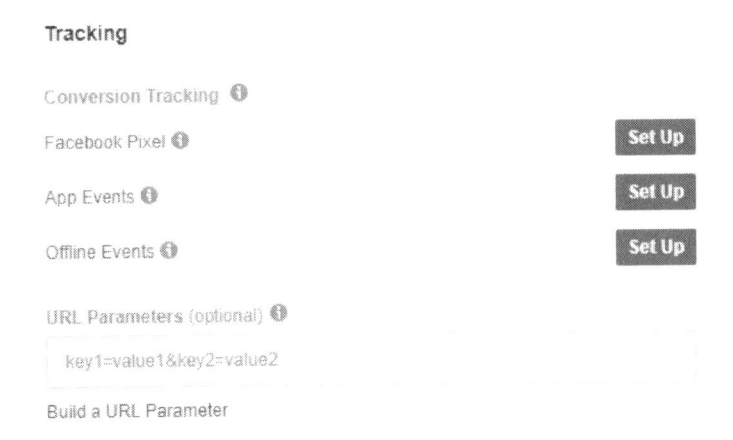

You may also want automated placement, meaning Facebook chooses where to place your ads based on your budget and objectives.

You can manually edit the placement of your ads if you like.

Placements
Show your ads to the right people in the right places.

- **Automatic Placements (Recommended)**
  Use automatic placements to maximize your budget and help show your ads to more people. Facebook's delivery system will allocate your ad set's budget across multiple placements based on where they're likely to perform best. Learn More

- **Edit Placements**
  Manually choose the places to show your ad. The more placements you select, the more opportunities you'll have to reach your target audience and achieve your business goals. Learn More

How to Optimize Facebook Ads

Now that you know how to create ads for your marketing campaigns, let's look at how to optimize them. To increase conversion rates, your ads have to be seen by as many target customers as possible.

Below are some tips that can help you optimize your ads and increase ad conversion rates.

Use Direct Calls-to-Action

Since you've already set advertising goals you want your ads to achieve, create direct CTAs that advance those goals.

Chapter 5: Facebook Advertising

If you want the target customer to sign up for your email list, use a "sign up" call-to-action. Here's an example of this kind of CTA:

> **ClickUp**
> Sponsored
>
> Ditch spreadsheets and save time managing social media, digital marketing, and SEO
>
> Try ClickUp™ Free Forever—100,000+ teams from companies like Google, Airbnb, Netflix, & Uber are more productive with Tasks, Docs, Goals, and more!
>
> Direct CTA
>
> CLICKUP.COM/MARKETING
> Try ClickUp™ Free Forever   Sign Up

When potential clients are confronted with direct CTAs, they're able to make decisions faster and take action.

Design a Great Landing Page

In chapter 2, we talked in-depth about landing pages. You can revisit the chapter to refresh your memory.

A great landing page is a key to increasing your lead conversion and generating more sales from ads. When your ads drive your leads to your landing page, they shouldn't have to struggle to figure out what you're offering or how it can benefit them.

For example, this ad tries to draw target clients to the website to increase brand awareness:

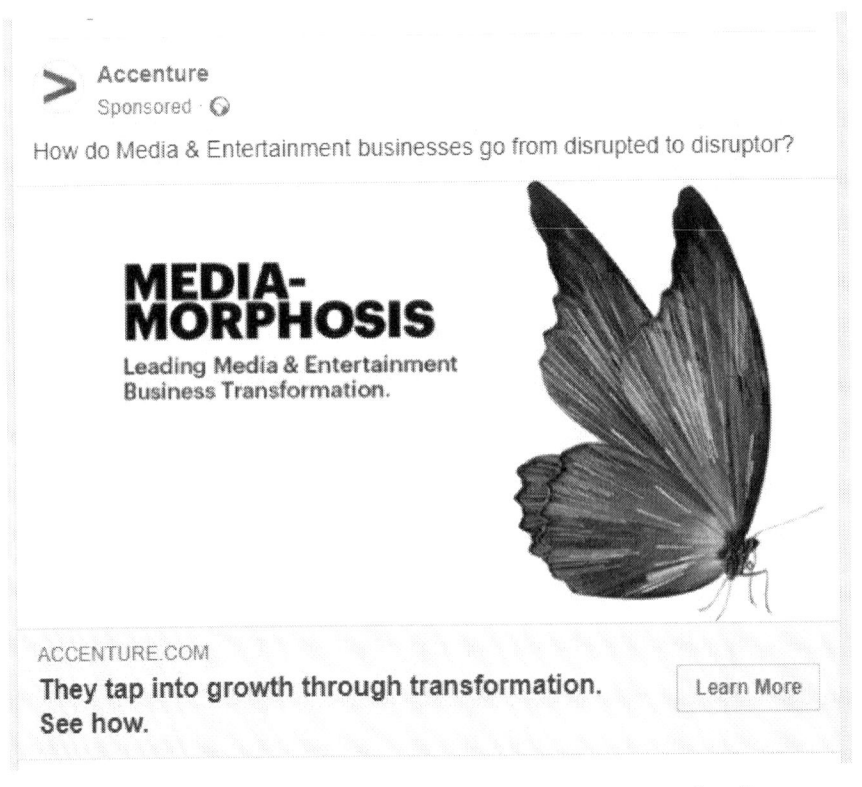

> **Accenture**
> Sponsored
>
> How do Media & Entertainment businesses go from disrupted to disruptor?
>
> **MEDIA-MORPHOSIS**
> Leading Media & Entertainment Business Transformation.
>
> ACCENTURE.COM
> **They tap into growth through transformation. See how.**   Learn More

I clicked the "learn more" CTA and was taken to a great landing page with more information.

Through ads like this one, more customers are introduced to brands and quickly understand what they offer.

Use Eye-Catching Images and Videos

Images and videos are very attractive and help create a first impression on potential customers. Target customers are more inspired to take action when they watch or see a visually appealing ad.

Research by Renderforest shows that 40% of users take action immediately after watching a video ad.

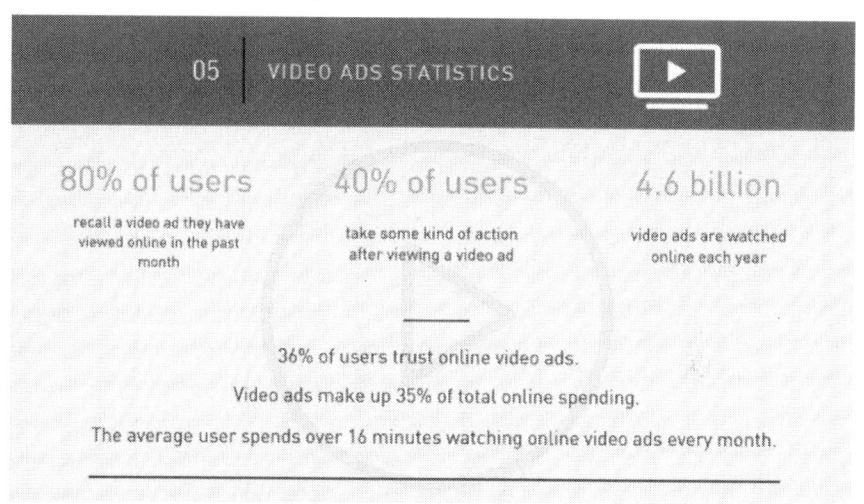

05 | VIDEO ADS STATISTICS

80% of users recall a video ad they have viewed online in the past month

40% of users take some kind of action after viewing a video ad

4.6 billion video ads are watched online each year

36% of users trust online video ads.
Video ads make up 35% of total online spending.
The average user spends over 16 minutes watching online video ads every month.

Research by Marketing Charts projects that brands will spend more than $61 billion on online video ads in 2021.

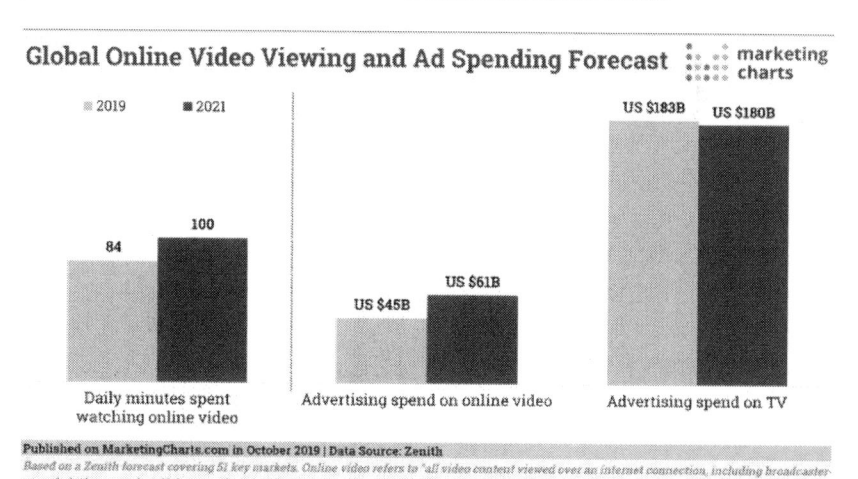

Global Online Video Viewing and Ad Spending Forecast — marketing charts

	2019	2021
Daily minutes spent watching online video	84	100
Advertising spend on online video	US $45B	US $61B
Advertising spend on TV	US $183B	US $180B

Published on MarketingCharts.com in October 2019 | Data Source: Zenith
Based on a Zenith forecast covering 51 key markets. Online video refers to "all video content viewed over an internet connection, including broadcaster-owned platforms such as Hulu, over-the-top subscription services like Netflix, video-sharing sites like YouTube, and videos viewed on social media".

This shows that more and more people are using online video ads to advertise their brands. If your ads aren't engaging and attractive, you're losing what may be your best chance to convert more leads to customers.

Use a Variety of Ad Formats

A/B testing is useful when it comes to optimizing your ads for different formats. Run your ads in different ad formats and find the ones with the highest conversion rates.

Using several formats helps you discover the types of ads that perform better and optimize them to engage more leads.

Target the Right Audience

Even the most stunning, well-made ad is useless if you fail to target the right audience. It has to get in front of the customers who need your services or products.

After all, these people are already searching for a solution to their challenge. Encourage them to take action because your brand has what they need. When you place the right ads before them, they'll learn more about your business and make their decisions easily.

Part of good targeting is using the right ad format and platform. You should target a larger audience to increase the chances of more people seeing your ads and becoming aware of your products and business.

Keep Ads Short and Direct

Ads must be short and to-the-point. Make it easy for the target market to stay focused on your message and know what action to take after reading or watching your ads.

The attention span of the target market is decreasing every day. With ever more competition from other brands offering the same services, this attention is shrinking.

More and more people are shopping online. Research by Statista shows that the number could reach 2.14 billion by 2021. More companies are making videos part of their marketing, and customers will shift their attention to the brands that create brief but captivating videos.

Number of digital buyers worldwide from 2014 to 2021
(in billions)

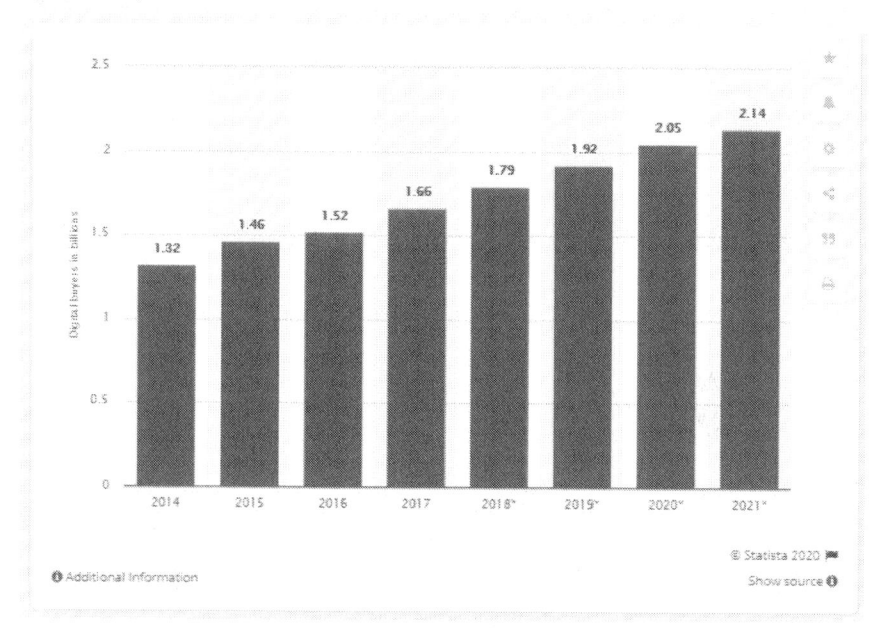

Year	Digital buyers (billions)
2014	1.32
2015	1.46
2016	1.52
2017	1.66
2018*	1.79
2019*	1.92
2020*	2.05
2021*	2.14

© Statista 2020

Create short-and-sweet ads that capture the attention of the viewers and draw them to your business. If you're using video ads, it's wise to keep them under two minutes. Shorter videos have higher engagement rates with potential clients.

Research by Marketing Land shows that marketing videos between 16 and 20 seconds have the highest engagement rates.

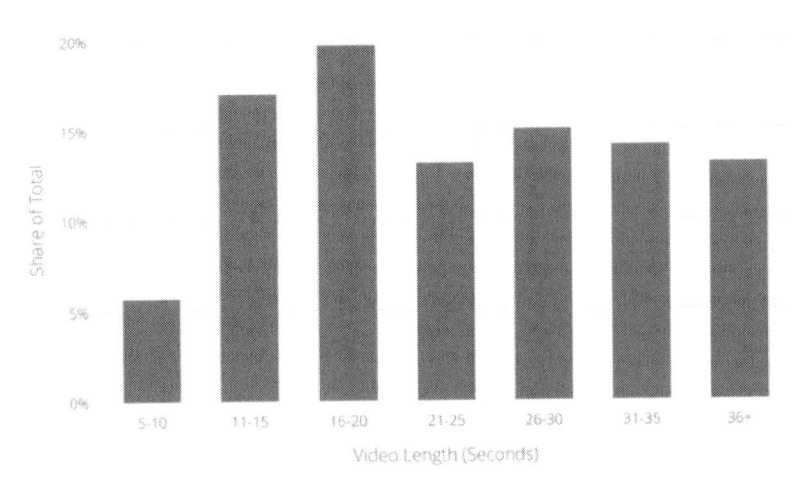

Facebook video ad length, ecommerce advertisers

The research also shows that the same Facebook video ad length has the highest conversion rate.

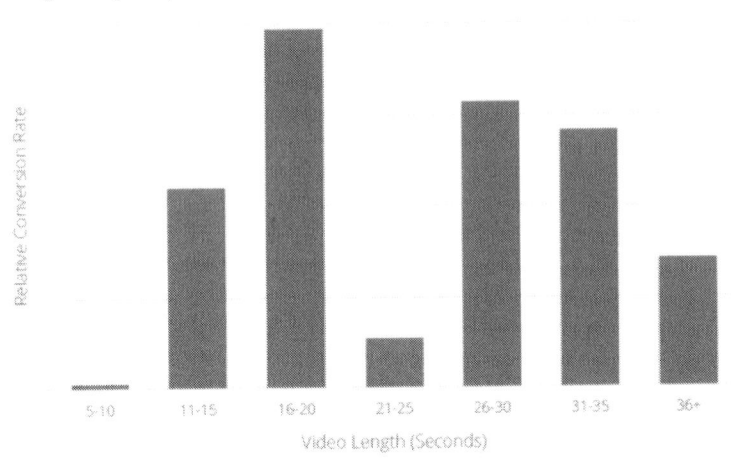

Facebook video ad conversion rates by length, ecommerce advertisers
Weighted by ad spend

Use Analytics to Improve Your Marketing

You're running your ads and have also been gathering analytics and monitoring metrics related to your ad performance.

To improve and optimize that performance, you have to convert these analytics into actionable insights and use them to improve your ads.

For instance, you've created an ad and used keywords that will help it rank high. You can collect your analytics and metrics, such as data about the times your ads appear when people are scrolling through Facebook.

You can note what times of day certain keywords are more or less effective, and use that information to choose keywords that will optimize your brand.

Segment Your Audience

Instead of trying to reach your entire audience at once, you can segment your ads so that each one is designed to reach a particular type of audience.

Since different members of your audience are in different buyer journey stages, segmenting will make it easy for the target market to make their individual decisions and commit to your business.

If for instance, a potential customer is in the awareness stage, you can create ads that target them to introduce your brand and explain how it can help them.

Research by Marketing Charts shows that 37% of shoppers look to social media for purchase inspiration.

Online Media Used for Purchase Inspiration

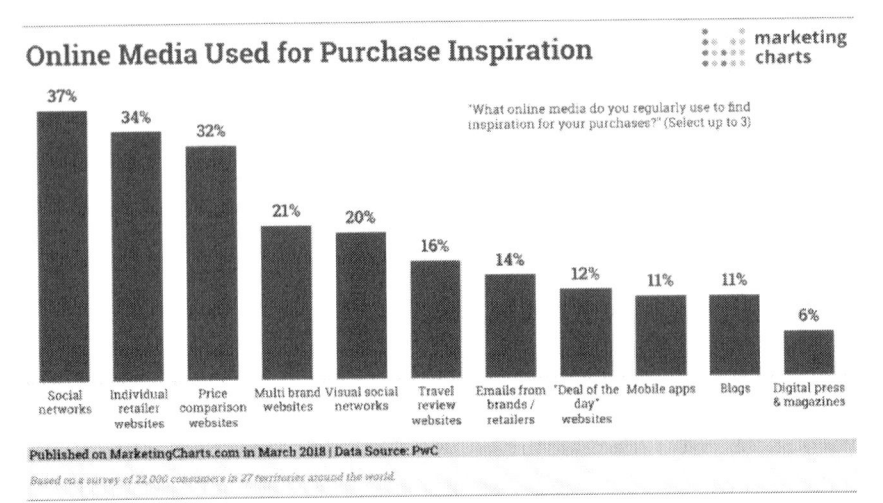

"What online media do you regularly use to find inspiration for your purchases?" (Select up to 3)

Source	%
Social networks	37%
Individual retailer websites	34%
Price comparison websites	32%
Multi brand websites	21%
Visual social networks	20%
Travel review websites	16%
Emails from brands / retailers	14%
"Deal of the day" websites	12%
Mobile apps	11%
Blogs	11%
Digital press & magazines	6%

Published on MarketingCharts.com in March 2018 | Data Source: PwC
Based on a survey of 22,000 consumers in 27 territories around the world.

Online media used by consumers around the world for purchase inspiration.

It seems some buyers view Facebook ads to get inspired to make a purchase online.

With segmentation, you can use that inspiration to engage them with your business and probably convert them into clients.

Another study by Clutch shows that 89% of businesses value Facebook as a great social site to grow their businesses.

The Social Media Platforms Businesses Value

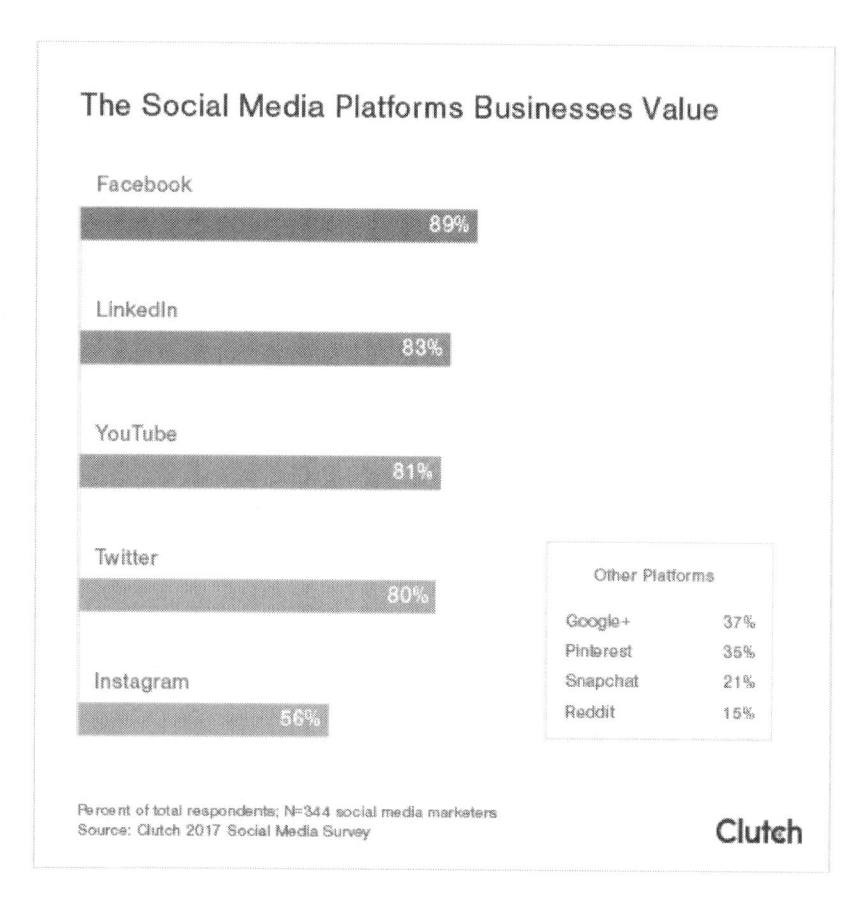

Platform	Percent
Facebook	89%
LinkedIn	83%
YouTube	81%
Twitter	80%
Instagram	56%

Other Platforms

Google+	37%
Pinterest	35%
Snapchat	21%
Reddit	15%

Percent of total respondents; N=344 social media marketers
Source: Clutch 2017 Social Media Survey

Clutch

If you're in the B2B space, most of your target clients see Facebook as a valuable business site. If you segment your ads to reach these target markets, it will be easy to get their attention.

Schedule Your Ads at the Right Time

Your ads won't always perform well and reach many target customers. To increase their reach, schedule your ads and optimize them for the right times.

This will ensure the greatest number of target customers sees them by displaying them when those people are most active on Facebook.

Choose the Right Objective for Each Ad

Every ad should be created to accomplish a specific purpose or objective. As you design each one, choose the objective that fits into your overall marketing strategy and furthers your goals. For a reminder of the list of Facebook Ads objectives, see "How to Start a Facebook Ads Campaign: Set Goals for Your Ads" earlier in this chapter.

When you plan your ads with the right objectives, the Facebook algorithm helps you optimize your ads to reach more target customers.

Now that we've covered the ins and outs of Facebook Ads, let's move on to user onboarding.

Chapter 6: User Onboarding

You've done the hard work of advertising your brand and now clients are coming to your business. To win their trust and retain them, you have to show them how your services will help them and how to best use the services to solve their pain points.

In this chapter, we'll discuss how to onboard new customers to your business. User onboarding is a brand's process of guiding new customers on how to use their services or products. It's a delicate step as you get your clients acquainted with your business. If it's not done right, brands lose a lot of new customers to their competitors.

Research shows that brands can lose up to 75% of their new customers the first week they start using their business.

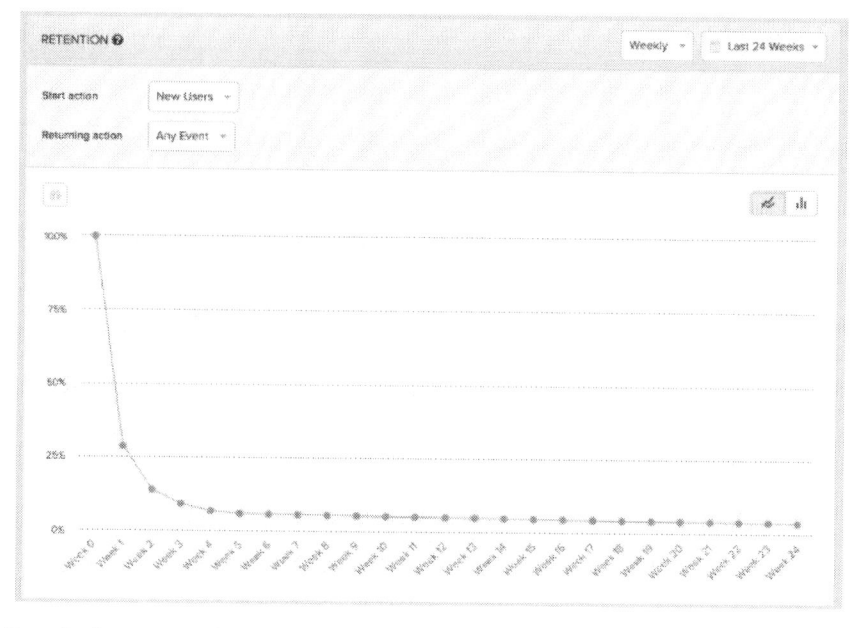

Localytics research shows that 25% of new app users left the business after using the app just once.

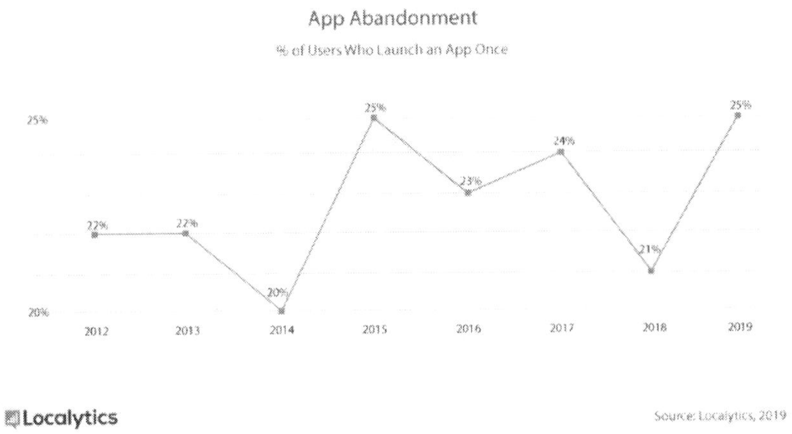
App Abandonment
% of Users Who Launch an App Once
25%
20%
22%
22%
20%
25%
23%
24%
21%
25%
2012
2013
2014
2015
2016
2017
2018
2019
Localytics
Source: Localytics, 2019

If your new users aren't well onboarded, you'll lose them shortly after they start using your services. To keep them coming back for more, guide them through a step-by-step process that makes understanding how to use your product easy.

Importance of User Onboarding

Besides retaining customers, these are some of the benefits of good user onboarding.

Increase Sales

Onboarding helps you generate more sales and grow your business.

Your new customers will be using your services or products to satisfy their business needs. Well, onboarded customers will become your retainer clients as they continually use your products or services. You'll be earning continuous income from these loyal customers.

Win Your Clients' Trust

When customers visit your business and are taught how to use your services, they trust your brand's offerings. They believe in your brand and engage with you as you help them solve problems.

User onboarding is a trust-building process. Your new customers learn more about your business and the different ways it addresses their challenges.

Chapter 6: User Onboarding

Provide More Value to Customers

You're in business to solve problems and make money doing it. To serve your customers better, you need to know more about their experience with your business. The onboarding process helps you find out how to provide more value to your customers. Learning more about their unique characteristics will help you improve your customer experience and offer better services or products.

Research by Invesp shows that 55% of customers spend more on brands that offer a better experience.

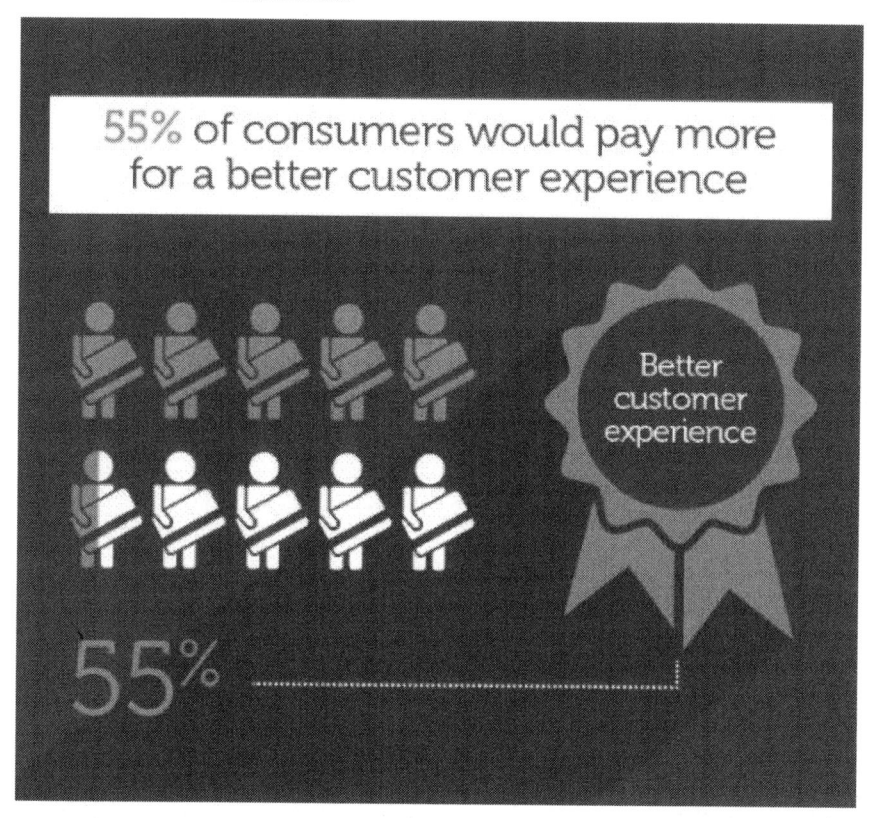

55% of consumers would pay more for a better customer experience

Better customer experience

55%

This shows how important customer experience is for your business growth. As you onboard your customers, you give them a great experience that motivates them to stick with your brand.

Improving customer experience also helps brands grow their sales through cross-selling and upselling. If your customers are thrilled with a product you offer, they'll likely be interested in one of your other products, or in an improved version of the original product.

Why Improve Customer Experience

The top three reasons why businesses proactively manage and invest in customer experience are to:

- Improve customer retention — 42%
- Improve customer satisfaction — 33%
- Improve cross-selling and up-selling — 32%

Addressing each of these reasons can positively impact bottom line revenue.

Image Source: https://www.superoffice.com/blog/customer-experience-statistics/

Show clients How to Use Your Services

Using some services or products can be complex. To help new customers know how to use the services, you have to onboard them.

This will make using your services easy rather than frustrating and time-consuming. A service that's easy to use is valuable and offers a better customer experience. You want to provide a solution to customers' problems, and that solution shouldn't introduce other problems.

Reduce Churn Rate

Customers use services, but if they can't really understand or see the value of using the software, they stop using it.

Research by Statista shows a 22% churn rate among online retail brands. When brands take their new customers successfully through the onboarding process, they reduce the churn rate and retain more customers.

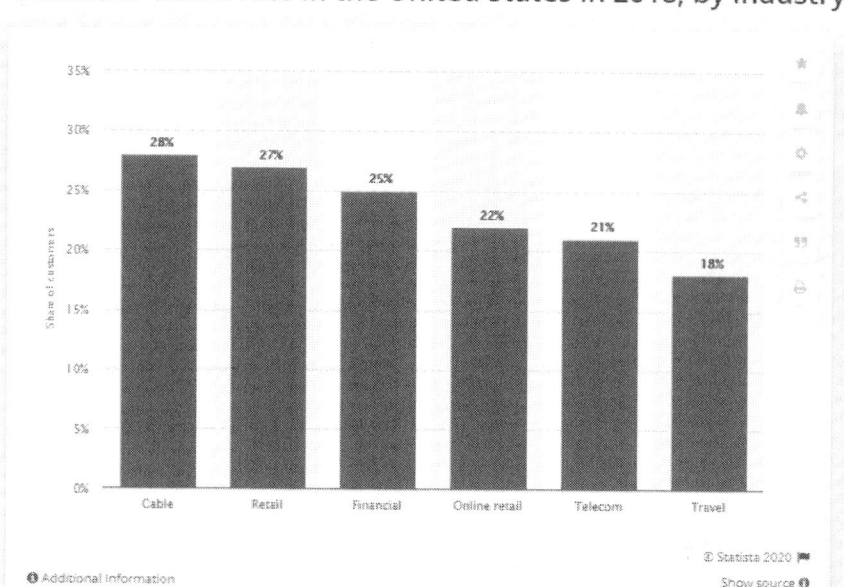

Customer churn rate in the United States in 2018, by industry

Industry	Share of customers
Cable	28%
Retail	27%
Financial	25%
Online retail	22%
Telecom	21%
Travel	18%

© Statista 2020

Increase Customer Engagement

It is through the onboarding process that many brands engage with customers as they incorporate them into their businesses.

The process gives your business another excuse to interact with potential customers and new customers. Engage with them as they seek to learn more about your brand's services. This interaction builds trust, which can lead to more sales and loyal clients who will be in constant need of your services.

Improve Product Adoption

Potential clients can hear about your product from other users who have had a great experience with your onboarding process. They may then decide to purchase your product or service. This brings in more sales and attracts new customers.

Different clients will adopt your product at different stages of the product adoption process. This curve shows the typical path of adoption of your services or products.

Product Adoption Curve

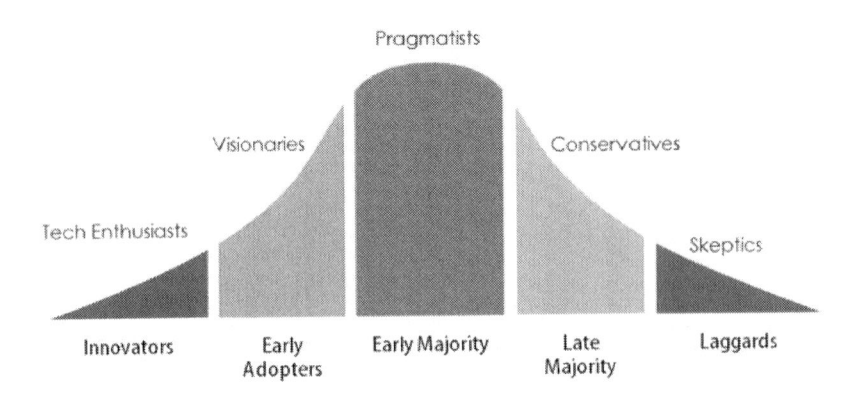

```
                    Pragmatists

           Visionaries          Conservatives

Tech Enthusiasts                          Skeptics

  Innovators    Early    Early Majority    Late      Laggards
               Adopters                  Majority
```

Several factors influence product adoption.

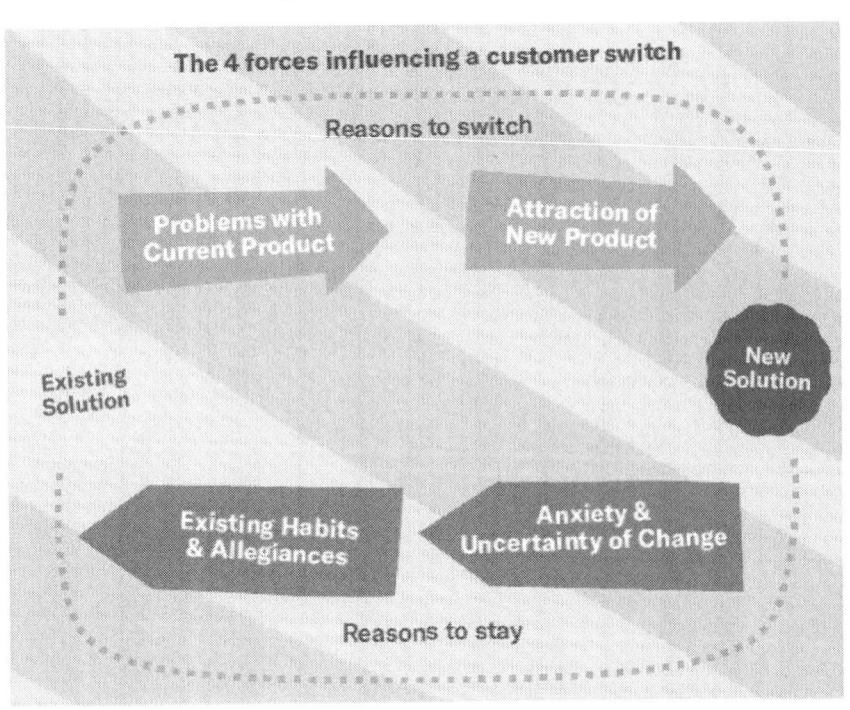

The 4 forces influencing a customer switch

Reasons to switch
- Problems with Current Product
- Attraction of New Product

Existing Solution → New Solution

Reasons to stay
- Existing Habits & Allegiances
- Anxiety & Uncertainty of Change

Image Source: https://www.intercom.com/blog/product-adoption/

Once your customers establish great habits with your products, they can help you bring in other clients. Their comments on your services or reviews can play a huge part in the product adoption process.

Increase Conversion Rates

When potential customers know how to use a product, they're more likely to convert and buy that product.

There are numerous ways to draw clients to your business. Below are the results of research by Episerver that show conversion rate by traffic source.

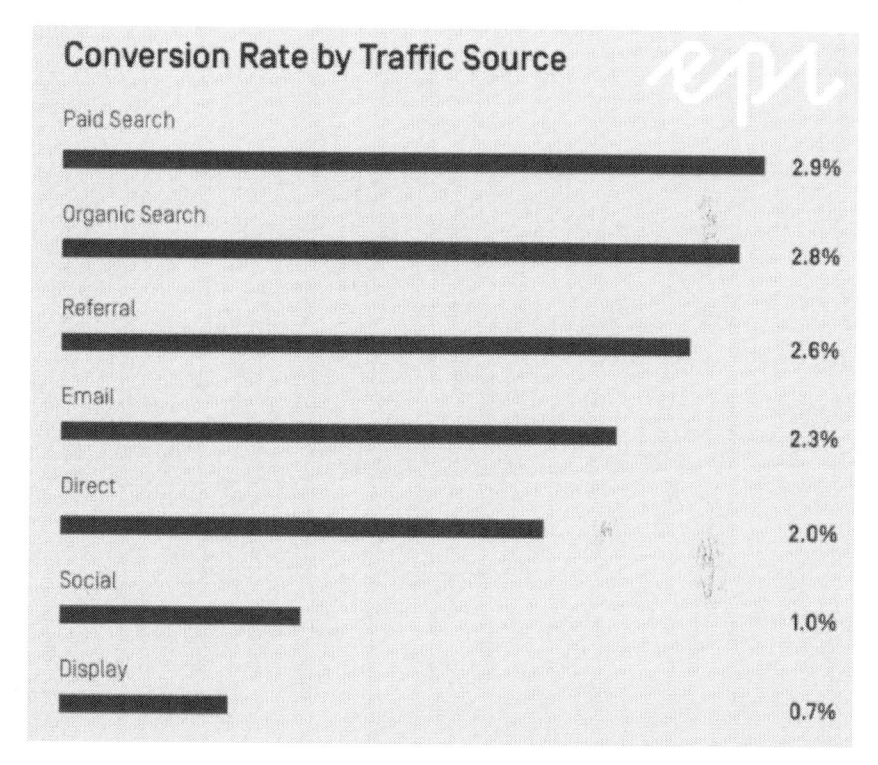

Conversion Rate by Traffic Source

Traffic Source	Conversion Rate
Paid Search	2.9%
Organic Search	2.8%
Referral	2.6%
Email	2.3%
Direct	2.0%
Social	1.0%
Display	0.7%

Guiding your customers through onboarding can help you get more conversions to boost the conversions from these sources.

To avoid losing newly acquired customers and reduce cart abandonment, stand by your customers as they begin using your product. This will help them get to know more about your business and your services.

Onboarding Metrics to Track

To see whether your onboarding process is progressing and bearing fruit for your business, here are some metrics to measure.

Customer Retention

Teaching your customers how to use your services or products and being there to answer their questions will reduce the rate at which they leave your business.

To measure your onboarding efforts, check your data and evaluate the number of customers you're retaining.

Research by Vonage shows that brands lose $62 billion due to poor customer service. Here are other reasons customers switch brands.

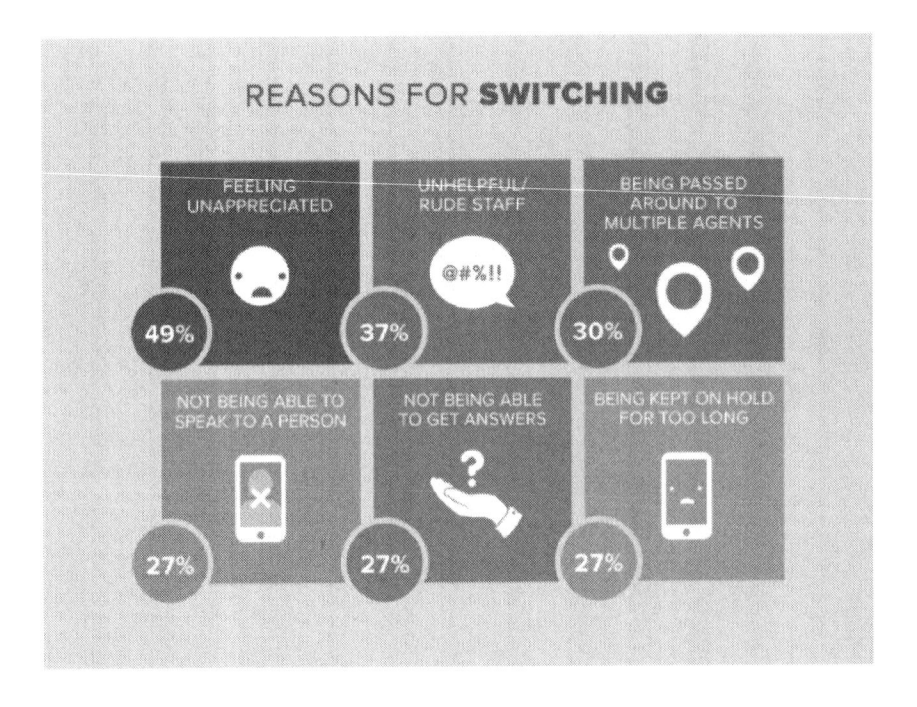

REASONS FOR SWITCHING

- FEELING UNAPPRECIATED — 49%
- UNHELPFUL/RUDE STAFF — 37%
- BEING PASSED AROUND TO MULTIPLE AGENTS — 30%
- NOT BEING ABLE TO SPEAK TO A PERSON — 27%
- NOT BEING ABLE TO GET ANSWERS — 27%
- BEING KEPT ON HOLD FOR TOO LONG — 27%

If you find that customers are leaving too often, make sure you offer a way for them to let you know why. Then you can use that information to adjust your onboarding process and keep customers around longer.

Chapter 6: User Onboarding

Conversion Rates

High conversion rates from your new and potential customers show that your onboarding process is performing well. New customers like your brand and services, enjoy learning how to use your product and believe they're getting value by using it.

Free Trial Conversions

Most SaaS brands offer a free trial of their services. The free trial can be for a week, two weeks, or a month to give customers adequate time to see how the product works before they decide to purchase.

Here's an example from the Hootsuite website.

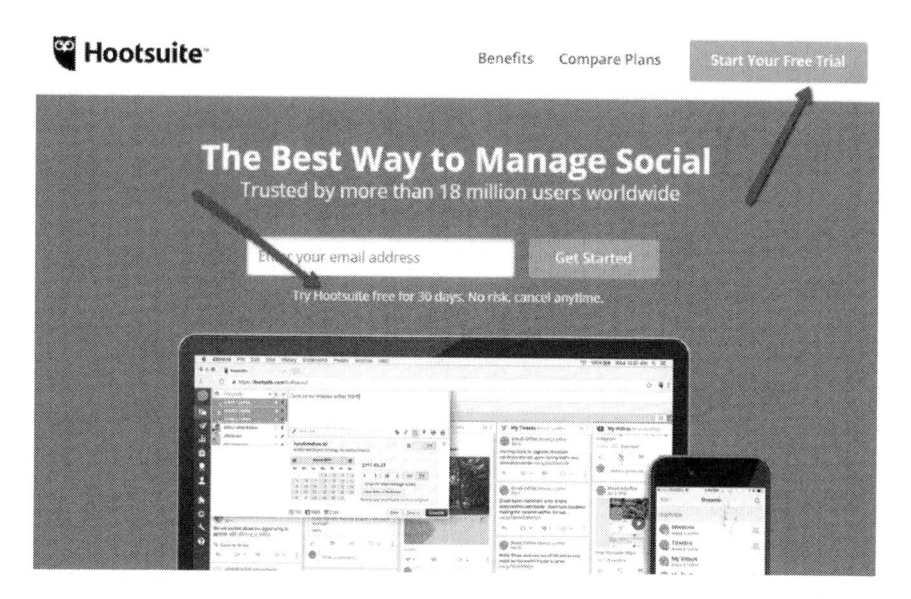

Giving your new customers services for free helps you build trust with them as you onboard them.

You can check the progress of your onboarding process by looking at the number of trial users who converted and became recurrent customers. If this number keeps decreasing even though you're still giving your customers free trial services and onboarding them, there's a problem with your onboarding process.

Customer Acquisition Costs

Acquiring new customers is very costly. If your customer acquisition costs are higher than those customers' projected expenditures on your business, it's not worth it.

Onboard and acquire customers who will spend more on your business and help you generate more revenue and profits. You may also need to revisit your customer acquisition and onboarding processes to root out inefficiencies.

Low Referral Rates

Customers will refer others to brands that have helped them achieve success. Since their onboarding experience influences their perception of success, it can affect your referral rates in a positive or negative way.

You can calculate the sales resulting from your referrals to see how you're doing. Increased referral rates and sales signify that more customers are using your services and bringing in more referral sales.

Here's how to calculate your referral rates:

$$\text{Referral Rates} = \frac{\text{No. of } referred \text{ purchases}}{\text{No. of } total \text{ purchases}}$$

Research by Invesp shows that customers referred by others are four times more likely to refer other customers to the same brand.

Customer Reffered by Other Customers Have:

37% higher retention rate

4 times more likely to refer more customers to your brand

Image source: https://www.invespcro.com/blog/referral-marketing/

To measure the success of your onboarding process, check your referral and conversion rates. Low referral rates are a sign that some aspect of your onboarding process is falling short.

Customer Response Time

Throughout the process of onboarding, you're in constant communication with your new and potential customers, and even your previous customers. The speed with which these customers provide feedback can indicate their enjoyment of your onboarding process.

You can use different types of surveys as you communicate and onboard your customers. Some perform better than others. Research compiled by

Survey Anyplace shows the variation in response rates among different methods of customer surveying.

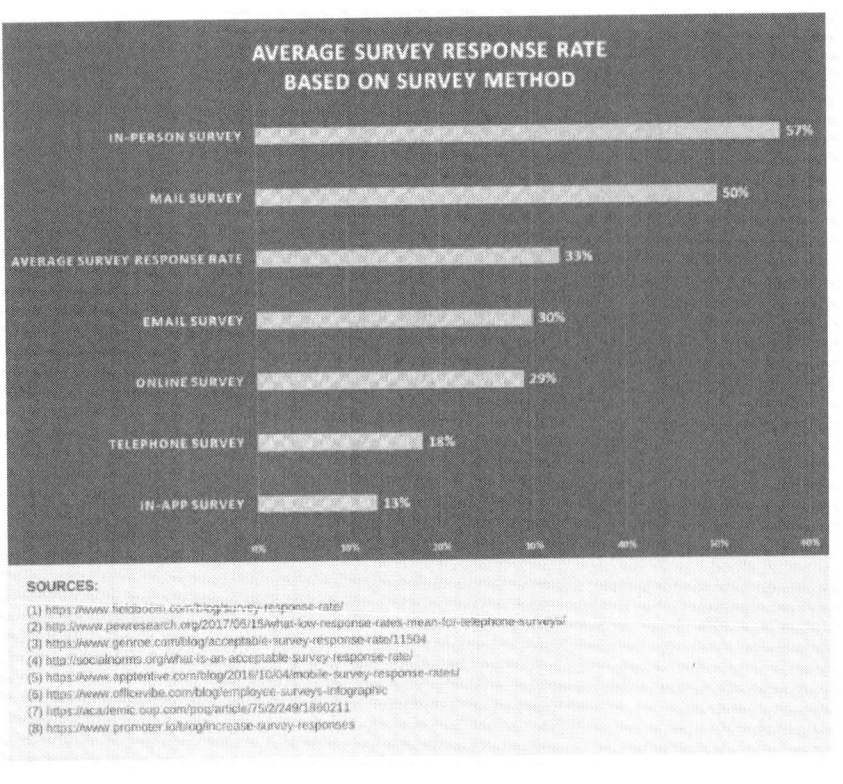

AVERAGE SURVEY RESPONSE RATE BASED ON SURVEY METHOD

Survey Method	Response Rate
In-Person Survey	57%
Mail Survey	50%
Average Survey Response Rate	33%
Email Survey	30%
Online Survey	29%
Telephone Survey	18%
In-App Survey	13%

SOURCES:
(1) https://www.fieldboom.com/blog/survey-response-rate/
(2) http://www.pewresearch.org/2017/05/15/what-low-response-rates-mean-for-telephone-surveys/
(3) https://www.genroe.com/blog/acceptable-survey-response-rate/11504
(4) http://socialnorms.org/what-is-an-acceptable-survey-response-rate/
(5) https://www.apptentive.com/blog/2016/10/04/mobile-survey-response-rates/
(6) https://www.officevibe.com/blog/employee-surveys-infographic
(7) https://academic.oup.com/poq/article/75/2/249/1860211
(8) https://www.promoter.io/blog/increase-survey-responses

Irrespective of your mode of communication, if response rates are low, it may have something to do with your onboarding process.

Customer Lifetime Value

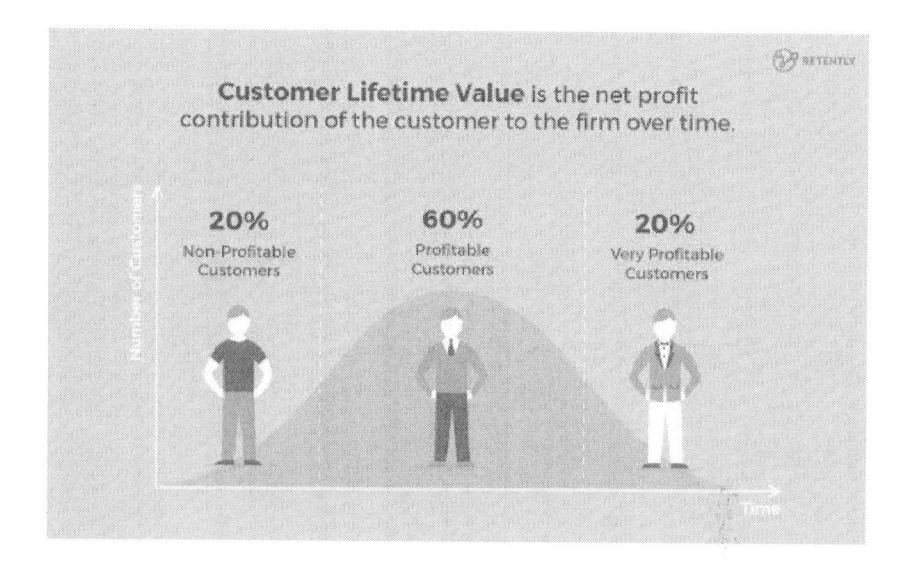

As we mentioned before, the onboarding process doesn't end with your new customers. Even customers who have been with you for a while are onboarded as you grow your business and offer updates or new services and products.

You can measure the success of your onboarding by tracking customer lifetime value. This is the profit you earn over time from a single client who uses your services repeatedly.

A high and continuous profit from a single customer shows that the customer values your brand and services. This client knows the value they're getting and appreciates the assistance you provide as they solve their problems. It's also an indicator that your customer onboarding process is performing well.

You can refer to chapter 3, "Ad Metrics to Measure: Customer Lifetime Value," for a reminder of how to calculate the metric.

High Bounce Rate

Your brand awareness and advertising campaigns are designed to draw your target customers to your brand. If they reach your website and bounce away after viewing very little your website, there's a problem.

This problem is probably mostly related to your web design and content, but your onboarding process can also contribute to the high bounce rate.

Your onboarding process starts long before customers reach your website. It starts with your marketing campaign. If they don't see any value from the time you start attracting them, there's a high chance they'll bounce.

You can reduce the bounce rate by welcoming your visitors with a video.

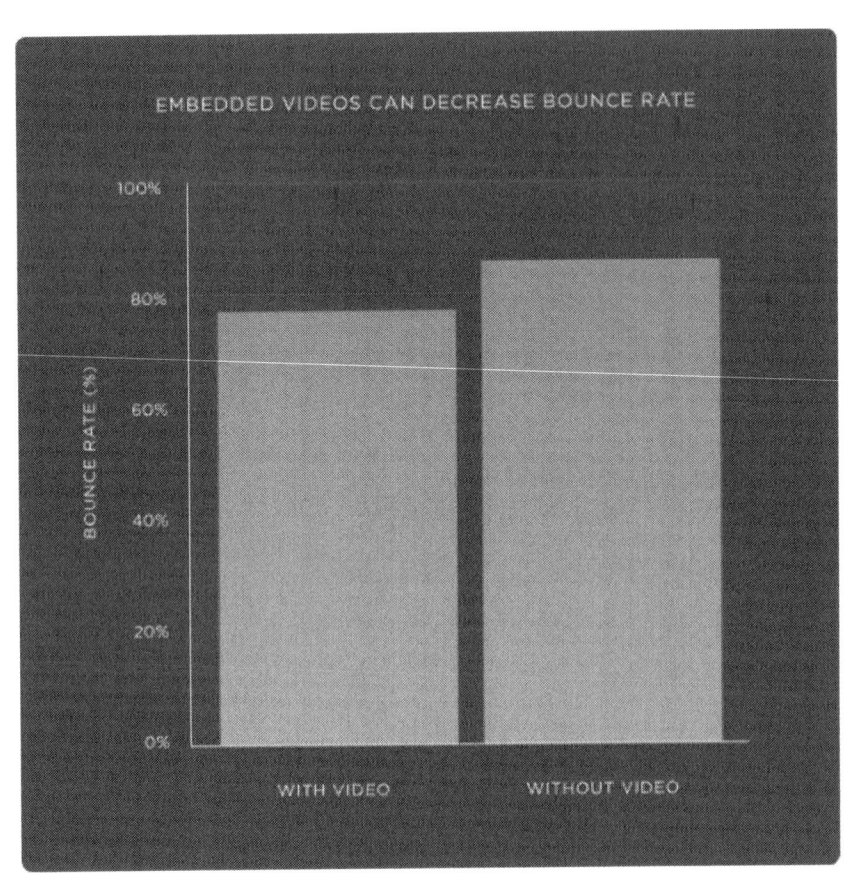

EMBEDDED VIDEOS CAN DECREASE BOUNCE RATE

As you also work on other factors, don't forget your website loading speeds. Slow website speeds can increase the bounce rate even if you're offering awesome services or products.

Research by Think With Google shows that the bounce rate increases with page load time.

As page load time goes from:

1s to 3s the probability of bounce increases 32%

1s to 5s the probability of bounce increases 90%

1s to 6s the probability of bounce increases 106%

1s to 10s the probability of bounce increases 123%

Onboarding Process Completion Time

How long will it take your new customers to understand and start using your services or products? That should be one of the first questions you ask yourself as you develop your onboarding procedure.

The less time it takes, the better for your business. New customers can be discouraged by a long, complicated onboarding process and leave your business.

It's important for new customers to be onboarded to your business as soon as possible, but don't overwhelm them in the process. A whirlwind speed won't give them enough time to understand what you're telling them and can be just as frustrating as a slow onboarding.

Feature Usage

Most SaaS tools have a collection of features they offer brands and these are mentioned during the course of their business marketing.

As you onboard new customers, it's essential to track the usage of all the features your business offers. This will help you know whether customers have a good understanding of these features.

For example, AWeber is an email marketing tool.

But the tool has many other features it offers alongside email marketing:

Chapter 6: User Onboarding

Email Newsletters Automatically create emails from your newest blog posts.	**Drag and Drop Editor** Choose from over 700 mobile responsive email templates.	**HTML Templates** Create and send professional email newsletters with ease.
Email Automation Easily create automated email sequences with our drag and drop editor.	**Tagging** Apply tags to trigger automated email campaigns based on clicks and opens.	**Team Hub** Enable multiple users to collaborate around a single account.

‹ ● ○ ○ ›

Split Testing Test subject lines, send times, email content and much more.	**Autoresponder Follow Ups** Send a sequence of automatically delivered emails.	**RSS to Email** Automatically create emails from your newest blog posts.
Integrations Connect your email list with your favorite online tools to automate your list growth.	**Sign Up Forms** Grow your email list with mobile responsive sign up forms.	**Email API** Connect third-party integrations with AWeber's API.

‹ ○ ● ○ ›

Mobile Apps Download our suite of mobile apps.	**Customer Service** Get account support when you need it.	**Subscriber Management** Easily collect, track and manage your subscriber list.
Subscriber Segmenting Create subscriber segments to send targeted emails and campaigns.	**Email Tracking** Track email performance with analytics like open rates, click-throughs and more.	**Email Deliverability Rate** Get industry-leading deliverability and ensure your emails make it to the inbox.

‹ ○ ○ ● ›

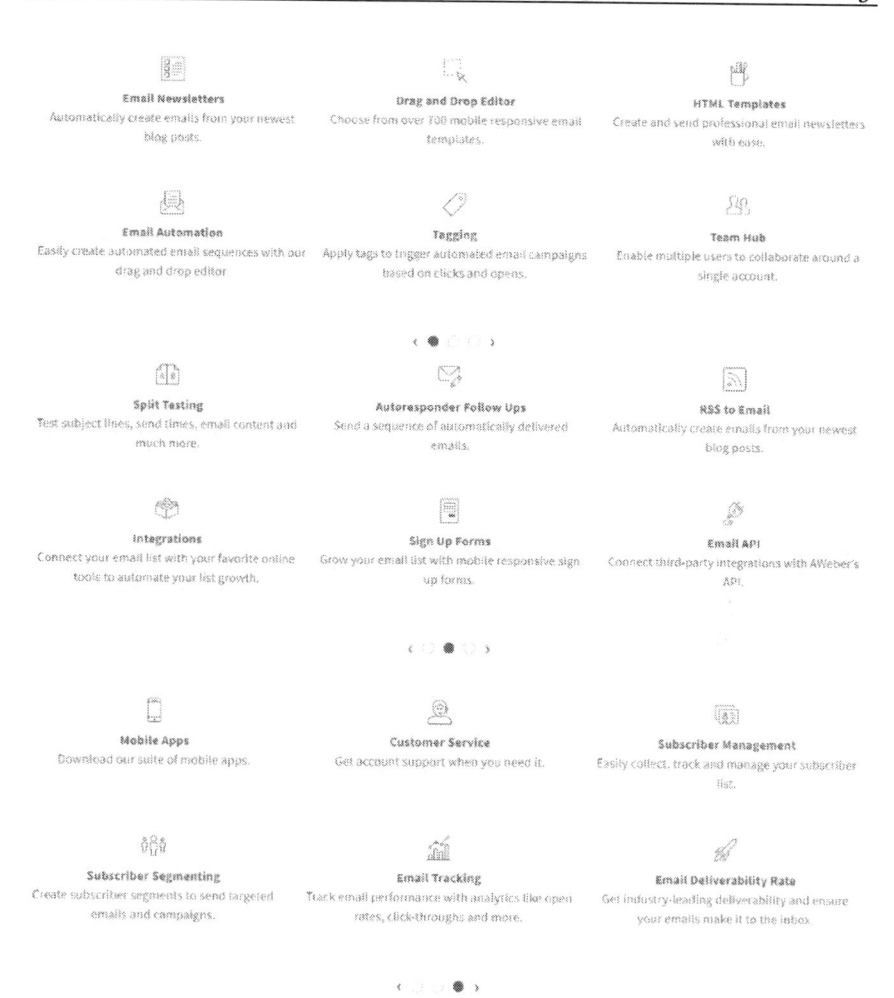

Users who actively use all of your software's features show that they're interested in your tool. They want to know all about it so they can use it effectively to solve their challenges.

If you see that users aren't engaging with all the features you provide, you may need to make sure your onboarding process is explaining those features more thoroughly.

Customer Progression

You can track another great metric to improve your onboarding process by asking, how are your customers progressing through your onboarding?

Are they curious and asking questions about your business services? Do they continually want to know more about your products and how the products can help them?

If they seem uninterested or, on the other end of the spectrum, ask many questions about even the most basic aspects of your services, your onboarding process may be difficult to work through or may not offer enough information.

Types of User Onboarding

Your new customers come to your business from different perspectives and have different levels of knowledge about your business and what you offer.

Here are some onboarding types your new customers may benefit from based on their pain points.

Account-Focused Onboarding

Some services require new customers to have an account, but creating the account and activating it can be hard. Brands use account-focused onboarding to show customers how to create and use an account.

Function-Oriented Onboarding

To teach your new users how your app or its core features function and how to use them, you need a function-oriented onboarding process. This will show customers how to align the app's features with their business and use it to meet their needs.

Benefits-Oriented Onboarding

Your new customers want to benefit from using your services or products. In a benefits-oriented onboarding process, you teach the customers the core benefits you offer and how they can gain them as they use your services or products.

Progressive Onboarding

New and existing customers using your services will need new training as you roll out updates.

In progressive onboarding, the business provides customers with more information to help them understand the services, especially any new features that have been added. Your customers will be in constant learning mode as you keep them abreast of new information.

How to Create a Great Onboarding Process

It's the goal of every business owner to see new customers become loyal and recurrent customers to their business. Here are some tips to achieve this as you onboard them to your business and win their trust.

Use Welcome Videos

Videos have a high conversion rate and engage your customers with your brand. Research by Statista, compiled by Oberlo, shows that 85% of internet users love video content.

Oberlo | Internet Users Everywhere Enjoy Video Content

85% of all internet users in the United States watched online video content monthly on any of their devices.
(Statista, 2018)

Another study by Wyzowl shows that marketers have an 88% return on investment with video content.

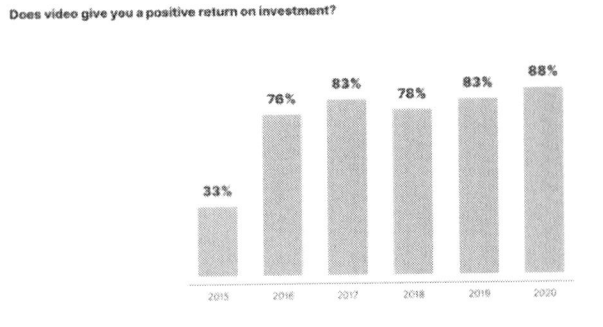

Does video give you a positive return on investment?

- 2015: 33%
- 2016: 76%
- 2017: 83%
- 2018: 78%
- 2019: 83%
- 2020: 88%

Source: Wyzowl State of Video Marketing Survey 2020 — wyzowl

The demand for video content keeps on growing every day. Research by Wyzowl shows that 59% of marketers plan to use video as part of their marketing.

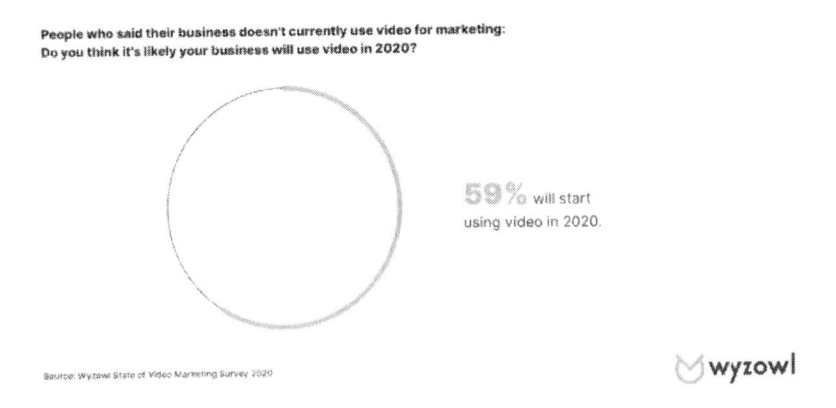

People who said their business doesn't currently use video for marketing: Do you think it's likely your business will use video in 2020?

59% will start using video in 2020.

Source: Wyzowl State of Video Marketing Survey 2020 — wyzowl

The above data shows how essential video is to your business marketing plan. As you onboard your customers, welcome them with video content. You can also include video content in your onboarding process.

Ensure that the videos are short, interesting, and highly informative. Provide all the information your customers will need as they start the onboarding process.

Use High-Quality Landing Pages

The quality of your landing pages plays a key role in your onboarding process. Don't send your new users to landing pages that are poorly designed or have slow loading speeds. Clients hate pages like these. Also, fill the pages with attractive, focused content to engage clients with your brand as they keep learning about your business offers and how you can help them.

You can check out chapter 2 to learn how to create high-quality landing pages.

Personalize Your Communications with Clients

Research by Gartner shows that personalization can help customers get a good deal and make the purchasing process less complicated.

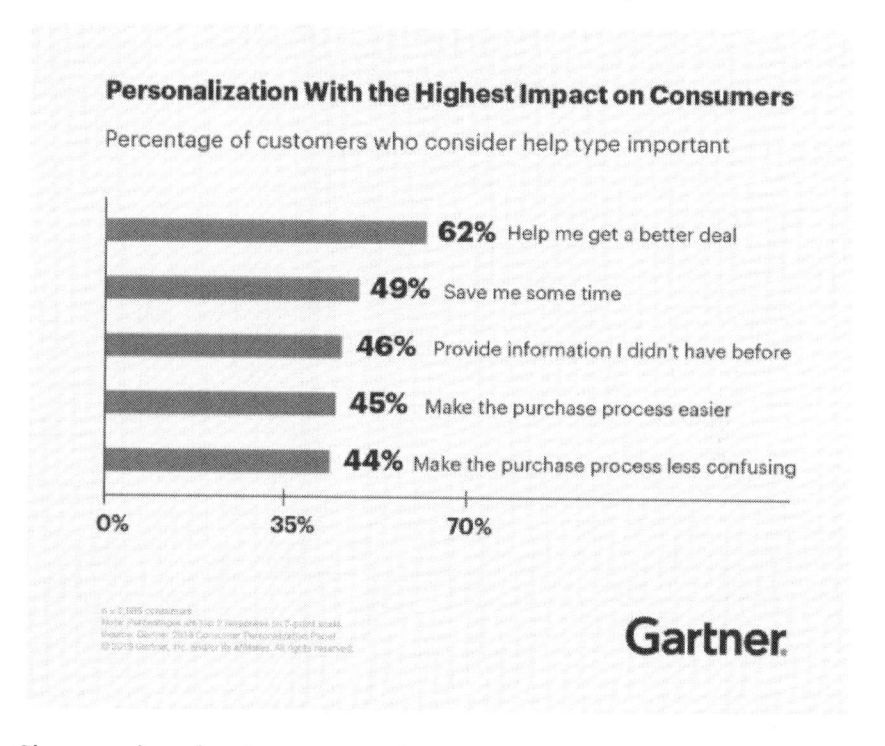

Personalization With the Highest Impact on Consumers

Percentage of customers who consider help type important

- 62% Help me get a better deal
- 49% Save me some time
- 46% Provide information I didn't have before
- 45% Make the purchase process easier
- 44% Make the purchase process less confusing

Gartner.

Since you've already segmented your new customers based on the information they gave you, there's no reason not to personalize your communication. Provide them with content that they need based on their level of understanding of your brand's services or products.

Include Testimonials from Previous Customers

It's vital to use every possible means to win the trust of your new customers.

One amazing way is to include testimonials from your past and current customers in your onboarding process. Here are some testimonial examples from Buffer clients:

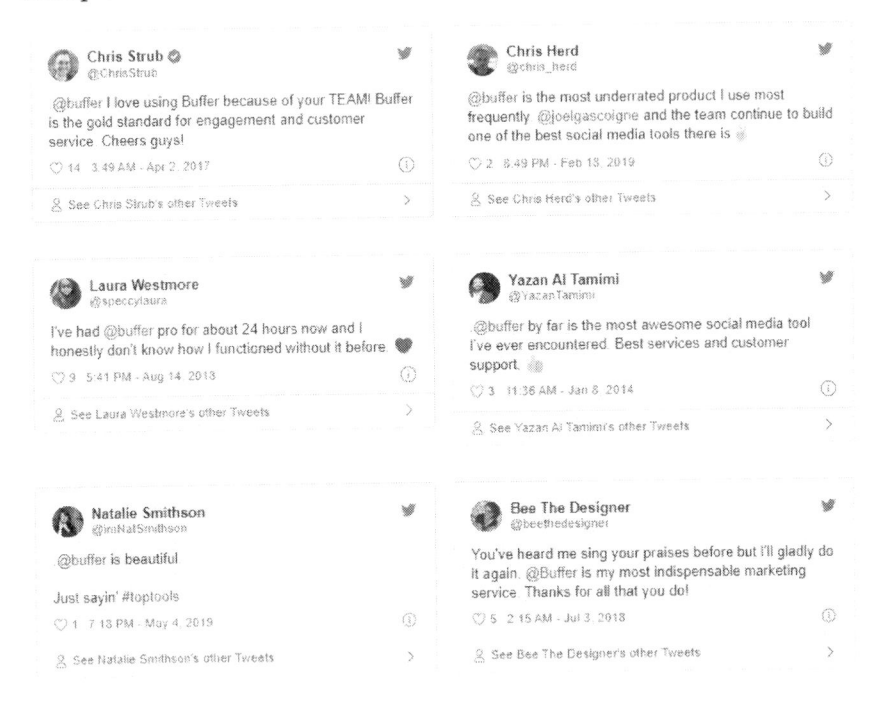

Chris Strub @ChrisStrub
@buffer I love using Buffer because of your TEAM! Buffer is the gold standard for engagement and customer service. Cheers guys!
♡ 14   3:49 AM - Apr 2, 2017
See Chris Strub's other Tweets

Chris Herd @chris_herd
@buffer is the most underrated product I use most frequently. @joelgascoigne and the team continue to build one of the best social media tools there is
♡ 2   6:49 PM - Feb 13, 2019
See Chris Herd's other Tweets

Laura Westmore @speccylaura
I've had @buffer pro for about 24 hours now and I honestly don't know how I functioned without it before
♡ 9   5:41 PM - Aug 14, 2013
See Laura Westmore's other Tweets

Yazan Al Tamimi @YazanTamimi
.@buffer by far is the most awesome social media tool I've ever encountered. Best services and customer support.
♡ 3   11:36 AM - Jan 8, 2014
See Yazan Al Tamimi's other Tweets

Natalie Smithson @imNatSmithson
@buffer is beautiful

Just sayin' #toptools
♡ 1   7:13 PM - May 4, 2019
See Natalie Smithson's other Tweets

Bee The Designer @beethedesigner
You've heard me sing your praises before but I'll gladly do it again. @Buffer is my most indispensable marketing service. Thanks for all that you do!
♡ 5   2:15 AM - Jul 3, 2013
See Bee The Designer's other Tweets

> **Chapter 6: User Onboarding**

> **Anshul Sharma**
> @lognmansh
> Have never seen as open and as transparent a company as @buffer, loved browsing your website and reading your blogs. Definitely a torch bearer in employee satisfaction, loved your company dashboard. learnt a lot today! ★★★★★
> ♡ 3   7:21 PM · May 7, 2019
> See Anshul Sharma's other Tweets

> **Life that Counts**
> @lifethatcounts
> @buffer seriously some of the best digital customer service I've had in maybe forever! @charityblendceo @the_agif you guys should connect with these guys! #SameHeart #SameMission #NPO #serve
> ♡ 3   2:36 AM · Apr 30, 2019 · Cullman, AL
> See Life that Counts's other Tweets

> **Lo-I33t-uh**
> @lolitatracy
> GAH. @buffer. You guys are KILLIN' IT with email content this week. I think I've learned more about #SMM the past few days than I have in the past month.
> ♡ 8   7:23 PM · Feb 10, 2019
> See Lo-I33t-uh's other Tweets

> **Nicolas Le Roux**
> @nico_lex
> So happy to be again a customer of @buffer, great API and so many improvements in the interface, the tool is awesome
> ♡ 4   7:15 PM · Jan 30, 2019
> See Nicolas Le Roux's other Tweets

> **Michael Orona**
> @CrazyBeanur
> .@buffer I love buffer!!! Huge time saver!
> ♡ 3   6:32 PM · Mar 6, 2019
> See Michael Orona's other Tweets

> **Richard Franks**
> @richardpfranks
> New @buffer for web is
> ♡ 7   12:56 PM · Feb 22, 2019
> See Richard Franks's other Tweets

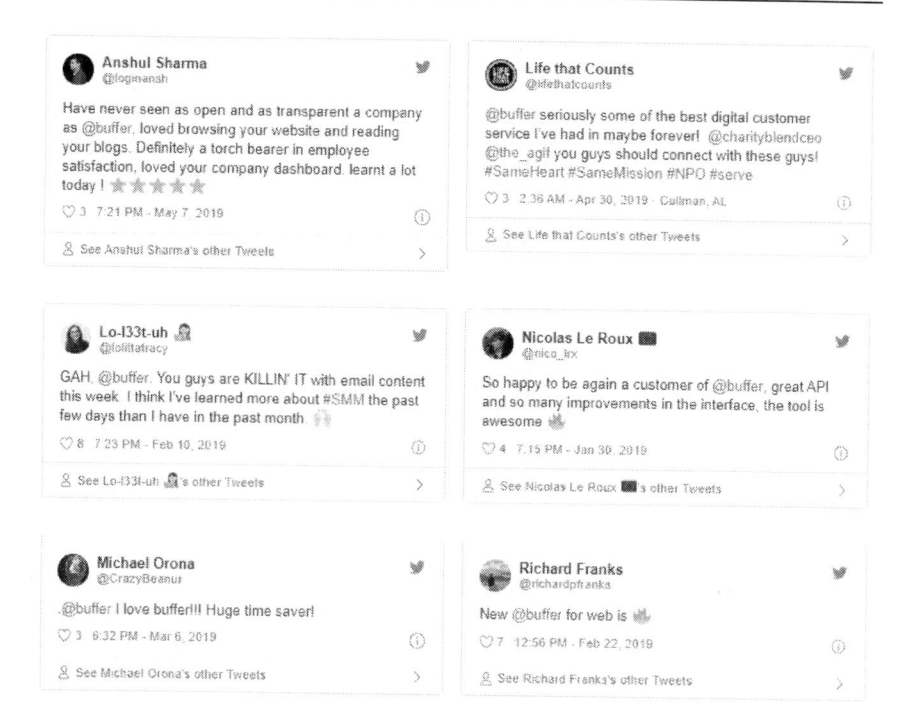

When clients see testimonials from other customers, they trust and engage more with your brand.

Use Multiple Communication Channels

Clients use more than one means of communication. As you onboard your customers, find several communication channels that can effectively reach them.

Remember that email is the best form of communication for most clients. At the same time, you shouldn't limit your customers to email as the only way to communicate. Pay attention to the mode of communication your customers prefer to use, and follow their lead.

Update Your Customers about Product Upgrades

Upgrades to your services or products help you keep offering your customers better services.

Once you add new features or upgrades, make sure you update your customers. You can also point out how the upgrades will help them keep succeeding.

If your upgrades come with additional costs, communicate that clearly to your customers. You may also want to offer discounts for early upgraders to motivate them to get on board.

Provide a Detailed Product Description

Your customers should have all the information they need both before and after they start using your services or products.

As a marketer, it's your job to provide customers with an in-depth description of your services. Show them all they need to see and learn about your business and how they can effectively use your business to solve their challenges.

To keep your new customers interested in your services or products, make product descriptions interesting and engaging. For example, if your product is software, you can include videos demonstrating how the software works alongside the description.

Watch Your Competitors

You're not the only business offering services in your niche. Why not visit your competitors' businesses and check out how they onboard their new and existing customers? This will help you gather some tips you can use in your business as you onboard your own customers.

Create a Detailed Buyer Persona

To serve your customers well, you have to know them. Develop an in-depth buyer persona to represent your target customers.

Once you know your customers on a personal level, you'll know what they need to overcome their challenges and you can guide them well. Your onboarding will provide them with relevant information about how your services or products will help them.

With a detailed buyer persona, you'll also make it easy for your customers to know and trust your brand as you onboard them because you'll have a better understanding of what they're looking for in a brand.

Best Tools for Onboarding

Below are some tools that can help you develop and improve your onboarding process.

UserIQ

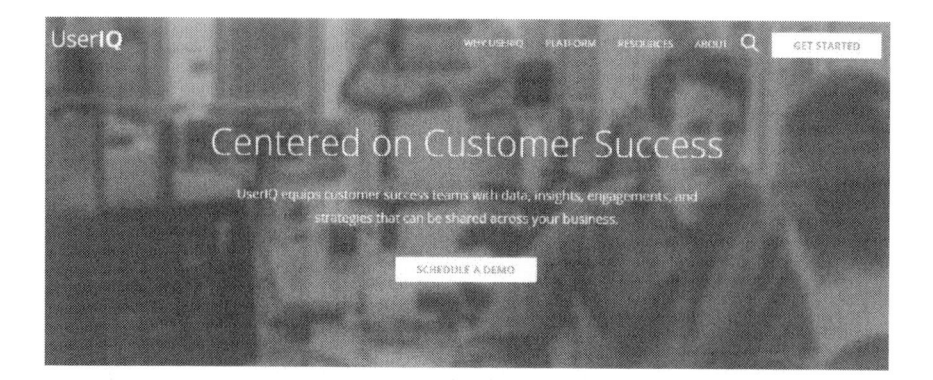

During the onboarding process, most customers just use the business once and then leave. With the UserIQ tool, you can reduce that churn rate and optimize your onboarding process.

It can help you deliver the right messages to the customer, get insights that will help you in the decision-making process, and engage customers with your business beyond that first interaction.

The tool includes a 30-day free trial, after which you can customize your pricing.

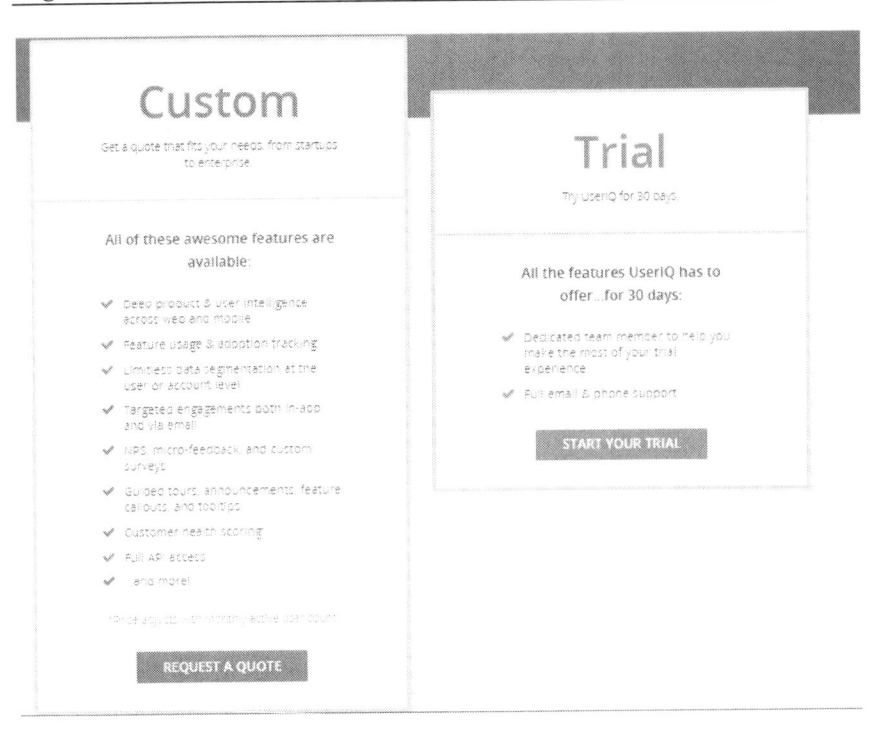

Intercom

Many brands lose customers as they onboard them to their businesses. The Intercom tool helps you engage and onboard your customers to retain them for the long haul.

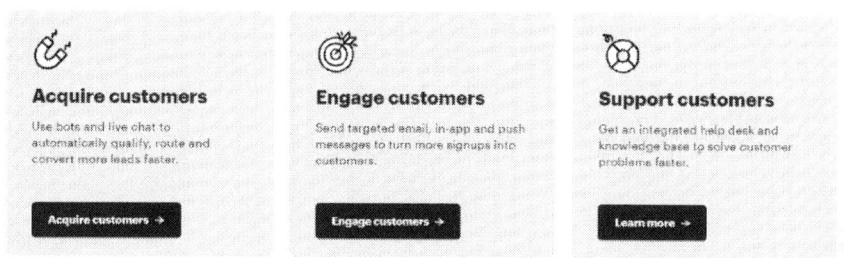

Chapter 6: User Onboarding

Perfect for sales, marketing, and support

Acquire customers
Use bots and live chat to automatically qualify, route and convert more leads faster.

Acquire customers →

Engage customers
Send targeted email, in-app and push messages to turn more signups into customers.

Engage customers →

Support customers
Get an integrated help desk and knowledge base to solve customer problems faster.

Learn more →

Here are some other apps you can integrate with this tool to make your brand marketing and onboarding easy:

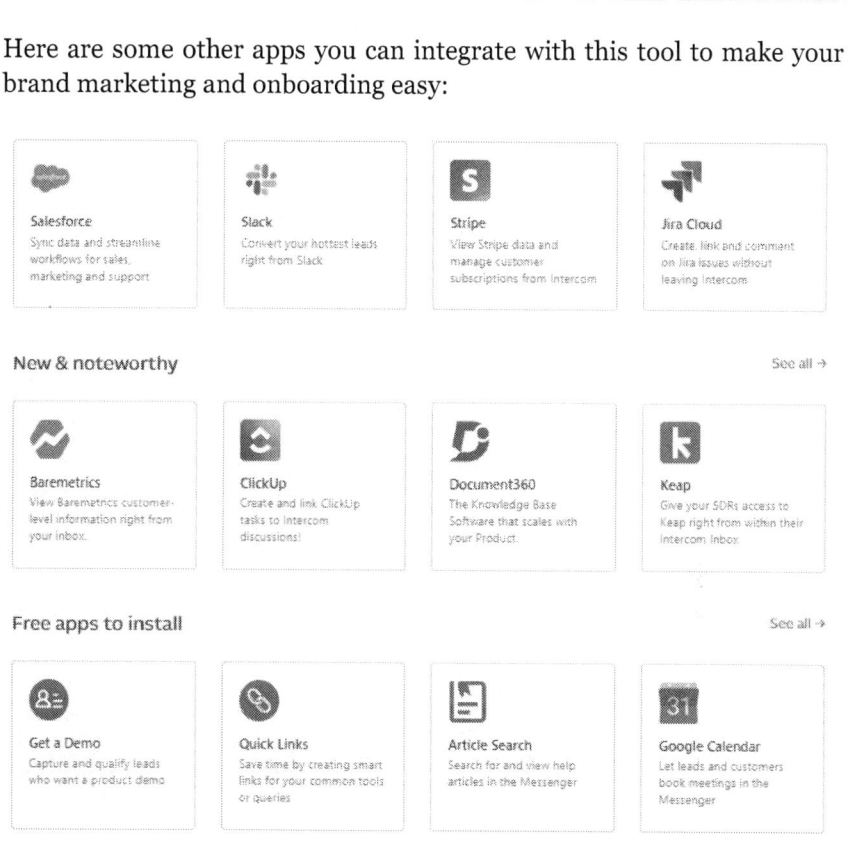

Salesforce
Sync data and streamline workflows for sales, marketing and support.

Slack
Convert your hottest leads right from Slack.

Stripe
View Stripe data and manage customer subscriptions from Intercom.

Jira Cloud
Create, link and comment on Jira issues without leaving Intercom.

New & noteworthy   See all →

Baremetrics
View Baremetrics customer-level information right from your inbox.

ClickUp
Create and link ClickUp tasks to Intercom discussions!

Document360
The Knowledge Base Software that scales with your Product.

Keap
Give your SDRs access to Keap right from within their Intercom Inbox.

Free apps to install   See all →

Get a Demo
Capture and qualify leads who want a product demo.

Quick Links
Save time by creating smart links for your common tools or queries.

Article Search
Search for and view help articles in the Messenger.

Google Calendar
Let leads and customers book meetings in the Messenger.

For support teams

Stripe
View Stripe data and manage customer subscriptions from Intercom

Jira Cloud
Create, link and comment on Jira issues without leaving Intercom

Quick Links
Save time by creating smart links for your common tools or queries

Zendesk Support
See Zendesk tickets or create new ones—without leaving your inbox

For sales teams

Salesforce
Sync data and streamline workflows for sales, marketing and support

Slack
Convert your hottest leads right from Slack

Outlook Calendar
Seamlessly book meetings with leads and customers

HubSpot
See HubSpot data in Intercom's Inbox and sync leads and conversations

For marketing teams

Google Analytics
Measure the impact of your Messenger on website conversions

Segment
Sync your user data from any app into Intercom

Marketo
Automatically send leads and conversations to Marketo

Zoom Webinars
Enable visitors and users to register for webinars in your Messenger

If you'd like to use the tool, here's the pricing model:

Chapter 6: User Onboarding

For basic chat and messaging		For automation and messaging at scale	
Start	**Grow**	♡ Chosen by 53% of businesses **Accelerate**	**Scale**
Basic live chat and outbound messaging.	Chat, targeted email, and self-service support.	Automated workflows, bots, and reporting.	Advanced workflows, permissions, and security.
Try for free	Try for free	Chat with us	Chat with us
from **$39**/month	from **$99**/month	from **$499**/month with annual plan	from **$999**/month with annual plan
• Includes 1 seat • Live chat • Targeted outbound chat • Team inbox • Slack integration See more	Everything in **Start** plus: • Includes 5 seats • Inbound & outbound email • Help center • Saved replies • Conversation ratings • HubSpot & GitHub integrations See more	Everything in **Grow** plus: • Includes 10 seats • Custom bots • Multiple team inboxes • Automated assignment rules • Multilingual help center • Team performance reporting • Salesforce & Zendesk Support integrations • Personalized onboarding See more	Everything in **Accelerate** plus: • Includes 10 seats • Service Level Agreement rules • Workload management • Role-based permissions • SSO and SAML integrations • Custom API rate limits • Tailored training sessions • Ongoing product consultation See more

Customize your plan with optional add-ons

Product Tours	**Advanced lead generation**	**Advanced customer engagement**	**Advanced support automation**
from **$199**/month	from **$499**/month with annual plan	from **$499**/month with annual plan	from **$249**/month with annual plan
Drive adoption with interactive tours inside your product.	Grow your pipeline with ABM and sales integrations.	Drive growth with automated multichannel campaigns.	Provide faster answers and automated actions with Answer Bot.
• Targeted guided tours • Video tours • Easy, code-free builder	• Account-Based Marketing • Salesforce Sandbox support • Clearbit Reveal & Marketo Integrations • Send apps in bots	• Push messages & notifications • Smart Campaigns • Message A/B testing & control groups • Clearbit Reveal & Marketo Integrations	• Automated answers to common questions • Resolution reporting • Send apps in bots
Add to trial	Chat with us	Chat with us	Chat with us

Proof

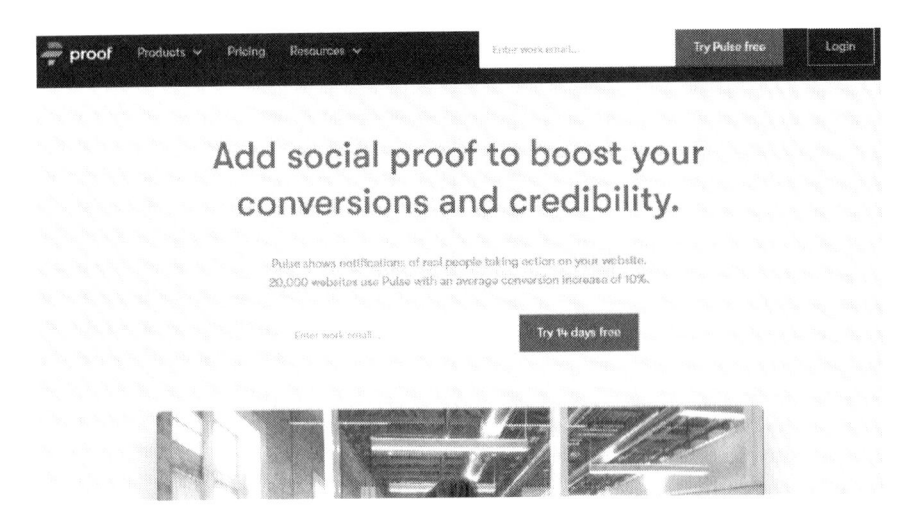

Social Proof offers a great way to win the trust and loyalty of your new customers. The Proof tool helps you take advantage of social proof, the tendency of potential customers to imitate the actions of others, as you onboard your customers and increase conversion rates.

The tool is also amazing for boosting the website experience for visitors as they interact with your website.

Here are some of its features:

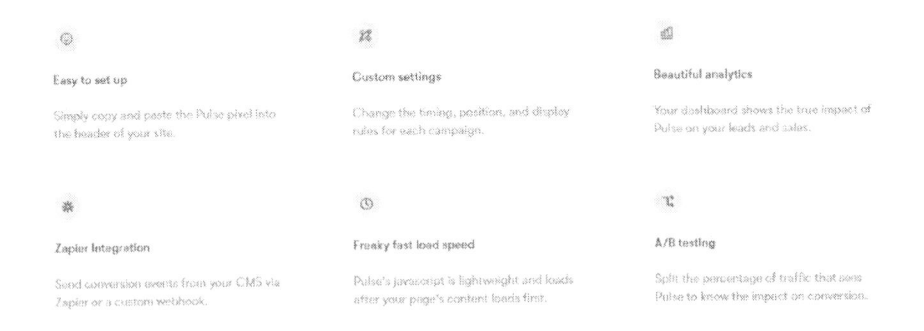

Easy to set up
Simply copy and paste the Pulse pixel into the header of your site.

Custom settings
Change the timing, position, and display rules for each campaign.

Beautiful analytics
Your dashboard shows the true impact of Pulse on your leads and sales.

Zapier Integration
Send conversion events from your CMS via Zapier or a custom webhook.

Freaky fast load speed
Pulse's javascript is lightweight and loads after your page's content loads first.

A/B testing
Split the percentage of traffic that sees Pulse to know the impact on conversion.

If you decide to use the tool, this is how much you will be spending. The cost depends on the number of monthly users:

Add social proof to boost your conversions and credibility.

How many unique visitors do you get per month?

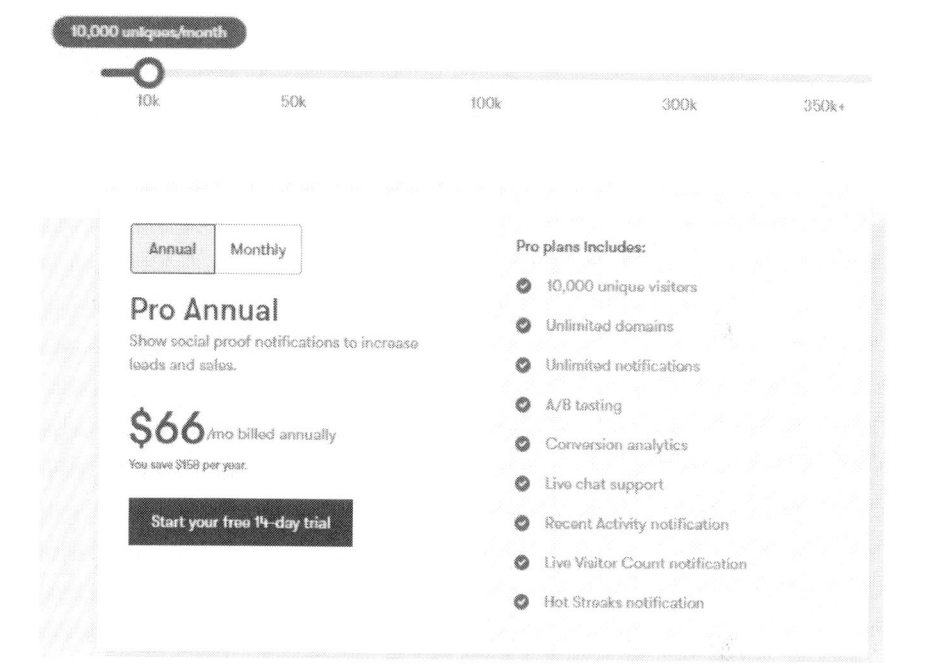

10,000 uniques/month

| 10k | 50k | 100k | 300k | 350k+ |

Annual | Monthly

Pro Annual
Show social proof notifications to increase leads and sales.

$66 /mo billed annually

You save $158 per year.

Start your free 14-day trial

Pro plans includes:
- 10,000 unique visitors
- Unlimited domains
- Unlimited notifications
- A/B testing
- Conversion analytics
- Live chat support
- Recent Activity notification
- Live Visitor Count notification
- Hot Streaks notification

Wistia

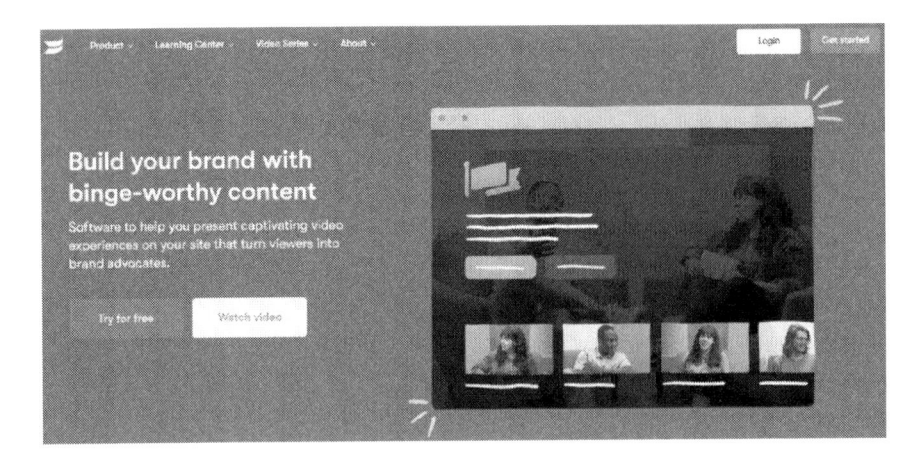

You'll need welcoming videos to introduce your customers to your business as you onboard them. Great videos can help you win your clients' trust, engage them and convince them that your product is what they need.

Wistia helps you create amazing videos.

Wistia helps you turn video viewers into brand advocates

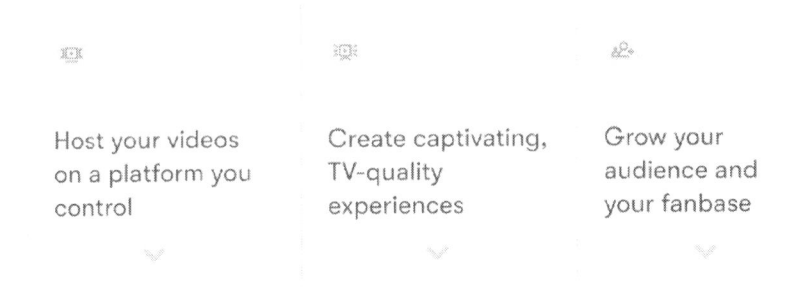

| Host your videos on a platform you control | Create captivating, TV-quality experiences | Grow your audience and your fanbase |

Chapter 6: User Onboarding

Here are the tools you can integrate with Wistia software:

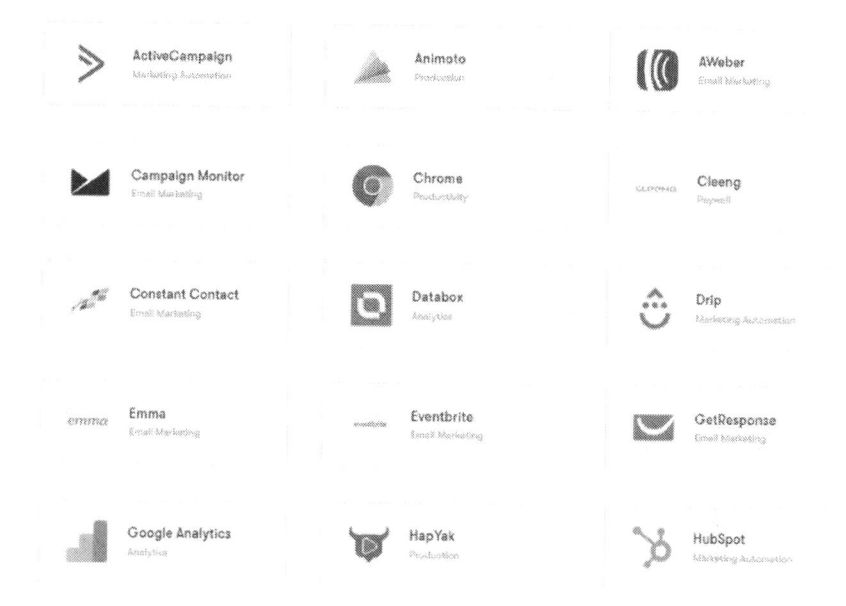

ActiveCampaign Marketing Automation	**Animoto** Production	**AWeber** Email Marketing
Campaign Monitor Email Marketing	**Chrome** Productivity	**Cleeng** Paywall
Constant Contact Email Marketing	**Databox** Analytics	**Drip** Marketing Automation
Emma Email Marketing	**Eventbrite** Email Marketing	**GetResponse** Email Marketing
Google Analytics Analytics	**HapYak** Production	**HubSpot** Marketing Automation

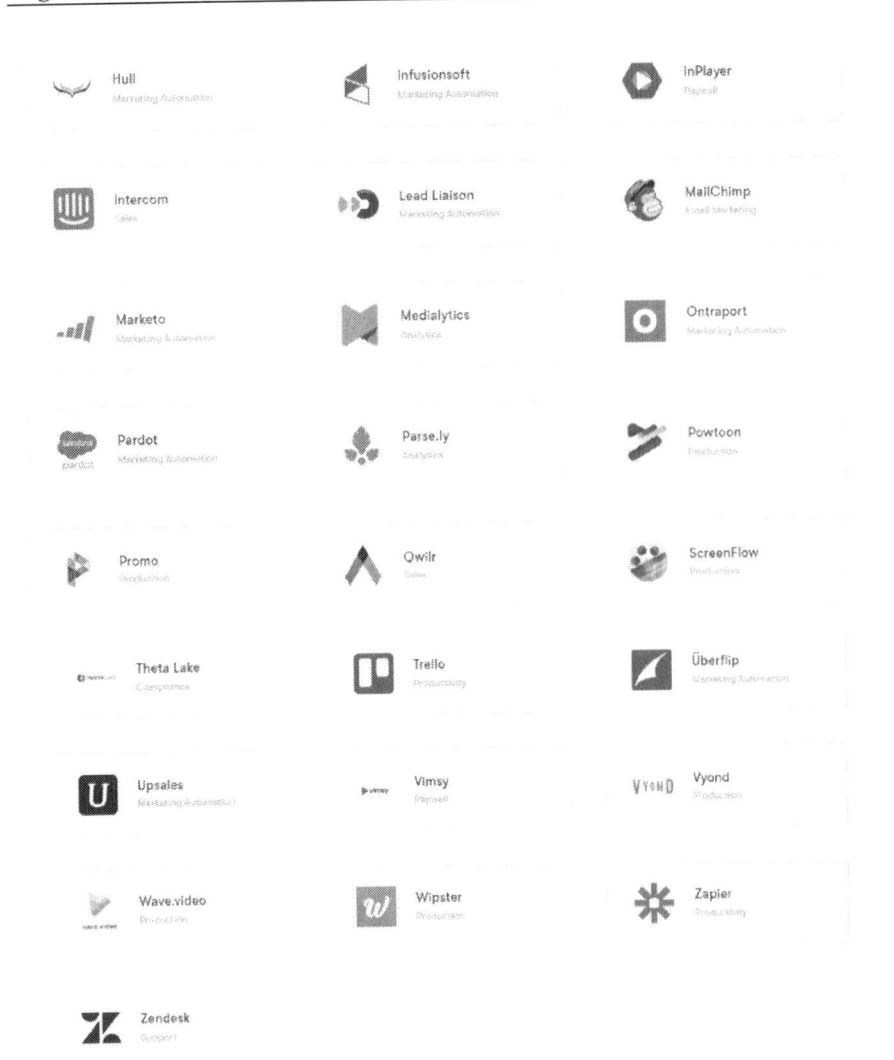

Hull Marketing Automation	Infusionsoft Marketing Automation	InPlayer Paywall
Intercom Sales	Lead Liaison Marketing Automation	MailChimp Email Marketing
Marketo Marketing Automation	Medialytics Analytics	Ontraport Marketing Automation
Pardot Marketing Automation	Parse.ly Analytics	Powtoon Production
Promo Production	Qwilr Sales	ScreenFlow Production
Theta Lake Compliance	Trello Productivity	Überflip Marketing Automation
Upsales Marketing Automation	Vimsy Paywall	Vyond Production
Wave.video Production	Wipster Production	Zapier Productivity
Zendesk Support		

Chapter 6: User Onboarding

Here's the pricing for the tool:

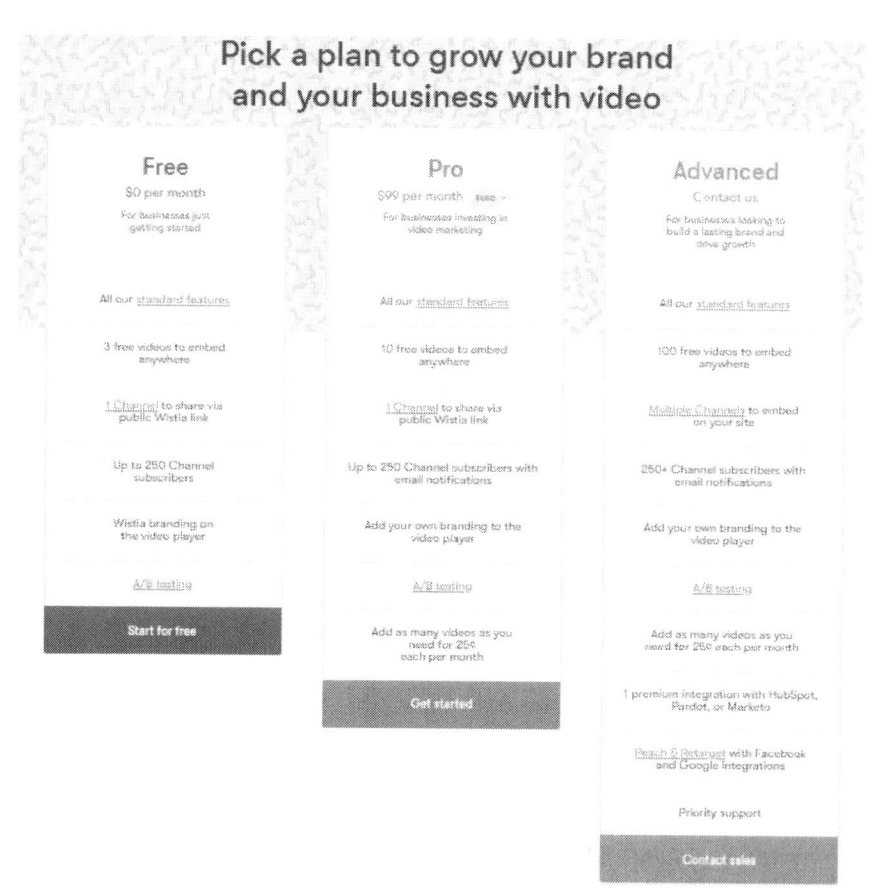

Pick a plan to grow your brand and your business with video

Free	Pro	Advanced
$0 per month	$99 per month	Contact us
For businesses just getting started	For businesses investing in video marketing	For businesses looking to build a lasting brand and drive growth
All our standard features	All our standard features	All our standard features
3 free videos to embed anywhere	10 free videos to embed anywhere	100 free videos to embed anywhere
1 Channel to share via public Wistia link	1 Channel to share via public Wistia link	Multiple Channels to embed on your site
Up to 250 Channel subscribers	Up to 250 Channel subscribers with email notifications	250+ Channel subscribers with email notifications
Wistia branding on the video player	Add your own branding to the video player	Add your own branding to the video player
A/B testing	A/B testing	A/B testing
Start for free	Add as many videos as you need for 25¢ each per month	Add as many videos as you need for 25¢ each per month
	Get started	1 premium integration with HubSpot, Pardot, or Marketo
		Reach & Retarget with Facebook and Google Integrations
		Priority support
		Contact sales

Bonjoro

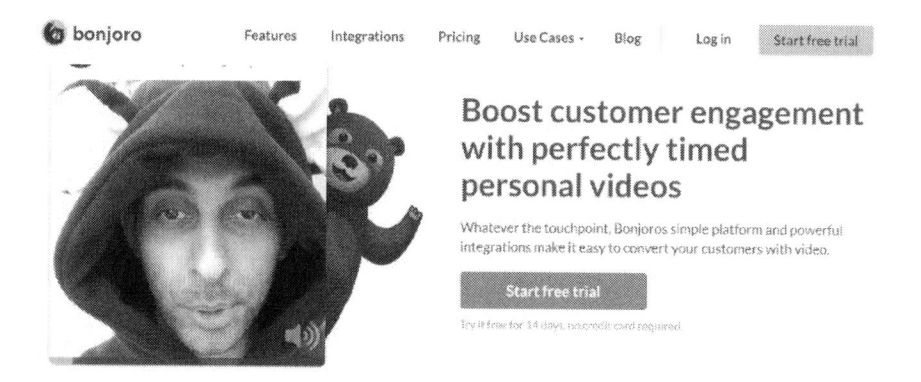

bonjoro — Features | Integrations | Pricing | Use Cases | Blog | Log in | **Start free trial**

Boost customer engagement with perfectly timed personal videos

Whatever the touchpoint, Bonjoros simple platform and powerful integrations make it easy to convert your customers with video.

Start free trial

Try it free for 14 days, no credit card required

343

You can use Bonjoro to personalize your business marketing campaigns. Send personalized videos to your customers as you onboard them to teach them more about your business solutions.

Bonjoro also lets you translate your video content into different languages to increase engagement with a variety of customers.

You can integrate the Bonjoro tool with the following apps:

- **ActiveCampaign** Grow your business with sales automation. See more >
- **ConvertKit** Email marketing for professional bloggers. See more >
- **Drip** Connect with the world's first Ecommerce CRM. See more >
- **Gmail** Send Bonjoros using your Gmail account. See more >
- **Hubspot** Connect to your Hubspot account. See more >
- **Intercom** Connect to the popular CRM. See more >
- **Keap** One place for everything. Happier customers everywhere. See more >
- **Mailchimp** Sync your mailing lists. See more >
- **MailerLite** Send Bonjoros to your subscribers. See more >
- **Microsoft (beta)** Send Bonjoros from your Microsoft account. See more >
- **Ontraport** Your marketing campaigns at-a-glance. See more >
- **Patreon** Thank your donors. See more >
- **SharpSpring** Marketing Automation: Powerful. Affordable. For Everyone. See more >
- **Shopify** Thank your customers for purchases made. See more >
- **Zapier** Connect Bonjoro to over 750 apps with Zapier. See more >

Chapter 6: User Onboarding

And here's the pricing structure for the tool:

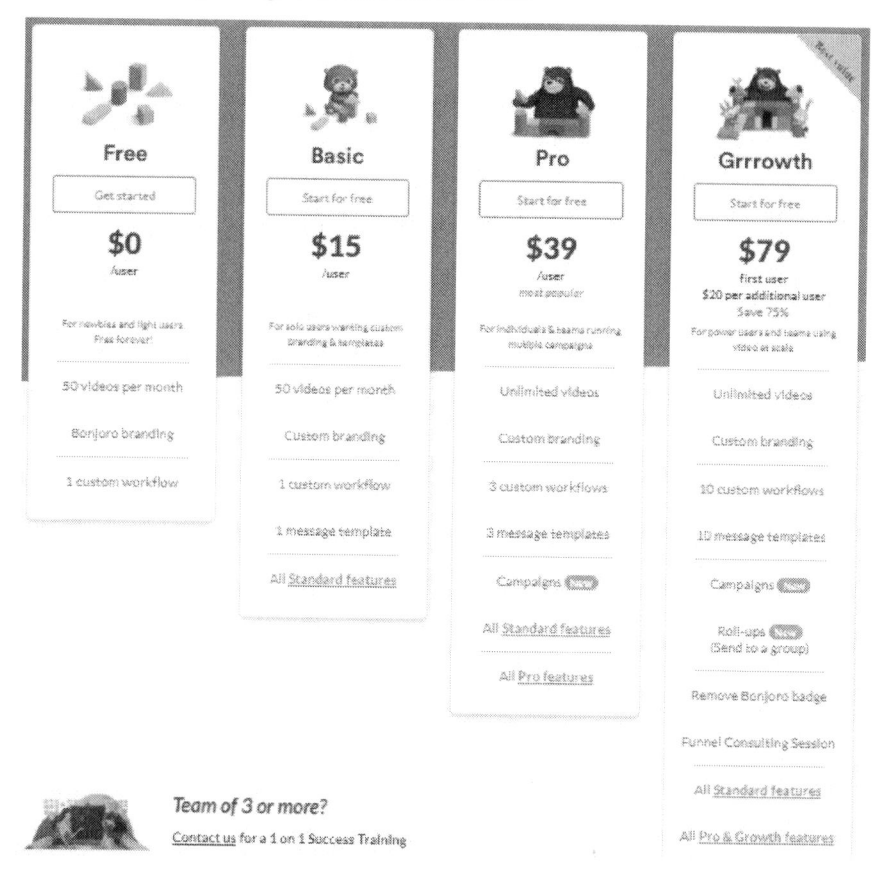

Free	Basic	Pro	Grrrowth
Get started	Start for free	Start for free	Start for free
$0 /user	**$15** /user	**$39** /user most popular	**$79** first user $20 per additional user Save 75%
For newbies and light users Free forever!	For solo users wanting custom branding & templates	For individuals & teams running multiple campaigns	For power users and teams using video at scale
50 videos per month	50 videos per month	Unlimited videos	Unlimited videos
Bonjoro branding	Custom branding	Custom branding	Custom branding
1 custom workflow	1 custom workflow	3 custom workflows	10 custom workflows
	1 message template	3 message templates	10 message templates
	All Standard features	Campaigns (New)	Campaigns (New)
		All Standard features	Roll-ups (New) (Send to a group)
		All Pro features	Remove Bonjoro badge
			Funnel Consulting Session
			All Standard features
			All Pro & Growth features

Team of 3 or more?
Contact us for a 1 on 1 Success Training

These are its standard and pro features:

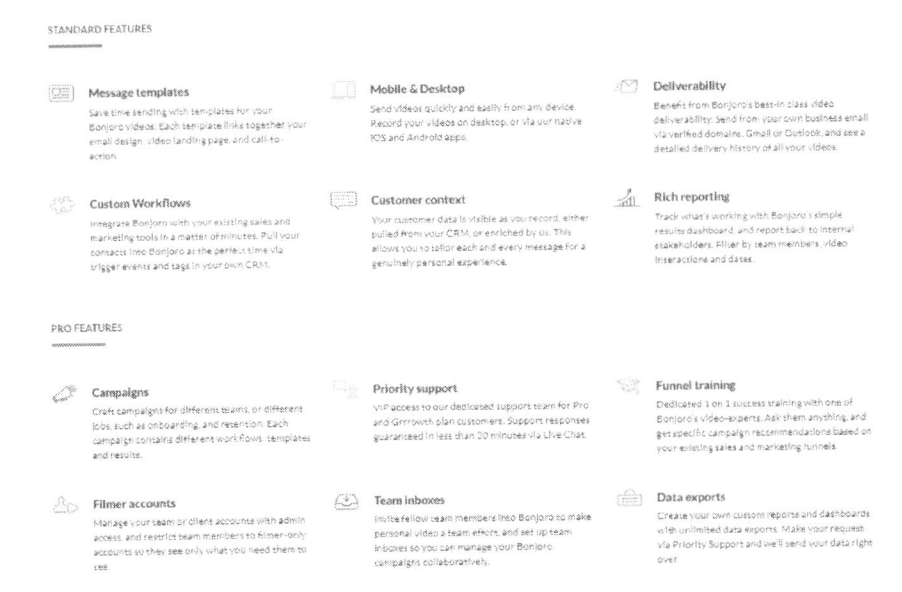

STANDARD FEATURES

Message templates
Save time sending with templates for your Bonjoro videos. Each template links together your email design, video landing page, and call-to-action.

Mobile & Desktop
Send videos quickly and easily from any device. Record your videos on desktop, or via our native iOS and Android apps.

Deliverability
Benefit from Bonjoro's best-in-class video deliverability. Send from your own business email via verified domains, Gmail or Outlook, and see a detailed delivery history of all your videos.

Custom Workflows
Integrate Bonjoro with your existing sales and marketing tools in a matter of minutes. Pull your contacts into Bonjoro at the perfect time via trigger events and tags in your own CRM.

Customer context
Your customer data is visible as you record, either pulled from your CRM, or enriched by us. This allows you to tailor each and every message for a genuinely personal experience.

Rich reporting
Track what's working with Bonjoro's simple results dashboard, and report back to internal stakeholders. Filter by team members, video interactions and dates.

PRO FEATURES

Campaigns
Craft campaigns for different teams, or different jobs, such as onboarding, and retention. Each campaign contains different workflows, templates and results.

Priority support
VIP access to our dedicated support team for Pro and Grrrowth plan customers. Support responses guaranteed in less than 30 minutes via Live Chat.

Funnel training
Dedicated 1 on 1 success training with one of Bonjoro's video-experts. Ask them anything, and get specific campaign recommendations based on your existing sales and marketing funnels.

Filmer accounts
Manage your team or client accounts with admin access, and restrict team members to filmer-only accounts so they see only what you need them to see.

Team inboxes
Invite fellow team members into Bonjoro to make personal video a team effort, and set up team inboxes so you can manage your Bonjoro campaigns collaboratively.

Data exports
Create your own custom reports and dashboards with unlimited data exports. Make your request via Priority Support and we'll send your data right over.

CloudApp

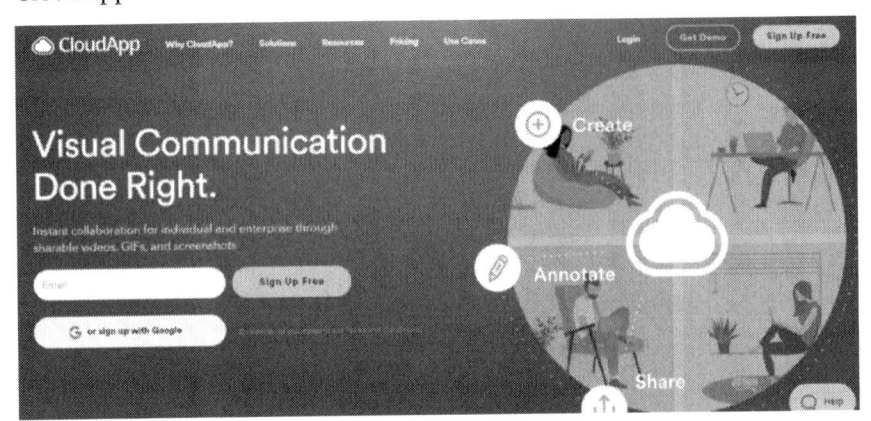

Screenshots of your product and excellent video content are some of the most effective ways to educate your customers. CloudApp helps you capture that information. Since it's a recording software, you can use it to record your computer screen and capture GIFs and images.

Chapter 6: User Onboarding

Here are some tools you can integrate with the software:

Asana
Complete tasks faster with visuals

Quip
Accelerate collaboration inside Quip

Pivotal Tracker
Become more agile in Pivotal Tracker

Microsoft Office
Better visual communication in Microsoft Office

GitLab
Speed up your workflow in GitLab

Help Scout
Better customer support in Help Scout

LiveAgent
Deliver delightful customer support in LiveAgent

Zoho Desk
Delight customers in Zoho Desk

Freshdesk
Close tickets faster using CloudApp with Freshdesk

Zoho CRM
Close more deals in Zoho CRM

Basecamp
Communicate better inside Basecamp

Mattermost
Collaborate faster with your team in Mattermost

Zendesk
Communicate more efficiently with customers

Jira Software
Better bug reporting in Jira.

Trello
Collaboration is More Fun When It's Visual

Zapier
Connect CloudApp to hundreds of other apps with Zapier

Sketch
Share your work and designs instantly

Adobe XD
Share designs faster from Adobe XD

Google Sheets
Make your spreadsheets more visual

Google Docs
Make your documents more visual

Google Slides
More engaging visual content for your slides

GitHub
Add an image or GIF to your pull requests to clarify

WordPress
Content is richer when it's visual

Slack
Collaborate faster with your team with CloudApp

347

This is the CloudApp pricing structure:

Amplitude

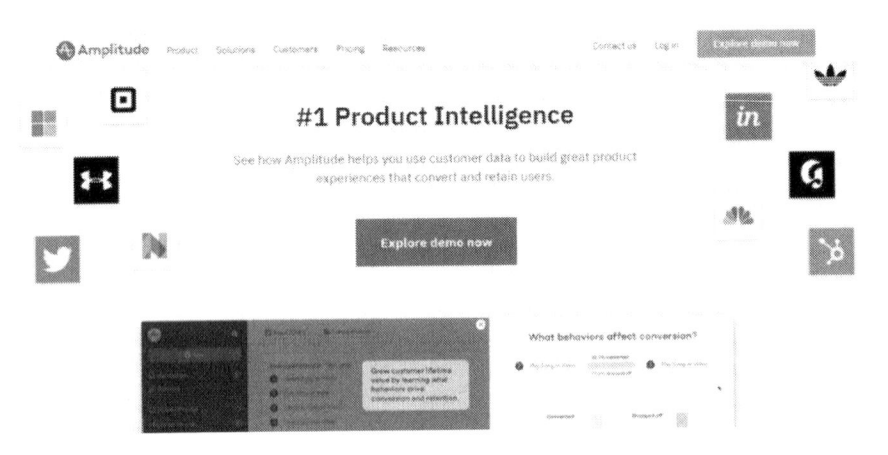

You need customer data to make decisions about how to advertise, interact with potential customers, and offer the best services or products.

Amplitude provides user analytics that show you how to serve your customers better. You can track your visitors and give them the best customer experience.

Visit the website for more details about its pricing structure, which includes three variations.

Chapter 6: User Onboarding

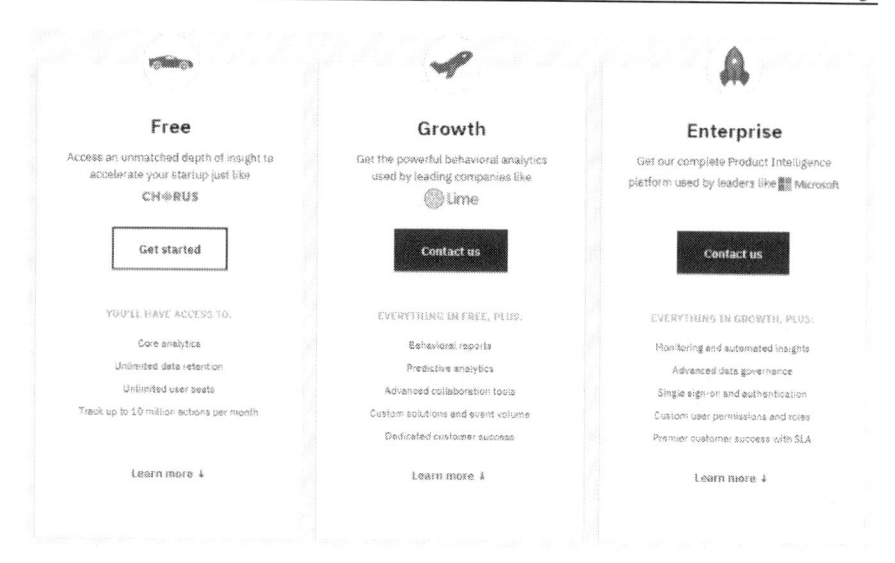

Here are some integrations for the Amplitude tool:

These are some other features of Amplitude:

Taxonomy
Build product trust with data integrity

- Expedite your QA and data validation process
- Define the rules for data collection
- Correct implementation errors without writing code

Learn more

Query
Direct data access for custom analytics

- Track and share any metric with custom queries
- Get raw access to your product data with Snowflake
- Benefit from Amplitude's merged users and clean schema

Learn more

Accounts
Accelerate SaaS product growth

- Identify features that drive account conversion
- Sync critical data from integrations like Salesforce and Zendesk
- Focus on the right accounts impacting ROI

Learn more

Scale
Access billions of user actions without compromise

- Sample your high volume user base without sacrificing accuracy
- Get instant answers at any event volume
- Customize your sampling rate

Learn more

Insight
Ship fast and learn more with automatic alerts

- Get notified on changes in product performance
- Closely monitor KPI trends and anomalies
- Instantly surface patterns in your product data

Learn more

Portfolio
Analyze engagement across multiple applications

- Automatically merge user IDs across platforms and products
- Understand how users move between platforms and products
- Get a single click executive view of a company's product health

Learn more

Optimizely

Optimizely   PLATFORM   SOLUTIONS   CUSTOMERS   SERVICES   PLANS   RESOURCES   LOG IN

Out-experiment. Outperform.

Optimizely is the world's leading experimentation platform, empowering marketing and product teams to test, learn and deploy winning digital experiences, every time.

IBM   hp   sky   GAP   AMERICAN EXPRESS   ebay

Chapter 6: User Onboarding

Optimizely helps you run A/B tests for your onboarding process. Different customers have different preferences, and to know what works best, you need to run tests.

You can use the tool to check different aspects of your marketing, such as your landing pages or website content, that help you attract and retain new customers.

The data you obtain from the testing can show you how to give your customers the best trust-building experience and increase your customer conversion rate.

Three levels of Optimizely are available to choose from:

Essentials	Business	Enterprise
Get started with the essential experimentation tools to help you optimize your web experiences.	Drive experimentation across all of your digital touchpoints and begin collaborating across teams.	Scale experiments 10X, with advanced collaboration, reporting, targeting, personalization & more.
✓ A/B Testing ✓ Visual editor ✓ Multi-page experimentation ✓ Platform security and compliance ✓ Analytics Integrations ✓ Stats Engine ✓ Support for Dynamic Websites	All Essentials features + ✓ Mutually exclusive experiments ✓ Multivariant testing ✓ Advanced targeting options ✓ Additional roles and permissions ✓ Extensions ✓ Program Management	All Business features + ✓ Personalization campaigns ✓ Behavioral targeting ✓ Product and content recommendations ✓ Third-party audiences ✓ Stats Accelerator ✓ Advanced Program Management

Totango

Accelerate Your Customer Onboarding Results

Enterprises that operate around their customers run customer success on Totango.

[Start for Free]

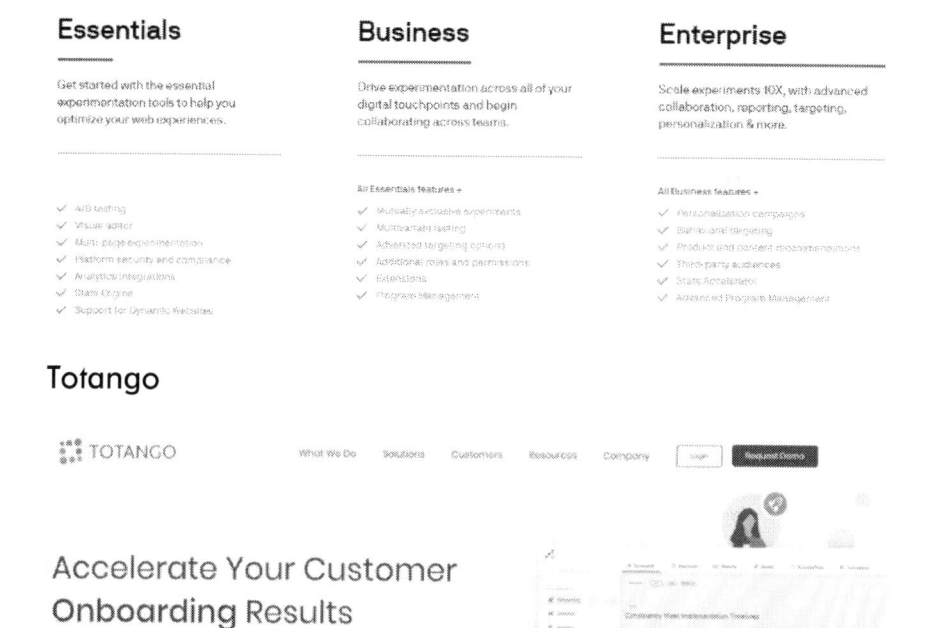

Totango is a great tool for increasing your customer conversion and ensuring your onboarding process achieves great results.

This tool can help accelerate the customer acquisition process. You can also use it to reduce the churn rate and identify upselling and cross-selling opportunities to grow your business.

Helpshift

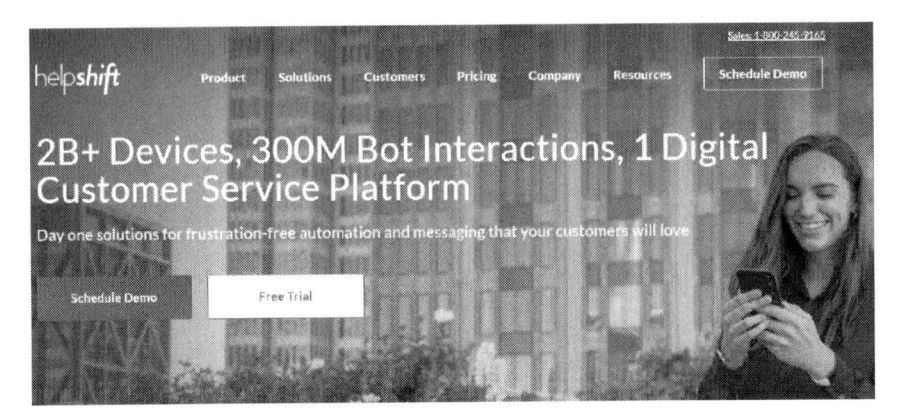

As you onboard your customers, you need to hear their views about your services. Helpshift provides great customer support for your brand.

Through several channels like live chat, messaging, bots, and a ticketing system, customers can ask questions if they need help and get timely answers.

Reach out to the company to request pricing for their services.

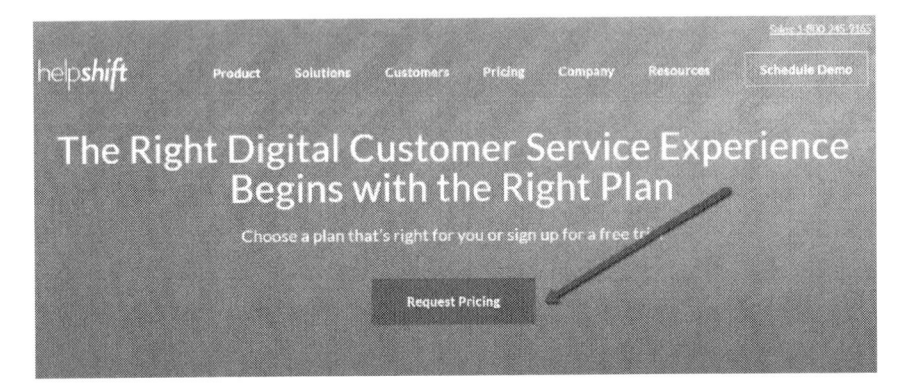

Clearbit

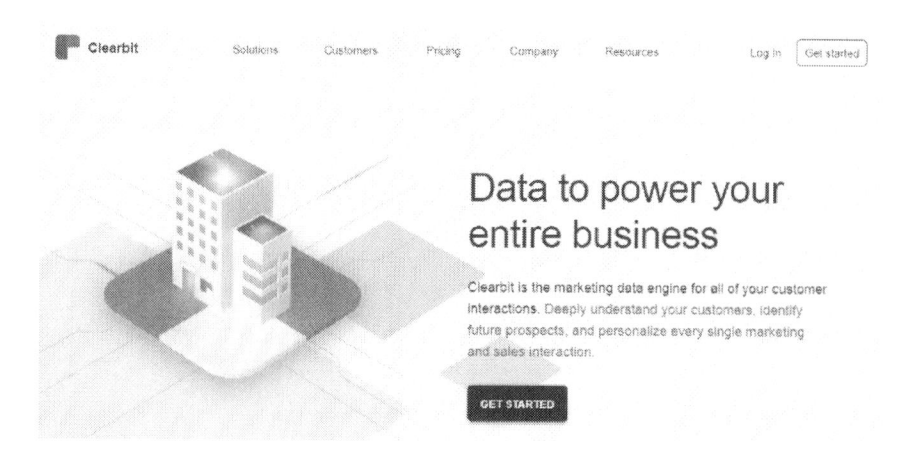

Clearbit is a great tool for interacting with your customers as you onboard them. It lets you personalize every step of your marketing and onboarding process. You get to know more about your customers and offer the most relevant services for their needs.

Here are the main solutions you can get from the tool and a list of other tools you can integrate with Clearbit:

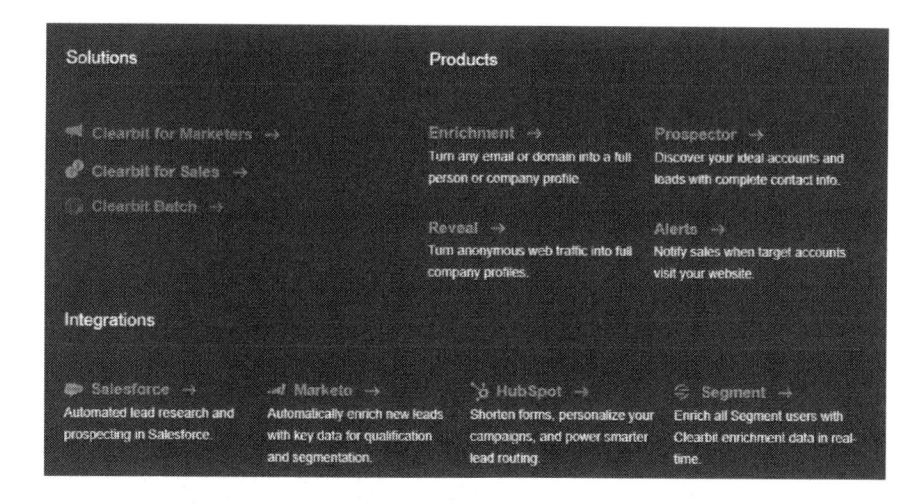

Solutions		Products			
Clearbit for Marketers →		Enrichment →		Prospector →	
Clearbit for Sales →		Turn any email or domain into a full person or company profile.		Discover your ideal accounts and leads with complete contact info.	
Clearbit Batch →		Reveal →		Alerts →	
		Turn anonymous web traffic into full company profiles.		Notify sales when target accounts visit your website.	
Integrations					
Salesforce →	Marketo →		HubSpot →		Segment →
Automated lead research and prospecting in Salesforce.	Automatically enrich new leads with key data for qualification and segmentation.		Shorten forms, personalize your campaigns, and power smarter lead routing.		Enrich all Segment users with Clearbit enrichment data in real-time.

Visit the website to get a quote.

Mixpanel

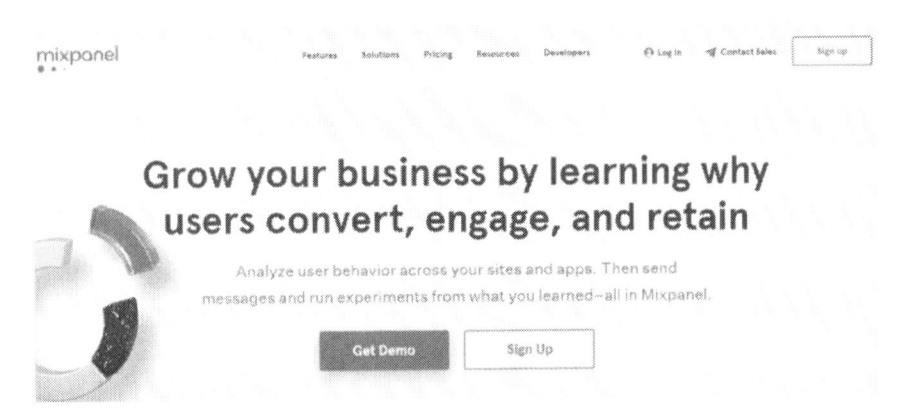

Learning about the behavior of your customers is a great way to get to know them better.

Mixpanel runs behavioral analytics to help you engage customers, give them the services they want, and retain them for the long term.

Mixpanel offers a three-level pricing structure:

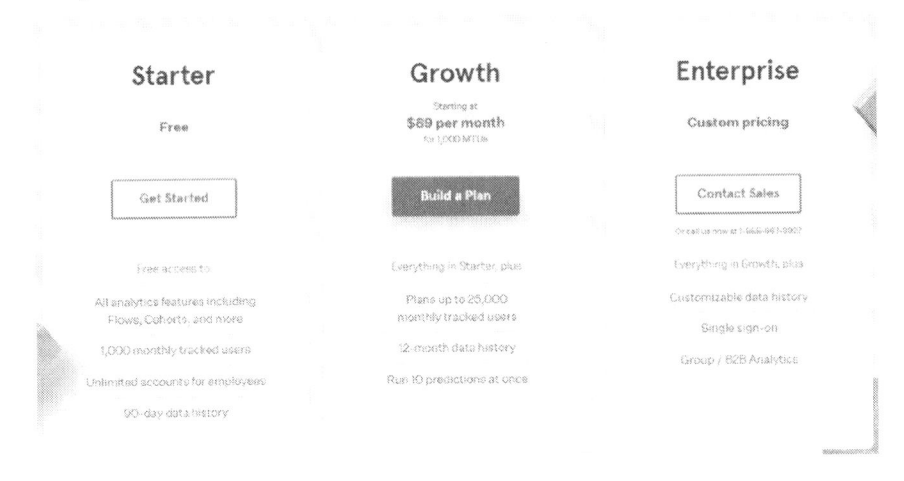

Chapter 6: User Onboarding

Segment

Collecting and analyzing customer data is a must-do for every brand. This tool helps brands collect and unify customer data from different sources.

With the tool, you can send customer data to any platform you want for analytics.

Over 100 platforms can integrate this tool, depending on what you want to learn from your customer data. This is how much the tool costs:

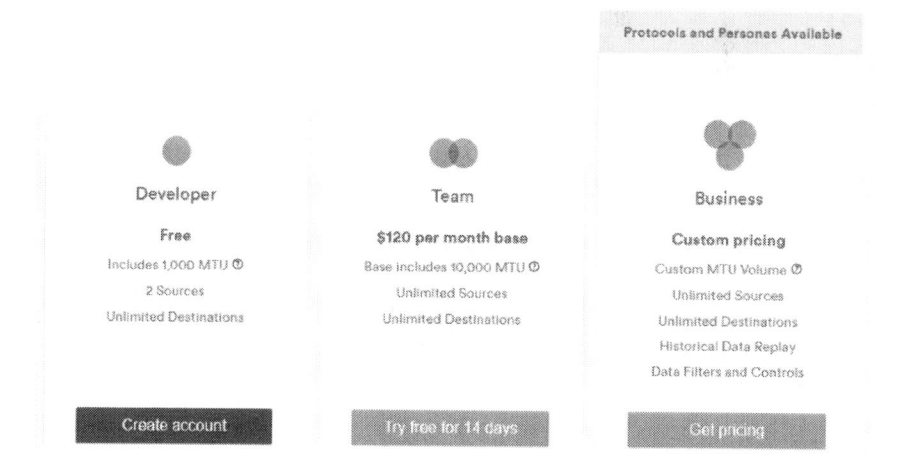

NeverBounce

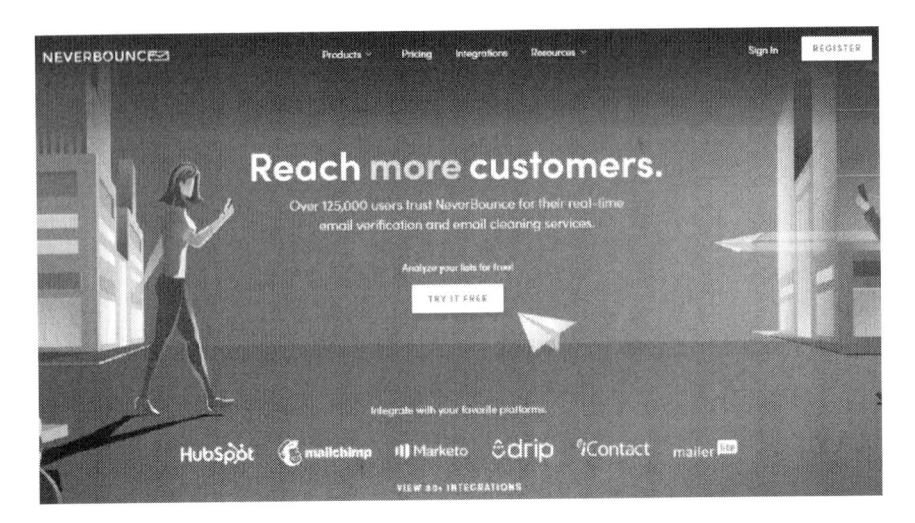

NeverBounce helps your brand verify emails as you onboard your customers and engage them in your services.

With verified emails, it's easy to reach your target customers and ensure that they get every email you send them. Visit the website to learn more about its pricing.

Here are some tools you can integrate with NeverBounce:

Chapter 6: User Onboarding

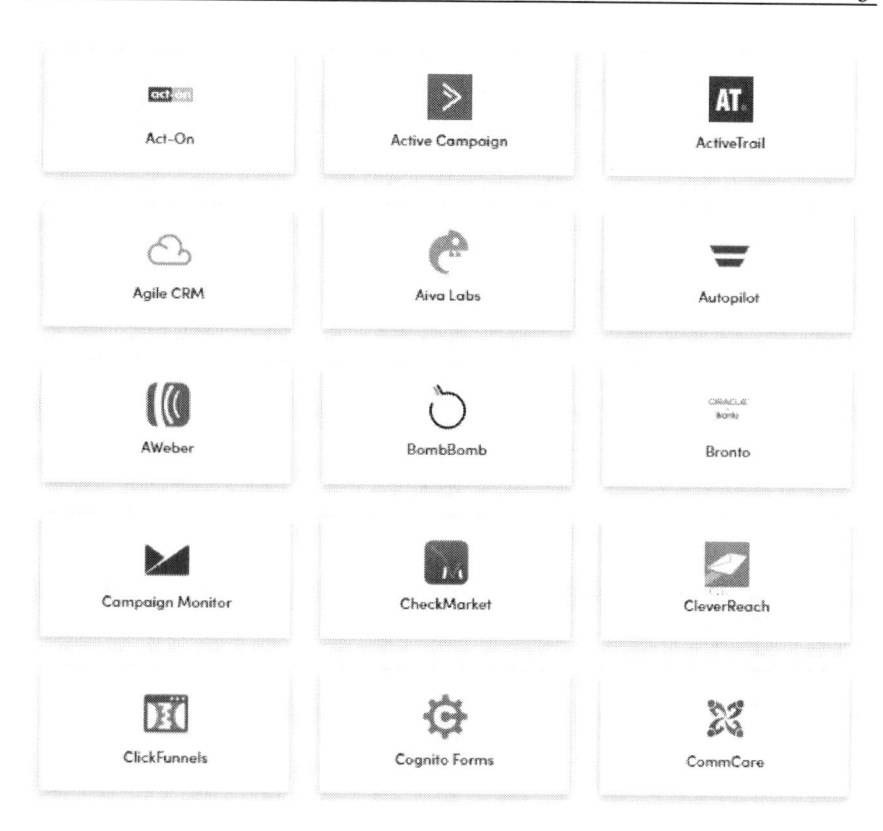

Act-On	Active Campaign	ActiveTrail
Agile CRM	Aiva Labs	Autopilot
AWeber	BombBomb	Bronto
Campaign Monitor	CheckMarket	CleverReach
ClickFunnels	Cognito Forms	CommCare

Appcues

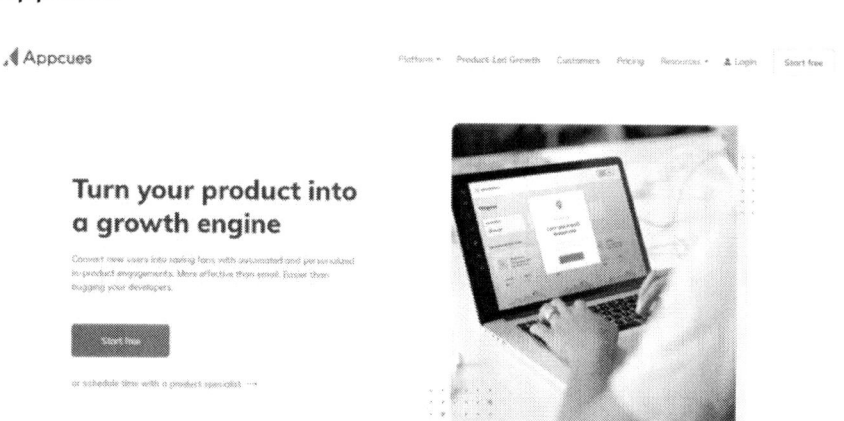

Turn your product into a growth engine

Appcues helps brands create personalized onboarding experiences for their customers that nurture them into their business.

You can use the tool to increase customer engagement with specific features of your services or products.

The tool's self-service guidelines help engage customers and build great customer experience. You can integrate it with other tools to help achieve your business goals.

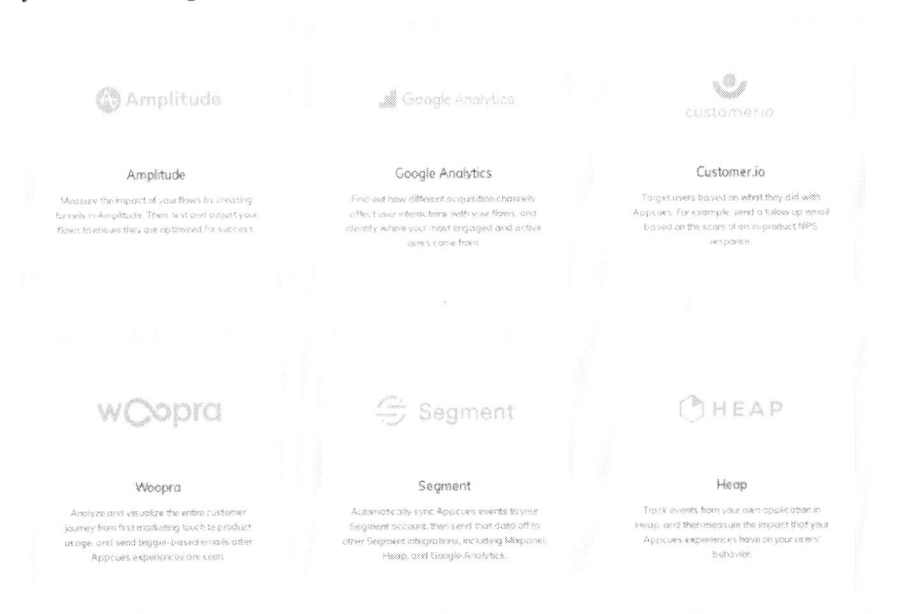

The pricing model depends on the number of users you want to involve in your business. Visit the website for more details.

Chameleon

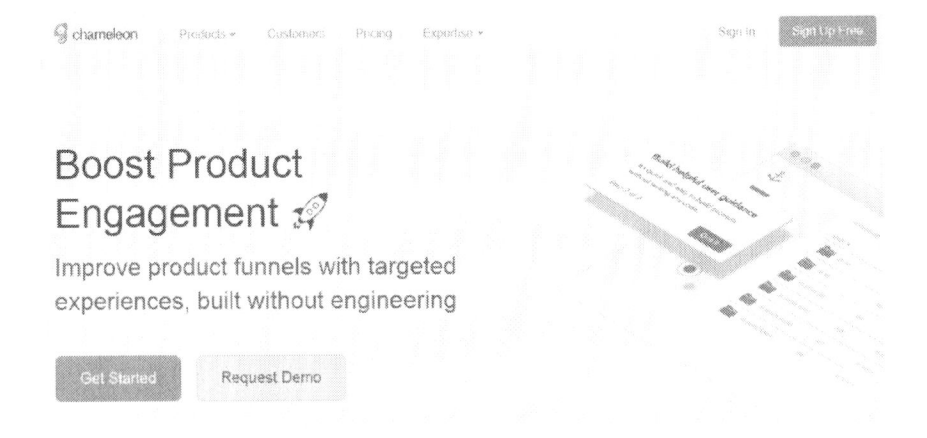

Chapter 6: User Onboarding

To increase conversions during the onboarding process, you need to boost product engagement. Chameleon provides great features to help with engagement. These include A/B testing to see what works best for your brand and surveys to collect information from your customers about the services they'd like to see.

You can also integrate Chameleon with other tools:

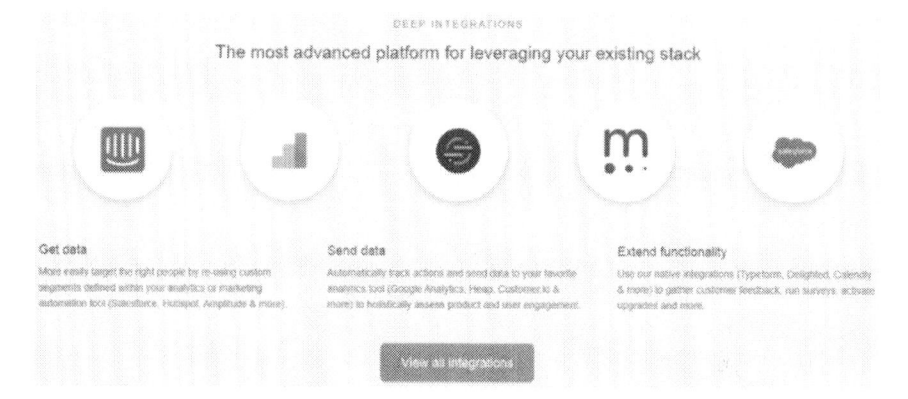

Here are the products that come with this tool:

And here are its costs, depending on the number of monthly users:

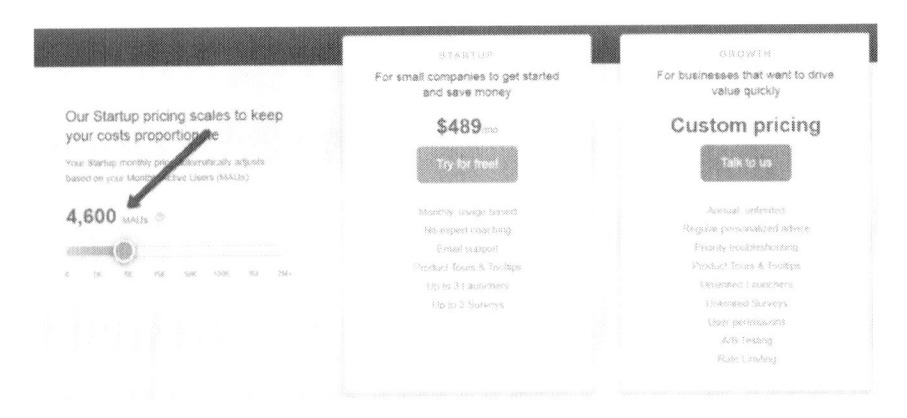

Tour My App

Increase user activation and engagement

Create in-application tutorials that guide your users as they use your web application

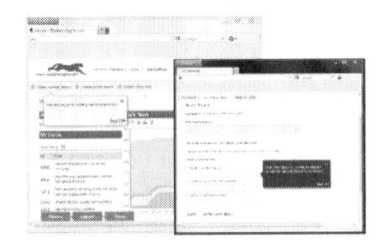

Use in-application guided tours to onboard new users, highlight features in your app, show a demo, or as a substitute for documentation. No coding required!

You can use the Tour My App to create educational tutorials that help increase user engagement with your services or products.

If you're looking to improve the onboarding process for your new customers, the tool provides a handy way to create product demos and display your app's features.

Here are some more details about Tour My App and what you can get out of it:

Chapter 6: User Onboarding

Engage your users

Improve user engagement by displaying in-app guided tours that help users perform tasks in your web application. Show a "getting started" tour when they log in for the first time. Highlight advanced or unused features when the time is right.

Better than documentation

Let us face it. Users don't read documentation. Users don't watch feature videos. What if you could explain features from within the application, as your users interact with them? Now you can, with Tour My App.

No coding required

Just add a few lines of Javascript to your pages, and then our powerful Tour Builder allows you to create and change tours through a GUI interface. Say goodbye to mucking around in code and re-deploying your app every time you want to make a change.

Fully interactive tours

Tour My App allows you to create completely interactive tours, where you can progress the tour when users perform specific actions, like clicking a button or typing some text.

Complete customisation

Tour My App allows you to customise every aspect of your tours. Change the colour scheme to match your site. Position the message box to the left, right, above or below the target item. Decide exactly when and how a tour should be displayed.

Easy to maintain

Tired of creating new tutorial videos or user documentation every time your UI changes? With Tour My App, it takes only minutes of pointing and clicking to update an existing tour to a new UI or to create a new tour.

Handles the little stuff

Tour My App supports tours that run across pages. It can manage dynamically loading elements and AJAX pages. It even keeps track of who has seen a tour so that it is not shown to them again.

Usage metrics

See how your users interact with the tours. Learn which steps cause users to quit a tour midway and how often each tour is run. Learn if you need to make changes to your tours and iterate.

What are you waiting for?

Get started today. View pricing and sign up!

Here's the Tour My App pricing structure:

Pricing & Sign Up

	Enterprise	Achiever	Performer (POPULAR)	Starter
	$250 Monthly	$75 Monthly	$24 Monthly	
# of Tours	Unlimited	Unlimited	Unlimited	Unlimited
Tour Runs	More than 50000 /month	50000 /month	10000 /month	1000 /month
Activity Stream	✓	✓	✓	✓
Funnel Analytics	✓	✓	✓	
Multilingual Tours	✓	✓		
Professional Services	Available at $100 /hr	Available at $100 /hr	Available at $100 /hr	
Price	Contact us	$250 /month	$75 /month	$24 /month
	Contact us	Sign Up for FREE 30 Day Trial	No credit card required. Choose plan later.	

Heap

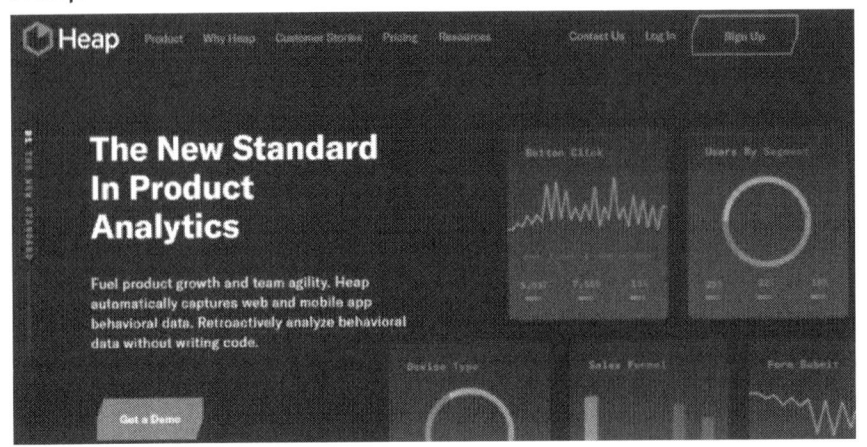

Heap can significantly improve your onboarding process. It helps increase user engagement and lower customer churn rate.

You can use it to analyze customer behavior and optimize your product analyses to increase conversions and sales.

Here's the Heap pricing model:

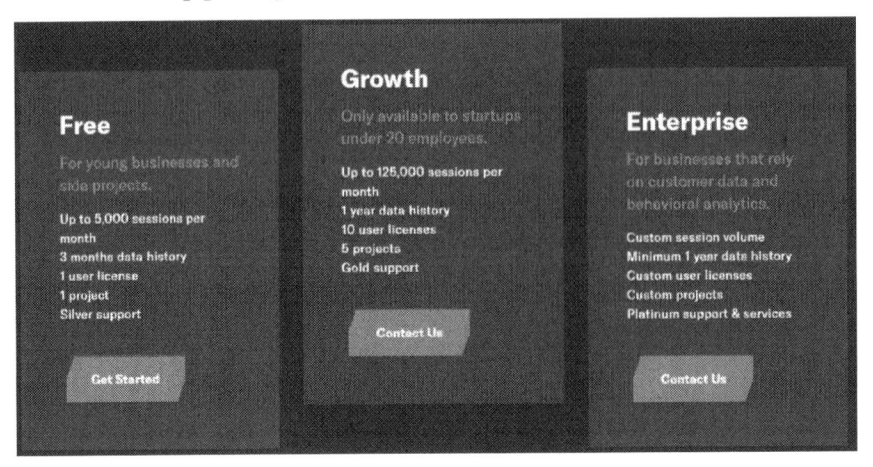

Chapter 6: User Onboarding

Localytics

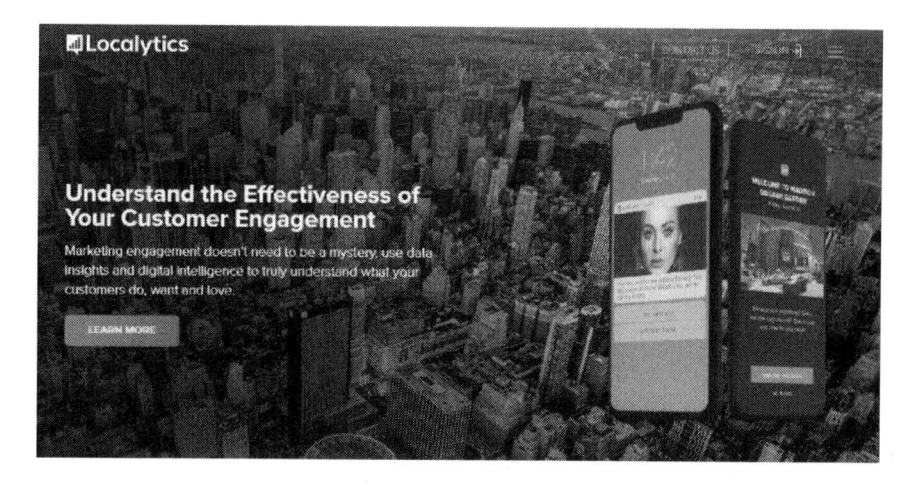

The onboarding process is a great time for brands to learn more about their customers so they can offer more tailored services.

You can use Localytics to help create your product experiment and engagement strategy. It supports you in your endeavor to offer the best services or products to your customers, build trust with them, and get recurrent revenue from your sales.

Here's some information about the tool and how it works:

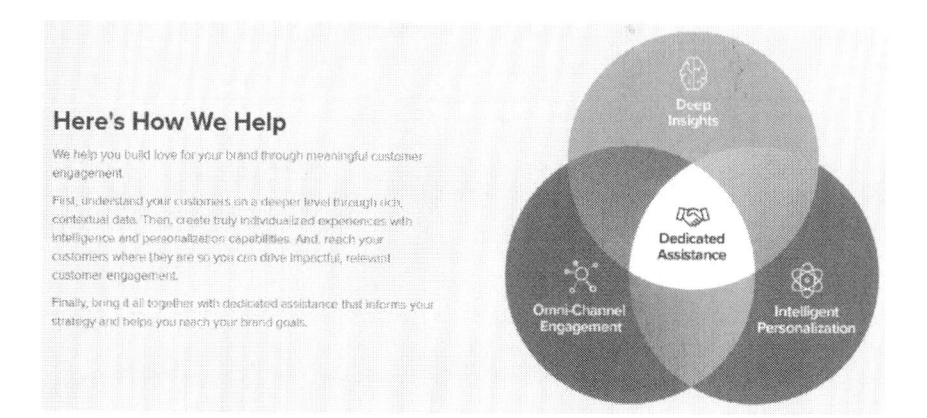

Help Scout

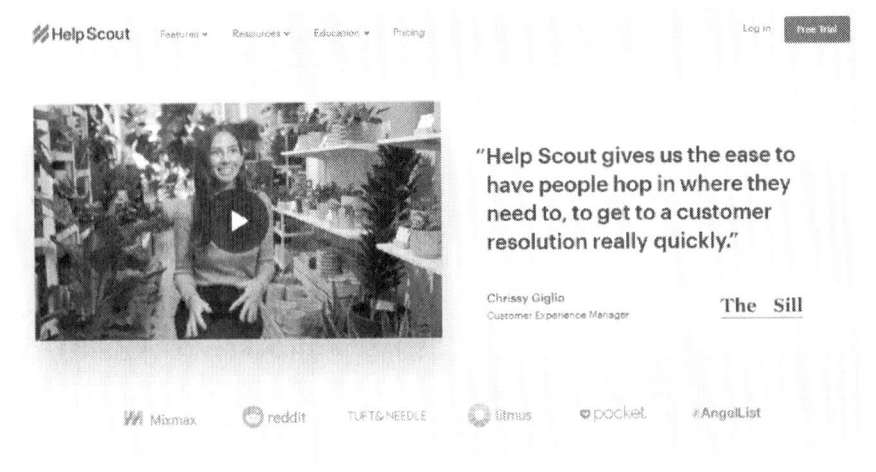

Online customers are very demanding and need answers right now. Help Scout offers a way for you to manage customer questions and provides an in-depth guide with answers to those questions.

You can use the tool to close deals through its live chat or engage your customers as you onboard them through its in-app messaging. It also gives insights into your customers as you serve them so you can understand them better.

You can integrate Help Scout with other tools to achieve your marketing goals as you onboard your customers. Here are some of those tools:

Chapter 6: User Onboarding

Docs	Slack	Mailchimp	Shopify
Olark	Capsule	Webhooks	Pipedrive
Highrise	WooCommerce	Mixpanel	OnePageCRM
Magento	Campaign Monitor	Hively	KISSmetrics
FullStory	Nicereply	Jira	Campfire
Salesforce	PipelineDeals	Constant Contact	BriteVerify
Bronto	Metorik	Churn Buster	Segment.io

365

And this is how much it costs:

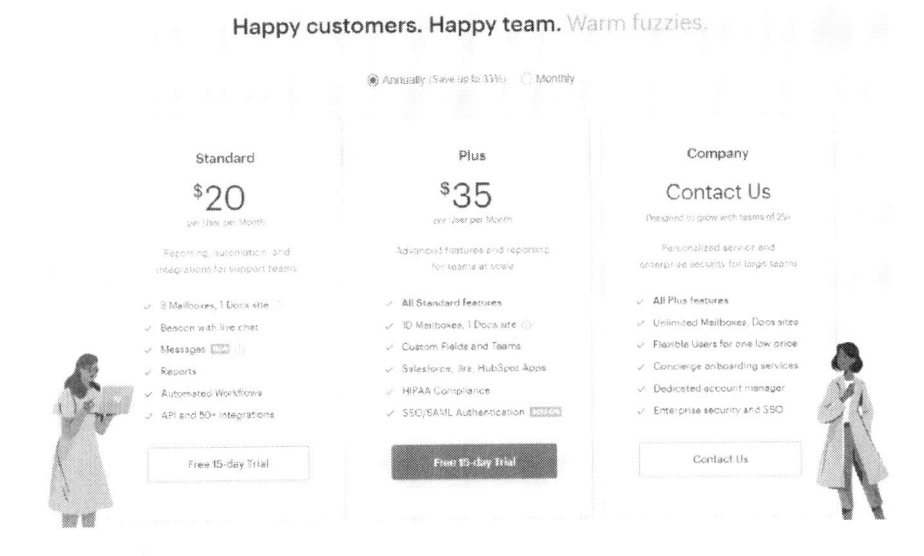

Zendesk

Zendesk is a CRM tool that creates and gathers community forums where you can engage your customers and help them solve their challenges during onboarding.

The tool also hosts self-service guides for customers, accompanied by a constant customer support team to answer any questions they may have.

Chapter 6: User Onboarding

Here's how much you'll pay for Zendesk:

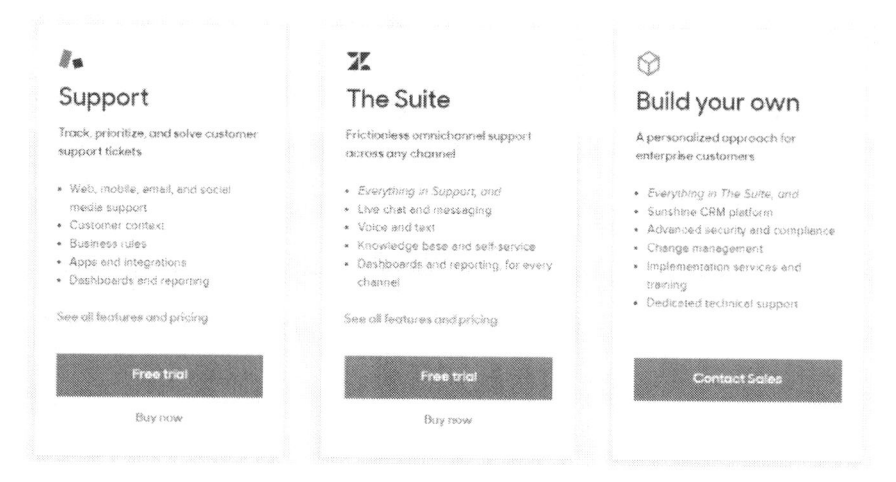

UserGuiding

As a brand, you have to carefully walk your customers through every step of the onboarding process.

UserGuiding has great features to help you do that. You can engage your customers through the product's messaging app.

The tool can also help boost product adoption. UserGuiding lets you collect customer feedback that's useful in your decision-making process.

Below is the cost of the tool:

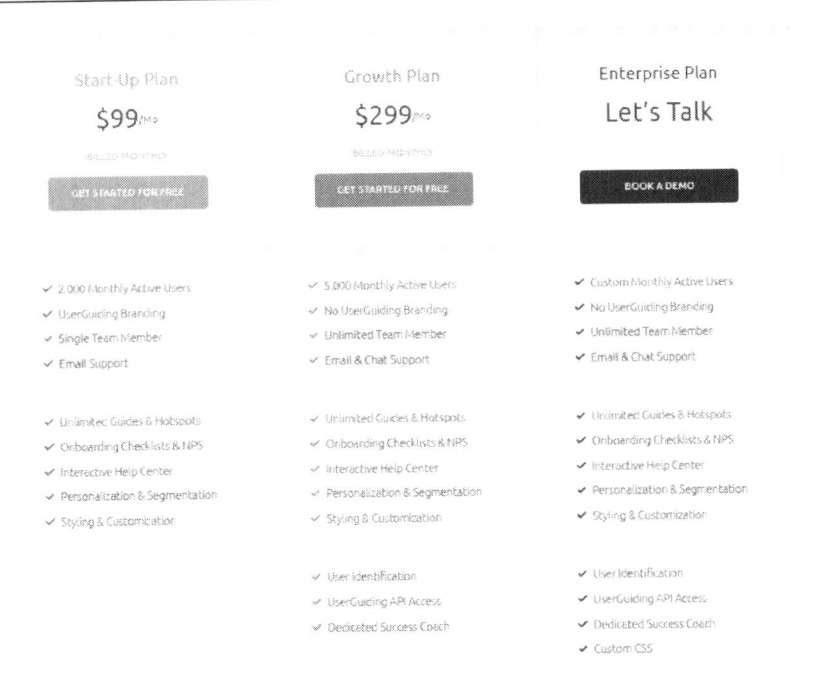

Start-Up Plan	Growth Plan	Enterprise Plan
$99/mo	$299/mo	Let's Talk
BILLED MONTHLY	BILLED MONTHLY	
GET STARTED FOR FREE	GET STARTED FOR FREE	BOOK A DEMO
✓ 2,000 Monthly Active Users	✓ 5,000 Monthly Active Users	✓ Custom Monthly Active Users
✓ UserGuiding Branding	✓ No UserGuiding Branding	✓ No UserGuiding Branding
✓ Single Team Member	✓ Unlimited Team Member	✓ Unlimited Team Member
✓ Email Support	✓ Email & Chat Support	✓ Email & Chat Support
✓ Unlimited Guides & Hotspots	✓ Unlimited Guides & Hotspots	✓ Unlimited Guides & Hotspots
✓ Onboarding Checklists & NPS	✓ Onboarding Checklists & NPS	✓ Onboarding Checklists & NPS
✓ Interactive Help Center	✓ Interactive Help Center	✓ Interactive Help Center
✓ Personalization & Segmentation	✓ Personalization & Segmentation	✓ Personalization & Segmentation
✓ Styling & Customization	✓ Styling & Customization	✓ Styling & Customization
	✓ User Identification	✓ User Identification
	✓ UserGuiding API Access	✓ UserGuiding API Access
	✓ Dedicated Success Coach	✓ Dedicated Success Coach
		✓ Custom CSS

WalkMe

WalkMe helps brands manage their customer experience and engage customers with their services or products.

With the tool, you can assist your customers as needed and direct them to take specific actions with your brand's services during the onboarding process.

Chapter 6: User Onboarding

Visit the website for more details about its pricing. These are the benefits you'll get from this tool:

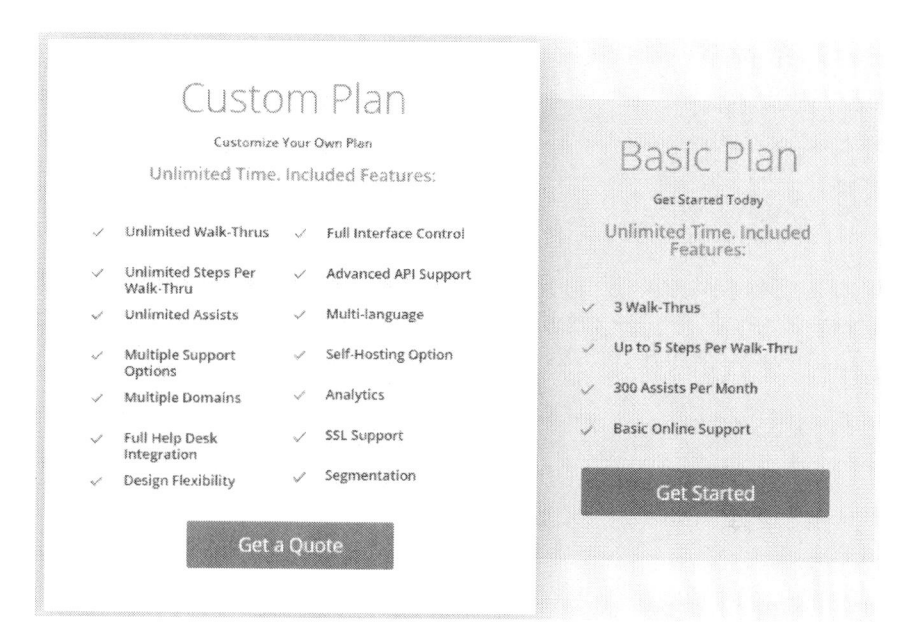

Custom Plan	Basic Plan
Customize Your Own Plan	Get Started Today
Unlimited Time. Included Features:	Unlimited Time. Included Features:
✓ Unlimited Walk-Thrus ✓ Full Interface Control	✓ 3 Walk-Thrus
✓ Unlimited Steps Per Walk-Thru ✓ Advanced API Support	✓ Up to 5 Steps Per Walk-Thru
✓ Unlimited Assists ✓ Multi-language	✓ 300 Assists Per Month
✓ Multiple Support Options ✓ Self-Hosting Option	✓ Basic Online Support
✓ Multiple Domains ✓ Analytics	Get Started
✓ Full Help Desk Integration ✓ SSL Support	
✓ Design Flexibility ✓ Segmentation	
Get a Quote	

Best Practices for Your App Onboarding Process

To make the most of your onboarding process, here are some practices you can adopt.

Monitor Customer Progress

Every customer is not at the same place in the buyer journey. Use in-app tools to monitor their progress and offer the best guidance according to their stage in the buying process.

Monitoring your customers' progress can also help you identify upselling and cross-selling opportunities you can use to increase your sales.

Help Customers Identify "Aha!" Moments ASAP

Your customers want to buy your products or services because they want to solve their challenges.

You want your customers to know more about your business and how it will help them in the shortest time possible. That means helping them reach and recognize their aha! moments quickly. These are the moments when they realize you're offering the solution they need.

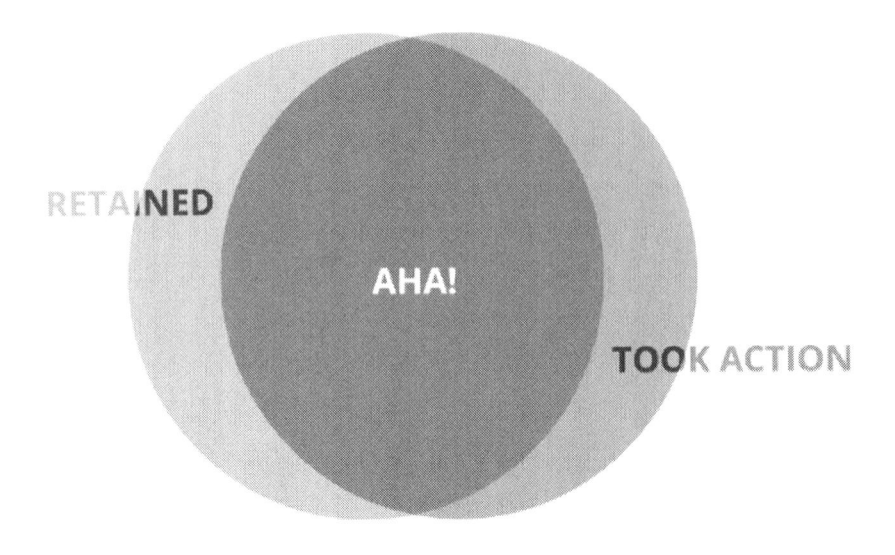

Image Source: https://mode.com/blog/facebook-aha-moment-simpler-than-you-think

The way to do this is to provide all the information the customer needs to understand what your services can do for them and why you're different from your competitors. This will help them take action sooner during the onboarding period and generate sales.

Monitor and Optimize Customer Feedback

Your customer feedback is what helps you understand what makes your customers tick. During onboarding, make sure you act on the feedback they give you and provide them with what they need.

Help Customers Understand Your Value Proposition

From the start, help your customers answer this important question: Why should I use this business's services and what will I get out of it?

Make it easy for new customers to understand your business and see the value you're offering.

Ensure Top-Notch Customer Service

Customer service is at the center of your business marketing. If you can't address your customers' needs, they'll go elsewhere. Here are some statistics related to customer service:

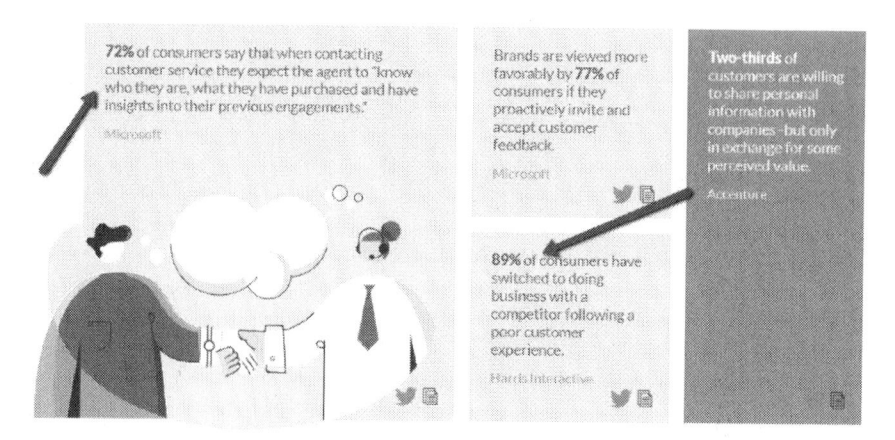

> 72% of consumers say that when contacting customer service they expect the agent to "know who they are, what they have purchased and have insights into their previous engagements."
> Microsoft

> Brands are viewed more favorably by 77% of consumers if they proactively invite and accept customer feedback.
> Microsoft

> Two-thirds of customers are willing to share personal information with companies - but only in exchange for some perceived value.
> Accenture

> 89% of consumers have switched to doing business with a competitor following a poor customer experience.
> Harris Interactive

Mistakes to Avoid during User Onboarding

There are some mistakes that can detract from your efforts to reach out to customers and convert them.

You don't want to put in all that work and then watch your customers end up with your competitors, do you? To avoid falling into that trap, avoid the following errors.

Not Addressing Customer Needs Immediately

When your customers have issues that need to be resolved, don't make them wait. Answer their questions in the shortest time possible.

Clients whose needs aren't addressed immediately leave and take up with a competitor. Your customer support team should be ready and available to answer questions 24/7.

Not Seeking Customer Feedback

Customer feedback tells you whether your customers are enjoying your services and what you can do to keep improving them.

Research by Statista shows that 27% of customers are frustrated by a brand's lack of effectiveness at offering their services.

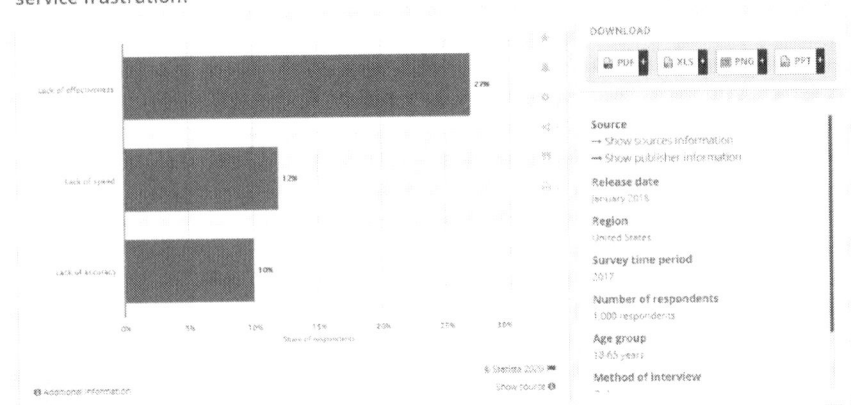

From your experience, what has been the one most common cause of your customer service frustration?

This lack of effectiveness is largely attributed to a lack of customer opportunity to provide feedback the brands can use to improve services.

Collect customer feedback and act on it as soon as you can to improve your customer experience, offer better products and services, and increase sales.

Confusing Customers with Too Much Information

Every step of onboarding is a learning process for your customers. Don't overwhelm your customers with too much information at once. It will bore them or frustrate them, and they'll probably lose interest in your services and seek out other businesses.

To keep new customers interested, give them information that's broken down into small bits. You can include video content as many people engage more with video content than with text-based content.

Neglecting Customer Follow-Ups

Don't make customers come to you with their problems. Reach out to see how they're doing. This will promote trust by demonstrating that you care for them and want to do your best to meet their needs.

Research by Invesp shows that 48% of salespeople don't do customer follow-ups.

The Importance of Sales Follow Ups
Statistics and Trends

48% of salespeople never even make a single follow up attempt

Checking in with customers can also motivate them to open up for more help, which can lead to cross-selling and upselling opportunities.

Making False Promises

When onboarding new customers, be open and honest with them. Don't promise what you can't deliver. That will disappoint them and you'll lose them to your competitors.

Deliver on what you promise or, even better, surpass your promises. That will strengthen the trust bond and encourage the customer to engage and use your brand's services or products even more.

That's a wrap for our discussion of user onboarding. To learn about A/B testing, let's head to the next chapter.

Chapter 7: A/B Testing

Experimenting is one of the best ways for many business owners to grow their online brands. A/B tests can show you what's working best in your business. You can use the test results to optimize lead generation, conversions, and sales.

A/B testing involves comparing "versions A and B" of something, running two different variations to see which performs or works best. In this chapter, we'll cover this process in-depth and explain how to use it to grow your business.

This approach to business improvement is on the rise as business owners want to know which of their methods produce the most growth. Research by FinancesOnline shows that the global A/B testing market is projected to be worth $1081 million by 2025.

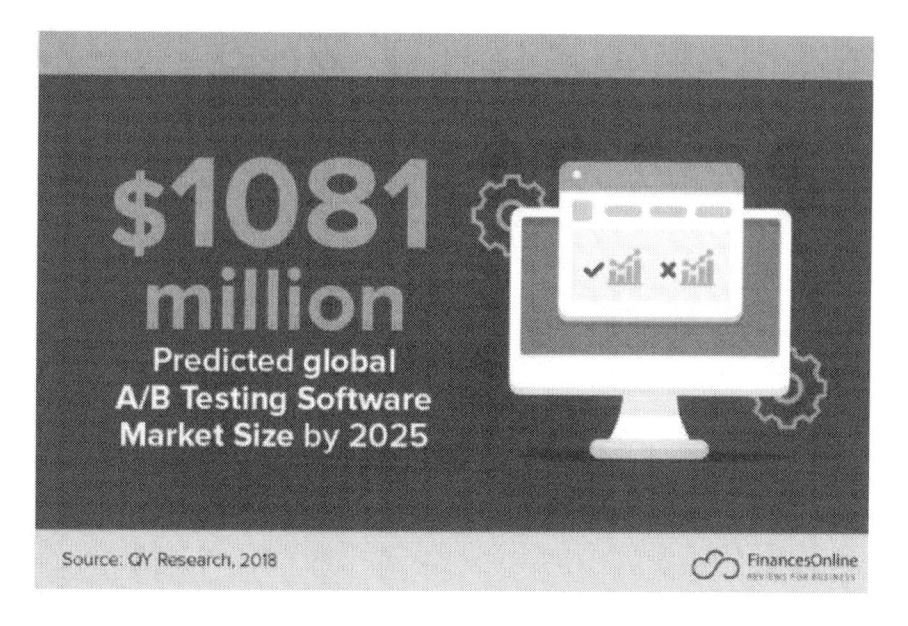

$1081 million
Predicted global A/B Testing Software Market Size by 2025

Source: QY Research, 2018   FinancesOnline

To start, we can look at the benefits that brands enjoy when they run A/B tests.

Benefits of A/B Testing

Increase Customer Engagement

Testing your business and website helps your customers and potential customers engage better with your brand.

The tests show you which versions of your content and customer interactions are most compelling so you can provide what your customers want. That will increase their product or service engagement as well as their knowledge about your business and what it can do for them.

Increase Customer Experience

Online buyers are very demanding. They like to do business with brands that give them the experience they want.

As a method to learn more about what's most important to their customers, many businesses run A/B tests. The tests help brands tailor the experience they provide.

And the research shows that customers are willing to pay more to buy from brands that give them the best experience.

Chapter 7: A/B Testing

55% of consumers would pay more for a better customer experience

Better customer experience

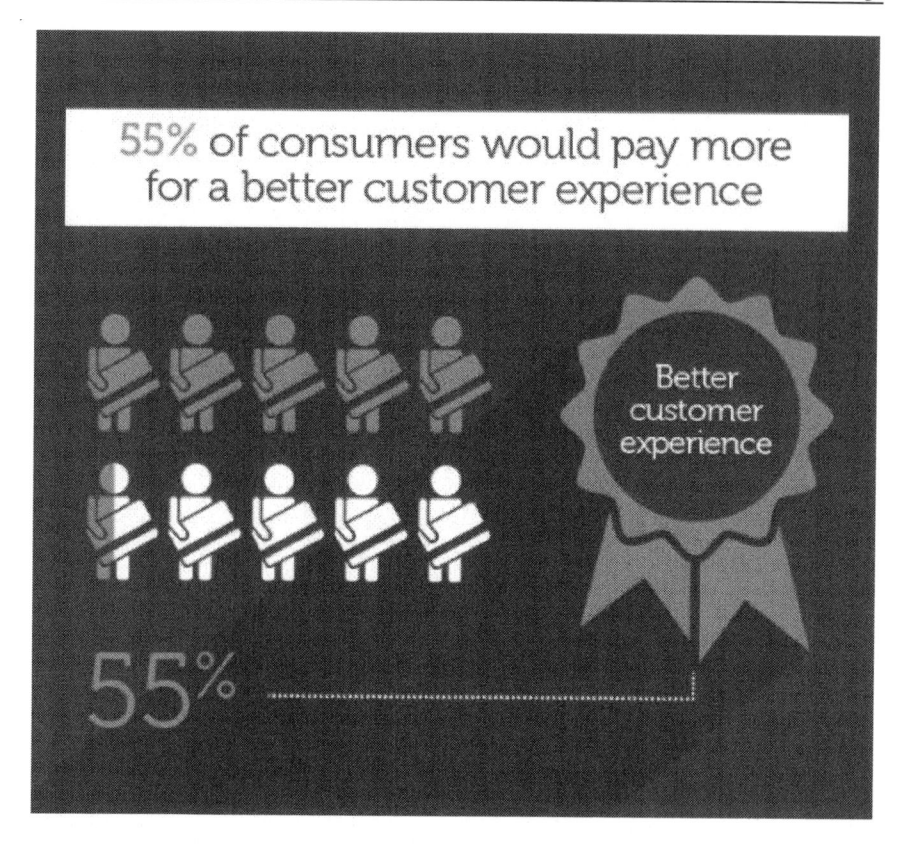

55%

Make More Sales

A/B tests help brands increase their sales and business ROI. When brands know what works best for them and optimize it, they attract more customers.

Businesses that acquire this knowledge offer the best value to their customers. Since the customers enjoy the services, they buy more.

Research by Statista shows that online sales are on the rise every day.

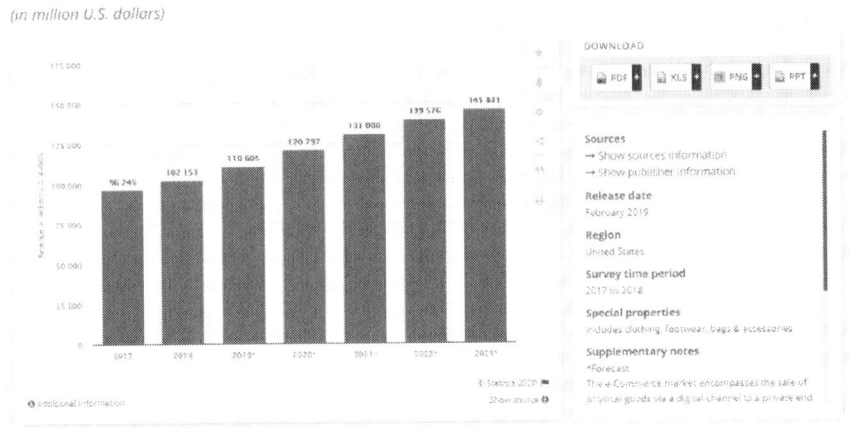

Apparel, footwear and accessories retail e-commerce revenue in the United States from 2017 to 2023
(in million U.S. dollars)

[Bar chart showing revenue growth from 2017 to 2023]

This increase in spending is due to brands knowing what their customers want and giving it to them.

Offering customers the best services will not only increase your sales, but will also make customers your brand ambassadors, and then they'll do some of your marketing for you.

Reduce Cart Abandonment

There are many reasons potential buyers abandon a cart during the shopping process. These are some of the reasons:

Reasons For Online Shopping Cart Abandonment

(Infographic showing: Presented with unexpected costs 56%; Was just browsing 37%; Found a better price elsewhere 36%; Overall price too expensive 32%; Decided against buying 26%; Website navigation too complicated 25%; Website crashed 24%; Process was taking too long 21%; Excessive payment security checks 18%; Concerns about payment security 17%; Delivery options were unsuitable 16%; Website time out 15%; Price presented in a foreign currency 13%; Payment was declined 11%. SOURCE: WorldPay)

When you run A/B tests, you'll know why your customers decided not to make a purchase. You'll devote attention to fixing the problem, and this will reduce the number of carts abandoned.

For example, in the chart above, one of the reasons is unexpected costs. To reduce the rate of cart abandonment, inform your potential customers about all the expenses they'll incur while they're shopping before they get to the cart. This will help them plan their spending and prepare them before it's time to click "Check out."

Generate Leads and Customers

Testing different variations of your website helps you increase lead generation and convert leads into customers.

For example, you may be losing clients because your website's landing pages load slowly. Research by Think With Google confirms that this is a common problem.

As page load time goes from:

1s to 3s the probability of bounce **increases 32%**

1s to 5s the probability of bounce **increases 90%**

1s to 6s the probability of bounce **increases 106%**

1s to 10s the probability of bounce **increases 123%**

Running tests on every aspect of your customer interaction will help you generate and convert more customers to your business.

Increase SEO Rankings

Search engine optimization is an essential factor in the success of every online business. Ranking high in search engine results helps a brand reach more target customers and increase website traffic. A/B tests can tell you what keywords rank high on your website. You can then optimize your site to increase its ranking and draw more potential customers.

How to Generate A/B Test Ideas

Here's a shortlist of the many different ways brands can get or generate ideas to run their A/B tests.

Your Competitors

You can check out your competition to see what types of ideas bring them good results, then use them for your business. You're competing for the same customers, so you can use those ideas to generate your A/B test ideas.

Use Your Performing Ads

Since running ads is a good way to reach out to customers, you can use your best ads to generate A/B test ideas.

Website Content

The web content you create for your brand can give you ideas for business optimization.

Ensure that the content you create is suitable for your target customers. Your content should be educational and easy to understand.

Surveys

You can send your target customers a survey that they can fill out to help you generate some ideas for your brand testing.

There are [many different tools you can use when sending your customers a survey](#) or questionnaire to fill out. Choose a tool that will help you collect all the data you need to design an accurate test.

Your Sales Team

Your team can be a great source of information for growing your brand. You can reach out to them and ask for help coming up with ideas for A/B tests to run on your branding strategy.

Since your team members have marketing experience and have been interacting with potential clients at different levels, they'll definitely have some ideas to contribute.

On-Site Customer Behavior

Your customers' behavior can give you tips for how to run your A/B tests for your business. You can monitor a variety of customer behaviors as they interact with your business website. This can be through blog content, website copy, or their comments on the website.

All these things will help you learn more about your customers and generate A/B tests that will show you how to draw them in.

Past A/B Tests

Maybe you've previously run some tests. You can revisit those tests to develop fresh marketing ideas. You might be surprised to find that your past tests can help you think of new ways to reach out to your potential customers.

Social Media Sites

These are other great sites you can use to reach your target customers. Research by Statista shows the most popular social sites:

Most popular social networks worldwide as of January 2020, ranked by number of active users
(in millions)

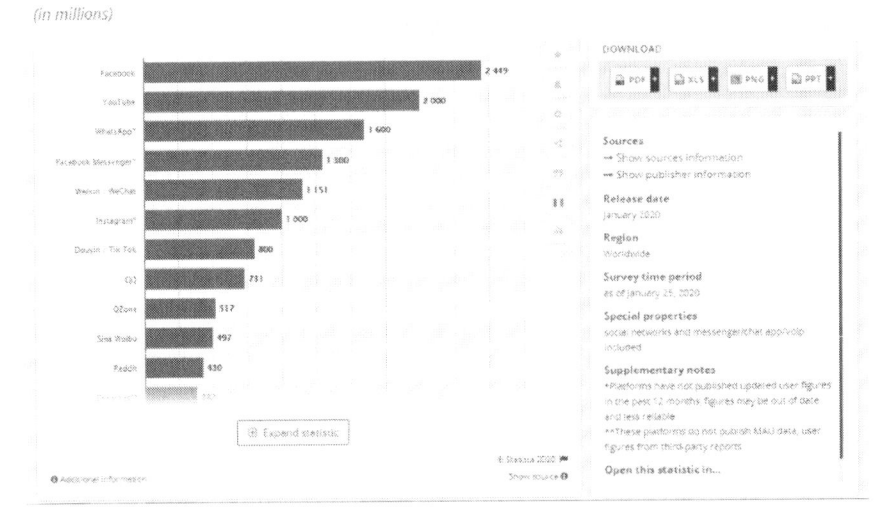

You can visit these sites and interact with your target customers for inspiration. These sites can be a great source of testing ideas as you learn how you can grow your brand and satisfy your customers.

Marketing Content to Test

There are many aspects of your marketing strategy that you can test as you grow and learn how to satisfy your customers. Here are some comparisons for testing your business website.

Trial Period

SaaS companies often give their new customers a free trial period to get acquainted with their services before they start a monthly subscription. For most brands, that's a one-month free trial period. Here's an example from Xero SaaS of 30-day free signup:

Try Xero FREE for 30 days!

Sign up fast, with unlimited users and no credit card required

First name

Last name

Email address

Phone number

Country

Kenya

☐ I'm not a robot reCAPTCHA

☐ I have read and I agree to the terms, privacy and offer details

Other brands give new customers a 14-day free trial. Here's an example from GoToMeeting:

You can try comparing a shorter trial period to a longer one to see which achieves better results.

Website Design/Themes

Your website design or theme is one of the most important components of your online brand. Customers hate poorly designed websites. Even if your services or products are spectacular, your customers will be turned off by inferior design.

To ensure your website design is effective and attractive to your potential customers, develop two different versions and run A/B testing to find out which design is most beneficial for your business.

Landing Pages

You can design different types of landing page copy and run them simultaneously on your website to see which version your customers like more.

Product Images

Customers interact with product images in various ways. Changing your product images can help attract new customers to your shop.

Colored visuals are excellent for drawing people to read the content.

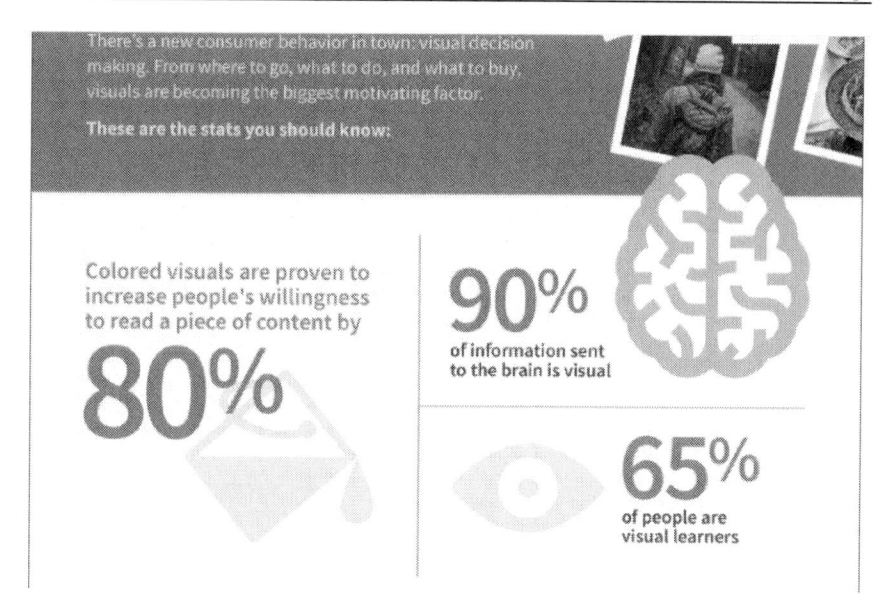

Image source: https://crowdriff.com/resources/blog/visual-marketing-statistics

You can design different product images and test them on your website to determine which images perform best.

Video and Audio

Videos are one of the customers' favorite ways to interact with businesses online. Brands that run video marketing campaigns can run different variations of their videos to see which ones attract the most customers.

If your brand has new welcome videos for onboarding, you can create several variations of these videos and compare their performance.

Content-Length

Different customers prefer different content length and depth. You can run some tests to see whether your customers want to read longer or shorter content and whether they'd like to see an overview or a lot of detail. Research shows that in-depth content ranks high in search engine results.

CONTENT TOTAL WORD COUNT

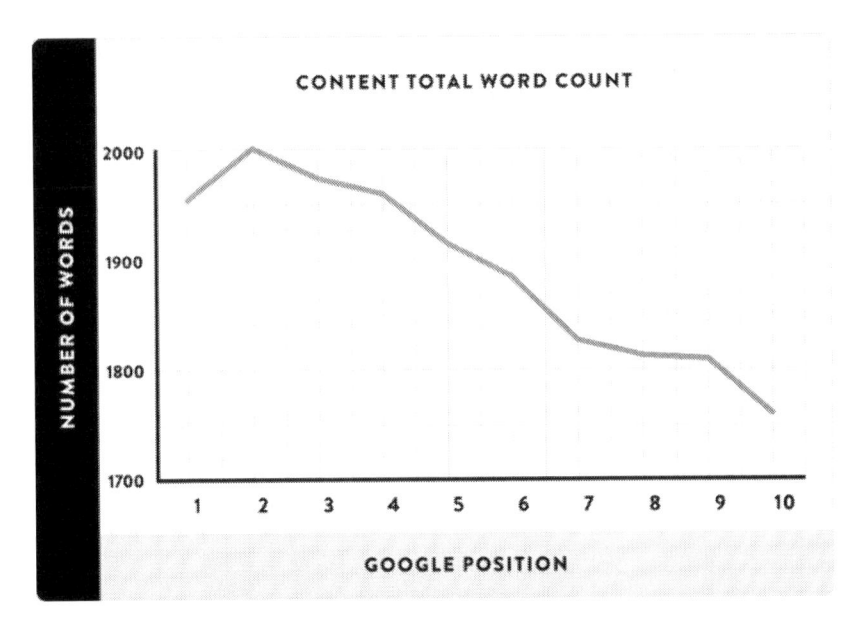

[Chart: Number of Words vs Google Position, showing word count decreasing from ~2000 at position 2 to ~1700 at position 10]

Compare the rankings of different variations on your content in the search engines. You can also compare how search engines rank different images, videos, sentence lengths, and paragraph lengths.

Your CTAs (Buttons and Colors)

As we explored in chapter 2, "Essentials of a Perfect Landing Page: Images and Videos," color preferences vary among individuals and groups, such as by gender.

Color is also an emotionally charged component of content and design, which means it can affect customers' buying decisions.

Compare the effects of changing, for example, CTA button colors. Change the hues you incorporate into other parts of your website and ads to see which ones attract your potential customers with ease.

Client Testimonials

One way to get more customers is to ask your existing customers for testimonials. To increase the chances of your potential customers reading your testimonials, you can post them in different versions. For instance, create some video testimonials and test their performance against text-based testimonials.

Chapter 7: A/B Testing

Use the results to inspire more potential customers to build trust with your business. Here's an example of Marketo testimonials:

Here are some examples of Buffer testimonials:

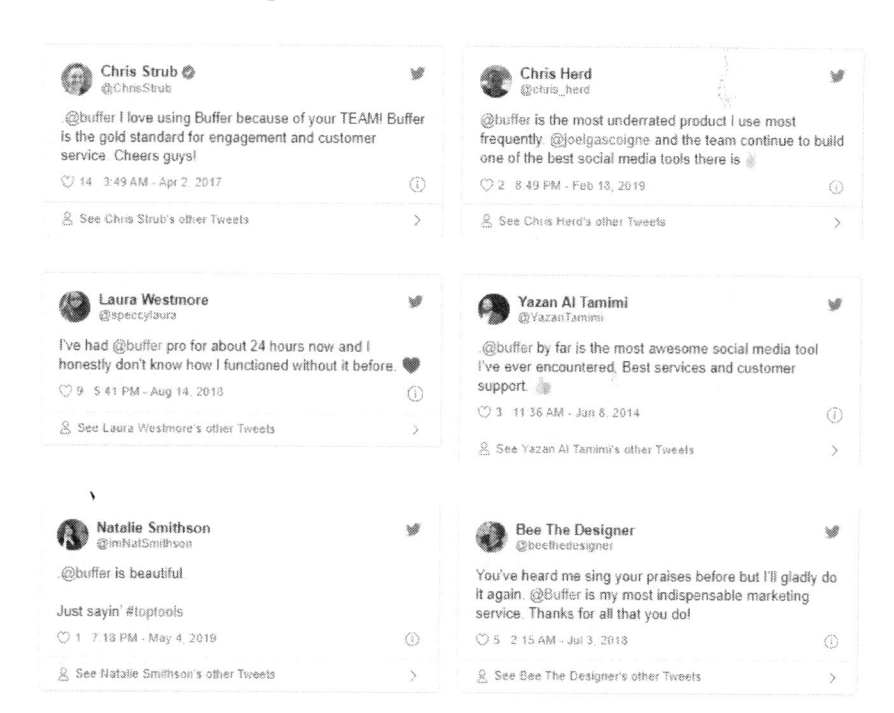

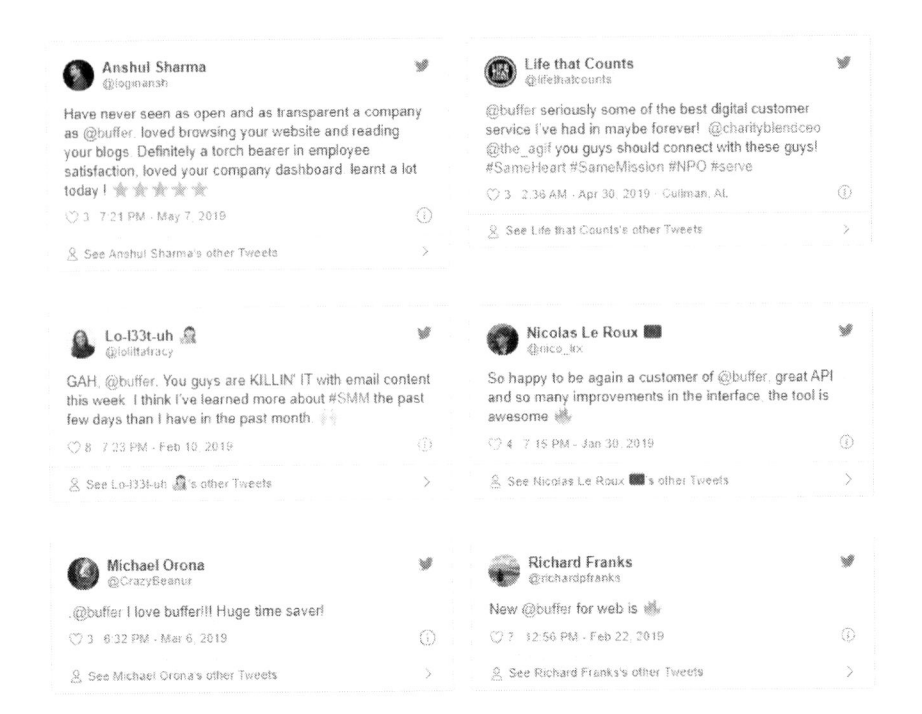

These two companies use different types of testimonials, but both are effective. You need to run testing to determine which approach is the best for your company.

Blog Headlines

As you seek to create blog content that many readers will enjoy, you'll want to invite readers in with a good headline for each post. Run A/B testing to see which version of a headline will be more attractive to readers.

CoSchedule is a great site you can use to analyze your headlines as you create your content:

Chapter 7: A/B Testing

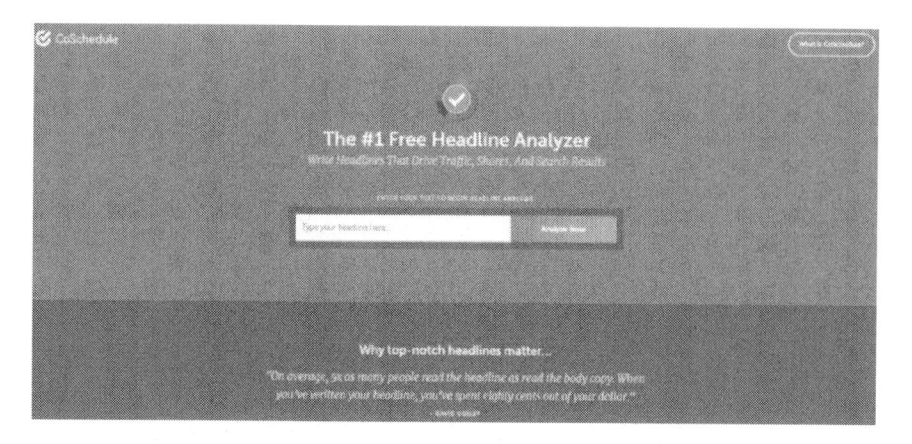

Live Chat on Your Website

You can test the viability of the live chat on your website. This will illuminate the importance of your live chat to your business growth.

Many brands lose new customers because they don't have a customer service system they can use to find solutions to their immediate challenges.

With a live chat, many lost customers can be regained as brand owners can both show they care and use the instant feedback from these conversations to come up with faster solutions to customer problems.

Email Copy

Email marketing is supremely effective for reaching customers and growing a business. Remember, the CMI found that 77% of content marketers use email campaigns. Email marketing has one of the highest ROIs of all marketing methods.

The average return for email marketing is **$38 for every dollar invested**, or an ROI of 3800%.

To increase your marketing returns, you have to create a high-quality email copy. You can run different versions of that copy to see which works best for your brand. From there, it will be easy to know the type of email campaigns that draw the most customers.

Sales Page Length

Different versions of sales pages perform differently. You can vary the length of these pages to see which ones customers prefer to interact with.

Provide one version of the sales pages with all the important information you think your customers will need, plus a detailed product description and other helpful information. Then create a shorter version with only the vital information. Run A/B testing to see which version gets more traffic.

Simplify the Checkout Process

A long, complicated checkout process can force your new customers to abandon their carts and shop with your competitors.

To shorten the process, consider reducing the number of fields you ask your customers to fill in before they make a purchase. For example, some customers hate to give all their private information just to buy a single item.

Including product images next to items in the checkout process can also make things simpler for customers as they order. Another way to ease checkout is to include more details about the pricing and shipping costs for new customers to help them avoid any hidden expenses. Remember, research shows that 61% of customers abandon carts because of extra costs.

Incorporate some of these features in your checkout page and test to see which ones result in the most completed purchases.

Font Size and Type

Font size and type can affect the way customers view your website, ads, and other content. You can run some tests to compare different font sizes in these settings. This will show you what your customers find attractive so you can produce content that draws them in.

Product Offers or Discounts

You can test different product offers or discounts to see which ones result in the most leads or conversions. This is a good way to learn how to price and market your products or services to your customers.

How to Choose A/B Testing Tools

Running an online brand can be hard, especially when you don't know the right tool to use or what makes a good tool to accomplish your business goals.

Here we list some factors you can consider when choosing among the many A/B testing tools on the market.

Pricing

Different tools vary in cost, usually based on the set of features you want. Before you decide to use a tool, ensure that you know all about its pricing structure.

You may find that one tool has everything you need for your A/B experiments but is too expensive for your business budget. Choose tools that won't put a damper on your business's operations or profit margins.

Features

Choose a tool that includes all the features you need for your experiments. A tool won't do you any good if it lacks the most important functionalities for the A/B tests you want to conduct.

Ease of Use

Some tools are more user-friendly than others. You'll want to find a tool that isn't needlessly complex and provides results that are easy to understand.

Ensure that your team knows how to use and get the most out of the tool you've chosen as they run your A/B tests.

Integrations

Running accurate experiments requires a coordinated effort. Your A/B testing tool should be easily integrable with a wide range of other tools to make testing easier as you determine the best way to market your business.

Customer Support

As a customer, you'll require support from time to time as you use the tool. Choose a tool that provides a 24/7 support team to help you solve any problems you run into. The team should be easy to access and available when you need immediate help.

Your Business Goals

Some tools are specially designed to run certain types of experiments. For example, if you want to run special tests on your landing pages, you might use Crazy Egg.

Other tools are perfectly designed to run specific tests on other aspects of your brand.

If you're only looking to test limited components of your marketing strategy, you can choose the tools that will give you the most accurate results for those components.

A/B Testing Tools

Below are some tools you can use when running A/B tests for your business.

Unbounce

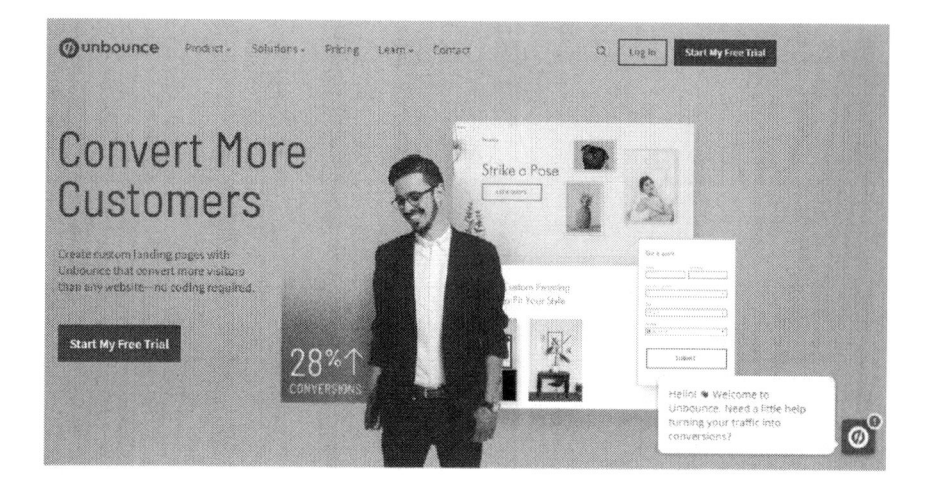

Unbounce is great for creating awesome, high-converting landing pages for your business.

The tool has a range of landing page templates you can choose from. Here are some of these templates:

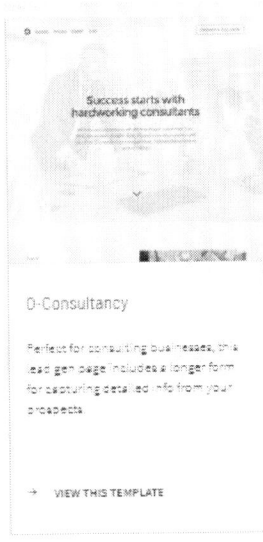

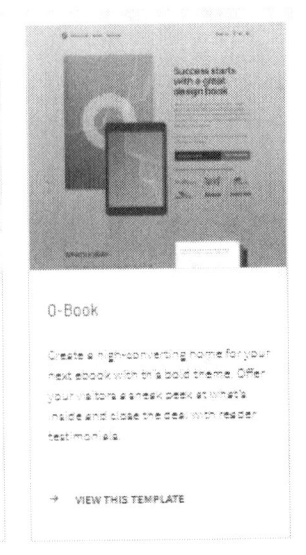

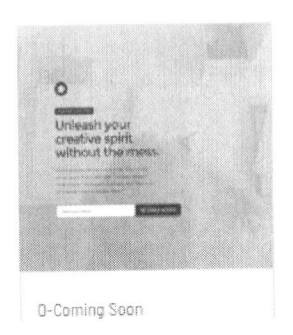

Here are some tools you can integrate with Unbounce:

Google Analytics

The Unbounce Script Manager supports Google Analytics. Just add your tracking ID and start monitoring your traffic and events (like button clicks and form fills).

Integrate with Zapier

Keep your workflow flowing. Using Zapier, you can send leads and data from your Unbounce landing pages to 1000+ supported apps via "Zaps."

→ Learn More

Integrate with webhooks

Create your own custom integrations by sending Unbounce form submissions to any server with webhooks.

Direct lead integrations

Automatically send leads to your CRM and marketing automation tools like Salesforce, Zoho, HubSpot, Mailchimp, and more—all without leaving the builder.

Branded lead email notifications

Send a real-time email notification to your team or clients every time a new lead comes in. Emails can be easily customized to match your brand.

Add more tracking and analytics

Need more than Google Analytics? Easily add and manage tracking like Facebook Pixels across all of your pages with Script Manager.

And here's the pricing model for the tool:

Enterprise	Premium (Recommended)	Essential
Starting from		
$399+ USD / mo	**$159** USD / mo	**$79** USD / mo
billed annually	billed annually	billed annually
Enterprise plans are custom-built to suit your needs. Partner with a Dedicated Launch Specialist and Customer Success Manager to maximize your ROI.	Scale up with double the landing pages, popups, and sticky bars of the Essential plan. Plus client sub-accounts, premium integrations, and AMP landing pages.	Just getting started? The Essential plan includes everything you need to build, test, and optimize for more conversions.
375+ Landing Pages	150 Landing Pages	75 Landing Pages
40+ Popups and Sticky Bars	16 Popups and Sticky Bars	8 Popups and Sticky Bars
Contact Us	Start My Free 14-Day Trial	Start My Free 14-Day Trial

Usability Hub

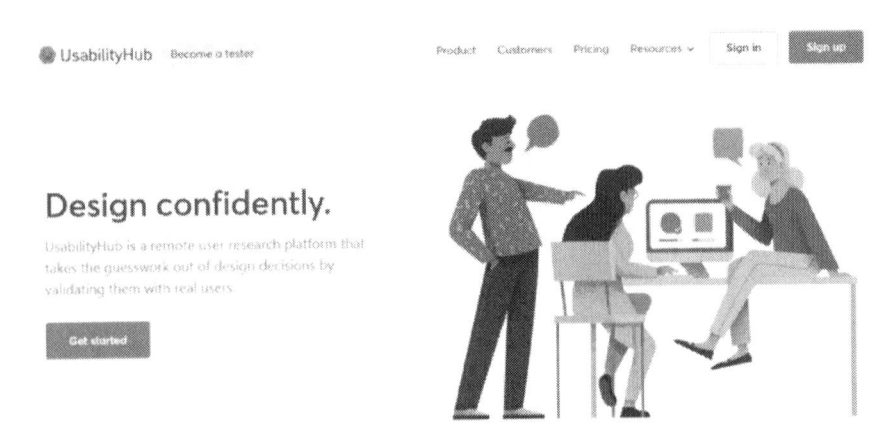

Usability Hub is a great user testing platform marketers use to test different aspects of their business marketing.

You can measure users' interaction with your landing page design to help increase engagement with target customers as they interact with your business.

Here's the tool's pricing model:

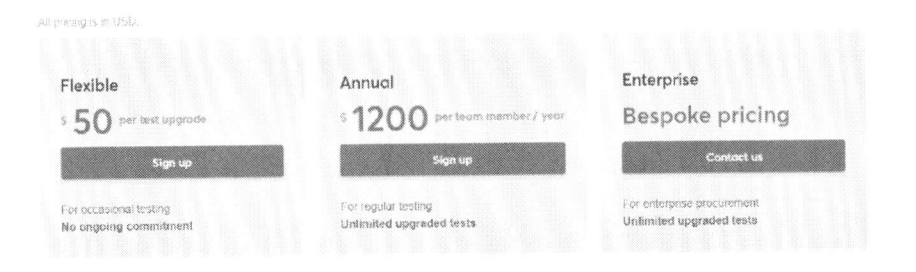

VWO.COM

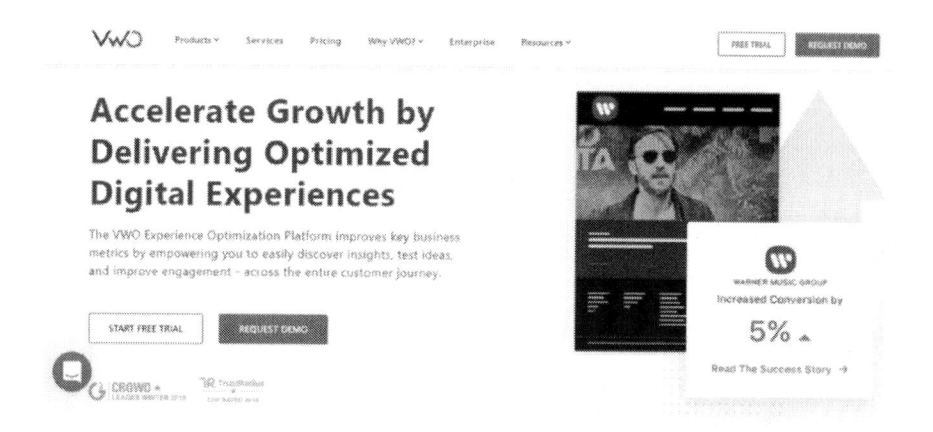

VWO.com gives you a superior way to run different A/B tests for your brand. It's a leader in the conversion optimization industry and can help you ensure a memorable customer experience for many potential customers.

Here are the popular guides you'll get with this tool:

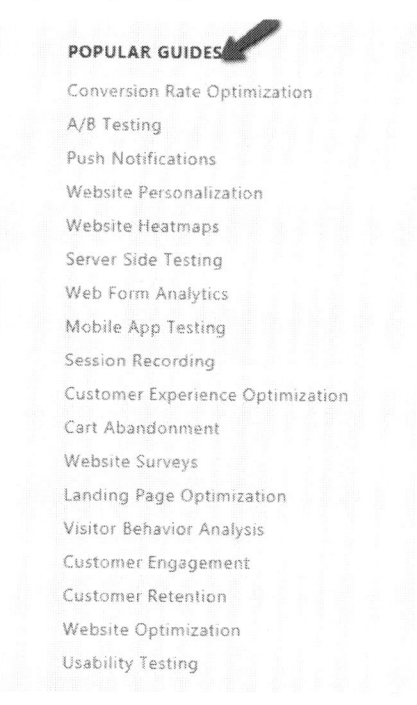

- Conversion Rate Optimization
- A/B Testing
- Push Notifications
- Website Personalization
- Website Heatmaps
- Server Side Testing
- Web Form Analytics
- Mobile App Testing
- Session Recording
- Customer Experience Optimization
- Cart Abandonment
- Website Surveys
- Landing Page Optimization
- Visitor Behavior Analysis
- Customer Engagement
- Customer Retention
- Website Optimization
- Usability Testing

And here's how much the tool costs:

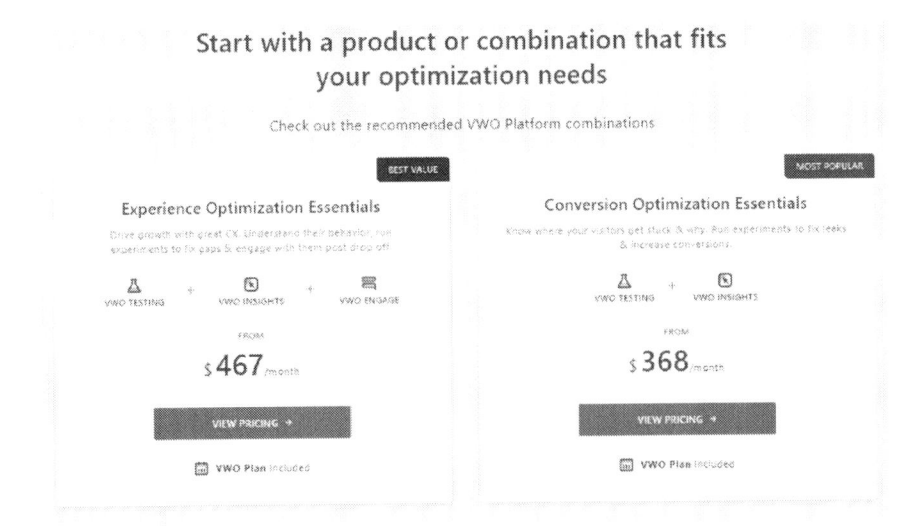

Convert

fa

Convert is one of the best tools you can use for your A/B tests. The tool does not store personal data and uses first-party cookies to track visitors.

It boasts an expert support team that will show you around as you learn how you can use it to grow your brand.

Here are more features you can get from Convert:

Chapter 7: A/B Testing

You can [integrate Convert with other tools](#) to help you achieve your desired goals. Here's how much the tool will cost:

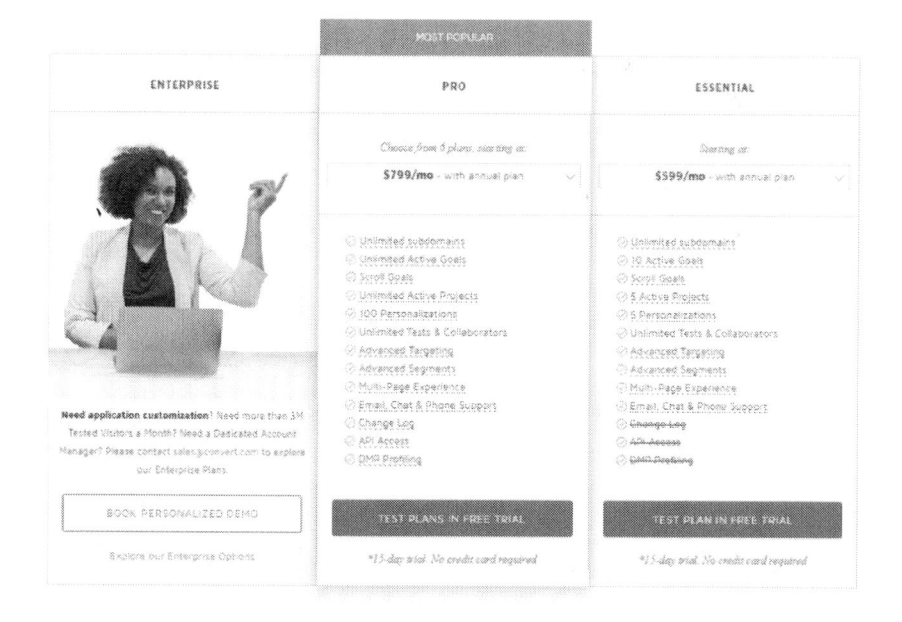

These are some testimonials from clients who have used Convert for their A/B testing:

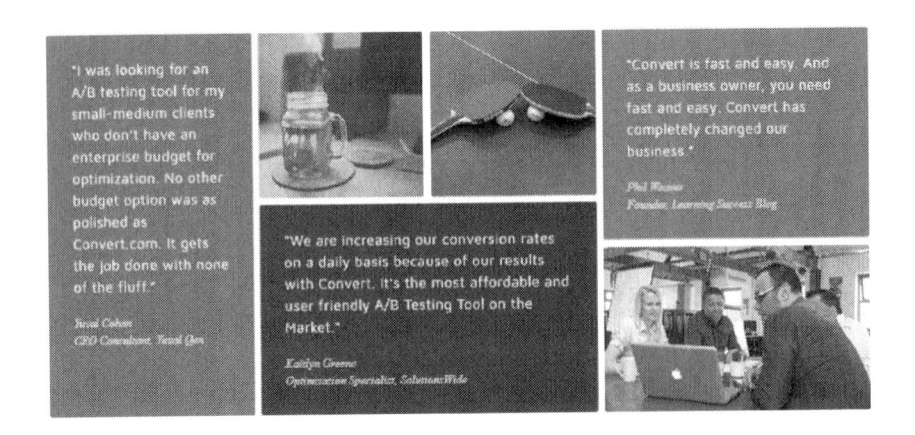

AB Tasty

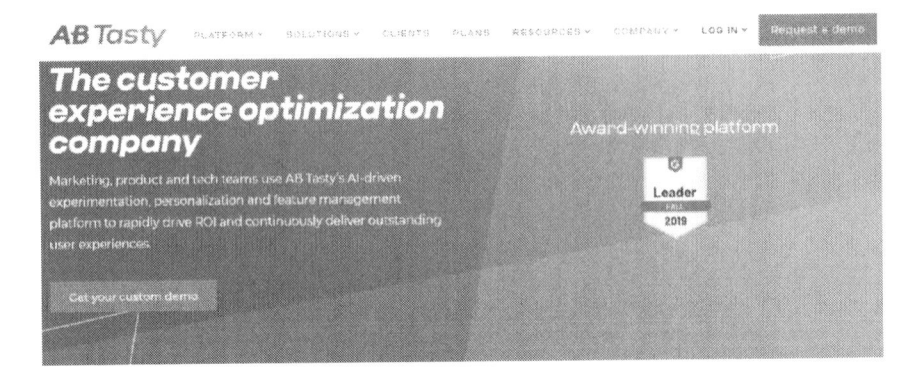

AB Tasty helps brands grow their ROI by providing magnetic experiences to their customers. The tool uses modern technology to run experiments that help brands grow their market and reach more customers.

It can help you understand user behavior and engagement to develop personalized solutions.

You can integrate AB Tasty with many other tools to streamline your A/B tests as you grow your business. Here are some of these great integrations:

Chapter 7: A/B Testing

CRM-onboarding & CDP

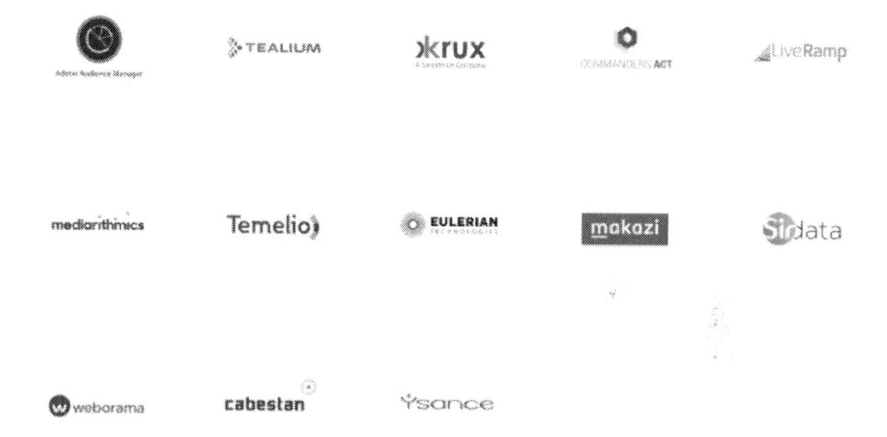

To learn more about pricing, fill out the form on the company's website:

Crazy Egg

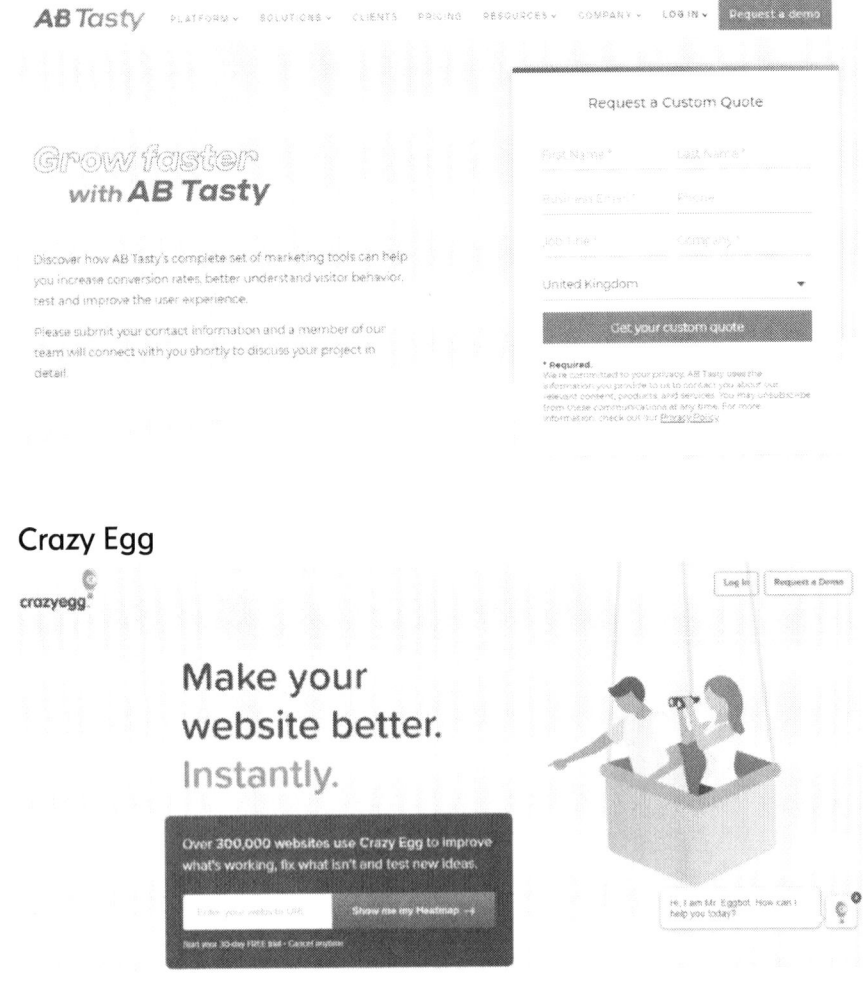

You can use Crazy Egg to increase website traffic and lead conversions. The Crazy Egg heatmap helps brand owners learn more about their visitors' behaviors and increase their conversion rates.

Chapter 7: A/B Testing

Get click data from website visitors with Crazy Egg heatmap reports.

It uses this data to show you which parts of a web page are attracting the most attention. The more clicks an area receives, the brighter (or hotter) its color will be.

Crazy Egg heatmap helps you figure out why people are leaving your website

No matter what precautions you've taken, visitors will inevitably encounter usability issues with your website. They'll click on things that aren't links, while also failing to recognize website elements that are actually meant to be clicked on.

Since the Heatmap report lets you identify what people are (and aren't) clicking on, you can use this data to identify such issues and improve usability.

All you need to do is review the data, and then do what the data is telling you to do.

Here's the Crazy Egg pricing structure:

Pricing

View Your Heatmap & Get Started In Less Than 60 Seconds

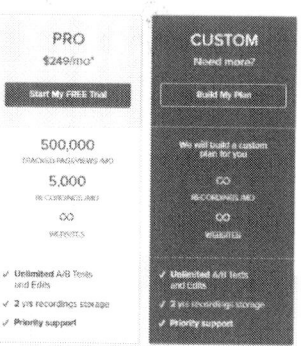

BASIC	STANDARD	PLUS (MOST POPULAR)	PRO	CUSTOM
$24/mo*	$49/mo*	$99/mo*	$249/mo*	Need more?
Start My FREE Trial	Start My FREE Trial	Start My FREE Trial	Start My FREE Trial	Build My Plan
30,000 TRACKED PAGEVIEWS /MO	75,000 TRACKED PAGEVIEWS /MO	150,000 TRACKED PAGEVIEWS /MO	500,000 TRACKED PAGEVIEWS /MO	We will build a custom plan for you
100 RECORDINGS /MO	500 RECORDINGS /MO	1,000 RECORDINGS /MO	5,000 RECORDINGS /MO	∞ RECORDINGS /MO
∞ WEBSITES	∞ WEBSITES	∞ WEBSITES	∞ WEBSITES	∞ WEBSITES
✓ Unlimited A/B Tests and Edits	✓ Unlimited A/B Tests and Edits	✓ Unlimited A/B Tests and Edits	✓ Unlimited A/B Tests and Edits	✓ Unlimited A/B Tests and Edits
✓ 3 mo recordings storage	✓ 1 yr recordings storage	✓ 2 yrs recordings storage	✓ 2 yrs recordings storage ✓ Priority support	✓ 2 yrs recordings storage ✓ Priority support

Oracle Maxymiser

Oracle Maxymiser: Testing and Personalization

Transform your business with Oracle Maxymiser's advanced website testing and personalization solutions. Remove the guesswork and make data-driven decisions on websites and mobile apps to create a seamless and connected customer experience. From simple A/B to complex multivariate tests, Oracle Maxymiser's intuitive self-serve interface, advanced personalization tools and recommendations, and robust insights make it easy.

Oracle Maxymiser provides a variety of tools marketers can use to grow their website traffic, engage more leads, and increase conversion rates.

Here are the main advantages of this amazing tool:

Six Key Attributes That Marketers Love and IT Trusts

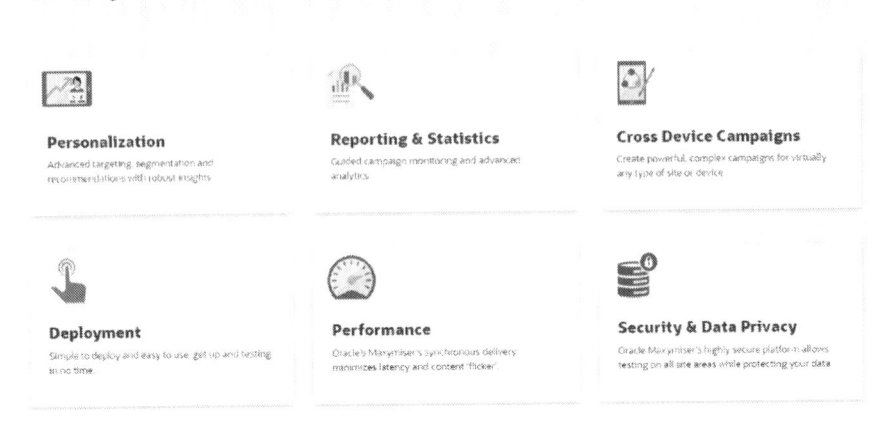

Personalization
Advanced targeting, segmentation and recommendations with robust insights

Reporting & Statistics
Guided campaign monitoring and advanced analytics

Cross Device Campaigns
Create powerful, complex campaigns for virtually any type of site or device

Deployment
Simple to deploy and easy to use, get up and testing in no time

Performance
Oracle's Maxymiser's synchronous delivery minimizes latency and content 'flicker'

Security & Data Privacy
Oracle Maxymiser's highly secure platform allows testing on all site areas while protecting your data

Zoho Pagesense

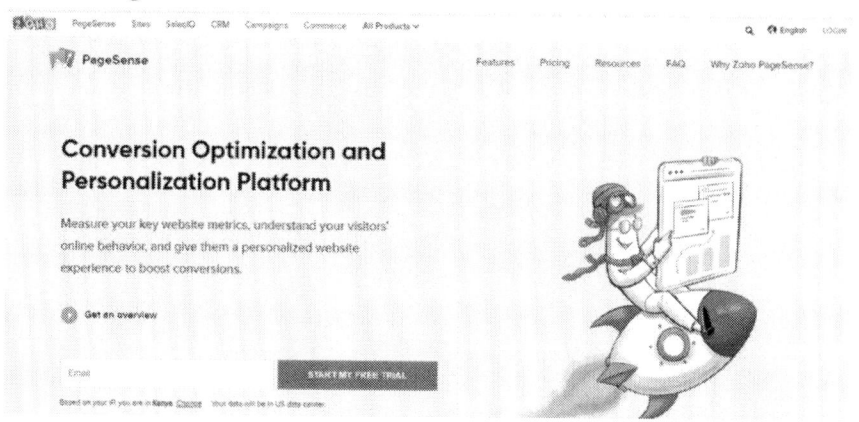

Tracking your key website metrics is vital to your business growth. This tool helps you monitor those metrics and engage with your customers.

To help with your A/B testing, here are some tools you can integrate with the Zoho Pagesense:

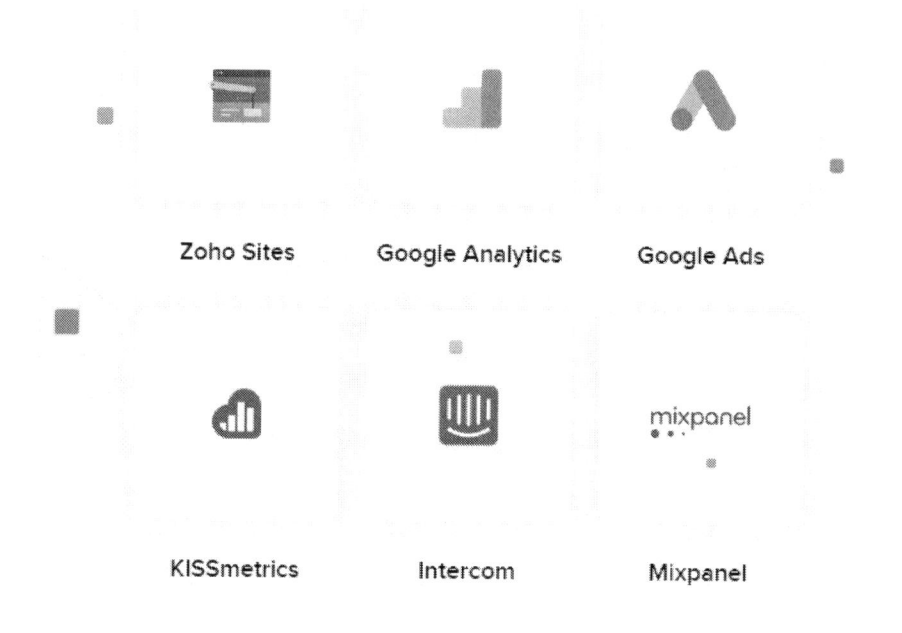

- Zoho Sites
- Google Analytics
- Google Ads
- KISSmetrics
- Intercom
- Mixpanel

And here's the pricing structure for the tool:

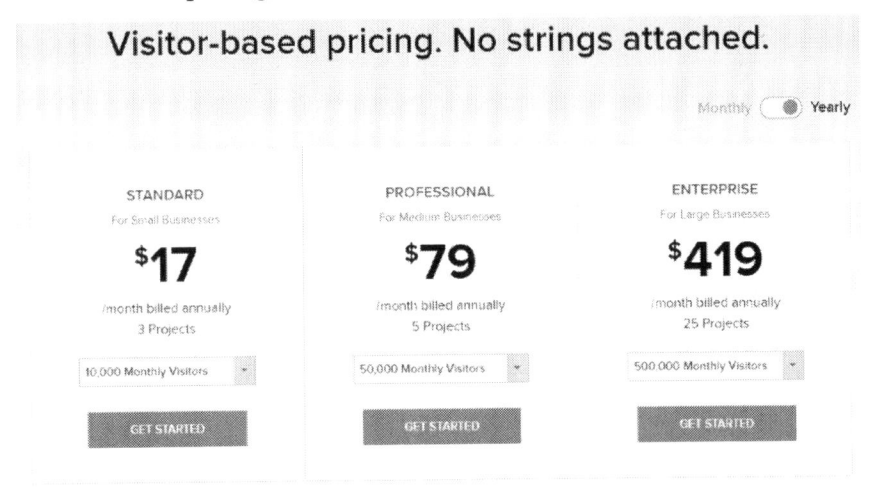

Visitor-based pricing. No strings attached.

Monthly / **Yearly**

STANDARD	PROFESSIONAL	ENTERPRISE
For Small Businesses	For Medium Businesses	For Large Businesses
$17	**$79**	**$419**
/month billed annually	/month billed annually	/month billed annually
3 Projects	5 Projects	25 Projects
10,000 Monthly Visitors	50,000 Monthly Visitors	500,000 Monthly Visitors
GET STARTED	GET STARTED	GET STARTED

These are the numerous features every user benefits from by using Zoho Pagesense:

Features you get
All plans include these pro features

- Heatmaps
- Scroll maps
- Attention maps
- Form Analytics
- Session Recording
- Goals
- Funnel Analysis
- A/B Testing
- Split URL

- Visual Editor
- Audience Targeting
- Report Segmentation
- Revenue Analysis
- Real-time Reporting
- Role-based Access
- Integrations
- Chrome Plugin
- URL Targeting

- Unlimited Users
- Unlimited Experiments
- Unlimited Domains
- Unlimited Pages

Chapter 7: A/B Testing

Adobe Target

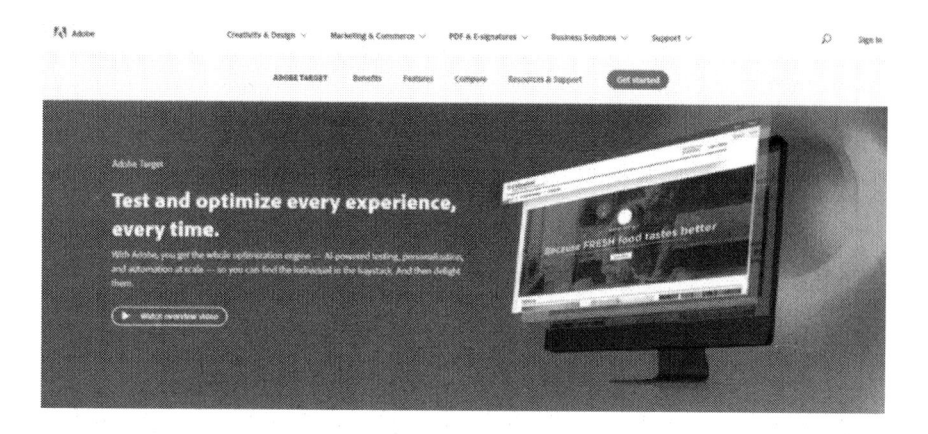

Adobe Target offers many features that help you conduct A/B tests and personalize your results to please your customers.

The tool has advanced AI-powered automation tools to ensure accurate testing. You can visit the features page to see the features it recommends for you.

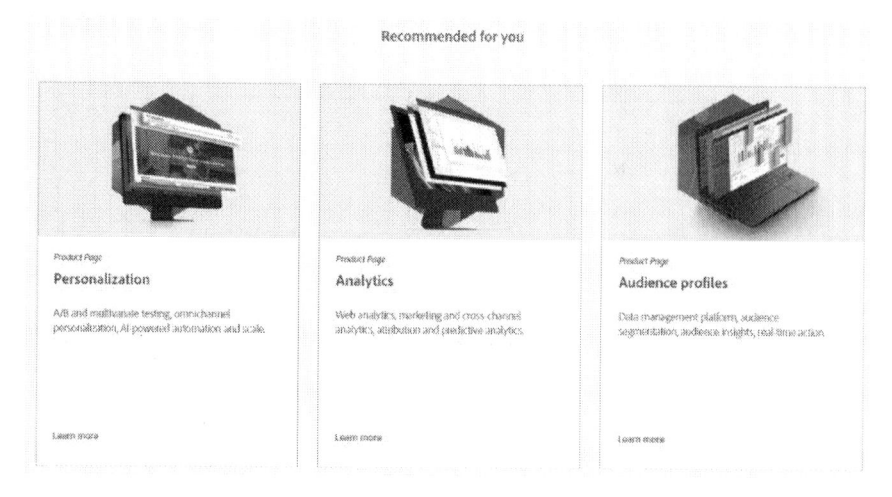

Visit the company's website to learn more about other features and its pricing model.

Splitforce

Splitforce is a fantastic tool for increasing user engagement with your app and boosting your sales and ROI.

Here's the cost of the various plans Splitforce offers:

Plans & Pricing

Upgrade, downgrade, or cancel anytime

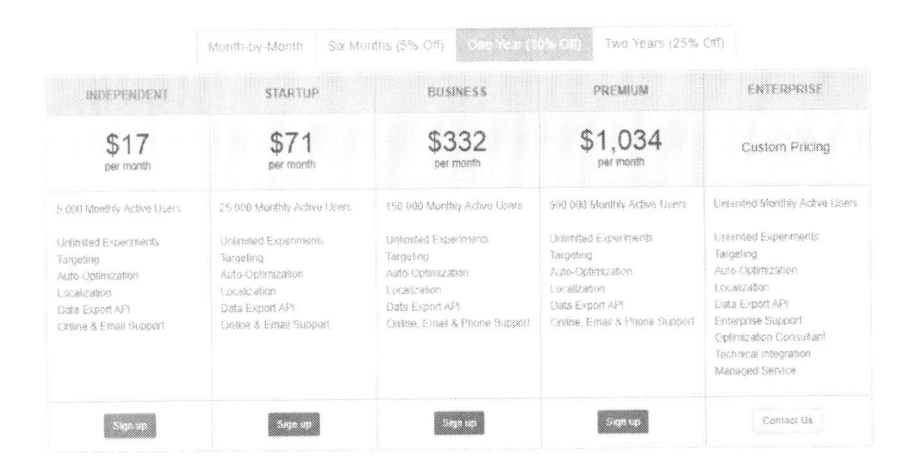

	INDEPENDENT	STARTUP	BUSINESS	PREMIUM	ENTERPRISE
Price	$17 per month	$71 per month	$332 per month	$1,034 per month	Custom Pricing
Users	5,000 Monthly Active Users	25,000 Monthly Active Users	150,000 Monthly Active Users	500,000 Monthly Active Users	Unlimited Monthly Active Users
Features	Unlimited Experiments, Targeting, Auto-Optimization, Localization, Data Export API, Online & Email Support	Unlimited Experiments, Targeting, Auto-Optimization, Localization, Data Export API, Online & Email Support	Unlimited Experiments, Targeting, Auto-Optimization, Localization, Data Export API, Online, Email & Phone Support	Unlimited Experiments, Targeting, Auto-Optimization, Localization, Data Export API, Online, Email & Phone Support	Unlimited Experiments, Targeting, Auto-Optimization, Localization, Data Export API, Enterprise Support, Optimization Consultant, Technical Integration, Managed Service
	Sign up	Sign up	Sign up	Sign up	Contact Us

ChangeAgain

ChangeAgain is integrable with Google Analytics to facilitate A/B testing. You don't have to be tech-savvy to use this tool, and you can set up your desired test in a very short time.

Chapter 7: A/B Testing

The easiest A/B test setup

Visual Editor
No Coding Required. Visual editor empowers you to easily change the headline, button, image or any other element to create multiple variations of your website without the help of a designer or a coder. You'll be amazed at how easy it is.

Simple one-time installation
Changeagain's installation process is dead simple. You need to put the JavaScript code snippet on your website only once and be assured of a lifetime of easy A/B testing.

Advanced HTML/CSS & JavaScript editing
We don't limit you to only make "visual" tweaks. You can make more sophisticated changes by using HTML, JavaScript, CSS and jQuery.

It also makes it easy to test, analyze, and optimize your website:

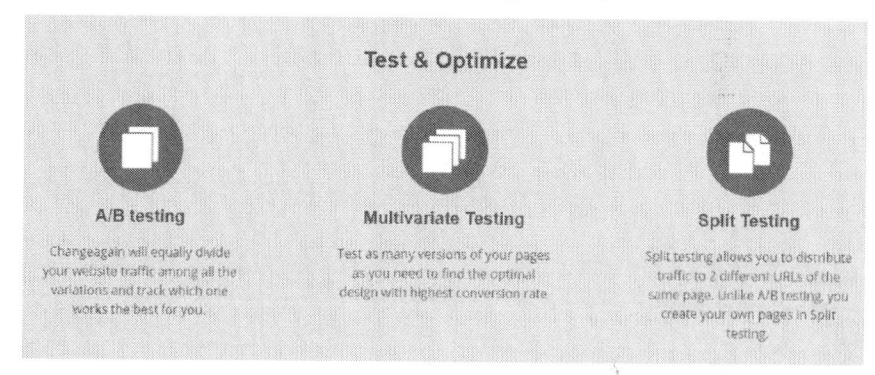

Test & Optimize

A/B testing
Changeagain will equally divide your website traffic among all the variations and track which one works the best for you.

Multivariate Testing
Test as many versions of your pages as you need to find the optimal design with highest conversion rate

Split Testing
Split testing allows you to distribute traffic to 2 different URLs of the same page. Unlike A/B testing, you create your own pages in Split testing.

Here are some other features you can get from the tool:

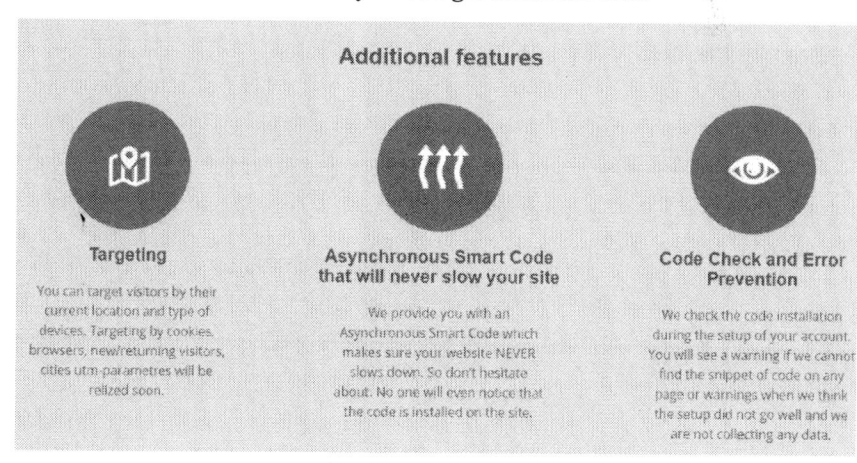

Additional features

Targeting
You can target visitors by their current location and type of devices. Targeting by cookies, browsers, new/returning visitors, cities utm-parametres will be relized soon.

Asynchronous Smart Code that will never slow your site
We provide you with an Asynchronous Smart Code which makes sure your website NEVER slows down. So don't hesitate about. No one will even notice that the code is installed on the site.

Code Check and Error Prevention
We check the code installation during the setup of your account. You will see a warning if we cannot find the snippet of code on any page or warnings when we think the setup did not go well and we are not collecting any data.

ChangeAgain has a great support team that's available for consultations around the clock if you experience any problems. This is how much the tool will cost if you use it:

Enterprise	Professional	Basic	StartUp
	$ 149 /month	$ 49 /month	$ 14 /month
Unlimited Web-sites	4 Web-sites	2 Web-sites	1 Web-site
Unlimited Online experiments	14 Online experiments	5 Online experiments	3 Online experiments
Unlimited Impressions	Unlimited Impressions	Unlimited Impressions	Unlimited Impressions
A/B tests/ Split tests	A/B tests/ Split tests	A/B tests/ Split tests	A/B tests/ Split tests
Google Analytics Integration	Google Analytics Integration	Google Analytics Integration	Google Analytics Integration
Mobile Adaptive experiments	Mobile Adaptive experiments	Unlimited Targeting	1 Country Targeting
Advanced Targeting	Advanced Targeting	All Devices Testing	Desktop Testing
Account Manager	Email and Skype Support	Email Support	Email Support
CONTACT US	GET FREE TRIAL	GET FREE TRIAL	GET FREE TRIAL

All plans include a 14-days free trial. No credit card required. Try it out without any commitment.

Optimizely

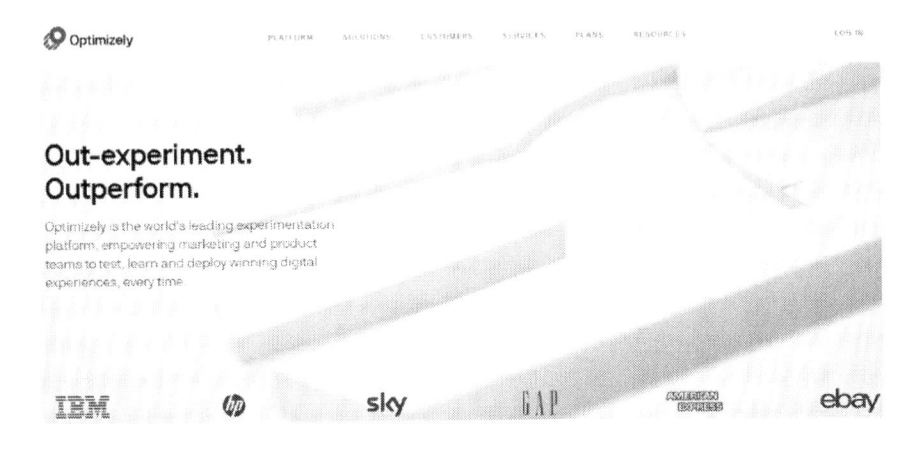

Out-experiment. Outperform.

Optimizely is the world's leading experimentation platform, empowering marketing and product teams to test, learn and deploy winning digital experiences, every time.

IBM · hp · sky · GAP · AMERICAN EXPRESS · ebay

Optimizely is good for running A/B tests to improve the performance of your website and business.

Chapter 7: A/B Testing

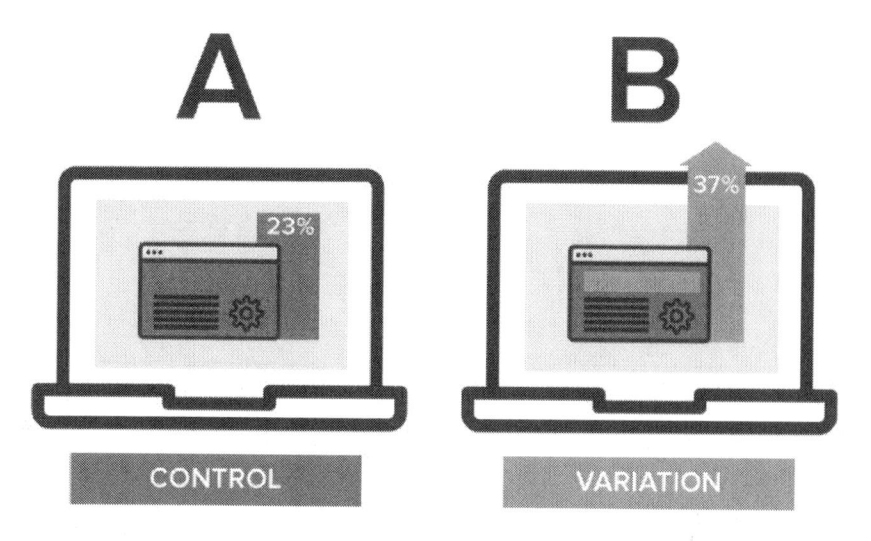

It collects data and offers insight to help you optimize your website and reach a large number of target customers.

Here's how A/B testing works with Optimizely:

How A/B Testing Works

In an A/B test, you take a webpage or app screen and modify it to create a second version of the same page. This change can be as simple as a single headline or button, or be a complete redesign of the page. Then, half of your traffic is shown the original version of the page (known as the control) and half are shown the modified version of the page (the variation).

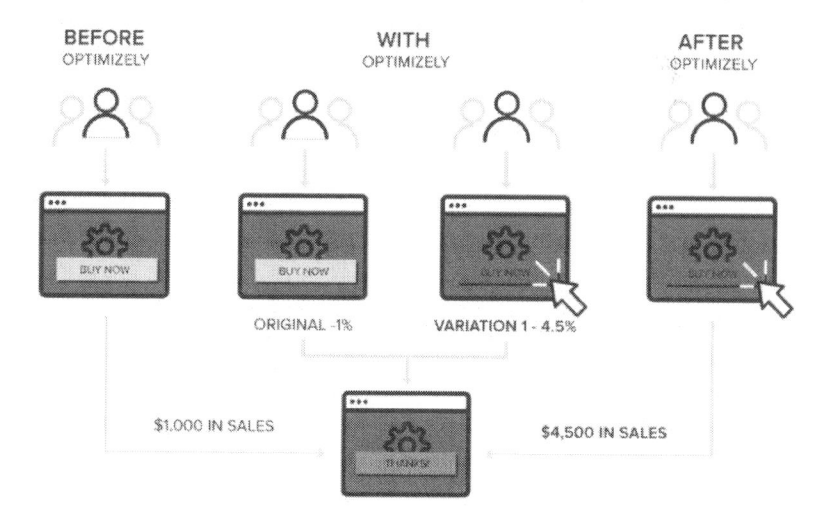

You can visit the Optimizely website to learn more about their pricing plans.

411

Leadformly

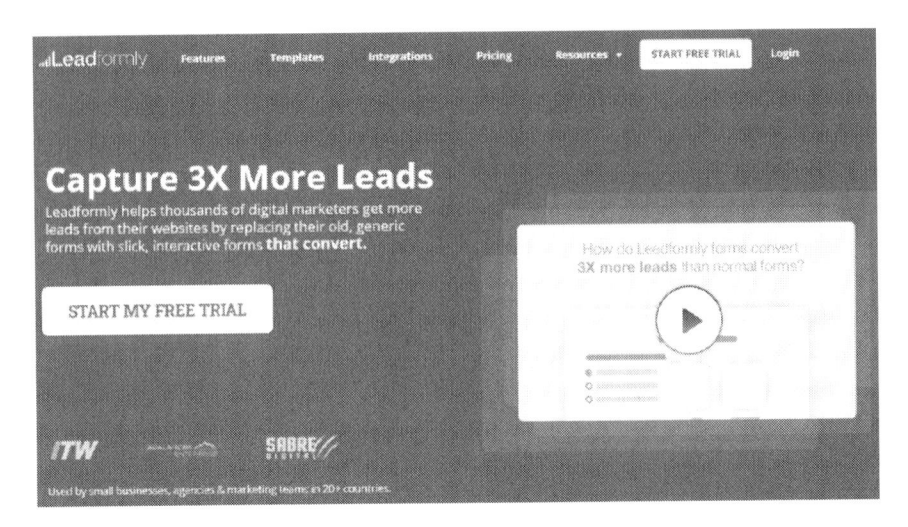

Leadformly lets marketers test and optimize forms on their website to generate more leads and attract more potential customers.

Here are some of the great features of this tool:

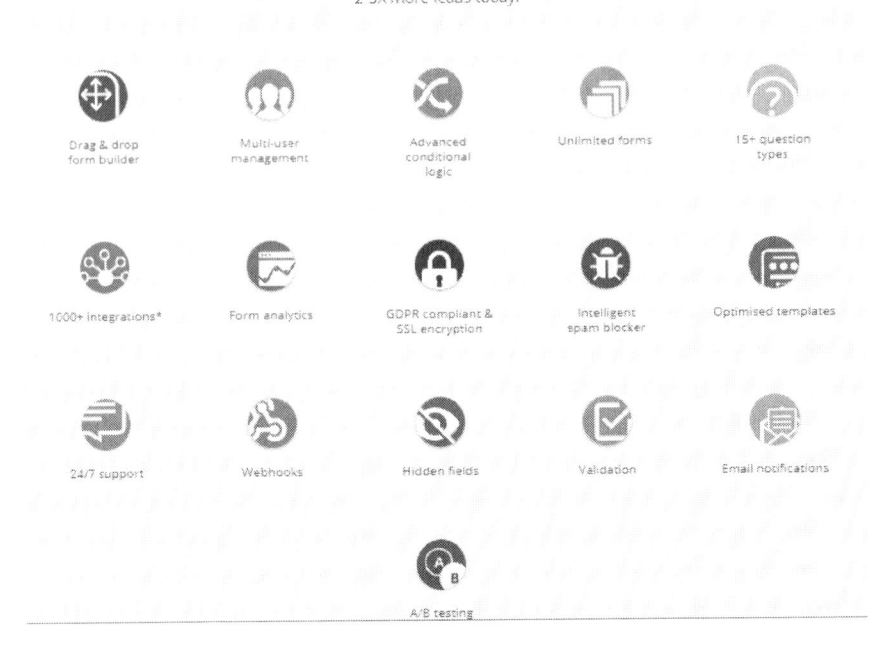

Chapter 7: A/B Testing

And these are the tools you can integrate with Leadformly to simplify your A/B testing:

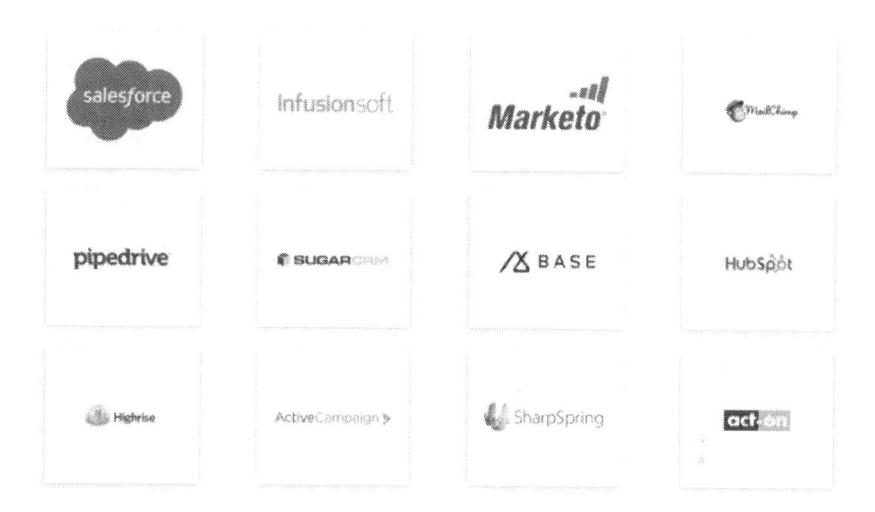

Here's the pricing structure:

	Essential	Growth	Team
How many leads could you capture with Leadformly? IN THE PAST 30 DAYS **No. of website visits** e.g. 10,000	$37 /month billed yearly Start your free trial	$74 /month billed yearly Start your free trial	$149 /month billed yearly Start your free trial
LEAD GENERATION			
No. of leads per month	Up to 250	Up to 1,000	Up to 25,000
No. of forms	Unlimited	Unlimited	Unlimited
Conditional logic	✓	✓	✓
Smart spam block	✓	✓	✓
Hidden fields	✓	✓	✓
Hidden fields	✓	✓	✓
Edit form HTML	✓	✓	✓
A/B testing	—	✓	✓
TEAM			
No. of users	2 Users	5 Users	10 Users
Email Notifications	✓	✓	✓
INTEGRATIONS			
Zapier (1000+)	✓	✓	✓
Webhooks	✓	✓	✓
REPORTING & ANALYSIS			
Analytics	✓	✓	✓

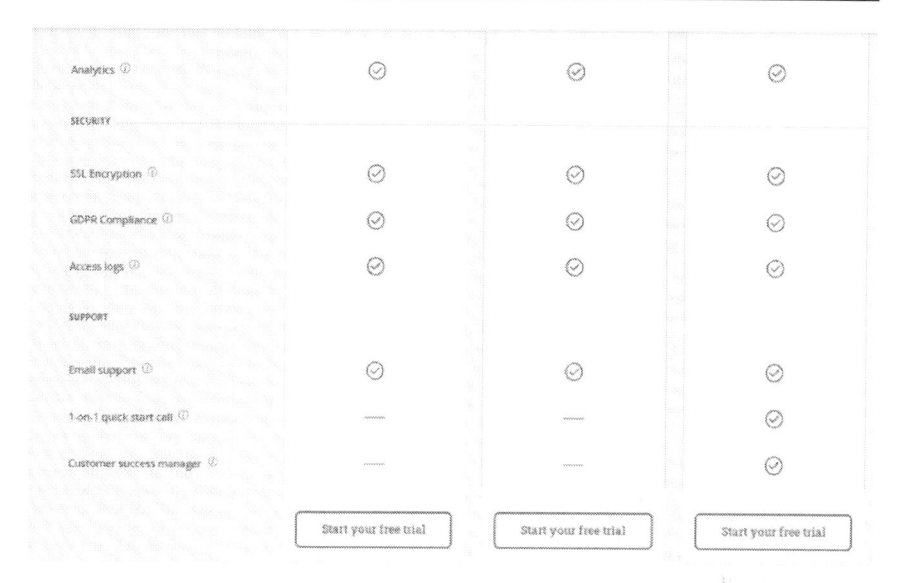

Nelio A/B Testing

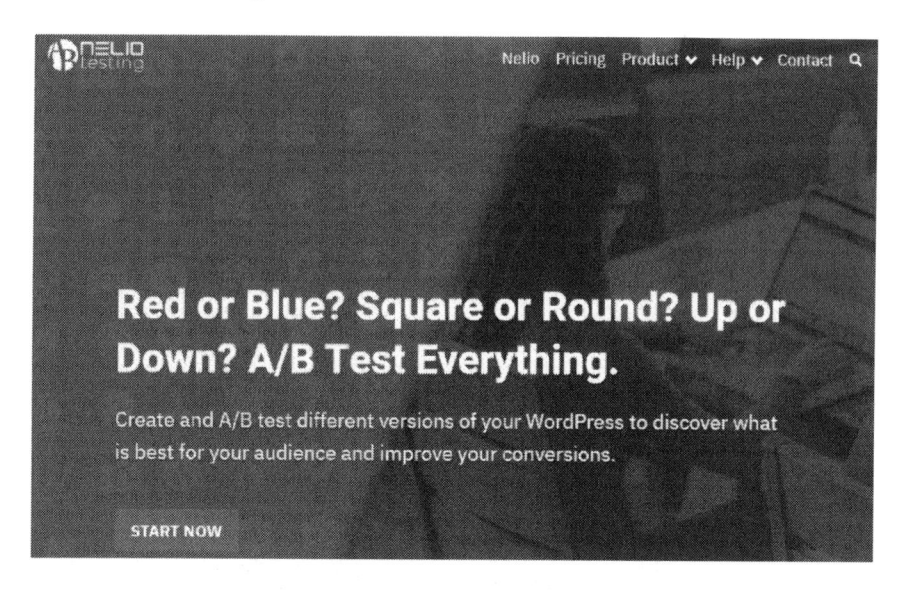

Nelio gives you all the features you need to run the A/B tests that will tell you what you need to know. Here are a few more of the advantages of using this tool:

Advantages of Nelio A/B Testing

Easy A/B Testing
Subscription plans for personal sites, business owners, or web agencies.

Visitors Become Customers
Increase engagement, interactions, and conversions today.

Zero Technical Knowledge
Not good at math? No coding skills? Don't worry, Nelio takes care of everything.

More Than Just A/B Testing
Test everything: pages, posts, products, custom types, headlines, widgets, themes, menus, heatmaps, and more.

Fully Automated
Automatically update your WordPress site to reflect the winning alternative.

Never Leave WordPress
Do everything from the WP dashboard. No need to use external tools.

This is how much you'll pay if you decide to use Nelio:

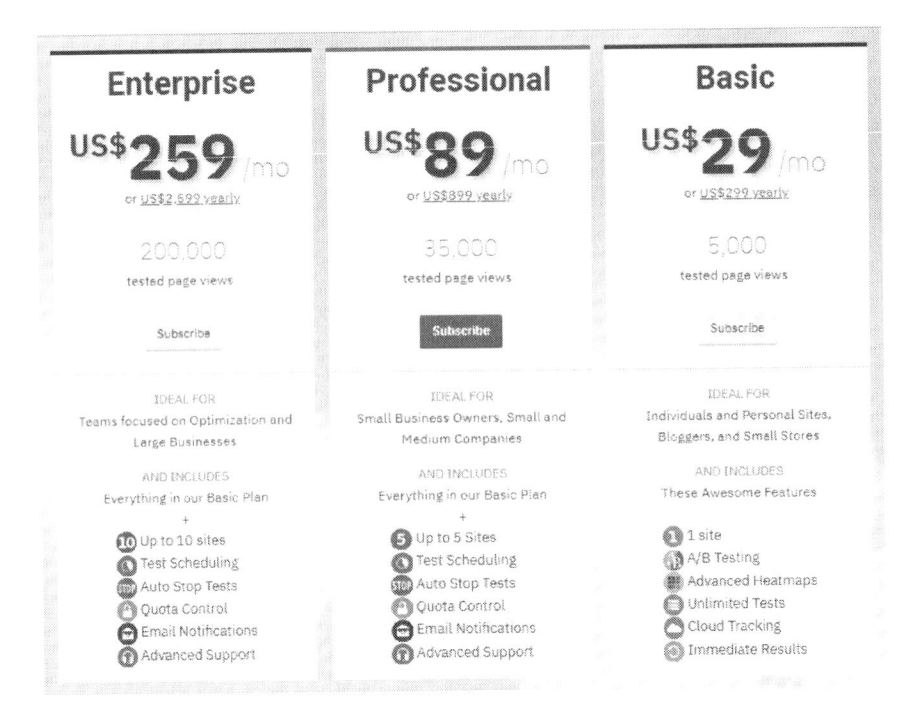

Enterprise	Professional	Basic
US$259/mo	US$89/mo	US$29/mo
or US$2,599 yearly	or US$899 yearly	or US$299 yearly
200,000 tested page views	35,000 tested page views	5,000 tested page views
Subscribe	Subscribe	Subscribe
IDEAL FOR	IDEAL FOR	IDEAL FOR
Teams focused on Optimization and Large Businesses	Small Business Owners, Small and Medium Companies	Individuals and Personal Sites, Bloggers, and Small Stores
AND INCLUDES	AND INCLUDES	AND INCLUDES
Everything in our Basic Plan +	Everything in our Basic Plan +	These Awesome Features
Up to 10 sites	Up to 5 sites	1 site
Test Scheduling	Test Scheduling	A/B Testing
Auto Stop Tests	Auto Stop Tests	Advanced Heatmaps
Quota Control	Quota Control	Unlimited Tests
Email Notifications	Email Notifications	Cloud Tracking
Advanced Support	Advanced Support	Immediate Results

Apptimize

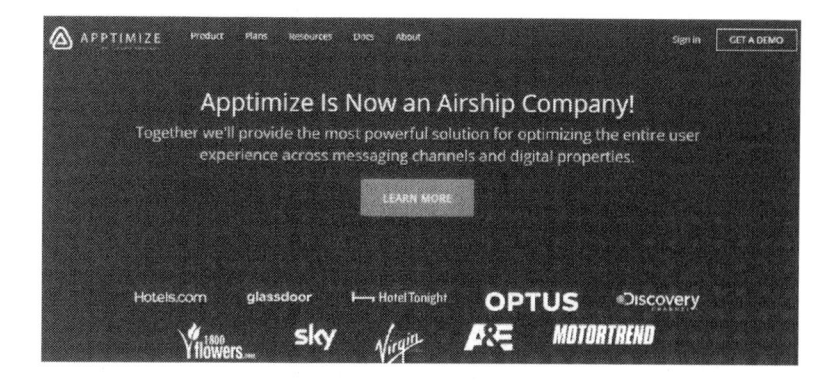

With Apptimize, you can track your users across different channels as you test and optimize your website to increase lead generation and conversion.

The tool can also tell you how every single test you run impacts the performance of your website and sales. It provides data you can use to bolster user engagement and trust, leading to higher sales and ROI.

Here's the tool's pricing:

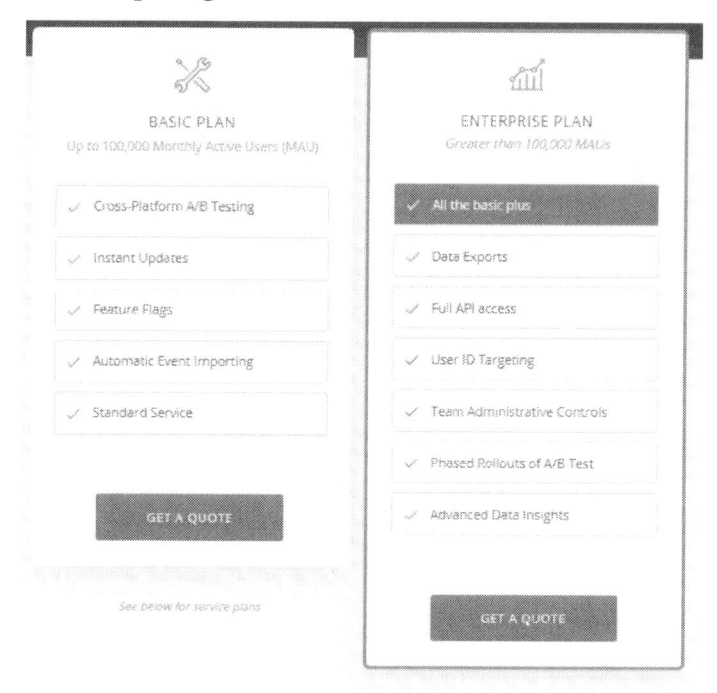

And these are the service plans you can choose from:

SERVICE PLANS

Feature	Standard	Silver	Gold
Email Support (9AM-5PM Pacific Time; Response by next business day)	✓	✓	✓
Technical Documentation	✓	✓	✓
Dedicated Customer Success Manager		✓	✓
Implementation and Onboarding		✓	✓
Technical Integration Services			✓
Dedicated Slack Channel			✓
Multi-day onsite training led by mobile strategists and forward deployed engineers			✓
Emergency Escalation Process with Guaranteed 2-hour Response Time for Tier 1 Issues			✓
Telephone Support			✓

Chapter 7: A/B Testing

Dynamic Yield

Dynamic Yield lets you run useful personalization tests for your brand. This personalization can be based on any kind of data you collect from your business and customers. The results will show you how to target customers in different buyer stages and improve the perceived value of your business.

Here are the different aspects of end-to-end personalization the tool provides for your business:

How to Run A/B Tests

Any A/B test you conduct needs to be accurate so you can analyze the data you collect and then use it to grow your customer base by marketing your services or products.

Here are some guidelines you can follow as you run your tests to grow your brand.

Set Goals/Objectives

Before you start, you need to decide what you want to achieve with your A/B tests. Always ask yourself, what do I want to accomplish by running tests on these aspects of my business? This question will keep your tests focused and help you make decisions that further your business objectives.

Choose the objectives or goals that you want the hypothesis testing to help you with. Here are some examples of marketing objectives:

OBJECTIVES OF ADVERTISING

1. Introduce a Product
2. Introduce a Brand
3. Awareness Creation
4. Acquire Customers
5. Differentiation
6. Brand Building
7. Positioning
8. Increase Sales
9. Increase Profits
10. Create Desire
11. Call to Action

Image source: https://www.marketing91.com/objectives-of-advertising/

Chapter 7: A/B Testing

For example, your objective might be to attract more customers to your business, so to accomplish that, you may decide to compare two versions of a web page to see which one attracts more.

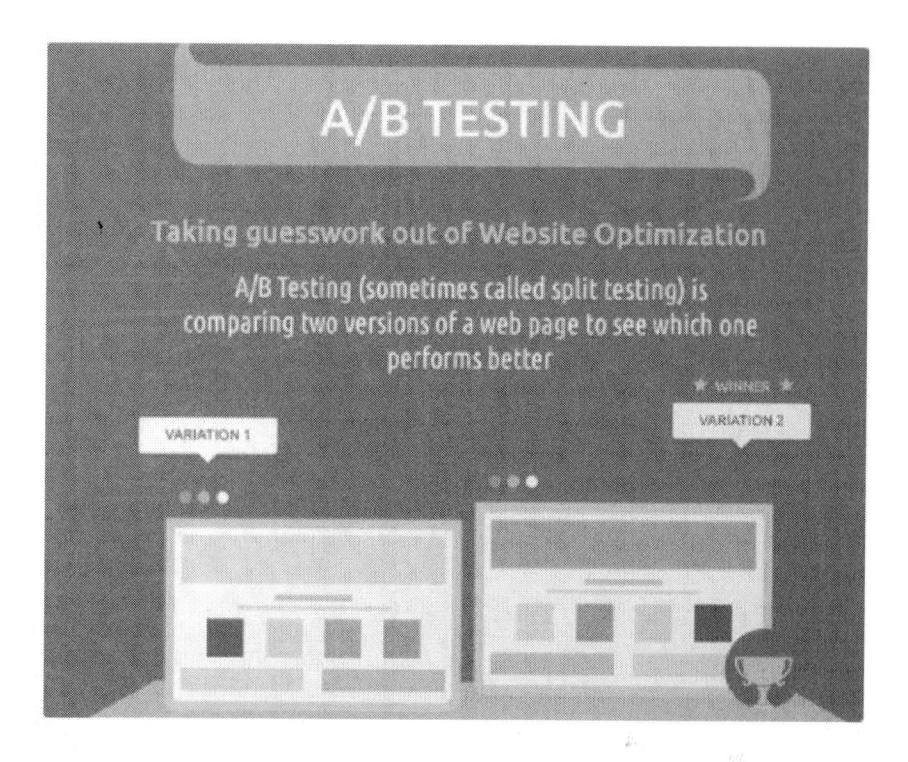

Image source: https://infographicjournal.com/step-by-step-guide-to-ab-testing/

Develop a Hypothesis

To run your tests effectively, you need to start with a hypothesis. You can collect some information to base your hypothesis on from your customers or target customers through surveys.

Then, run tests that focus on your customers' needs to see if your hypothesis is true. Remember, your business is not about you, but about your customers. You must do whatever you can to provide the best services or products to them.

As you develop your hypothesis, make sure it's valid. That means it needs to be a statement you can prove correct or incorrect by testing. Running your tests on an invalid hypothesis can affect your testing process and business operations.

Design a Testing Strategy

Now that you've decided on the objectives you want to achieve and you have a hypothesis based on your customer data, determine the best way to confirm or deny your hypothesis. This will help you run your tests to get the most meaningful results and achieve your objectives in the shortest possible time.

Analyzing the customer data will also help you give customers a high-quality product or content as you test for better ways to serve them and help them resolve their issues.

Create Variants

You've now analyzed all your data and you know which test to start with. You can go ahead and create the different variants, such as the two comparable web pages, for the specific test that you want to run. Don't make the mistake of running too many tests at the same time.

Select a Suitable A/B Testing Tool

Once you've designed variants for the tests you want to conduct, you can select and use the tool that will help you get the most accurate results.

Remember, there are many tools you can use for your A/B testing. But these tools are not all the same and can give you different results. Review the previous section about factors to consider when choosing an A/B test tool.

Run Your A/B Tests

You're ready to begin your tests. As you run the experiments, collect data that will help you make the right decisions about how to grow your brand. You'll need the assistance of a team that can analyze the data you collect to develop a marketing plan or make adjustments to your current plan.

Document all the tests you run for your business. This will eliminate the need to repeat the tests you've already conducted.

A/B Testing Mistakes to Avoid

Making mistakes as you run your A/B tests can negatively affect your business growth and customer service. As you make your plans and run these tests, these are the errors you don't want to commit.

Not Optimizing Your Tests

Your aim for the tests is to reach many potential customers who will see them and provide data that helps you build your brand. If your tests aren't optimized for search engines, you won't reach many potential customers. This will affect how you interact with and search for your target customers and may cause you to lose some clients to your competitors.

Many potential customers are now using smartphones to access the company information they need before making purchases.

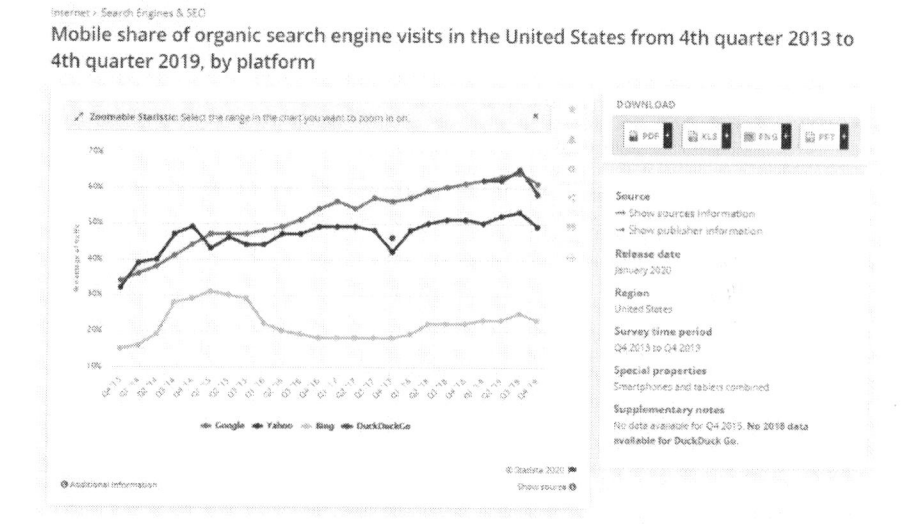

Mobile share of organic search engine visits in the United States from 4th quarter 2013 to 4th quarter 2019, by platform

STATISTICS ON THE TOPIC	
Mobile audiences and access Mobile apps Mobile social Mobile media Mobile commerce	**MOBILE INTERNET TRAFFIC AS SHARE OF TOTAL GLOBAL ONLINE TRAFFIC** 51.65%
	MOBILE SHARE OF TOTAL DIGITAL MINUTES IN THE UNITED STATES IN 2017 65%
	APP SHARE OF TOTAL MOBILE MINUTES IN THE UNITED STATES IN 2017 87%

As you run your tests, ensure that your potential customers can access them on their mobile devices. Your tests should also be optimized for search engine rankings.

Making it easy for the target customer to find your tests can help you compile the information you need to make your business operations successful.

Running Too Many Tests at Once

This is a big mistake many brands make as they run their A/B tests. Running too many tests simultaneously will affect the data you collect as well as your focus and concentration on the tests. It will negatively affect the whole testing process, which can cause problems for your business.

Running too many tests at the same time is also costly and can lower your profits if the tests fail.

Conduct a limited number of tests each time and carefully collect all the data that can help you improve your marketing. Act on the data you collect to offer better services or products to your customers and grow your business.

Ending Tests Too Soon

Sometimes getting accurate results from your tests can take some time. If you make the mistake of concluding your tests too soon, you lose the chance to find out how to grow your business.

To collect all the information you need, run the tests for a substantial time period. This will help you determine what works and how you can use it to reach your customers.

Incorporating Too Many Variables

Running your tests with too many variables can confuse your target customers and muddle your data. It's best to stick to one pair of variables per test.

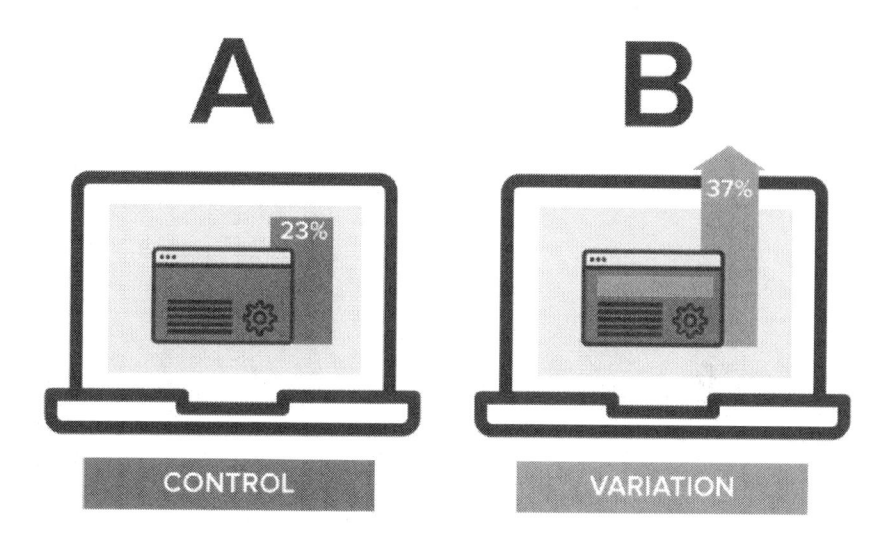

Make it easy for the target customers to interact with the tests and engage with your brand.

With too many variables, some variables may not see enough traffic, which can affect the number of target customers who interact with your tests and skew your results.

Setting Your Expectations Too High

Every marketer expects to grow their business once they've run some A/B tests on particular aspects of their website. However, it isn't wise to set those expectations too high.

For example, expecting to make more than $20,000 per month after simply testing your landing pages is unrealistic. Set marketing goals that are achievable for the tests you're running.

Running Tests Too Soon

Sometimes you may need faster business results, and this forces you to run tests before you've seen the results of your previous strategy changes. That's a big mistake.

Once you've completed a test, take some time out to analyze the data you collected and apply it to your business. Wait to conduct another test until after you see the effects of the one you've already done.

Not Tracking Results/Metrics

Many brands run A/B tests but don't track metrics to see if their business is achieving the goals they set. This mistake can affect business operation and corrupt the whole testing process. It's crucial to keep tabs on business metrics as you run A/B tests.

Changing the test parameters as you run the tests

This seems like a no-brainer, but it can affect the results of your testing. It's not a good idea to change the parameters you started with in the middle of your A/B testing. Keeping parameters consistent will help you collect unbiased data that you can rely on as you make business decisions.

Changing the parameters can also confuse the target customers and affect their decision-making process during the testing period.

Giving Up Too Soon When Tests Fail

You can try your best to run meticulous A/B tests, but sometimes tests fail. Giving up too soon once things start to look bad can affect your marketing and business operations.

Marketers are encouraged to try their best as they conduct tests. If they don't get the desired results, we recommend that they continue giving their best effort and let the testing continue until they get results.

Not Developing a Hypothesis

The A/B testing hypothesis plays a crucial role in the design of your A/B tests. Starting without a hypothesis leads to running these tests blindly and affects the results you generate for your business.

A hypothesis helps guide you throughout the testing process, data collection, and analysis to keep your business growing.

Trusting Other Marketers' Test Results

As you run your tests, don't trust the results other marketers got in their A/B experiments. Similar brands may have run tests like the one you want to run. Don't assume you'll get the same results they did. Your results may vary even though you're in the same industry.

For example, a certain company can change its CTA color button and increase its conversions by 60%. Don't expect to get that conversion rate if you follow up and implement the same tests.

Not Testing Everything on Your Website

Many different aspects of a website can affect the success of your online business, lead generation, new customer conversion, and sales. Running just one or two tests for the whole website is a mistake and can affect your business.

Run tests on every part of your marketing strategy. Just don't make the mistake of running all the tests at once. These different tests will help you see how to satisfy your target customers and offer better services or products for them.

Running Tests on the Wrong Pages

You can choose excellent variables for your tests, but if you run those tests on the wrong pages, they can slant your results.

Before running your tests, ensure that you've designated the right pages for the type of testing you're doing. This will help you get the right results to achieve your objectives.

Conclusion

We hope you've enjoyed acquiring your newfound knowledge of digital marketing tools and strategies. Let's quickly review what you've learned so you'll be ready to get started.

Why Digital Marketing Matters

Below are some statistics for growth marketing:

KEY DIGITAL MARKETING GROWTH STATS *2019*

4.7% — Global online ad spend is set to grow 4.7% this year, up from the 4% forecast in December 2018.

14% — Location-based marketing is set to grow 14% to $24.4 billion in ad spending this year.

43% — Nearly half of advertisers plan to increase spending on influencer marketing by April.

39% — The average revenue per Snapchat user rose from $1.21 in 2018 to $1.68 in 2019.

110% — Social referral traffic to retail ecommerce sites has grown 110% in two years.

500% — TikTok's in-app sales surged 500% to $9M in May from a year earlier.

Image Source: https://www.socialmediatoday.com/news/2019-key-digital-marketing-growth-stats-infographic/558413/

These statistics make it clear that brands are rapidly growing and reaching their online customers to further their business objectives.

Producing awesome products or services isn't all it takes to attract the number of customers you need to succeed. You have to make sure the customers who will be interested in your product know about it by marketing your brand to generate leads, walk them through all the buyer stages, and convert them into customers.

To do this, you need to understand your customers well at each stage. This will make you an effective marketer who engages customers as you nurture them and increase your business's sales and ROI.

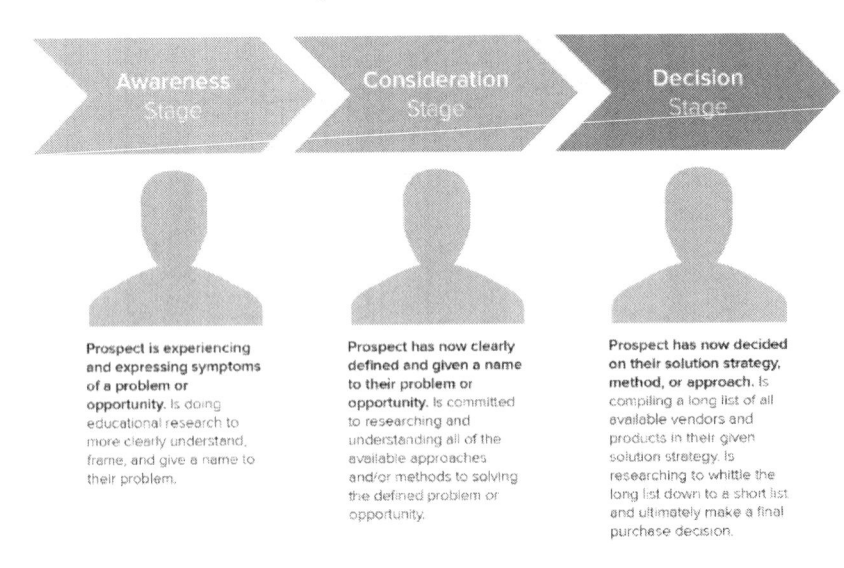

Awareness Stage	Consideration Stage	Decision Stage
Prospect is experiencing and expressing symptoms of a problem or opportunity. Is doing educational research to more clearly understand, frame, and give a name to their problem.	Prospect has now clearly defined and given a name to their problem or opportunity. Is committed to researching and understanding all of the available approaches and/or methods to solving the defined problem or opportunity.	Prospect has now decided on their solution strategy, method, or approach. Is compiling a long list of all available vendors and products in their given solution strategy. Is researching to whittle the long list down to a short list and ultimately make a final purchase decision.

Image Source: https://blog.hubspot.com/customers/apply-the-buyers-journey-to-your-inbound-strategy

Having a great buyer persona will help you create high-quality content that attracts your target customers to your brand, earns their trust, and increases your conversion rates.

Conclusion

Growth Marketing Strategies

This book has introduced you to a lot of useful guidelines for how to strategize as you promote your product or service and reach out to your customers.

Let's review some of the strategies you've learned.

Customer Diversification

You're in business to create products or services that will help your customers solve their pain points and help you make profits. Learning to diversify your market reach can help you learn more about your customers and know the best ways to reach them.

Throughout the A/B Testing chapter, you learn about how to test your marketing strategy so you can improve it and reach a variety of target customers.

Understanding diverse customer behaviors also plays a significant role in your new customer onboarding. Even a great relationship between a manager and an employee can improve the employee's work ethic.

> 72% of employees say one-on-one time with their direct manager as the most important part of any pre-boarding or onboarding process
> - Enboarder

In the same way, you must strive to forge a relationship with your customers that makes them want to work with you. Showing that you care about your customers and taking time to understand their motives and behaviors can help you successfully onboard them and encourage them to become loyal to your business.

Product Development

Customer needs change every day. As a marketer, you need to be coming up with new product improvements and developments to help address your customers' challenges.

Remember, you're not the only business in the market. You have to find ways to stand out from your competition. One great way is to create high-quality products or services that your customers will love. Innovative product development will keep attracting more target customers to your business.

As you help them solve their problems, they'll become your retainer clients and you keep making profits from the sale of services or products to them.

Market Penetration

Cultivating a prominent presence in the market with new services or products can help you reach more target customers and convert them into clients.

This book has shown you many different means to reach the market and generate more customers for your business. Now that you know how to do it, take action.

The process of reaching out to B2B customers in particular and converting them into clients is long and complicated. Throughout the book, you've learned about ways to reach these customers.

Remember, if customers don't build trust with brands, they tend to do business with them just once and then leave for their competitors. Statista's research shows a [22% churn rate for online retailer brands](#).

Conclusion

Customer churn rate in the United States in 2018, by industry

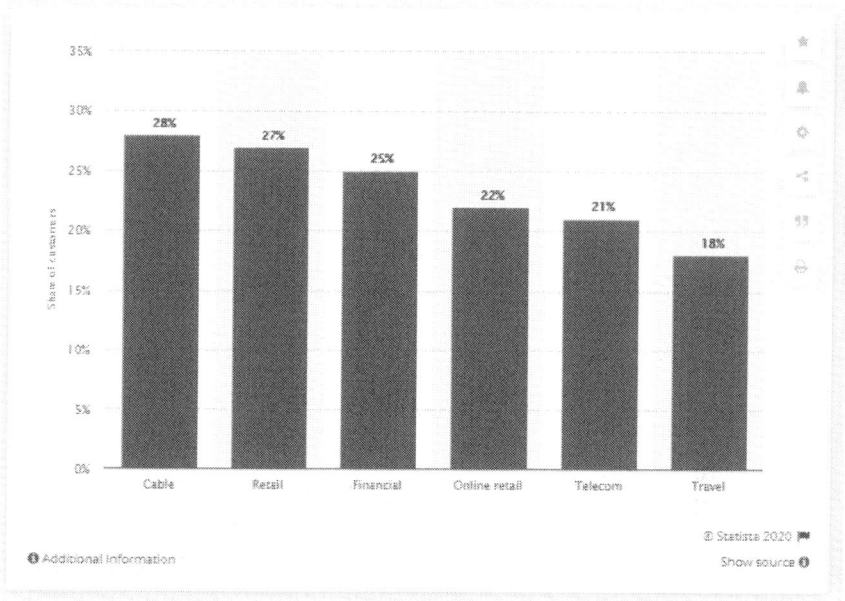

Industry	Share of customers
Cable	28%
Retail	27%
Financial	25%
Online retail	22%
Telecom	21%
Travel	18%

© Statista 2020

Content Marketing

Content is key to online business growth. As a business owner or marketer, you need to know the right kind of content to produce for your customers in their different buyer stages. These are some factors to remember for successful content production.

A Documented Strategy

Producing content regularly and by following a documented strategy is a vital contributor to business growth. However, very few brands do this. Research by the CMI shows that only 38% of brands have a documented content marketing strategy.

Percentage of B2B Marketers Who Have a Content Marketing Strategy

- 37% — Yes, and it is documented
- 38% — Yes, but it is not documented
- 19% — No, but plan to have one within 12 months
- 6% — No, with no plans to have one within 12 months

Base: B2B content marketers; aided list.

Develop a documented strategy for your content production. This ensures that the content you create helps your business achieve its objectives and targets the right audience at the right time.

Effective Distribution

As you produce the content, be careful to distribute it through the channels that most effectively promote your business. A study by the CMI shows that distributing content through the right channels makes a big difference in the content's success.

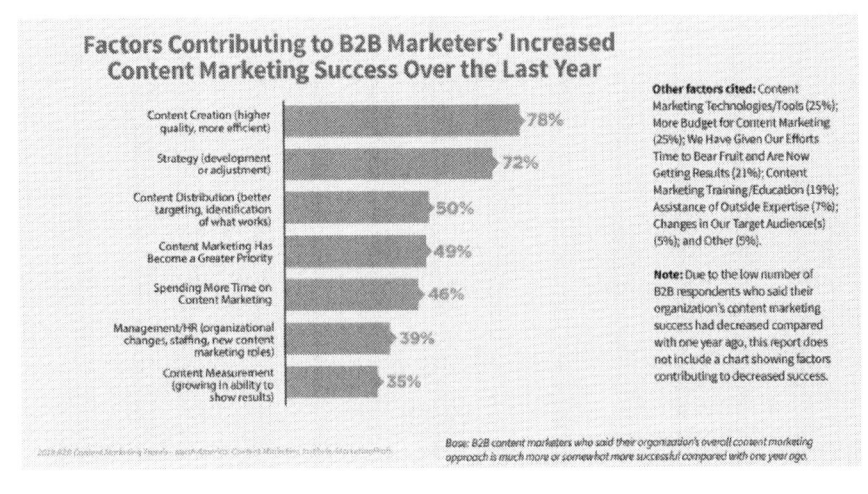

Factors Contributing to B2B Marketers' Increased Content Marketing Success Over the Last Year

- Content Creation (higher quality, more efficient): 78%
- Strategy (development or adjustment): 72%
- Content Distribution (better targeting, identification of what works): 50%
- Content Marketing Has Become a Greater Priority: 49%
- Spending More Time on Content Marketing: 46%
- Management/HR (organizational changes, staffing, new content marketing roles): 39%
- Content Measurement (growing in ability to show results): 35%

Other factors cited: Content Marketing Technologies/Tools (25%); More Budget for Content Marketing (25%); We Have Given Our Efforts Time to Bear Fruit and Are Now Getting Results (21%); Content Marketing Training/Education (19%); Assistance of Outside Expertise (7%); Changes in Our Target Audience(s) (5%); and Other (5%).

Note: Due to the low number of B2B respondents who said their organization's content marketing success had decreased compared with one year ago, this report does not include a chart showing factors contributing to decreased success.

Base: B2B content marketers who said their organization's overall content marketing approach is much more or somewhat more successful compared with one year ago.

Conclusion

And don't forget to monitor the content marketing metrics that will tell you how well your strategy is working.

Commitment

Brands also need to be dedicated to content production for their business and target customers. Research shows that only 36% of organizations are committed to producing content.

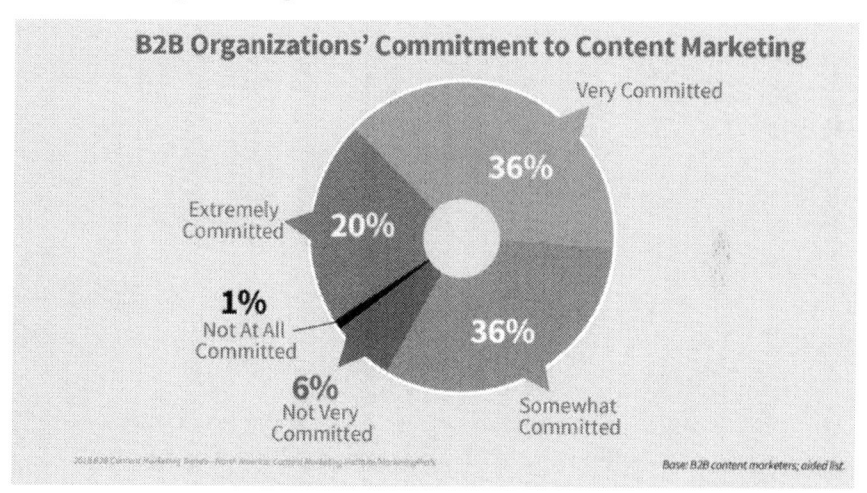

B2B Organizations' Commitment to Content Marketing

- Very Committed: 36%
- Somewhat Committed: 36%
- Extremely Committed: 20%
- Not Very Committed: 6%
- Not At All Committed: 1%

Brands should seek to produce high-quality content that informs and helps their target customers—regularly. For example, customers lose interest in a blog when no new posts appear for a long time.

Commitment to top-notch content production will also keep your B2B brand in the game of lead generation and conversion as the process of getting new customers is long and complicated.

Customer Engagement Preferences

The consumption of content is also changing. Most target users are consuming more video content than text-based content.

Video is the #1 form of media used in content marketing strategy

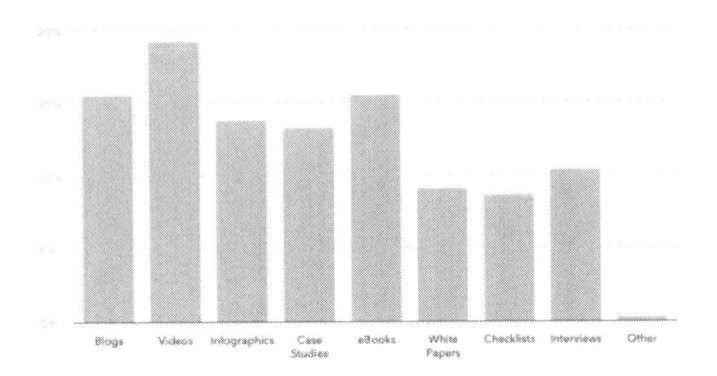

[Bar chart showing content types: Blogs, Videos, Infographics, Case Studies, eBooks, White Papers, Checklists, Interviews, Other]

As you create content, include some video to keep your target customers engaged with your brand. Also, create a variety of different text-based content for your readers, and incorporate images and color.

Most readers go through several different content types before engaging with a business. Demand Generation research shows that 40% of potential buyers interact with at least three different content types.

HOW MANY PIECES OF CONTENT HAVE YOU TYPICALLY CONSUMED BEFORE ENGAGING WITH A SALESPERSON WHEN YOU ARE AMID MAKING A PURCHASE DECISION?

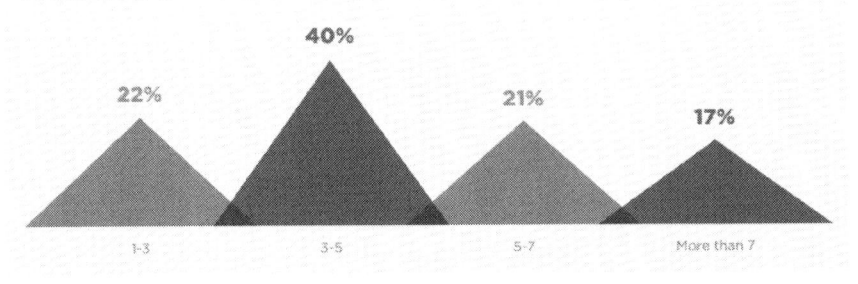

1-3	3-5	5-7	More than 7
22%	40%	21%	17%

Eye-catching content that offers some uniqueness and variety is better at grabbing and holding customers' attention, which makes them more likely to engage with your business, and for longer.

Conclusion

Search Engine Optimization

As you keep building on your knowledge of how to increase your brand awareness and reach more target customers, don't forget the most essential part of it all—SEO.

Investing in SEO will help your target customers find your business and any content you publish with ease. They'll be attracted to your brand, engage with it, and probably convert into customers.

Hubspot research shows that only 63.6% of brands globally invest in SEO.

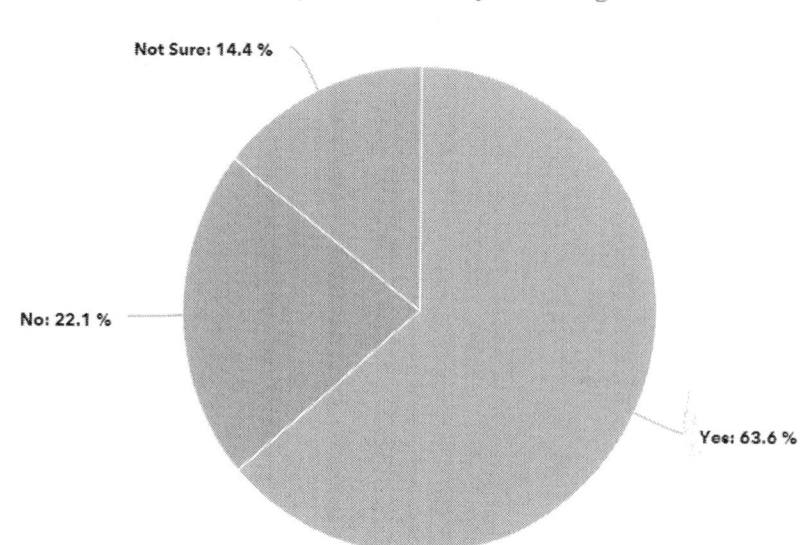

Global Companies Actively Investing in SEO

Not Sure: 14.4 %
No: 22.1 %
Yes: 63.6 %

If you've been neglecting this area of your business, it's high time to get to work on it. There are many different tools you can take advantage of in your pursuit of SEO.

Facebook Ads

Social sites are becoming some of the best marketing sites online brands can use to attract new customers. Apart from content marketing, brands are making ads and posting them on these social sites. In chapter 3, we covered techniques for making appealing ads. We also discussed the best channels for publishing your ads to reach more leads.

The number of monthly active users on social sites is rapidly increasing. If brands create high quality-ads and advertise them on these sites, they can see rapid business growth.

For example, here's a chart showing the increase in Facebook's number of active users:

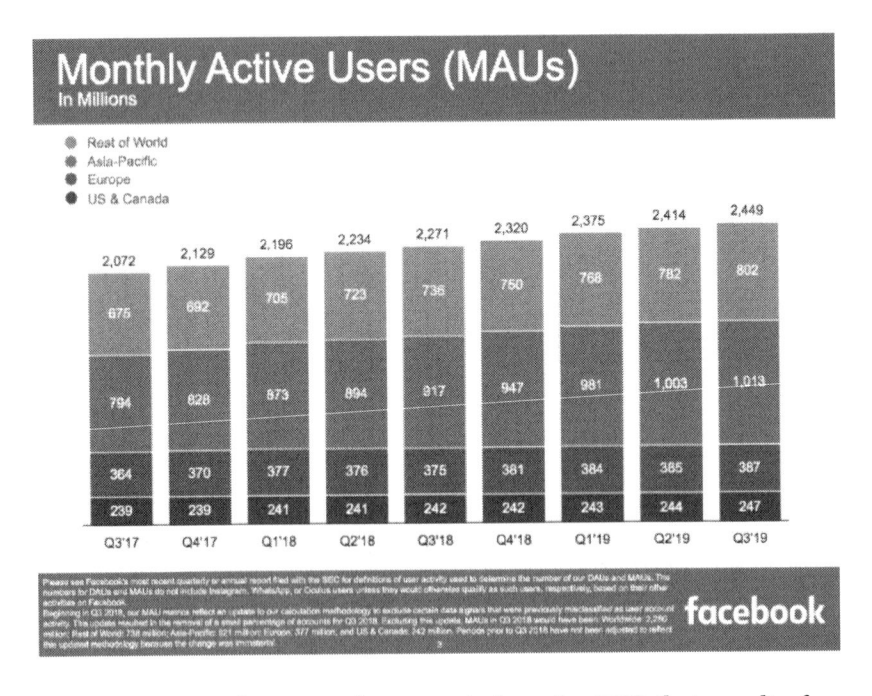

Monthly Active Users (MAUs)
In Millions

- Rest of World
- Asia-Pacific
- Europe
- US & Canada

Region	Q3'17	Q4'17	Q1'18	Q2'18	Q3'18	Q4'18	Q1'19	Q2'19	Q3'19
Total	2,072	2,129	2,196	2,234	2,271	2,320	2,375	2,414	2,449
Rest of World	675	692	705	723	736	750	768	782	802
Asia-Pacific	794	828	873	894	917	947	981	1,003	1,013
Europe	364	370	377	376	375	381	384	385	387
US & Canada	239	239	241	241	242	242	243	244	247

facebook

As you run your ads, remember to calculate the ROI that results from your advertising efforts. Research shows that 40% of businesses struggle to prove that their marketing brings an ROI.

Conclusion

What are your company's top marketing challenges?

Challenge	Percentage
Generating traffic and leads	63%
Proving the ROI of our marketing activities	40%
Securing enough budget	28%
Identifying the right technologies for our needs	26%
Managing our website	26%
Targeting content for an international audience	21%
Training our team	19%
Hiring top talent	16%
Finding an executive sponsor	7%

STATE of INBOUND

Also, learn all you can about ad channels and how to run ads on them before advertising on these channels. This will help you get a high return on investment from your ads.

Hiring experts in that field to help you run your ads can also be beneficial for your brand. One excellent example is Voy Media. We'd love to help you with your Facebook advertising.

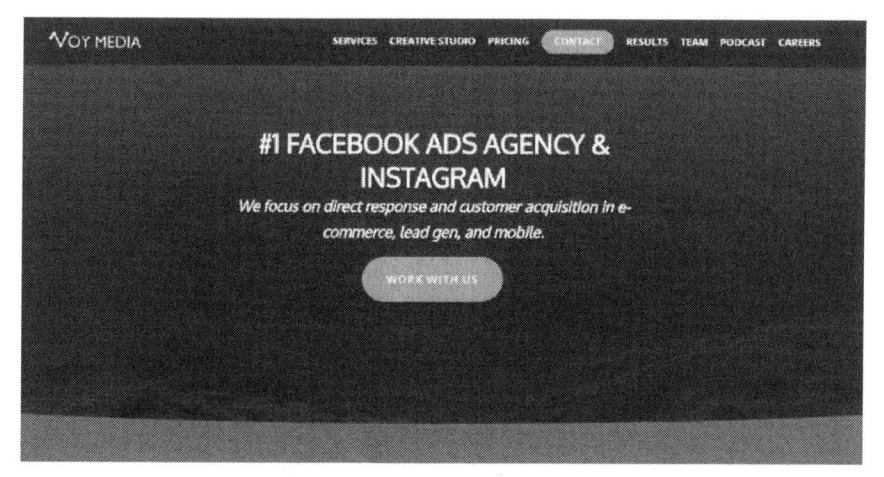

VOY MEDIA

SERVICES CREATIVE STUDIO PRICING CONTACT RESULTS TEAM PODCAST CAREERS

#1 FACEBOOK ADS AGENCY & INSTAGRAM

We focus on direct response and customer acquisition in e-commerce, lead gen, and mobile.

WORK WITH US

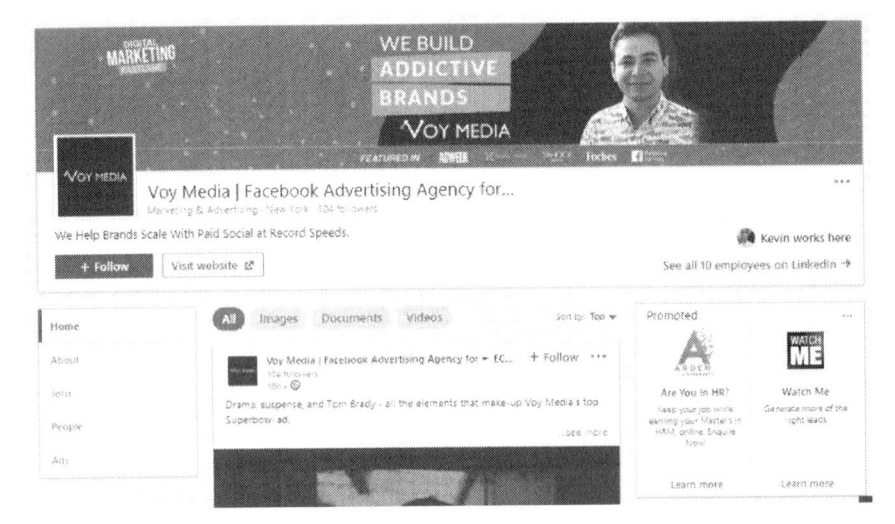

As you aim to grow your business, devote your efforts to retaining all your existing customers by providing the best customer experience they can get anywhere.

Research by Invesp shows that brands have a 70% probability of selling to their existing customers.

> The probability of selling to an existing customer is 60-70%, while the probability of selling to a new prospect is 5-20%.
>
> **60-70%** Existing Customer
>
> **5-20%** New Customer

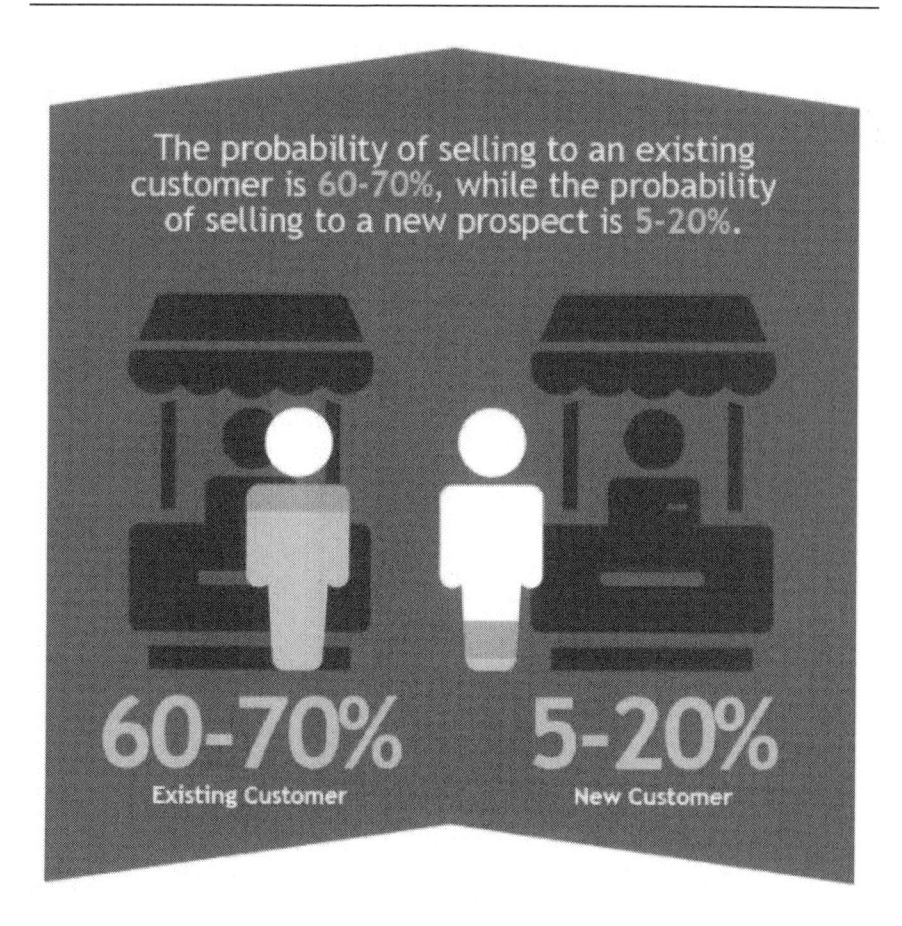

Business Websites

As you grow your business and reach out to more customers, don't forget to make your website a top priority.

Invesp has found that [89% of businesses use their websites to generate new customers](#).

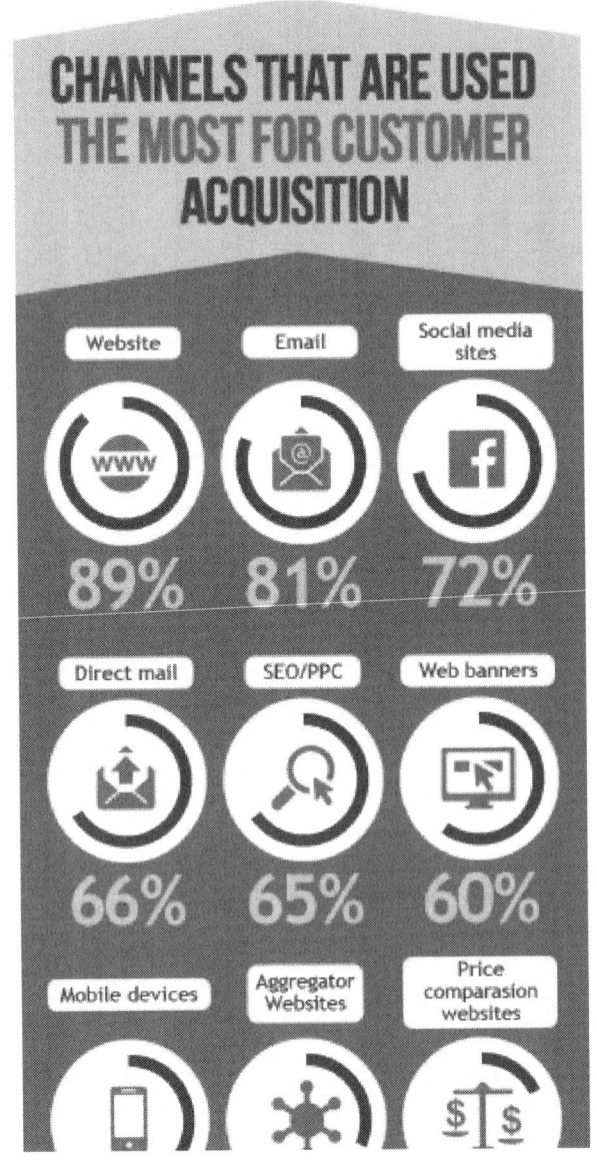

CHANNELS THAT ARE USED THE MOST FOR CUSTOMER ACQUISITION

Website	Email	Social media sites
89%	81%	72%

Direct mail	SEO/PPC	Web banners
66%	65%	60%

Mobile devices | Aggregator Websites | Price comparasion websites

Let's remind ourselves of some key components of a good business website.

Superb and User-Friendly Design

The importance of appearance and intuitiveness to your website can't be overstated. Look for a great designer who can design the site using attractive themes and designs and make it as user-friendly as possible.

Landing Pages

In chapter 2, we discussed landing pages in detail. Review that chapter before you begin work on this part of your site.

Your business's landing pages are the most delicate aspect of your website. It's worthwhile to invest in a professional copywriter who can develop your landing page copy.

You may also want to create separate landing pages for your different campaigns. MarketingSherpa research shows that 48% of marketers create a new landing page for each campaign.

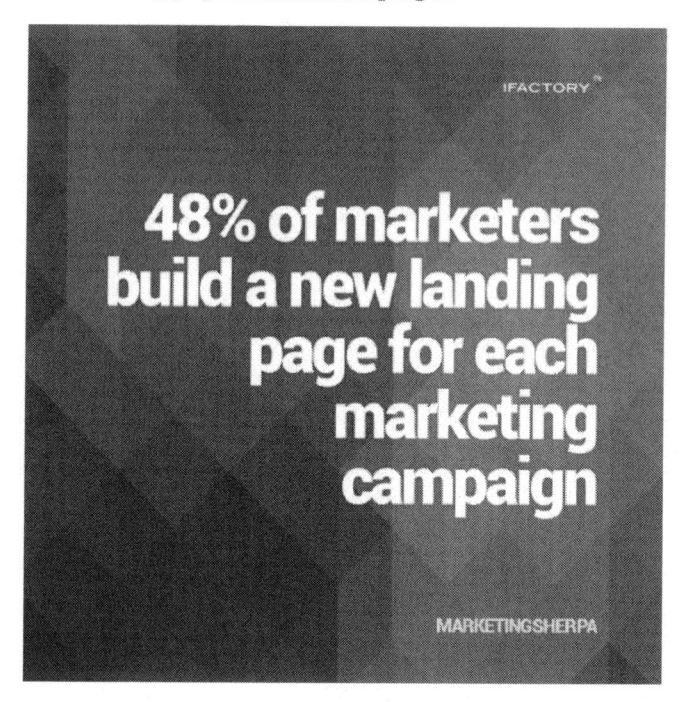

Image Source: https://ifactory.com.au/insights/why-should-i-use-landing-pages/

Your landing pages are meant to help your target customers understand your services or products and why they should use them instead of your competitor's.

Trustworthiness

Online business is all about trust-building. Your entire business should be centered around trust because customers will leave the moment they feel they can't trust your business. If target customers don't feel secure or trust your website when they land on it, they won't stick around.

Conversely, target customers love to do business with trustworthy companies. One way to earn the trust of your target clients is to include trust seals on your landing pages and other parts of your website. See chapter 2, "What Makes a Great Landing Page? Trust Symbols," for some examples. You can also include SSL certificates on the site.

Loading Speed

Your ads and other marketing channels can send a lot of traffic to your website. However, if your target customers arrive there to find that the site isn't professional or takes ages to load, they won't waste time there, and your competitors will enjoy doing business with them.

Research shows that websites with loading speeds of 3 seconds or less are fast enough to avoid turning customers away.

Conclusion

Slow website loading speeds increase your bounce rate and this can affect the growth of your business.

Content Usability

Enhancing your content usability can also reduce the bounce rate of your website. Here are some factors to consider when it comes to the usability of your content:

ENHANCE USABILITY

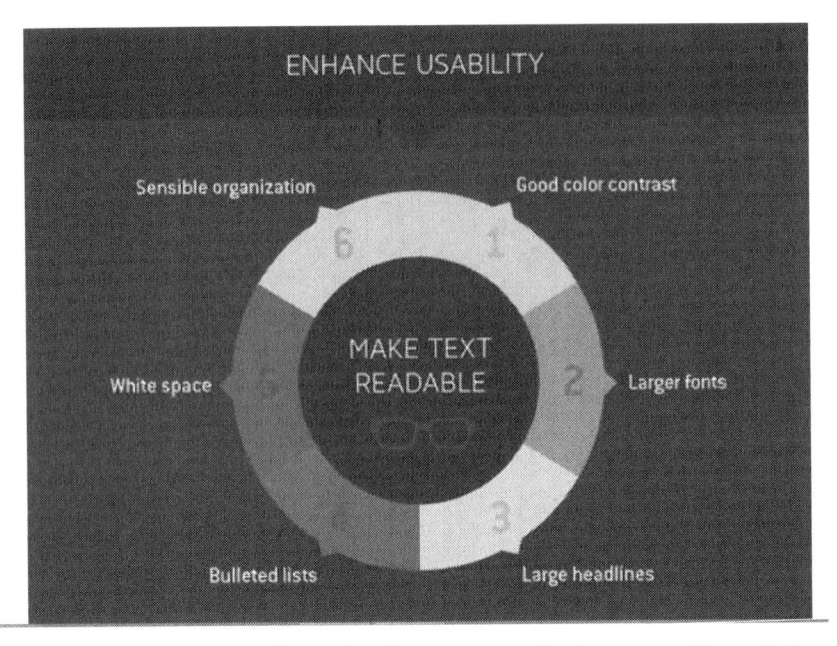

- Sensible organization
- Good color contrast
- Larger fonts
- Large headlines
- Bulleted lists
- White space

MAKE TEXT READABLE

A wall of text is always off-putting, but content that's easy to digest helps you keep customers' attention as you explain how your business's services or products will help them solve their pain points.

That concludes our review. You have the knowledge, and now it's time to put it to good use. Go forth and market!

If you have any questions or comments about this book or need help check out https://voymedia.com or email kevin@voymedia.com.

Printed in Great Britain
by Amazon